Making Medical Decisions for the Profoundly Mentally Disabled

Basic Bioethics
Glenn McGee and Arthur Caplan, editors

Making Medical Decisions for the Profoundly Mentally Disabled

Norman L. Cantor

The MIT Press
Cambridge, Massachusetts
London, England

MIT Press books may be purchased at special quantity discounts for business or sales promotional use. For information, please e-mail <special_sales@mitpress.mit .edu> or write to Special Sales Department, The MIT Press, 5 Cambridge Center, Cambridge, MA 02142.

This book was set in Sabon by Graphic Composition, Inc.
Printed on recycled paper and bound in the United States of America.

Library of Congress Cataloging-in-Publication Data

Cantor, Norman L.
    Making medical decisions for the profoundly mentally disabled / Norman L. Cantor.
        p. cm.—(Basic bioethics)
    Includes bibliographical references and index.
    ISBN 0-262-03331-3 (hc. : alk. paper)
    1. Mental health laws—United States. 2. Medical ethics—United States—
Decision making. 3. Informed consent (Medical law)—United States. 4. Right to
die—Law and legislation—United States. 5. Conservatorships—United States.
I. Title. II. Series.

KF480.C36 2004
344.7304'4—dc22

                                                                2004057805

10   9   8   7   6   5   4   3   2   1

Contents

Series Foreword

We are pleased to present the fifteenth book in the Basic Bioethics series. The series presents innovative works in bioethics to a broad audience and introduces seminal scholarly manuscripts, state-of-the-art reference works, and textbooks. Such broad areas as the philosophy of medicine, advancing genetics and biotechnology, end-of-life care, health and social policy, and the empirical study of biomedical life are engaged.

Glenn McGee
Arthur Caplan

Acknowledgments

This book has had a long gestation period. I started seriously contemplating the legal and moral status of profoundly disabled persons at least sixteen or seventeen years ago. Consequently, many people have, over the years, made useful comments through conversations or writings. I am grateful to them all, but I particularly thank the following groups and individuals: participants in faculty colloquia at Rutgers University School of Law, Newark, and Seton Hall University School of Law; participants in the Disability Ethics Network organized by New Jersey Health Decisions; Carl Coleman and Lance Stell for reading portions of the manuscript; a long string of helpful research assistants, most recently Julie Newman and Janice Goldberg; my very able and valuable secretary Bobbie Leach; and Dean Stuart Deutsch of Rutgers Law School for financial support from the Dean's Research Fund.

Versions of chapters 2 and 4 previously appeared as articles in the *Annals of Health Law* and the *Journal of Legal Medicine,* respectively. I am grateful to the editors of those journals. Finally, I am grateful for the encouragement of the editors connected with the MIT Press, particularly Art Caplan and Glenn McGee.

Making Medical Decisions for the Profoundly Mentally Disabled

Introduction

This book is about surrogate decision making on behalf of people with profound mental disabilities—those men, women, and children whose mental functions are so limited that they cannot make considered choices about important matters affecting their lives.(Profound mental disabilities can have various causes, including retardation, autism, cerebral palsy, epilepsy, spina bifida, and other neurological impairments.) Profoundly disabled persons[1] are adults who have been profoundly retarded or severely brain damaged since birth, but some are fatally stricken infants who will not survive early childhood or older children with severe, lifelong cognitive disabilities. This book focuses on the U.S. law that governs decisions made on behalf of profoundly disabled[2] persons—the law that determines which issues are subject to surrogate decision making, who can decide on behalf of the incapacitated person, and, especially, what decision-making standards or criteria are applicable. Yet law is grounded in ethics, philosophy, economics, and politics, factors which influence the applicable legal boundaries and therefore are included in the ensuing discussion.

Who are the profoundly disabled persons at the center of this book? For the most part, they are people whose cognitive functioning places them in the bottom of the ranges applicable to the mentally retarded. Mental retardation is roughly defined as a condition of significantly subaverage intelligence (an intelligence quotient of less than 70) coupled with substantial impairments in at least two areas of social behavior.[3] Most retarded persons, however, have enough cognitive capacity to make at least some medical decisions for themselves. The contemporary approach is to assess decision-making capacity according to the complexity of the particular issue at hand and to grant self-determination to any person, regardless of mental disability, who can understand the nature and consequences of that issue and is capable of exercising considered choice. Even under an approach that seeks to maximize the self-determination opportunities of the mentally disabled, however, some persons are so mentally impaired that they can make virtually no medical decisions for themselves. A small percentage of mentally disabled persons have an IQ that is below 30, qualifying them as severely or profoundly retarded.[4] A century ago, persons who possessed a mental age of two years or less would have been labeled "idiots," and those who had a mental capacity equivalent to a three- or four-year-old would have been labeled "imbeciles."[5] Today, the harsh labels are gone, and strenuous efforts are made to communicate effectively with severely disabled persons and to involve them in decision making to the maximum extent feasible. Still, some persons are so severely cognitively disabled that any important decision affecting them must ultimately be made by some surrogate. That category of surrogate decision making forms the heart of this book.

Cognitively disabled persons have an enormous range of interests about which decisions sometimes have to be made. There are lifestyle matters (such as living location, supportive services, and education), bodily integrity matters (including a wide range of medical interventions), relational matters (daily interpersonal associations, including sexual interactions), property matters (involving disposition of personal or real property), and even civic matters (such as voting or jury service). Not every matter that affects a disabled person is subject to surrogate decision making. The profoundly disabled may be excluded from certain subject areas because the area involves a social institution whose objectives would be frustrated by inclusion of the profoundly disabled. Social institutions such as voting and jury service demand individualized, deliberative effort at levels of cognitive and communicative function that are lacking in the profoundly disabled. They reasonably require a minimum level of deliberative function because of the important public interests involved.[6] Any adverse impact on excluded profoundly disabled persons is attenuated. Unlike medical or lifestyle decisions that have an immediate effect on the incapacitated subject of the decision, the inability to cast a vote or serve on a jury is unlikely to impact the personal well-being of the excluded profoundly disabled person.

Another category of matters is excluded from surrogate decision making despite the clear potential effect of these matters on disabled persons.

An established legal principle treats certain choices—including certain legal prerogatives—as so personalized, so dependent on an individual's personal weighing of values and considerations that they are beyond the realm of surrogate decision making.[7] Marriage is a prime example. If a person is profoundly disabled and unable to comprehend the nature of the connections and commitments involved in marriage, no surrogate will be permitted to select a lifetime mate on behalf of the disabled person. Other examples include the adoption of a child and the making of a last will and testament. In all these instances, the potential impact of bad decisions is so great and the role of personalized preferences so critical that the preclusion of surrogate decision making seems reasonable.

This book concentrates on serious medical and surgical decisions that affect the bodily integrity of profoundly disabled persons—including the withholding or withdrawal of life support, procreation-related matters (abortion and sterilization), organ or tissue donation, and participation in medical research. All of these subject matters pose hard issues regarding surrogate decision making. Some of these bodily interventions are so fraught with hazards of exploitation that some sources argue that they ought to be excluded from the realm of surrogate decision making. Chapter 2 addresses those claims for the exclusion of surrogate choice, with particular reference to the withdrawal of life support and sterilization. Chapter 5 addresses similar concerns about exploitation in contexts where medical procedures ostensibly benefit parties other than the disabled patient—organ or tissue donation and participation in nontherapeutic medical research. Again, the question of whether surrogate decision making should be precluded in these contexts arises.

Even if a serious medical matter such as removal of life support is deemed subject to surrogate decision making on behalf of a profoundly disabled person, hard questions arise about the framework for such decision making. Who is entitled to act as surrogate decision maker—a family member, a close friend, a judicially appointed guardian, medical personnel, an institutional ethics committee, or a court (chapter 3)? What standard should the surrogate apply—substituted judgment, best interests, or some other (chapter 4)? If best interests, what factors within a best-interests test are appropriate? How can a profoundly disabled patient's best interests be measured—i.e., how does a surrogate assess the relevant benefits and burdens when the experiential reality of the person may be so unfathomable that the surrogate is tempted to project his or her own discomforts onto the disabled ward? Should the interests of others, especially family members, help determine the medical fate of a profoundly disabled patient? What significance should be attributed to the expressions of the incapacitated patient related to the contemplated medical procedure (chapter 6)? And what role does human dignity play in shaping the fate of the profoundly disabled medical patient?

Profoundly disabled persons may lack the capacities of reflection, communication, and interpersonal interaction that our culture commonly associates with rights-bearing persons. Indeed, some moral philosophers contend that a gravely demented human lacks the minimum cognitive ability to qualify as a person. From that perspective, the absence of personhood usually connotes diminished moral stature and might even impel disqualification from the equal legal status that a democratic society guarantees to its citizens. So before fleshing out the decision-making framework that is legally applicable to the profoundly disabled, it is necessary to determine whether profoundly disabled humans are, in fact, persons. In chapter 1, I examine the notion of personhood and offer both practical and theoretical reasons why profoundly disabled humans are entitled to the full legal and moral status of persons.

This ongoing premise—that profoundly disabled humans are persons entitled to full legal and moral status—dictates that a variety of rights and protections be extended to ensure the well-being and dignity of profoundly disabled persons. Yet that full stature "does not entail that they [the profoundly disabled] are to be treated exactly like project pursuers [persons whose cognitive capacity permits the formulation and pursuit of personal plans]."[8] All persons need not be treated identically. Sometimes people's differences are relevant to the way in which other people and legal rules relate to them. For example, although disabled persons are protected against unfair discrimination, a blind person need not be admitted to airline pilots' school. In the case of profoundly disabled people, their severely limited mental capacities mean that their rights have to be adjusted in ways that are appropriate to their capacities. The details of these situations are explored later in this book, but I sketch at this point some of the ways in which profoundly disabled persons may—consistent with law and morals—be subject to different treatment than other persons.

As persons under the Fourteenth Amendment, profoundly disabled people enjoy full protection of their constitutional liberty interests. Yet profoundly diminished mental capacity affects how the concept of liberty gets implemented. Many constitutional liberties seem to involve autonomous choice among options available to the rights holder. Examples include a person's prerogatives to determine whether to employ contraception, whether to bear a fetus to term, and whether to reject life-sustaining medical intervention. Profoundly disabled persons do not have the capacity to exercise such choices themselves, at least not in the reasoned and deliberative manner to which the autonomy model aspires. Do autonomy-based rights extend to the nonautonomous? If so, how can those rights be exercised? Are profoundly disabled persons entitled to have surrogates make fundamental medical choices for them? A competent person has a constitutional right to reject life-sustaining medical intervention, but can a never competent person have a right to have a surrogate exercise a comparable choice on his or her behalf—at least in some circumstances?

Chapter 2 addresses the relationship between autonomy-based rights and mentally incapacitated persons. There I contend that Fourteenth Amendment liberty should be deemed to include a right of mentally incapacitated persons to have conscientious surrogates make potentially beneficial medical choices. In other words, while profoundly disabled persons cannot have a right to make their own choices (as do competent persons), they may have a right to have some important choices made on their behalf.

Because of the differential in deliberative capacity between competent and profoundly disabled persons, there are also differences in the force attributed to their respective voices. When people have sufficient mental capacity to be autonomous, their voice is ordinarily controlling. That is, competent persons can articulate their medical choices, and those decisions generally become determinative of the medical course to be followed.[9] The voice of a profoundly disabled person does not always have the same overarching status as an autonomous voice. Chapters 5 and 6 consider if and when a surrogate decision maker is permitted to override a profoundly disabled person's objections to a course of medical treatment. Chapter 5 discusses instances when the will of a profoundly disabled person must be upheld and chapter 6 shows how, in the context of serious medical choices, the uttered preferences or feelings of a profoundly disabled person are always entitled to respect—that is, to be considered by surrogates acting on behalf of the disabled person.

Another concomitant of profound mental disability is vulnerability to manipulation. Capacitated persons who surround the profoundly disabled person may be able to manipulate or direct the expressions and preferences of the disabled person. That power can be exercised in good or bad ways. Moreover, the profoundly disabled person is often subject to binding surrogate control of his or her medical fate (as when parents make basic medical decisions on behalf of their immature children). Some surrogates may be tempted to consider the interests of affected third parties, not just those of the disabled person. This vulnerability that is connected with mental disability might dictate that special protections be extended to medical decision making done for, rather than by, profoundly disabled persons. Chapter 3 addresses who gets to make critical medical decisions for such persons, and Chapter 4 speaks to the legal standards that bind the surrogate decision maker.

According to conventional wisdom, American law dictates that a surrogate must adhere to the vulnerable patient's best interests when serious medical choices are in issue. I argue in chapter 4 that "best" interests should be neither the moral nor legal mandate. The venerable formula of best interests of the patient is a misnomer of sorts. While a surrogate decision maker must indeed consider and respect the interests of a disabled ward, that surrogate is not always compelled to follow the very best course for the disabled ward to the exclusion of interests of family or others close to the ward. In some instances, other persons' interests can properly come into play.

At the same time, a serious legal and moral question arises about surrogate decision making that primarily benefits others, as when someone authorizes a tissue donation by a profoundly disabled person or permits that person's participation in nontherapeutic medical research. What moral theory enables a surrogate to deviate from the patient's best interests? To what extent can the surrogate derogate the disabled person's interests in favor of the interests of others? Chapter 5 examines the relation between "altruistic" medical decisions and the interests of mentally disabled persons. That chapter explores possible rationales for surrogate decisions that do not primarily promote the disabled patient's interests and outlines limits that protect disabled patients against unconscionable exploitation.

I contend throughout this book that the concept of intrinsic human dignity meaningfully informs the moral and legal bounds of decision making on behalf of profoundly disabled persons. Chapter 1 rejects the notion that humans with extremely low cognitive ability do not qualify as "persons" enjoying full moral stature and asserts on their behalf a concomitant right to be treated with human dignity. That chapter sketches the concept of intrinsic human dignity that I claim helps to shape the bounds of decision making on behalf of profoundly disabled humans. Succeeding chapters then show how intrinsic human dignity impacts on surrogate decision making. Chapter 2 examines the relation between autonomy-based rights (such as choice of medical treatment) and profoundly disabled persons who, as never competent beings, cannot make their own medical choices. I claim that while profoundly disabled persons cannot be entitled to make their own medical decisions, they have a right to have a conscientious surrogate make important medical decisions on their behalf. Part of the claim is that the exclusion of surrogate choice leaves every never competent patient in a medical limbo that sometimes constitutes an intolerably undignified and inhumane status. Human dignity also influences the decision-making standards that bind surrogates. Chapter 4 indicates how the notion of best interests of a never competent patient can and does incorporate intrinsic human dignity, even though the profoundly disabled person may not sense the indignity involved. The notions of intrinsic dignity and respect for persons also influence the role that disabled persons' voices play in surrogate decision making. Chapter 6 explains how respect for the intrinsic dignity of profoundly disabled humans compels attention to their preferences and feelings, even if those persons cannot make binding autonomous choices.

Another possible dictate of full moral status (and respect for human dignity) is that the profoundly disabled person be treated as an end and not exclusively as an object.[10] Does law embrace the Kantian imperative against using persons solely as a means? Is the Kantian imperative of human dignity violated by surrogate choices—such as authorization of an organ donation or participation in nontherapeutic medical research—that do not primarily benefit the disabled ward? What does it mean to be treated solely as a means? Does full moral status for never competent persons carry a duty or obligation to make modest sacrifices on behalf of the general community? Does justice within families or justice within communities permit surrogate decisions that impose net burdens on a ward? If surrogates can make some choices that are not beneficial to that ward, what protects the profoundly disabled ward against abusive exploitation? I contend in chapter 5 that basic human dignity serves as an important source of limitations when surrogates seek to make "altruistic" medical choices for profoundly disabled persons. Human dignity thus functions as a protection for profoundly disabled persons just as it does for all other bearers of full moral stature. At the same time, I suggest (in chapters 1 and 4) that the concept of dignity as applied to profoundly disabled persons is not identical to the concept applied to autonomous persons.

In short, in this book I try to show the relevance of intrinsic human dignity to various aspects of medical decision making for the profoundly disabled. Sometimes the concept of human dignity serves as an ultimate protection for the profoundly disabled ward against exploitation by a surrogate decision maker (as when nontherapeutic medical research is in issue). Sometimes that concept impels a right of access to a surrogate's decision about an important medical issue that is facing the profoundly disabled person (as with end-of-life medical decisions).

Any reliance on the concept of dignity provokes rigorous opposition. The main objection to using the concept of intrinsic human dignity in the context of surrogate decision making is the subjectivity or malleability that is supposedly attached to any definition of core human dignity. Efforts to ground social norms in an independent concept of human dignity are frequently dismissed as too indeterminate and culturally variable to be useful.[11] Ruth Macklin dismisses notions of human dignity as "mere slogans that add nothing to an understanding of [any] topic."[12] Deryck Beyleveld and Roger Brownsword label the concept of human dignity "something of a loose cannon, open to abuse and misinterpretation," particularly when used as a justification for curbing autonomy.[13]

Commentators sometimes see human dignity as such a malleable term that it produces contradictions among important human interests. For example, freedom of expression may be integrally related to human dignity, but it is sometimes used in a manner (deprecating persons on the basis of color or gender) that offends human dignity. Autonomy may be an important element of human dignity, but if a dwarf autonomously chooses to be tossed about as a part of public entertainment, intrinsic human dignity is offended. A similar tension about the dictates of human dignity appears in the context of end-of-life medical treatment. For some people, death with dignity means a patient's prerogative to secure the removal of medical life support (or even access to a poison) to avoid extreme debilitation or suffering during a dying process. For others, death with dignity means tolerating suffering as redemptive or as an integral part of human life, so that any acceleration of a dying process is incompatible with human dignity.[14] According to the latter perspective, all human life is dignified, and no suffering or debilitated condition can rob a person of his or her intrinsic human dignity. Divergent visions of human dignity also arise around the issue of surrogate authorization of tissue or organ donation from a mentally incapacitated person. Some persons argue that recognizing a profoundly disabled person's intrinsic dignity requires that he or she be allowed to donate an organ to a critically ill donee. For them, it is integral to a profoundly disabled person's humanity that the person be allowed to act in an altruistic way. Others argue that any such nonvoluntary donation constitutes the exploitation of a person in a fashion that is incompatible with intrinsic human dignity.

To me, the claim that human dignity is too inherently subjective and malleable to be useful is unconvincing. The same arguments have been made against using liberty or equality as binding legal norms. Despite the vagueness of those terms, American jurisprudence has usefully embraced the notion of "fundamental aspects of liberty" under the Fourteenth Amendment due process clause and the notion of "suspect classifications" under the equal protection clause.[15] Yes, there may be imprecision, cultural variability, and evolution in fixing the bounds of intrinsic human dignity. But that doesn't mean that the concept is fatally indeterminate or unusable as anything more than a grandiose yet impractical ideal. Even in a pluralistic society with diverse visions of human stature, I suggest, the evolving traditions and collective conscience of the people provide guides for assessing intrinsic human dignity without reliance on transitory opinions or trends. As is the case with the concepts of equality and liberty, the definition of intrinsic human dignity must be based on widespread understandings and must stand up to critical reflection.[16] An individual's subjective notion of intrinsic dignity does not meet that standard and cannot become the norm for surrogate decision making on behalf of profoundly disabled persons.[17] I suggest that intrinsic human dignity is a meaningful concept when grounded in the wisdom and experience of generations and modified by evolving norms that earn widespread acceptance and withstand critical examination.[18]

Germany offers an illustration of how a jurisprudence of intrinsic human dignity can be constructed. Article 1(1) of Germany's Basic Law (which is tantamount to a constitution) establishes that government must respect the inviolable human dignity of all people. Fifty years of jurisprudence have fleshed out that concept of dignity and established that it is not dependent on intellectual capacity and that it can be applied in cases of torture, the death penalty, and certain aspects of autonomy such as choice of sexual identity.[19] Of course, intrinsic dignity varies across cultures. American attitudes toward the death penalty and toward publications that humiliate or defame a person diverge from the German approaches. For example, American jurisprudence values free expression so greatly that it tolerates speech degrading persons which German jurisprudence would condemn as a violation of human dignity.[20] The point is that the apparent vagueness of human dignity does not preclude the development of a jurisprudence that gives meaningful content to the term.

Any discussion of surrogate decision making for the profoundly disabled—including examination of the role of intrinsic human dignity—must be attuned to our long cultural history of mistreatment of the mentally disabled. Victimization of mentally impaired people has taken many forms. There has always been a degree of ostracism and obloquy associated with people who are noticeably different and strange. In the mid-nineteenth century, the mentally retarded were often relegated either to alms houses or state training schools, where they were prone to abuse. Moral deficiency was attributed to the mentally retarded, and efforts were made to segregate and train them in order to compensate for their supposedly pathological tendencies.[21] By the late 1870s, social interest in heredity grew, and heredity was commonly linked with so-called feeblemindedness, moral degeneracy, and crime. Custodial institutionalization (as opposed to institutional training before release to the larger world) became more common in the interests of protecting the feebleminded from themselves and protecting society from the hereditary increase of this type of person.[22]

For many decades, mentally disabled people were viewed as an unproductive social burden and a menace because of their supposed moral weakness and reproductive proclivity. Between 1890 and 1920, a eugenics movement emerged with the object of controlling the social menace by preventing reproduction—using institutionalization, prevention of sexual relations within institutions, and involuntary sterilization if necessary.[23] By

1920, many people doubted the scientific foundation underlying the eugenics movement, but some states continued to pass laws that authorized involuntary sterilization.[24] In 1927, the Supreme Court upheld the constitutionality of such laws, with Justice Holmes declaring that society ought to be permitted to avoid being "swamped with incompetents" and that three generations of imbeciles (in the family of the person marked for sterilization) were enough.[25] Even in the 1920s, as the institutional approach to the retarded began to incorporate plans for their eventual return to the community, some institutions viewed sterilization as a prerequisite to release. Science eventually discredited any strong causal link between heredity and mental retardation.[26] Yet as late as the 1940s, some voices in the mental health community still regarded forced sterilization of even the moderately retarded as wise social policy. And an occasional voice supported involuntary euthanasia of "the completely hopeless [severely retarded] defective."[27] A psychiatrist urging euthanasia viewed it as "a merciful and kindly thing to relieve the defective [person]—often tortured and convulsed, grotesque and absurd, useless and foolish, and entirely undesirable—of the agony of living."[28] By the 1950s, the view of the mentally retarded as menaces and pariahs may have dissipated, but the retarded were still subject to benign neglect and sometimes abuse in overcrowded and dilapidated institutions.[29]

In the second half of the twentieth century, substantial changes occurred in social response to the mentally disabled. Warehousing the developmentally disabled in isolated, abusive institutions became increasingly viewed as inconsistent with basic human dignity. Legislation, litigation, and public exposes sought to ameliorate the conditions of the institutionalized and to guarantee supportive services that would maximize the self-sufficiency and potential of those institutionalized.[30] The language of rights quickly surfaced. Advocates of the developmentally disabled fought for rights not only to decent physical accommodations and freedom from undue restraint, but to adequate treatment and habilitation and jobs as well.[31]

Beyond the notion of a right to physical well-being and to beneficial services that maximize human potential, another kind of right surfaced in the late twentieth century regarding mentally disabled persons. This was a right to have the same kind of options regarding medical treatment as fully able persons have. As applied to the profoundly disabled population, this had to mean that medical choice would be exercised by a surrogate. That is an important issue within this book—the question of when and how a right that ostensibly involves autonomous personal choice can possibly apply to profoundly disabled people. Before facing the issue of a profoundly disabled person's possible right to surrogate medical choice, it is important to establish the status of the profoundly disabled human being as a full rights-bearing person. That is where this book about surrogate decision making begins.

1

The Moral Status of the Profoundly Disabled: Persons or Something Less?

Suppose a child is born who, throughout his life, will be profoundly retarded. . . . How shall we describe such human beings? Is it best to say that they are no longer persons? Or is it more revealing to describe them as severely disabled persons?[1]

The Concepts of Personhood and Full Moral Status

Personhood in our culture carries important consequences. In the legal context, personhood ensures maximum legal protection for profoundly mentally disabled beings. The Fourteenth Amendment of the U.S. Constitution, for instance, protects all "persons" against deprivation of life, liberty, or property without due process of law and safeguards persons against invidious or arbitrary government discrimination. Beyond constitutional protection, public discourse often refers to basic or natural or intrinsic "rights" in the sense of certain inviolable moral entitlements or protections.[2] Some or all of those morally grounded benefits might also be confined to "persons," although nonpersons with a diminished moral status may still receive significant protections. In the context of health-care ethics, a central theme is respect for persons, meaning adherence to certain protections and forms of solicitous treatment associated with human dignity.[3] Implicit in that ethical entitlement to respect is a judgment that all persons have full moral status. In moral philosophy, the term *person* is often associated with beings that have special value or importance—that is, full moral status. Because of these important implications of personhood, it is critical to determine at the outset of this book whether profoundly disabled human beings qualify as persons—as beings entitled to full moral and legal status.[4]

Resolving whether profoundly disabled humans have full moral stature has considerable importance in the domain of surrogate decision making that occupies this book. As the introduction suggests, some states might seek to exclude entire subject matters of medical decision making affecting the profoundly disabled (such as sterilization or removal of life support) from the realm of surrogate control. If the profoundly disabled are persons and thus entitled to maximum legal status and protection, they may oppose such categorical exclusion and claim a right to have such disputed decisions made by surrogates on their behalf. For example, an incapacitated person who needs a sterilization operation to avoid harsh medical consequences or to maximize sexual freedom has a strong interest in having sterilization chosen for him or her. Access to a full range of surrogate medical choices therefore affects the well-being of profoundly disabled humans. Such personal-welfare interests underlie a possible constitutional right to surrogate choice (which I call a *right to constructive choice*). Discussion of a claim of entitlement to constructive choice occupies a central place in chapter 2.

The concept of personhood can come into play in various other ways when surrogates are accorded authority to make certain medical decisions on behalf of the profoundly mentally disabled. An example is end-of-life decision making. If profoundly disabled beings are not persons, then decisions to terminate life-sustaining medical intervention (and thereby precipitate death) are facilitated. This factor has already surfaced in the debates surrounding the medical handling of grievously disabled infants, with some commentators asserting that infants, as nonpersons, have no entitlement to the customary presumption that life should be preserved.[5] If profoundly disabled infants have full moral status, then they get the same respect for their lives and well-being as children and adults.[6]

The possible implications of treating profoundly disabled humans as nonpersons also resound in the context of the medical handling of permanently unconscious human beings. The most extreme view is that a permanently unconscious human being, having no capacity to experience his or her environment or to have interactions with other beings, lacks a critical qualification for human existence and ought to be deemed dead.[7] An alternative view is that a permanently unconscious being is alive but has been reduced to a nonperson who lacks customary human interests in continued life, such as experiencing an environment or relating to other be-ings. A decision to withdraw life support is then apparently consistent with the unconscious nonperson's own limited interests. If the permanently un-conscious being is indeed a nonperson, a surrogate's effort to dictate the withdrawal of life support would be reinforced (given the diminished moral stature of a nonperson). Some commentators offer that account to explain why American law generally allows life support to be withdrawn from a patient in a permanently unconscious state even though the patient is not suffering and arguably has an interest in living because of the remote chance of a miraculous recovery.[8] If the permanently unconscious patient is not a person, then the interests of surrounding family and caregivers— that is, "real" persons—may assume greater importance in resolving the patient's fate. An incapacitated patient's medical fate is not ordinarily de-cided by reference to the burdens on family associated with treatment or nontreatment. But the absence of personhood in the patient could allow family interests not only to come into play but to become prominent or even dominant.[9] Moreover, if the permanently unconscious being is deemed a nonperson, perhaps it would be justifiable to harvest organs from the un-conscious being or to conduct medical research on that being before end-ing life support.

Absence of personhood could also affect the role that third-party inter-ests—particularly parents' and siblings' interests—play in determining the medical course for the profoundly disabled being in a variety of medical situations. Other examples (beyond the context of permanently uncon-scious patients) show how the diminished moral stature of a human being would help determine society's willingness (and perhaps moral entitle-ment) to subjugate that being's interests to the needs of other human be-ings.[10] It is self-evident that a *person's* interests in bodily integrity, personal well-being, and self-determination preclude harvesting nonvital tissue (a kidney or bone marrow) without personal consent—even if another per-son's life or several persons' lives could be saved. In other words, a person's medical course is not shaped by a utilitarian calculus encompassing social interests.[11] But if a profoundly disabled being is a nonperson, shouldn't a surrogate be able to approve the performance of a nontherapeutic medical experiment to benefit future generations of people? Wouldn't a profoundly disabled being's status as a nonperson determine the prioritizing of access to scarce medical resources or to other societal goods that facilitate people's opportunities to flourish?[12] And what about harvesting of nonvital tissue to benefit a real person?

An illustrative case arose with regard to anencephalic newborns—infants born without upper brains and fated to live short, insentient lives devoid of human interaction. Some commentators urged that an anencephalic baby's parents be allowed to consent to harvesting the baby's organs to benefit other children.[13] The American Medical Association's Council on Ethical and Judicial Affairs initially endorsed such a practice,[14] although the council later withdrew its approval. In this instance, the deathlike (that is, nonperson) status of the anencephalic being contributed to the commentators' willingness to allow an organ harvest—a willingness to exploit a living human's body for the benefit of others.

The moral stature of a profoundly disabled being is relevant to other issues in the context of surrogate decision making. An important question (to be explored in chapter 6) is the significance of the voice of the profoundly disabled patient—the expressions uttered by the nonrational patient, including those that either assent to or oppose a proposed medical intervention. These expressions cannot reflect the considered judgment of an autonomous person, but they might still reflect the will and feelings of a person. Establishing the profoundly disabled as persons with full moral status can help to determine the import to be attributed to their expressions.

Denying personhood (and full moral significance) to profoundly disabled humans would not mean depriving them of all moral status. At the very least, as sentient beings they would be entitled to be protected against needless suffering.[15] And their human status would limit the nature and extent of exploitation of profoundly disabled humans to satisfy the needs of others. That is, there might have to be important interests of "real" persons at stake in order to justify any exploitation of human nonpersons. Still, treatment as nonpersons would substantially truncate the interests of profoundly disabled humans.[16] Their lives might not be protected against nonpainful death. Their interests would be secondary in the allocation of societal resources. "Real" persons' interests would naturally enter into surrogate medical decision making and perhaps receive even heavier weighting than the nonperson's interests.

Treatment of the profoundly disabled as being nonpersons and having inferior moral status would also affect public attitudes and empathy. The interests of humans somehow get more respect when acknowledged as being connected to persons.[17] Lainie Friedman Ross comments that a severely retarded individual is deserving of respect but is "owed less [respect] than that owed to a fully actualized person."[18] Some philosophers would accord rights to mentally disabled persons to a degree "proportionate to the degree to which they approach being" full persons (meaning beings who are capable of acting as moral agents).[19] This phenomenon of diminished respect flows in part from people's tendency to identify with and respect most highly those beings who most resemble themselves. This is not to say that human beings don't count morally unless they are perceived as persons but only that there is a tendency to respect their interests less—to attribute less weight to their interests than to those of others—if personhood is deemed lacking. That tendency might well affect surrogate medical decision makers who are acting on behalf of the profoundly disabled.[20]

Criteria of Personhood

If the potential importance of personhood to shaping the rights of the profoundly disabled is acknowledged, then the issue becomes the criteria for personhood. A central task of moral philosophy is to identify a set of characteristics that distinguish "persons" from other living beings.[21] That task is not necessarily confined to distinguishing human beings from nonhuman animals. Considerable controversy exists about whether all live human beings qualify as persons (with concomitant full moral status). A number of philosophers contend that personhood requires a level of intellectual function that would exclude some or all profoundly disabled beings. For those philosophers, neither mere existence as a human being nor sentience (capacity for pleasure and pain) suffices for personhood.

While many philosophers regard high intellectual function as the principal determinant of personhood (and as the element that gives humans special moral value), there is no consensus about the precise level of intellectual function that is necessary and sufficient to confer personhood. Some philosophers look to autonomy and rationality (capacity to reflect and act on reason) as the key determinant.[22] Others demand greater intellectual capacity, such as a capability to make life plans and projects or a capability to communicate with others by language. Some go further and demand moral agency—the capacity to ponder and grasp moral principles—as a prerequisite to personhood.[23] Along those lines, Tom Beauchamp reserves moral personhood to those who "understand moral reciprocity and communal expectation."[24] At a less demanding level, some philosophers look to self-consciousness—awareness of personal identity over time—as the key element.[25] Self-consciousness is sometimes given a refined meaning— "reflective consciousness"—under which a person must not only be aware of self but also aware of having personal experiences. James Walters goes further, including in his definition of self-consciousness "the capacity to be aware of one's distinctive self as a relatively autonomous being among other such selves."[26]

Any position viewing high intellectual capacity of the human mind as the key to personhood and concomitant full moral status would exclude some profoundly disabled beings. Some profoundly disabled people are so severely neurologically damaged that they cannot reason or communicate, although they can experience pleasure and pain.[27] Others have the capacity for rudimentary autonomy, yet their mental function is so limited that they cannot qualify as moral agents: "Ethical reasoning depends upon certain kinds of cognitive as well as emotional capacities, including complex intellectual skills required to universalize and empathize."[28] Even a less demanding standard than moral agency—one that requires psychological continuity (a consciousness of personal identity over time)—would exclude at least some profoundly disabled beings from personhood.[29] This would especially be so under a definition of self-consciousness that requires "reflective consciousness" as opposed to mere sensory awareness of self and of an environment.[30] The status of a profoundly disabled being would also be uncertain under a view that treats capacity for human relationships as the key to personhood.[31] The nature of the intellectual or emotional capacities deemed critical to human relationships would then determine the status of profoundly disabled beings.

Other philosophical conceptions of the criteria necessary for personhood are more expansive and would clearly encompass the profoundly disabled (even if they would exclude some other human beings). One example is a position that accords personhood to any conscious human being who is capable of interacting on any level with other humans.[32] While permanently unconscious humans would then be excluded from personhood,[33] virtually all profoundly disabled humans would be included despite their very limited cognitive capacity. Another expansive position acknowledges the personhood of any human being who is sentient and capable of experiencing pleasure or pain.[34] An even more expansive position—one that is often grounded in a religious perspective—upholds the intrinsic value of any live human being, even a permanently unconscious one.[35] Such a position would accord full moral status and concomitant rights to any live human being, no matter how profoundly disabled.

If a high level of mental function distinguishes the human species and makes human beings worthy and valuable, why should profoundly disabled persons be treated as persons with full moral stature? One approach is to deny that personhood is grounded in any particular criterion such as high intellectual function. Many philosophers insist that all human beings are persons and that all humans are equally worthy and valuable regardless of intellectual level. One basis for that position is religious faith. According to the book of Genesis, humans are unique in being created in the image of God. This supposedly gives all humans a divinelike status (although the divinelike qualities are usually cognitive elements such as reason, judgment, and moral concern).[36] Even though the godlike qualities involve intellectual capacity, the human species as a whole is deemed worthy because of its generally high intellectual capacity and because all species members are viewed as possessing a "radical" intellectual potential from conception.[37] From that perspective, nonactualization of human potential does not negate that original radical capacity. The reality, though, is that some human beings lack cognitive capacity or even the potential for developing such capacity from the moment of conception. Attributing high mental function (or potential function) to all species members therefore rings hollow.

Some secular philosophers also contend that all human beings, regardless of intellectual function, have full moral status. That premise is sometimes based on intuition or moral (nonreligious) faith.[38] For example, Lois Shepherd calls concern and respect toward helpless beings "an essential part of being human, of existing."[39] Peter Byrne speaks of a "humanist perception" that all humans are morally equal.[40] Jean Elshtain posits a sort of secular golden rule of moral reciprocity. Each human must respect even the most debilitated humans because anyone could end up in such a debilitated condition.[41]

The Legal and Moral Status of the Profoundly Disabled

We have seen two theories of personhood—one grounded in intellectual function and the other in species membership. Which of those visions prevails? And why? For starters, I agree with Hilde Lindemann Nelson that personhood is largely a cultural construct that is reflected in social practice.[42] American society recognizes as persons with full moral status all live human beings, even those who cannot articulate their feelings and emotions so that their personalities are the product of interpretation by the people around them. That social construct does not even require consciousness for full moral status, as attested by the treatment of permanently unconscious humans as persons.

Using social practice as a key mark of personhood would seem to present grave threats of abuse, as historically illustrated by slavery and the holocaust. My response is that social practice cannot be an exclusive determinant and must be subjected to critical scrutiny. As part of that scrutiny, the concept of intrinsic human dignity must serve as a limit or check when social practice excessively contracts the criteria of personhood. When social practice expands the definition of personhood (for example, by including some nonhuman animals), no moral violation generally takes place. Perhaps intrinsic human dignity would be offended by an overly expansive definition of personhood (for example, treating rocks as persons), but certainly the inclusion of profoundly disabled humans within the category of persons does not constitute an offense to human dignity. Nor does inclusion of all humans derogate the status of nonhumans.[43]

American society has constructed a version of personhood that includes all live human beings as rights-bearing persons with full moral stature. Law currently treats even the most profoundly disabled human beings as persons. Constitutional protection of persons attaches at live human birth.[44] The U.S. Supreme Court adhered to that position when it refused to view a woman's exercise of procreative choice via an abortion as impinging on the interests of a person protected by the Fourteenth Amendment. That is, the Court did not treat an unborn fetus as a person with equal status to the mother. While the Court declared that government might generally preclude postviability abortion, the government's interest was deemed to be protection of a *potential* person rather than an actual person.

Courts and legislatures generally strive to safeguard the interests of born-alive humans without regard to level of intellectual function.[45] The traditional *parens patriae* authority is oriented toward protecting vulnerable people. Within that framework, a profoundly disabled human is no "less worthy of dignity and respect in the eyes of the law than a competent person."[46] That approach is evident in the legal response to permanently unconscious beings at both ends of the trajectory of human existence— anencephalic newborns and adults who have deteriorated to a permanently vegetative state (PVS). (Both a patient in a permanently vegetative state and an anencephalic infant retain lower-brain function and thus are not dead under a whole-brain standard for declaring death.) The law consistently treats permanently unconscious beings as persons entitled to respect.[47] In a 1992 Florida case,[48] parents of an anencephalic infant sought judicial authorization to have vital organs removed from their newborn in order to donate those organs to other critically ill infants whose lives could be salvaged. The parents argued that their anencephalic newborn, permanently lacking neocortical function and totally unable to interact with his environment, was for all practical purposes dead and ought to be declared dead to permit some human gain to be extracted from an otherwise unmitigated tragedy. (Apparently, the organs would be less suitable for transplant if surgeons waited until the anencephalic infant became totally brain dead.) The court summarily rejected the parents' plea for permission to transplant organs. The judge made clear that as long as the infant had even rudimentary, autonomic brain function, he would be regarded as a live person and protected against killing, by organ harvest or otherwise, even for the purpose of salvaging another human life or lives. A similar attitude solicitous of the well-being of an anencephalic infant prevailed in a federal district court in Virginia in 1993.[49] That court ruled that an anencephalic infant was protected by federal legislation prohibiting discrimination against the disabled. According to the court, a hospital's withdrawal of a life-sustaining respirator from the anencephalic infant (counter to the mother's wishes) would constitute unlawful discrimination against a disabled person.

A similar judicial attitude treats a PVS patient as a person entitled to protection against abusive treatment or invidious discrimination. All states deem a patient who is in a permanently vegetative state to be alive and entitled to continued life support unless a conscientious surrogate determines by some acceptable criterion that life support should be withdrawn. In most jurisdictions, that criterion is either best interests of the patient (a judgment that the insensate patient would be better off dead than alive) or substituted judgment (a determination that the patient, if miraculously capable of decision, would opt for death rather than a permanently insentient limbo). A few states are more restrictive, precluding removal of life support unless the PVS patient had previously expressed such a wish. In *Cruzan v. Director, Missouri Department of Health,*[50] the parents of a Missouri woman who had been rendered permanently unconscious as a result of an automobile accident sought judicial authorization for withdrawal of life-sustaining medical intervention (a tube supplying artificial nutrition) from their daughter. The state insisted on clear and convincing evidence of the now incompetent patient's prior wishes as a precondition to withdrawal of life support. The parents asserted their insentient daughter's liberty-based right to have her medical fate determined by a conscientious guardian. The U.S. Supreme Court, in upholding Missouri's insistence on clear and convincing evidence, relied on the public interest in protecting vulnerable persons (including permanently unconscious patients) against possible exploitation. To the majority (in a five to four decision), Missouri at least had a rational reason for insisting on prior instructions from the patient. No member of the Court hesitated in accepting permanently unconscious patients as persons deserving of legislative and constitutional protection.[51]

What are the reasons for the established practice of treating profoundly disabled humans as rights-bearing persons with full moral status? There are a number of explanations—some emotional, some practical, and some theoretical. On an emotional plane, one consideration is a "sentimental regard that we tend to have for beings of our own kind."[52] Many people have an instinctive emotional affinity toward beings who at least look like they are fellow persons: "We find it revolting to even think about killing a newborn baby whose anatomical features are so like our own,"[53] even if the newborn possesses only primitive intellectual function. Jane English comments on species affinity: "Our psychological Constitution makes it the case that . . . our ethical theory . . . must prohibit certain treatment of persons who are significantly personlike."[54] This emotional factor helps account for the practice of fully respecting profoundly disabled beings. (A similar emotional affinity may help account for the Supreme Court's construction of "viability" as the point at which states can protect a fetus from abortion;

a third-trimester fetus bears a strong physical resemblance to newborns and thereby strikes an emotional chord in observers.[55])

Another, perhaps less persuasive, reason to accord maximum moral status to the profoundly disabled is their role in enhancing the emotional lives of other persons.[56] People can form strong attachments to fellow humans—even those who operate at a dismal intellectual level. Mary Anne Warren calls this factor "transitivity of respect"—a notion that society ought to respect the fact that some persons love and attribute full stature to profoundly disabled beings.[57] In other words, society ought to accept the moral significance that some persons attribute to profoundly disabled beings. This rationale for legally protecting the profoundly disabled—as contributors to social relations—seems less persuasive for two reasons. Nonhuman animals serve a similar function, and no consensus yet supports personhood or comparable rights for even higher-functioning animals. And if the status of a profoundly disabled being is dependent on social contacts, some such beings might be excluded from protection because they had been abandoned by parents or other family. Unless healthcare providers or others have bonded with the isolated being, full moral stature might be found lacking—a clearly undesirable result.

Other, more practical reasons exist for deeming profoundly disabled humans to be persons with full moral status regardless of their low level of intellectual function. Even philosophers who tend to associate personhood and full moral status with high intellectual function find "social considerations" or a general public interest in imputing full stature and rights to the profoundly disabled.[58] For example, an instrumental rationale is available. Societal solicitude toward helpless and vulnerable human beings (even nonpersons) may help cultivate sentiments of sympathy and caring within the general population.[59] Protection of the profoundly disabled can also be viewed as a symbolic reminder of the sanctity of human life. Reluctance to neglect or abandon any human being conveys a social message about the worth of all human life. The further claim is that there is symbolic importance in how society treats frail and vulnerable beings; by protecting the profoundly disabled, society seeks to promote an atmosphere where the infirm are well treated and secure. Exclusion of certain human "nonpersons" from full protection and respect would risk eroding respect for humans who qualify as persons but are still intellectually marginal.[60]

Other social interests are promoted by according full stature and rights to profoundly disabled beings. If personhood and rights-bearing status were reserved to humans who have a particular level of intellectual function, hazards would exist regarding a possible arbitrary fixing of the relevant line and an arbitrary or abusive application of such a line. How much permanent brain dysfunction warrants exclusion from the human community? Even if a clear, coherent line were theoretically establishable, its administration might still be problematic. Here's an example. At one point, physicians at a Loma Linda, California, medical facility were willing to use anencephalic infants as potential organ donors.[61] The definition of anencephaly seemed clear—including total absence of neocortical or upper-brain function. Yet the Loma Linda staff received numerous calls from outside physicians volunteering newborns who, while exhibiting serious deficits, retained significant intellectual function. Treatment of all human beings as rights-holding persons safeguards against the arbitrary exclusion of some helpless individuals. In short, good practical reasons exist to treat profoundly disabled humans as rights-bearing persons with full moral stature.

These "practical" considerations justify the legal system's attribution of full rights-bearing status to all live humans. Is there also a theoretical basis for according full *moral* status to all human beings? As noted, some moral philosophers regard a high level of intellectual function (rationality, autonomy, or moral agency) as the key to personhood and full moral status. And many people's intuition may be that richer experiential lives "count for more."[62]

This spectrum of intellectual thresholds for personhood seem somewhat arbitrary. (Each propounder of a requisite level of intellectual function has a rationale, but none of them seems convincing.) One of the common elements in this spectrum is that most of the suggested levels of intellectual function would exclude many if not most profoundly disabled individuals. That fact makes it worth asking whether any theoretical basis other than religious faith reinforces the practical reasons for including all humans as persons.

Alan Gewirth has articulated a theory that is capable of rationalizing full moral status for almost all profoundly disabled humans. Gewirth sees purposive or goal-oriented behavior as the characteristic that makes persons special and worthy.[63] However, Gewirth himself doesn't clearly fix the level of intellectual function necessary for being a purposive agent and in at least some writings seems to deny full moral stature to profoundly disabled humans.[64] Evelyn Pluhar adapts Gewirth's approach to full moral status in a way that clearly attributes full moral significance to almost all profoundly disabled humans.[65] Pluhar defines *purposive behavior* (which she agrees is the key to full moral status) as including all "conative" beings—those who are goal directed and have desires, even basic desires for survival, food, shelter, and companionship. For her, that level of purposive agency is possessed by any human with even very low-level intellectual abilities.[66]

What makes purposive behavior and conscious desire the keys to full moral status? In a way, Gewirth and Pluhar do not look so much at characteristics that make beings particularly worthy of protection but, rather, try to assess moral harm. To some extent, Pluhar relies on intuition in saying that profoundly disabled but purposive people are morally significant. (I already noted the emotional factor that helps account for legal protection for profoundly disabled humans.) Perhaps the further point is that to Gewirth and Pluhar, frustration of purposive behavior (by death or inhumane treatment) just seems to be a significant enough harm to warrant empathy and concern. Some philosophers in defining moral harm tend to ask whether the being whose status is in issue is capable of valuing his or her own existence.[67] From their perspective, frustration of conscious humans' desire to live constitutes a moral wrong because it deprives them (without justification) of something that they value.[68] For Pluhar, there is no hierarchy of moral harm in killing a highly intelligent person as opposed to a mentally disabled person. "A bright, young human adult loses a complex network of relationships and has her life plan aborted. A significantly retarded human of the same age loses just as much from *his* perspective. Each loses *all that is precious*, all that matters to him or her."[69]

All this appeals to me. I like John Keown's suggestion that a person is anyone "having the ability to achieve some purposeful or self-directed action or to achieve some goal of importance to him or her self."[70] For me, this formulation focuses on the "common nature" of human beings—their mental capacity. The fact that the profoundly disabled have impaired brain function and don't reach an intellectual level that is typical of humans doesn't negate their common humanity. While I readily understand a position that attributes full moral status to every member of the human species—even permanently unconscious ones—some cognitive function seems to me like an integral part of a common human nature. In effect, the purposiveness position deprives permanently unconscious humans of moral status and confers full moral status on any conscious human being who is capable of purposive behavior, even toward basic or simplistic goals. Any profoundly disabled person who does not meet the suggested criterion for moral status (conative conduct) would still receive full legal protection for the practical reasons cited above. The current legal structure goes further and protects even permanently unconscious humans. As is developed in chapters 2 and 4, this does not mean that permanently unconscious beings must be kept alive. In most states, a surrogate may remove life-sustaining medical intervention from a permanently unconscious human. I will go further and argue that preservation of permanently unconscious persons violates intrinsic human dignity. First, let me explain what I mean by intrinsic human dignity.

The Role of Intrinsic Human Dignity

I argued earlier that all humans have full legal status and that virtually all humans (excluding primarily the permanently unconscious) have full moral status as persons. An important concomitant of personhood is entitlement to respect for dignity.[71] For reasons already cited, profoundly disabled persons get that respect for dignity even though they lack the intellectual capacity that generally characterizes the human species.

Because human dignity plays an important role in resolving the issues that are addressed in this book, I need to better explain at the outset what I mean by human dignity. After all, human dignity means many things to many people, as the term *dignity* is used in varied senses. People can comport themselves with an air of dignity—that is, with a certain calm and composure. Another meaning of dignity has to do with enjoyment of a secure environment and protection of well-being. Some commentators see the provision of decent living conditions as a central requirement of respect for human dignity. Their object is to secure for all persons the material conditions in which the human spirit can operate and flourish.[72] In that vein, the Universal Declaration of Human Rights treats economic security as being indispensable for human dignity and the development of personality. A similar concern about a humane and nurturing environment was certainly part of the legal attack that was launched in the United States in the 1970s against the poor conditions in which the mentally retarded were living in public institutions.[73] The provision of decent living conditions may be a worthwhile goal for humanists, but only at an extreme level of deprivation is human dignity implicated.

More commonly, the concept of human dignity functions as an intrinsic value or an inherent stature that demands respect. That notion of dignity as an inherent stature underlies and informs many human rights. Respect for human dignity helps account for concepts such as freedom and justice and for rights such as bodily integrity, physical security, freedom of speech and conscience, freedom of association, privacy, and personal mobility.[74] As the introduction to the Council of Europe's Convention on Human Rights explains: "human dignity constitutes the essential value" that underlies various human rights protected by the Convention.[75] I am interested in exploring (at this point and in the rest of the book) the nature and degree of the respect that flows from the intrinsic dignity of human beings. What conduct toward human beings is so disrespectful of their moral stature that it violates intrinsic human dignity? What core of respect, what minimum norm of behavior, is morally owed to every human being? And how does that norm get applied to profoundly disabled persons?

Many commentators stress a strong link between dignity and autonomy, in part because they value human intellectual capacity for considered choice as a key human attribute.[76] For those commentators, upholding autonomy is a basic aspect of respecting human dignity. This veneration of autonomy extends to medical decision making for persons who are fully competent, competent to make *some* medical decisions, or formerly competent. An ethic that upholds autonomy dominates both medical mores and the legal framework governing medical interventions affecting task-competent persons. Traditional legal doctrine requiring informed consent for medical interventions underscores the importance that our culture attaches to self-determination. Personal choice in medical decision making is such an integral element of American culture that it has even been acknowledged to be part of fundamental liberty under the Fourteenth Amendment— among the "choices central to personal dignity and autonomy" that qualify for special constitutional protection.[77] Many courts have recognized that the upholding of a competent patient's medical choice is integral to human dignity.[78]

Autonomous choice also plays an important role in determining the medical fate of formerly competent persons. Every state has recognized what I call "prospective autonomy"[79] via laws that compel adherence to advance medical directives—personal instructions issued by competent persons to govern their postcompetence medical handling.[80] Even for previously competent persons who fail to articulate their medical choices in advance, law often seeks to honor self-determination in shaping the standards that are imposed on surrogate decision makers. Substituted judgment is a common legal approach that instructs a surrogate decision maker to implement the medical course that the now incompetent patient would have chosen; that projection of the patient's wishes is grounded on the patient's own values and preferences when available.[81]

Most persons do not articulate postcompetence medical preferences in advance. In the absence of prior expressions, many states direct a surrogate decision maker to adhere to the incompetent patient's best interests. In jurisdictions where "best interests" is supposed to govern postcompetence medical decisions, a strong self-determination current is still present. The previously competent patient's own values and preferences are deemed highly relevant to defining the now incompetent patient's best interests. When those values and preferences are undiscernible or indeterminate, the patient's best interests are determined by an examination of the factors that most competent people deem crucial to their postcompetence medical handling—principally, the avoidance of extreme pain and other intolerably demeaning conditions. Thus, even under an objective best-interests formula, surrogates are in a sense required to honor self-determination by applying factors (benefits and burdens) that most people would want considered. This is part of an effort to project what the now incompetent patient would have wanted by assuming (in the absence of contrary indications) that this formerly competent patient would want his or her well-being promoted and by defining well-being according to how most competent persons would define their own postcompetence well-being.

An ethic of human dignity focused on self-determination cannot readily be applied to persons who have never been competent. It is true that the prevailing medical and legal approach is to honor the maximum self-determination possible for mentally disabled persons. This means upholding their decisions when they can understand the nature and consequences of the particular medical decision in issue. However, profoundly disabled persons, as I have defined them, have never had sufficient cognitive function to understand the nature and consequences of serious medical issues. Nor have they adopted philosophical or religious values that might guide medical decisions on their behalf. The central ethic in surrogate decision making for the never competent cannot therefore be autonomy. Conventional wisdom and many judicial opinions assert that ethical focus shifts to the never competent person's best interests—meaning personal well-being in the sense of physical and psychic integrity.

Chapter 4 addresses in detail the best-interests formula as it has been applied to serious medical decisions for profoundly disabled persons. It explains how law purports to apply a best-interests formula geared to the well-being of the never competent person as assessed by a reasonable person—a competent person who is making a considered choice while facing the circumstances that affect the never competent patient, and assuming the perspective (as far as possible) of the never competent patient. (This in essence is also the standard that is applied to a formerly competent patient who never indicated personal values or preferences to guide postcompetence decision making.)

This usage of a best-interests formula—with its focus on the well-being of the never competent person—is supported by a couple of theories that are consistent with human dignity. First, the common law traditionally regards government as having a *parens patriae* protective duty toward helpless persons. This is certainly a pervasive theme when formal guardians have been judicially appointed to make surrogate medical decisions for a never competent person or when a judge is charged with making the ultimate decision on behalf of a never competent patient.[82] A strict best-interests formula is customarily articulated in those contexts. Second, a patient's best interests are commonly viewed as an appropriate and humane default standard for surrogate decision making where never competent persons cannot make binding personal choices.[83] That is, considered choice by a profoundly disabled person is impossible, but the courts assume that any human being, no matter how mentally disabled, would want to have their own interests protected and promoted. Respect for persons therefore includes protection of the well-being interests of never competent persons.

While both these perspectives seem to dictate a surrogate's strict adherence to a ward's personal interests, practice does not necessarily follow that narrow course. My own perspective (to be further explained in chapter 4) is that best interests is not the standard that always governs surrogate medical decisions on behalf of never competent persons. I suggest in chapters 4 and 5 that the term *best* interests of the incompetent person does not really mean the maximum possible promotion of the patient's interests and that the interests of other persons may sometimes come into play.

Whatever the precise bounds of the best-interests legal standard, the point remains that one element of human dignity—respect for autonomy—has diminished importance in the context of serious medical decisions on behalf of profoundly disabled persons. Yet an absence of autonomy by no means relegates the profoundly disabled person to an undignified status.

A different aspect of human dignity occupies a central role in shaping the medical fate of profoundly disabled persons. I call this critical element *intrinsic human dignity*—meaning a core conception of basic respect to which every human being is entitled, regardless of cognitive capacity.[84] That notion of basic respect for every human being serves as an ultimate moral constraint on the surrogate treatment of profoundly disabled persons. That normative sense of human dignity, an inviolable core of respect, has been acknowledged in numerous legal contexts ranging from various international conventions on human rights to the constitutional jurisprudence of several countries.[85] For example, Canadian jurisprudence recognizes that "human dignity has an absolute core that may not be infringed."[86]

An integral part of human dignity is freedom from demeaning or degrading treatment. The full moral status of persons insulates them against unjust debasement and unwarranted contempt or humiliation, at least at extremes.[87] But not every offense to a person's dignity—not every frustration of will or subjection to embarrassment—is violative of intrinsic human dignity. My concept of intrinsic human dignity refers only to conduct that is so disrespectful and degrading of a person that it intolerably assaults core human dignity—that is, it violates an irreducible minimum of respect owed every human being.[88] Prison inmates are relegated to living conditions that are demeaning and undignified, but only when the conditions become so degrading as to be intolerably inhumane do they violate intrinsic human dignity. Bodily integrity is an important dignitary interest, but only when that interest is egregiously invaded—as with rape, torture, or other unjustified bodily encroachments—is core human dignity violated. As the European Council has explained, every unprovoked use of physical force against a person in custody may be degrading and deplorable, but only when police conduct causes intense physical or mental suffering or takes particularly repugnant forms does it become violative of the provision of the European Convention on Human Rights that protects intrinsic human dignity.[89]

A similar conception of core matters entitled to special protection appears in the context of competent persons. While autonomy is certainly linked to dignity, not every constraint on personal choice violates intrinsic human dignity. Only when *fundamental* liberty interests (such as freedom of conscience or choices about marriage and procreation) are intolerably invaded or denied does core human dignity get violated.

How do we differentiate between run-of-the-mill infringements of dignity and impingements on inviolable, core human dignity? In each culture, the definition of core human dignity is fixed by the collective conscience of the community as informed by experience and critical reflection. There is an inevitable element of cultural variability. One culture's notion of a fundamental freedom—as with polygamy, abortion, driver's licenses for women, or euthanasia—may offend human dignity in another culture. Some cultures will deem dwarf throwing or participation in degrading peep shows or clean-shaven faces for men to be intolerably demeaning; others will not. At the same time, some universal norms of human dignity— for example, a ban on slavery—prevail across cultures. And each culture will have some elements of dignity that it considers inviolable.

A core conception of human dignity is relevant to several situations (addressed later in this book) in which profound mental disability necessitates surrogate control of serious medical decisions. As is shown in the next chapter, the concept of intrinsic human dignity can provide a basis for a claim that mentally incompetent persons are entitled to have a surrogate decision maker choose for them, at least as to medical decisions that can benefit the incompetent person. That is, it may be violative of human dignity to exclude certain categories of medical decisions (for example, contraception or end-of-life decisions) from surrogate authority. The notion of intrinsic human dignity thus promotes broad access to all kinds of surrogate medical decisions that may prevent profoundly disabled persons from reaching an intolerably demeaning or undignified condition.

Intrinsic human dignity is also relevant in defining the protective legal standard (commonly articulated as the "best-interests" standard) that binds surrogate decision makers when they make important medical decisions on behalf of profoundly disabled persons. In chapters 4 and 5, I argue that the applicable legal standards permit some consideration of third-party interests, such as those of integral family members. At the same time, I assert that while surrogate decision makers may properly consider third-party interests in certain areas, such as tissue donation or participation in non-therapeutic research, intrinsic human dignity imposes significant protections against unconscionable exploitation of profoundly disabled persons. Finally, intrinsic human dignity informs how surrogate decision makers must treat the voice or expressions of the profoundly disabled (Chapter 6). In short, I contend in this book that the normative force of intrinsic, core human dignity informs in several respects the legal and moral framework for surrogate decision making on behalf of profoundly disabled persons. I now address how intrinsic human dignity relates to a profoundly disabled person's entitlement to a surrogate's determination about an appropriate medical course.

2

The Profoundly Disabled as Rights Holders: No Rights, the Same Rights as the Fully Capacitated, or Some Rights?

Attributing the "Same Rights" to the Profoundly Disabled

The notion of a constitutional right to make important medical decisions dates to the middle of the twentieth century. In 1965, the U.S. Supreme Court in *Griswold v. Connecticut*[1] indicated that certain unenumerated but fundamental elements of liberty, including a prerogative to make certain personal choices, are protected by the federal Constitution. (In *Griswold*, the Court struck down a Connecticut ban on the use of contraceptives by married couples, finding that access to contraception is part of a fundamental liberty interest within marital privacy.) Cases and commentators promptly sought to apply that liberty rationale to a competent patient's rejection of life-sustaining medical intervention.[2] They relied on the legal doctrine of informed consent as establishing traditional respect for personal medical choice in an effort to bolster the claim to fundamental liberty status for terminal medical choices. *Roe v. Wade*, in 1973, added impetus to the claim by reinforcing the constitutionally protected status of intimate personal choices, including a joint patient-physician decision to terminate a pregnancy.[3]

In the landmark *In re Quinlan*[4] case in 1976, the New Jersey Supreme Court ruled that a competent patient does indeed have a constitutionally protected right to decline or accept life-sustaining medical intervention. Furthermore, the court found that this liberty right had application even in the context of a patient mired in a permanently unconscious state. According to Chief Justice Hughes's opinion, "[T]he only practical way to prevent destruction of the right"[5] (meaning the now incompetent patient's right to decline treatment) was to permit a conscientious guardian to determine how the patient would exercise the right in the circumstances at hand. Accordingly, a devoted father was deemed entitled to decide, on behalf of his permanently unconscious daughter, whether to withdraw respirator support.

A number of other courts followed suit and subscribed to the position that a surrogate should be able to exercise choice on behalf of the now incompetent patient so that the constitutional right to decline treatment would not be lost.[6] The exercise of substituted judgment by a surrogate—seeking to replicate what the now incompetent person would decide if he or she were miraculously competent—was seen as a necessary means to preserve the patient's constitutional prerogative.[7] Some courts even declared that incompetent persons enjoy "the same right" to make medical decisions as competent persons.[8] And a similar approach emerged in cases dealing with sterilization determinations on behalf of mentally incapacitated persons. Courts that were considering sterilization sought to preserve the disabled patient's right to choose contraceptive means.[9] They did so by authorizing sterilization at least when the court agreed with the patient's guardian that sterilization would serve the disabled patient's interests.

Numerous commentators questioned the extension of a right to reject medical treatment to a decisionally incapacitated person. For them, the patient's constitutional prerogative is grounded in autonomous choice—a personalized weighing of options reflecting the patient's own values and preferences. An incompetent patient by definition could not have the capacity to understand the alternatives and to exercise informed choice. A typical query: "Whatever rights an incompetent person may be said to possess, how can autonomous choice be one of them when incompetency means precisely the inability to exercise choice?"[10] For these commentators, personal freedom to choose could not survive incompetency. For them, "proxy exercise of the right of self-determination is simply not possible."[11]

This critique of applying notions of self-determination and substituted judgment to decisionally incapacitated persons is certainly unconvincing in the context of previously competent patients. If a person, while competent, either made a prospective choice, as in an advance medical directive, or articulated values and preferences sufficient to guide postcompetency medical decisions, then self-determination is indeed respected when a surrogate implements the now incompetent patient's wishes. Prospective choice may not be as robust as contemporaneous choice because the advance decision maker may not have the detailed information and experience that would normally aid and instruct a medical decision. Yet a person who is anticipating future medical situations may have well-developed values about intolerable suffering or indignity that can be implemented even after the person has become incompetent. So a surrogate meaningfully promotes an incapacitated patient's self-determination when an end-of-life medical decision is grounded on values (such as religious principles or personal convictions about dignity) that the patient previously embraced.

When a previously competent patient's prior expressions and values are murky or opaque regarding end-of-life treatment preferences, however, autonomy in the sense of actual weighing of options is no longer possible. Even then, efforts can be made to reach decisions that would likely reflect the now incompetent patient's wishes as reasonably projected. I would argue that constructive preference—imputing choices to a formerly competent patient based on what the vast majority of competent persons would want done for themselves in the circumstances at hand—is a meaningful way of promoting the patient's likely preferences in end-of-life care.[12] I have little sympathy with the commentators who have categorically condemned the application of notions of self-determination and substituted judgment to the context of formerly competent medical patients.[13]

But the subject of inquiry in this book is profoundly disabled persons. How can substituted judgment and surrogate efforts to implement a patient's constitutional liberty interests be meaningfully applied to a person who has never been able to make considered choices about medical issues or to formulate important values relevant to such issues? Can such a person have "the same right" to refuse medical treatment as a capacitated person?

Several courts have suggested that even profoundly disabled persons enjoy "the same panoply of rights and choices" as fully capacitated persons. The first articulation of that sentiment came from the Massachusetts Supreme Judicial Court in *Superintendent of Belchertown State School v. Saikewicz*,[14] which was decided scarcely six months after *Quinlan*. Joseph Saikewicz was a sixty-seven-year-old resident of an institution for the developmentally disabled. He was severely retarded, with a mental capacity to function at the level of a child two years and eight months old. Joseph was dying of leukemia, and the question arose of whether to administer chemotherapy in the hope of producing a remission that could last from four to thirteen months. The Massachusetts court ruled that a court (as

opposed to the head of the institution) should resolve Joseph's medical fate
and that the applicable decision-making standard would be substituted
judgment—requiring a determination of what Joseph would want to do if
miraculously competent and fully aware of all the circumstances. The court
declared that incompetent persons must be accorded "the same panoply of
rights and choices" as competent persons because the mentally incapacitated share the "same dignity and worth" as the capacitated.[15] A few courts
have followed the course set by *Saikewicz* and have applied a substituted-
judgment standard to end-of-life decisions on behalf of patients who have
always been profoundly disabled.[16] And a few courts have taken a similar
approach with regard to sterilization decisions and abortion decisions on
behalf of profoundly disabled persons.[17]

The notion that profoundly disabled persons have the *same* right to
choose as the abled is inaccurate. The right to refuse medical intervention
is, in part, grounded in self-determination—a weighing and choosing
among competing options. As mentioned, substituted judgment implements self-determination if the now incompetent patient previously articulated actual choices about end-of-life care or expressed preferences or
values sufficient to project what course of medical treatment that patient
would likely choose for himself or herself. Yet a profoundly disabled person has never been able to make autonomous choices. A surrogate cannot
implement a never competent patient's right of self-determination.[18] (As
is discussed in chapter 6, there are good reasons for a surrogate decision
maker to gather and consider evidence about a profoundly disabled patient's feelings and preferences regarding prospective medical treatment,
but they do not include honoring the patient's own autonomous choice.)

Many courts and commentators have recognized the problematic of applying notions of autonomy and substituted judgment to the profoundly
disabled. Commentators commonly note that capacity for autonomous
decision making is a prerequisite to a right to self-determination,[19] and
they scorn the application of a substituted-judgment formula to infants or
to profoundly disabled adults who lack mental function beyond that of an
infant or a young child.[20] Any notion of determining what a person with a
mental age of two years and eight months (the level of mental function of
Joseph Saikewicz) would decide on his or her own behalf is dismissed as a
figment of the imagination.[21] Most courts, when asked to apply substituted
judgment to an infant or to a profoundly disabled adult, have therefore

rejected the idea as involving an "unrealistic" or "impossible" task. That judicial response has been forthcoming in a variety of medicolegal contexts—the provision of life-sustaining medical intervention,[22] petitions for sterilization,[23] and organ donation.[24] All these sources repudiate the logic of imputing self-determination to profoundly disabled beings and of claiming that a surrogate is exercising "the same right" to control medical intervention as a competent patient.

Other critics couple the apparent illogic of ascribing autonomy-based rights to never competent persons with suspicions about the abuses that supposedly ensue from surrogate decisions on behalf of this vulnerable population. The perceived hazards are several. Roger Dworkin notes a risk that surrogate decision makers would act according to utilitarian concerns—that is, the interests of society or surrounding persons—rather than the disabled patient's interests.[25] Others, including advocates for the disabled, fear substituted judgment as a cover for exploitation based on prejudice and stereotyped views of the quality of life experienced by the profoundly disabled.[26] These critics commonly worry about the hazards of imputing indeterminate feelings or preferences to the profoundly disabled. They cite the Nazi justifications of euthanasia—that it was in the interests of the euthanized and was what the victims would want if they could express their wishes. (More later about the hazards of abuse that accompany surrogate decision making. I shortly discuss state efforts—based on concern for vulnerable disabled persons—to exclude entire areas of decision making from the hands of surrogates acting for the profoundly disabled.)

Saying that the profoundly disabled cannot enjoy "the same right" as the decisionally capacitated does not mean that they have no constitutional rights or even no liberty-based constitutional rights. Liberty in the sense of autonomous choice is not the only aspect of liberty important to profoundly disabled persons. Even a constitutional prerogative that normally involves autonomous choice has constitutionally cognizable elements that are highly relevant to a profoundly disabled person. Consider the right to refuse medical intervention. That right is now established as a fundamental aspect of liberty under the Fourteenth Amendment.[27] The right has at least three components: an interest in self-determination (that is, in making a choice about treatment), an interest in well-being (that is, in having net interests advanced by a decision about treatment), and an interest in maintenance of bodily integrity (that is, freedom from unnecessary bodily invasion). (This interest in bodily integrity is really part of a broader interest in preserving personal dignity.) While the profoundly disabled person cannot exercise the self-determination component, the other two personal interests that underlie a right to reject treatment—well-being and bodily integrity—are still present for the profoundly disabled patient. And while the disabled person's self-determination is not exercisable by a surrogate acting for a never competent person, a surrogate can meaningfully implement the other two elements within the right to refuse treatment. A conscientious surrogate can seek to determine whether a medical intervention will promote the net interests (well-being) of a profoundly disabled patient and whether the patient's bodily integrity (or dignity) will be needlessly compromised by the contemplated medical procedure.

The same analysis applies to abortion and sterilization decisions. Never competent persons have important potential interests (bodily integrity, physical well-being, and procreative capacity) in these medical options even if self-determination is an impossibility. To quote one case: "The interests of the incompetent which mandate recognition of procreative choice as an aspect of the fundamental right to . . . liberty do not differ from the interests of women able to give voluntary consent to [sterilization]."[28]

All this explains what prompted the *Saikewicz* court to talk about "the same panoply of rights and choices" for a sixty-seven-year-old adult who had always had the mentality of a three-year-old. The court erred in talking about substituted judgment (when the patient had never been able to make a considered judgment) and about the "same" right to choose as a competent person (when the patient could never exercise self-determination). But the court was surely correct in its conclusion that permitting a surrogate to choose whether to initiate life-sustaining treatment was integral to respecting the "dignity and worth" of the profoundly disabled Joseph Saikewicz.[29] Only in that way could Joseph's well-being and dignitary interests in bodily integrity and avoidance of suffering—all of them integral parts of the constitutional right to reject treatment—receive the consideration they deserve. Only in that way—permitting surrogate choice regarding potentially beneficial medical options—can a never competent person have access to important benefits available to other persons.

In some instances, a person's well-being is promoted by being allowed to die, as when proffered treatment will prolong a dying process dominated by suffering or by deterioration to an unconscious or barely conscious status. Categorical exclusion of surrogate choice to reject life-sustaining treatment on behalf of a profoundly disabled person then prejudices the well-being interest of that patient. The same phenomenon occurs when a medically indicated abortion or sterilization is in issue. That is, a state prohibition on surrogate consent to sterilization can seriously prejudice the well-being of a mentally disabled person whose physical condition would be jeopardized by pregnancy or childbirth.

A profoundly disabled person's human dignity interests can be jeopardized by exclusion of surrogate choice. This can occur in at least two ways. First, the exclusion of surrogate choice may leave the patient to linger in an intrinsically undignified state, the passive object of bodily invasions and manipulations, as in the case of permanent unconsciousness. That specter of a demeaning limbo prompted a Florida court to declare that "terminally ill incompetent persons . . . have the same right to refuse to be held on the threshold of death as terminally ill competent persons."[30] A profoundly disabled, dying person may not have the capacity to personally refuse further life support, but that person surely has an interest in avoiding an undignified death. Second, denial of access to the same range of potentially beneficial medical options as would be enjoyed by a decisionally capacitated patient denies the profoundly disabled patient's equal status with other persons and thereby offends that patient's dignitary interest in equal treatment—unless there is a convincing reason for the differential handling. The Massachusetts Supreme Judicial Court commented in *Saikewicz*: "To presume that the incompetent person must always be subjected to what many rational and intelligent persons may decline is to downgrade the status of incompetent persons by placing a lesser value on his [or her] intrinsic human worth and vitality."[31] Years later, that court made a similar observation about indignity in the context of sterilization: "To take away the right to obtain sterilization from persons who are incapable of exercising it personally is to degrade those whose disabilities make them wholly reliant on other, more fortunate, individuals."[32]

The story of Sheila Pouliot illustrates how a state's preclusion of surrogate choice can implicate human dignity.[33] Ms. Pouliot was a forty-three-year-old woman, chronically disabled by mental retardation and cerebral palsy. She had lived with her family for many years, but at the critical period in 1999 she was living in a New York State facility for the developmentally disabled. In the months preceding her last hospitalization, she had suffered recurrent episodes of gastroesophagal reflux disease, aspiration pneumonia, and gastrointestinal bleeding. On December 21, 1999, Ms. Pouliot was admitted to University Hospital in Syracuse, New York, suffering from aspiration pneumonia, gastrointestinal bleeding, severe abdominal pain, and a nonfunctioning intestine.

Sheila Pouliot's sister Alice served as representative of Sheila and her family. Alice determined, in conjunction with the hospital's medical staff, that Sheila was unavoidably dying, was permanently reduced to a semiconscious state, and was unable to digest artificial nutrition. Thus, further medical intervention, including artificial nutrition and hydration (ANH), would only prolong Sheila's dying process. The hospital ethics committee concurred. Comfort care, including morphine sulfate, was provided for Sheila's abdominal pain and for pain secondary to various muscle contractures and dislocated joints.

That medical course was followed for several days until the state attorney general's office intervened. The attorney general insisted that New York law would not permit removal of artificial nutrition and hydration from a person in the absence of his or her clear prior instructions declining life support in the circumstances at hand. Sheila Pouliot, as a never competent person, could never meet that standard. In the wake of that legal intervention, the physicians renewed artificial hydration and administration of a glucose solution intravenously. For the next seven weeks, Ms. Pouliot lingered, unable to relate to her environment and occasionally moaning, crying, and grimacing with pain (despite substantial pain-relief medication). She swelled up with total body edema until her skin began to break down in several places. Finally, on March 3, 2000, the family and medical staff secured a court order permitting removal of all life support. Sheila Pouliot died with the attorney general's office still scrambling to pursue an appeal and to prevent removal of the artificial hydration that had swelled Ms. Pouliot to a caricature of her former self. Her course of dying was inconsistent with both medical standards of palliative care and with humane and compassionate care.[34] That course of dying, supposedly required by New York law preventing a surrogate from removing artificial nutrition and hydration from a never competent person, surely deprived Sheila Pouliot of intrinsic human dignity.

A Constitutional Claim to Appropriate Medical Options

A connection between access to surrogate choice (regarding important medical issues) and intrinsic human dignity is thus clear. Do the incapacitated person's dignity interests, coupled with an interest in well-being tied to a medical option, rise to a constitutional plane? Could a profoundly disabled person be constitutionally entitled to a surrogate medical decision? The U.S. Supreme Court has acknowledged a connection between constitutional liberty and surrogate decision making on behalf of a mentally disabled person. In 1988, the Supreme Court noted (in a case unrelated to medical treatment) that the rights of incapacitated persons sometimes are "only meaningful as they are exercised by agents [surrogates] acting with the best interests of their principals in mind."[35] Implicit in that quote is recognition that a best-interests-of-the-incapacitated-patient formula allows surrogates to consider the well-being, bodily integrity, and dignity interests that partially underlie the profoundly disabled patient's constitutional liberty interest in issue. Other sources have also recognized the important interests of incapacitated persons in securing needed medical options. Courts considering end-of-life treatment for the profoundly disabled have sometimes noted that while self-determination or free choice are not relevant to lifelong disabled persons, surrogate choice can prevent such persons from being "stripped of basic rights" or from being rendered "passive subjects of medical technology."[36] Surrogate decision making that employs a best-interests standard at least ensures that the profoundly disabled person will benefit from reasoned choice—consideration of the possible gains or harms of a contemplated medical procedure—thereby promoting that person's constitutionally based interests in well-being, bodily integrity, and dignity.

Most courts that have spoken to the issue therefore allow a surrogate to make end-of-life medical decisions on behalf of profoundly disabled persons and dictate the application of a best-interests standard for decision making. Even courts that articulate a substituted-judgment standard—that is, a standard that purports to replicate what the incompetent patient would decide—tend to modify that approach in its application to profoundly disabled persons. In 1992, the Massachusetts Supreme Judicial Court (the court that had decided *Saikewicz* in 1976) admitted that substituted judgment is "a legal fiction" as applied to a never competent person and is retained in an effort to vindicate the patient's "liberty interests" including the rejection of treatment.[37] The court presumably meant liberty interests such as bodily integrity and dignity rather than self-determination because the very fiction that was acknowledged by the court was the attribution of autonomous judgment to Joseph Saikewicz.

When applied to a profoundly disabled person, the substituted-judgment standard inevitably gets transformed into a best-interests approach. That transformation took place in *Saikewicz* itself when the court ended up deciding Joseph's medical fate by emphasizing the prospective negative effects of pain and anxiety, as would be done under a best-interests formula. And in deciding the medical fate of a small child stricken with leukemia, the Massachusetts court admitted that in such a context the substituted-judgment and best-interests standards are "essentially coextensive."[38]

A similar melding or blending of the substituted-judgment and best-interests standards can also apply to other medical issues involving profoundly disabled persons. In a case considering the sterilization of a profoundly disabled woman, the New Jersey Supreme Court talked about substituted judgment on behalf of the woman but ended up articulating a formula that dictated careful attention to the same criteria as in a best-interests approach.[39] One justice of the court called this a best-interests analysis that was "cloaked in a substituted-judgment formulation."[40] The melding of substituted judgment with best interests has also occurred in at least one case involving the transplantation of a kidney from a profoundly disabled person to a desperately ill sibling.[41]

All this is not surprising in light of the illogic, previously noted, of using substituted judgment to try to replicate decisions of persons who have always lacked capacity to make autonomous decisions. As Joel Feinberg has noted,[42] a profoundly disabled person with the mental function of a small child cannot grasp the concepts of continued existence and death that are necessary to form a judgment or preference regarding life-sustaining medical intervention. The best that can be done is to charge a conscientious surrogate with considering and balancing the incapacitated patient's interests, including prospects for pleasure, pain, and satisfaction. While a profoundly disabled person, lacking autonomy, cannot have "the same rights" as a capacitated person, that person retains important interests (such as well-being and dignity) that deserve respect even if the disabled person cannot decide when and how to advance those interests. Does the presence of those interests translate into a constitutional right to have a surrogate exercise choice on behalf of a profoundly disabled person? That issue is confronted in the following section.

A Constitutional Right to Some Surrogate Decision on Behalf of the Disabled Person?

In 1981, John Garvey argued in the *Harvard Law Review* that decisionally incapacitated persons should be accorded a constitutional right to have important medical decisions made on their behalf by bonded surrogates.[43] His argument was that the incapacitated have a cognizable liberty interest in beneficial treatment in various medical contexts and that such an interest can be implemented only by allowing surrogate choice. According to Garvey, government should be foreclosed from interfering in decisions by surrogates who have caring ties to an incapacitated patient so long as the surrogate is acting consistently with the interests of the patient. Parents or other closely connected surrogates would be entitled to make judgments about appropriate treatment choices, and those judgments could be supplanted only if they were demonstrably contrary to the helpless patient's interests.

Some other commentators (and some courts) have a very different perspective on surrogate decision making for the profoundly disabled. They view the profoundly disabled as vulnerable and subject to arbitrary and abusive manipulation in medical decision making, even by surrogates with close family ties to the patient.[44] They perceive even bonded surrogates as having significant conflicts of interest about a variety of medical decisions that are critical to a disabled patient's life or well-being. For example, if the issue is life-sustaining medical intervention, a family may be under considerable stress from the actual or prospective burden of caring for a severely handicapped person. If the issue is sterilization, the family may be influenced by the specter of monitoring the disabled person's behavior or even caring for what the family regards as deficient potential offspring. If the issue is organ donation, the family may be wracked by pressures to salvage a desperately ill relative of the incapacitated potential donor. According to some advocates of the disabled, family members may be subject to prejudice against the handicapped, with an accompanying tendency to undervalue the handicapped person's life and to project sentiments onto the disabled person that match the family members' interests and preferences. In the context of life-sustaining medical intervention, these advocates fear quality-of-life determinations from the perspective of people who are oriented to independence and self-sufficiency as ideals. In the context of sterilization, they fear insensitivity toward the disabled person's interests in procreation or in remaining free from unwanted bodily invasions. Because of the perceived hazards of exploitation of vulnerable populations like the profoundly retarded, these sources would foreclose whole categories of decisions—such as removal of life support or sterilization—from the hands of the surrogate decision makers responsible for profoundly disabled persons.[45]

Can Garvey's notion (of a constitutional right of an incapacitated person to have a surrogate decision) prevail in the face of these concerns by advocates of the disabled? Is a state constitutionally compelled to allow a surrogate to assess and seek to effectuate a profoundly disabled person's interests in important medical issues, or may a state foreclose surrogate decisions in potentially hazardous subject areas such as withdrawal of end-of-life care, sterilization, and participation in experimental medical protocols?

In at least two subject areas—sterilization and life-sustaining medical interventions—a few states have sought to either exclude or radically constrain surrogate decisions for the decisionally handicapped.[46] The apprehension about sterilization is most understandable in light of its long and checkered history. In this book's introduction, I noted the eugenics movement that peaked in the United States between 1900 and 1930. Part of the agenda of that movement was the passage of involuntary sterilization laws affecting primarily the "feebleminded" residents of state institutions. The first such statute was adopted in Indiana in 1907, but approximately thirty-two states followed suit in the period up to 1940.[47] The justifications for these laws were varied. The prime rationale was protection of society by avoiding the birth of assertedly inferior beings who would become burdens on the state either because of their dependency or antisocial conduct and who would go on to produce similar offspring. Preventing misery and suffering to prospective offspring was another rationale for the legislation. (The assumption was that feebleminded parents would be incapable of decent child rearing.) The laws also supposedly promoted the well-being of the feebleminded potential parents who might thrive without the burdens of parenthood for which they were ill-suited to deal. While some state courts invalidated local involuntary sterilization statutes,[48] the U.S. Supreme Court upheld the Virginia statute in 1927,[49] and a few courts upheld such statutes against constitutional attack as late as the 1970s.[50] During the first half of the twentieth century, approximately 60,000 people were compulsorily sterilized.[51]

By the second half of the twentieth century, the picture regarding compulsory sterilization had dramatically changed. The scientific underpinnings of the eugenics movement were in disrepute. The perception had grown that any effort to sterilize in wholesale fashion the institutionalized mentally retarded was grounded in prejudice and stereotyped images of sexual predators or creatures with uncontrolled sexual appetites.[52] Commentators cast doubt on the constitutional viability of nonvoluntary sterilization laws both because of evolving Supreme Court jurisprudence protecting procreational choice and because of the "potential for social oppression and invidious discrimination" embodied in such laws.[53] Many of the statutes providing for compulsory sterilization had lapsed, been repealed, or fallen into disuse by the 1950s.

The central issue in the 1960s and 1970s became whether courts had inherent jurisdiction to authorize parents or other guardians to consent to sterilization on behalf of profoundly disabled persons. During that period, the predominant judicial response—in a series of rulings that the courts lacked authority to authorize such operations, at least in the absence of enabling legislation—was negative.[54] These courts had a lingering revulsion toward the period when large numbers of mentally retarded people had been involuntarily sterilized despite the shaky basis of the underlying eugenic theory and its shoddy application in practice.[55] Also, by the late 1960s and early 1970s, procreation was well established as a fundamental aspect of liberty under the Fourteenth Amendment. A number of courts therefore expressed special reluctance to authorize sterilization of a disabled person—a possible deprivation of a constitutional prerogative—even when the parent or guardian argued that sterilization would be in the patient's best interest.[56] Today, most of the states that had refused in the 1970s to find inherent jurisdiction to authorize sterilization of a mentally disabled person have changed their law. Statutes or cases now permit sterilization where a court finds that the surgery will serve the incapacitated person's best interests. Only one state appears to continue to exclude all surrogate authorization of sterilization.[57]

The question under discussion is whether a state's exclusion of surrogate consent to important medical matters such as sterilization is constitutional. That constitutional issue can be raised regarding a number of states that have severely restricted surrogate decisions seeking to remove life-sustaining medical care from profoundly disabled persons. The judicial phenomenon started in New York in 1981.[58] The patient, John Storar, was a fifty-two-year-old, profoundly retarded man dying of bladder cancer. His mother opposed continuation of blood transfusions because they caused extreme pain and discomfort to the uncomprehending patient. New York's highest court refused to uphold the mother's determination. Absent a prior declaration from the patient expressing a preference about life-sustaining care, the court refused to permit a surrogate decision to end life support. New York's restrictive approach continued in 1988.[59] This time the patient, Mary O'Connor, was a seventy-seven-year-old woman who had suffered a series of devastating strokes that left her totally helpless and barely conscious—unable to recognize and relate to her surrounding loved ones or caregivers. Her daughters opposed the installation of tubes providing artificial nutrition and hydration, arguing that this formerly vital woman would never have wanted to be maintained in this totally debilitated status; they cited statements that O'Connor had made to that effect. Nonetheless, New York's highest court ruled against the daughters. According to Chief Judge Saul Wachtler (a jurist who later did jail time for threats and harassment), New York would not allow the removal of life support from an incapacitated patient without clear and convincing evidence that the patient, while previously competent, had chosen such a course with regard to the circumstances now present. O'Connor's prior statements were not focused enough on her present circumstances to satisfy the clear-and-convincing-evidence standard. A single concern moved the New York court—apprehension of abuse or exploitation of helpless populations. Judge Wachtler asserted that "no person or court should substitute its judgment as to what would be an acceptable quality of life for another."[60]

Since 1988, several other state courts have joined New York in demanding clear and convincing evidence of the incapacitated patient's prior preferences before allowing the withdrawal of life-sustaining medical intervention.[61] A couple of these courts apply their restrictive approach only to incapacitated persons who are still conscious. That is, these courts would permit a surrogate to withdraw life support from a permanently unconscious patient but not from a patient who retains any measure of consciousness, at least not without clear prior expressions. The whole approach that demands clear prior expressions has a devastating impact on profoundly disabled persons. Never competent persons, by definition, could never have supplied the requisite prior expressions.

The consequences of this restrictive approach to end-of-life care are addressed shortly. Note first that this restrictive approach to terminal decisions raises a constitutional issue that is similar to the one raised by the previously mentioned exclusion of sterilization from the realm of surrogate decision making. Does wholesale exclusion of a subject matter from surrogate decision making violate a profoundly disabled person's right to liberty where the disputed decision has the potential to benefit the disabled person?

Certain cases in the 1980s, in the contexts of both end-of-life and sterilization decisions, supported the notion that a decisionally incapacitated person might have a constitutional right to have a surrogate choose a medical course on the incapacitated person's behalf. Recall that *Saikewicz* in Massachusetts in 1977 asserted that a dying, profoundly disabled cancer patient should have a right to the "same range of choices and options" that an autonomous patient would have. That idea flourished in the 1980s—first in cases involving severely disabled women whose parents or guardians sought judicial authorization of sterilization and later in the jurisprudence of death and dying.

In re Grady,[62] decided by the New Jersey Supreme Court in 1981, is illustrative.[63] Lee Ann Grady was a nineteen-year-old who was so severely mentally impaired by Down's syndrome that she could not understand pregnancy and would never be able to care for a child. Her parents sought judicial endorsement of their determination as guardians that Ms. Grady's interests would be promoted by sterilization. The parents felt that such reliable contraception would facilitate Lee Ann's move to a desirable group-home setting. Writing for the court, Justice Morris Pashman saw the issue as how to "preserve the personal freedom of one incapable of exercising it by allowing others to make a profoundly personal decision on her behalf."[64] Justice Pashman understood that the patient could never exercise autonomous choice but felt that freedom to have a surrogate opt for a result beneficial to the patient's interests was critical both to the patient's well-being and to her constitutional interests. He noted the coexistence of Ms. Grady's two liberty interests—in procreating and in not procreating.[65] He observed that a competent person has a constitutional right to choose between the two courses and that such a critical choice would impact on the choosing person's well-being. To Justice Pashman, a disabled person's inability to choose for herself "should not result in the forfeit of this constitutional interest [procreating or not procreating]" or in inadequate attention to her best interests.[66] The exercise of surrogate choice would then be the only way to preserve the benefits of a considered decision about Ms. Grady's procreational future and about her well-being with or without sterilization. The court ruled: "When an incompetent person lacks the mental capacity to make that choice [regarding sterilization], a court should ensure the exercise of that right [liberty to procreate or not to procreate] on behalf of the incompetent in a manner that reflects his or her best interests."[67] (Best interests was adopted as the operative inquiry on the assumption that a never competent person—if miraculously able to express a choice— would want to have her interests furthered when medical choices are made for her.) The opinion added:

We do not pretend that the choice of [Lee Ann Grady's] parents, her guardian ad litem or a court is her own choice. But it is a genuine choice nonetheless—one designed to further the same interests she might pursue had she the ability to decide herself. We believe that having the choice made in her behalf produces a more just and compassionate result than leaving Lee Ann with no way of exercising a constitutional right.[68]

(The Court also dictated safeguards aimed at preventing exploitation by the surrogate decision maker. The matter of protecting the profoundly disabled against abuse is picked up later in this chapter.)

Several courts adopted *Grady's* perspective that the failure to permit surrogate choice regarding sterilization would deny a patient's constitutional right to procreational choice and might seriously jeopardize a disabled patient's well-being.[69] For example, the Massachusetts Supreme Judicial Court, in finding that equity courts have inherent authority to act in a mentally disabled person's best interests (including authorization of sterilization), reinforced its conclusion by noting that a contrary conclusion would impinge the disabled person's constitutional rights. The opinion explained: "government deprives a mentally retarded individual of his or her right to privacy [meaning liberty to avoid procreation] if it denies the person the opportunity to exercise that right [by means of a conscientious surrogate who considers various means of contraception]."[70]

That case was decided in 1982, a year after *Grady*. Three years later, the California Supreme Court used similar reasoning in invalidating a legislative framework that had purposefully excluded a sterilization option from the prerogatives of conservators (guardians) acting on behalf of mentally disabled people. In *Conservatorship of Valerie N.*,[71] the court declared that the legislative denial of an opportunity to have a surrogate opt for sterilization had deprived developmentally disabled persons of procreative choice—a fundamental liberty interest—in violation of both the federal and state constitutions. The court noted not just the disabled person's constitutional interests at stake, but the practical interests in having a procreative decision that would best promote personal growth and development. According to the majority opinion: "An incompetent developmentally disabled woman has no less interest in a satisfying or fulfilling life free from the burdens of an unwanted pregnancy than does her competent sister."[72] In effect, the California Supreme Court found that a profoundly disabled person has a constitutional right to have a critically important medical decision made on her behalf.

An intermediate appellate court in California in 1988 employed similar reasoning in the context of an end-of-life decision on behalf of a now incompetent patient.[73] The patient, William Drabick, was a forty-four-year-old male mired in a permanently unconscious state as a result of severe brain damage incurred in an automobile accident several years earlier. His brother as conservator (guardian) sought judicial approval of the removal of a life-sustaining feeding tube. The intermediate appellate court (the highest court to consider the matter, as the California Supreme Court declined review) ruled that the now incompetent patient had a right to have a surrogate make a choice about continued life support according to a standard or guideline that reflects the patient's interests. The court acknowledged that Mr. Drabick could not currently (and did not previously) make a conscious choice and so invoking a right to choose in some sense involves a legal fiction. According to the court, though, the absence of capacity to choose ought not entail forfeiture of William's fundamental interest in sound medical-treatment decisions.[74] The court explained: "It would be more accurate to say that incompetent patients retain the right to have appropriate medical decisions made on their behalf. An appropriate medical decision is one that is made in the patient's best interests, as opposed to the interests of the hospital, the physician, the legal system, or someone else."[75]

By embracing a surrogate choice that reflects the patient's interests rather than a technological imperative to do everything possible to preserve life, the court saw itself as promoting "respect for persons."[76] For the *Drabick* court, incapacitated as well as capacitated persons ought to be entitled to the exercise of treatment options that would advance their personal interests.[77] The connection between respect for persons and access to beneficial surrogate choice thus echoed a theme first uttered in *Saikewicz* in 1977 and repeated in the *Grady* and *Valerie N.* cases previously described. The notion is that government exclusion of a potentially beneficial medical option treats the incapacitated patient like an object whose feelings and emotions don't matter—a living organism that must be preserved no matter how much suffering or indignity might be entailed.[78] The accompanying blow to personal well-being and dignity warrants recognition of a constitutional right to a surrogate decision when a mentally disabled person's critical medical interests are at stake. The previously described saga of Sheila Pouliot illustrated the inhumane consequences of ignoring such a right.

In 1990, the United States Supreme Court put a significant crimp in the argument that a profoundly disabled person has a federal constitutional right to have critical medical decisions made by a surrogate acting according to the patient's interests. The relevant case is *Cruzan v. Missouri Department of Health,*[79] and it involved a review of Missouri's policy on decision making for incompetent medical patients as applied to a twenty-nine-year-old woman named Nancy Beth Cruzan. Ms. Cruzan's parents had sought judicial endorsement of their request to physicians to end the artificial nutrition and hydration that were sustaining their daughter, who was lying in a permanently unconscious state as a result of brain damage sustained in an automobile accident years earlier. Missouri's highest court—in contrast to cases like *Quinlan* and *Drabick* in other states—refused to authorize the removal of life support in the absence of "clear and convincing evidence" that the now incompetent patient had previously dictated such a medical course.[80] The Missouri court upheld the state's "unqualified interest" in preserving life, fearing that without prior instructions from the patient, surrogate decision makers would be making arbitrary quality-of-life determinations. The court perceived no impingement of the unconscious patient's constitutionally protected liberty interest because, according to the court, exercise of that interest required an autonomous patient or some clear choice by a previously autonomous patient.

Ms. Cruzan's parents sought redress in the United States Supreme Court. They argued that Missouri's restrictive policy for allowing the removal of life support denied their daughter liberty in violation of the Fourteenth Amendment. Her parents contended that part of her liberty interest was to have choices about her medical treatment in a permanently unconscious state made for her in a way that best reflects her interests and values.[81] (One of the personal interests to be protected by a surrogate would be freedom from unwarranted bodily invasions.) According to the parents and their supporting *amici curiae,* Ms. Cruzan should be constitutionally entitled to an individualized decision about her medical treatment by people who know her previously formed values and preferences, love her, and care about her best interests—all without the restrictive requirement of clear and convincing evidence that this young woman had previously made an explicit determination about maintenance of life support in case of permanent unconsciousness.[82]

In an opinion for five members of the Court, Chief Justice Rehnquist upheld the constitutionality of Missouri's insistence on clear and convincing evidence of the now incompetent patient's prior wishes as a prerequisite to removal of life support.[83] While assuming that a competent patient would have a constitutionally protected liberty interest in refusing unwanted medical treatment (in which case, state interference with a patient's choice would be subjected to strict judicial scrutiny), Chief Justice Rehnquist showed no similar solicitude for end-of-life decision making on behalf of a now incompetent patient. While he did not specify the precise standard of judicial scrutiny that was applicable to Missouri's restriction on surrogate choice, in essence he applied a rational-basis standard of review. (The rational-basis standard dictates judicial deference to any plausible, legitimate governmental interest that underlies a legislative policy—even if the policy is ill considered and unsound.) Using that undemanding approach, he had little trouble finding some legitimate and rational basis for Missouri's restriction on surrogate decision making. Chief Justice Rehnquist viewed the state's insistence on clear and convincing evidence as "a procedural safeguard to assure that the action of the surrogate conforms as best it may to the wishes expressed by the patient while competent."[84] Missouri's insistence on personal choice also made some sense to Chief Justice Rehnquist as a prophylactic against potential abuse in surrogate decision making or arbitrary quality-of-life determinations. Because of such legitimate concerns about abusive or arbitrary decision making, Rehnquist did not think that the Constitution requires states to confer broad "substituted judgment" authority on surrogates.[85]

For several reasons, the Supreme Court's five to four determination in *Cruzan* constitutes bad jurisprudence. For starters, the Missouri policy was arbitrary in that, at least as applied to permanently unconscious patients like Nancy Beth Cruzan, it accomplished the opposite of its intended result. The Missouri approach that insisted on clear prior expressions was aimed at implementing the now incompetent patient's wishes. Yet by confining removal of life support to the relatively rare instance when a patient previously spelled out such a course, the state mandated life support for the permanently unconscious Ms. Cruzan, even though the overwhelming likelihood is that the patient herself would have wanted life support discontinued.[86] (That conclusion flows from data showing that approximately 90 percent of people consistently prefer death to the insentient limbo of permanent unconsciousness.)[87] In other words, by precluding the removal of life support from Nancy Beth Cruzan, the chances were better than nine to one that the state was contravening her wishes.[88] Chief Justice Rehnquist conceded that the Missouri approach may have frustrated Ms. Cruzan's actual wishes and lamely responded, "[T]he Constitution does not require general rules to work faultlessly."[89]

It is true that the Constitution doesn't require that legally imposed presumptions or default rules be faultless. An age line (such as a minimum-age requirement for voting) is constitutional even though the age line, in its pursuit of maturity in voting, excludes some young but mature persons and includes some old but immature persons. Most or at least many persons below the age line would indeed be immature. So the age line generally (albeit inexactly) promotes the object of enhancing voter maturity. Similarly, a mandatory retirement policy can have a perverse effect in ousting some still capable workers, but if fixed at a sufficiently advanced age, it also rids the employer of many workers whose capabilities have declined with age. By contrast, Missouri's policy as applied to permanent unconsciousness would have a perverse effect of contravening the desires of the patient (albeit desires not fully articulated) in approximately 90 percent of the cases.[90] Chief Justice Rehnquist argued that a life-affirming presumption is defensible because a mistaken judgment to withdraw life support is irremediable.[91] Yet a mistaken (in the sense of contrary to the patient's wishes) judgment that maintains life support accomplishes an irreparable injury in three respects—contravening the patient's likely will, preserving an existence that the patient would deem intolerably undignified, and soiling the survivors' memories of the once vital patient: "[C]ontinuing treatment for a patient who would have wanted treatment stopped is as unfortunate as discontinuing treatment for a patient who would have wanted treatment continued."[92] If promoting the wishes of the now incompetent patient is the ultimate goal, it makes much more sense—in the absence of clear prior expressions from the patient—first to examine the patient's values and goals and then, if they are not definitive, to follow what a strong majority of people would want done in the circumstances at hand.[93]

Justice Brennan, dissenting in *Cruzan*, picked up on the perverse impact of a state's insistence on clear prior expressions as a prerequisite to any removal of life support.[94] Brennan acknowledged a state interest in providing Ms. Cruzan with a treatment course that would mirror her personal wishes. But he castigated the state and the Supreme Court majority for using evidence of clear prior expressions as the sole determinant of her likely wishes. For Justice Brennan, Missouri's framework discarded evidence of Ms. Cruzan's values, ignored meaningful (even if less than carefully articulated) prior expressions, and thereby deprived her of a "right to a decision as closely approximating her own choice as humanly possible."[95]

Cruzan's defects extend beyond this glaring discrepancy between the object of accomplishing the patient's wishes and the means chosen by Missouri to accomplish that object. Chief Justice Rehnquist's majority opinion pays scant attention to the forfeiture of critical interests that takes place when government precludes withdrawal of life support from an incapacitated patient absent clear prior expressions. (Missouri's policy forecloses surrogate resort to the unconscious patient's best interests, including interests of constitutional dimension such as bodily integrity, avoidance of suffering, and human dignity.)

The majority's inadequate attention to Ms. Cruzan's constitutional interests did not escape Justice Stevens. Justice Stevens's *Cruzan* dissent highlighted the harm to constitutionally cognizable interests caused by Missouri's narrow decision-making scheme and condemned the majority for neglecting those interests.[96] Justice Stevens pointed to an incapacitated patient's interest in bodily integrity and a concomitant right to be free of unwarranted bodily invasions, matters that were sacrificed by Missouri except for the extraordinary patient with the foresight to issue unambiguous prior instructions. Justice Stevens also recognized the incapacitated patient's interests in avoiding suffering (which probably were not applicable to the unconscious Ms. Cruzan), in being remembered as a vital individual (that is, in preserving her lifelong image), and in obtaining a life closure consistent with her own values, beliefs, and preferences (even if those preferences are not spelled out in detail).

In the case of a permanently unconscious patient like Ms. Cruzan, the patient also has an important interest in having her intrinsic human dignity respected. Ms. Cruzan's counsel accurately portrayed the degrading limbo to which Missouri seemed to be condemning her: "Her unconscious biological shell will be maintained by strangers in a sterile hospital room for 30 years, devoid of thought or perception and without hope of recovery. Such a choice will severely compromise her dignity for the rest of her days and will have devastating life-long effects for her family."[97] Justice Stevens responded appropriately. He labeled Missouri's neglect of Ms. Cruzan's various interests—other than biological existence—as a denial of personhood,[98] thus recalling the admonition of state cases like *Saikewicz* and *Drabick* that respect for persons demands that surrogates be allowed to consider the incapacitated patient's interests and that a technological imperative to keep the patient alive at all costs should not be imposed.[99] Justice Stevens clearly appreciated the important connection between human dignity and mentally incapacitated patients' access to surrogate medical decisions that would potentially benefit the patients.

By contrast, the *Cruzan* majority, in upholding Missouri's approach demanding clear prior expressions, showed little appreciation for the consequences of that approach on debilitated, dying patients. In Nancy Beth Cruzan's instance, she was unconscious and therefore unsensing of the various affronts to her interests perpetrated by Missouri's rule. Other dying patients, even if mentally incapacitated, can acutely experience the affronts involved. Philip Peters has commented: "The irrebutable presumption [absent clear prior expressions] that all lives are worth living will condemn many patients to unnecessary treatment, suffering, indignity, or pointless existence."[100] The negative consequences are perhaps starkest with regard to the suffering experienced by some still conscious patients. American courts have generally recognized that for some dying patients the burdens of continued existence outweigh the benefits and that conscientious surrogates may sometimes make such a judgment and order a cessation of life-sustaining medical intervention.[101] Recall the case of Sheila Pouliot, the profoundly disabled woman who lingered semiconscious for two months, grotesquely swelled up and unable to interact with her environment except to moan in pain—because New York law would not allow removal of life support from a dying person in the absence of clear prior instructions. Consider also the case of infants who are born with certain grave deficits that will inexorably cause their deaths in infancy or early childhood. In some such instances, continued existence entails almost constant medical intervention and unremitting suffering. Solicitude for the infant demands that some surrogate be able to put an end to medical intervention that is prolonging extreme and unremitting suffering.[102] Even the federal regulations that are aimed at narrowing medical decisions not to treat afflicted newborns leave some leeway for nontreatment where intervention would be "virtually futile and inhumane."[103]

To sum up *Cruzan,* the U.S. Supreme Court's willingness to uphold Missouri's approach to end-of-life decision making for the mentally disabled imperiled both the constitutional interests of incapacitated patients like Nancy Beth Cruzan and the temporal welfare of other, conscious dying patients. While Chief Justice Rehnquist's opinion accepted the premise that a competent Ms. Cruzan would be constitutionally entitled to reject life support,[104] the prerogative of ending medical intervention that prolongs a dying process could be preserved in Missouri only by the extraordinary prescience of the young woman in anticipating and spelling out in advance her desires concerning medical intervention in a permanently unconscious state. Once Ms. Cruzan lost decision-making capacity without clear advance instructions, her incompetent status allowed the state to erect a "protective" bar to any terminal decision despite the contravention of her likely wishes and impingement of her bodily integrity and dignity interests. Missouri's concern about exploitation of vulnerable patients provided (according to Chief Justice Rehnquist) a sufficient constitutional justification—that is, a rational basis—for its policy.

What *should* the Supreme Court have done in *Cruzan?* What constitutional doctrine should have been crafted to deal with medical decision making for a now incompetent patient? The better jurisprudential course would have been to acknowledge a formerly competent person's strong liberty interest in having her preexisting values and preferences (not just explicit end-of-life expressions) control postcompetence medical decisions and to recognize every incapacitated patient's constitutional right to have her contemporaneous well-being considered by a surrogate decision maker who is operating on the patient's behalf.[105] Justice Stevens set a fitting course when he suggested that the Constitution (meaning Fourteenth Amendment liberty) "requires the State to care for Nancy Cruzan's life in a way that gives appropriate respect to her own best interests."[106] Appropriate respect in this context means having a conscientious surrogate consider the patient's various interests (including prior values and preferences, as well as current well-being).[107] For profoundly disabled, never competent persons, prior values and preferences can never have an autonomous force,[108] so that a surrogate's focus must be on the patient's well-being. Consideration of current well-being, in turn, means surrogate weighing of the various benefits and burdens that are associated with the medical choice being contemplated, with the patient's net best interests serving as the surrogate's decisional guide. In end-of-life contexts, a surrogate ought to be able to sometimes conclude that the disabled patient would be better off dead than alive because of unremitting suffering or grievous debilitation (to the point of intrinsic indignity), so that life support should be withdrawn. A best-interests formula respects the incapacitated patient's interests by permitting a range of beneficial options that are similar to those available to competent patients and by making room for both the patient's well-being and intrinsic dignity to be considered as integral factors. (The contents of the best-interests formula, including human dignity, is discussed further in chapter 4.)

I am aware of only one context in which the Supreme Court has required, under the rubric of liberty and substantive due process, that a state permit a surrogate to implement an incapacitated person's constitutional interests. Several cases dealing with abortion require that a regulating state—in seeking to impose a parental-notification requirement—must provide a judicial bypass process that enables a judge to rule on the best interests of any minor seeking an abortion, including an immature minor who lacks the capacity to make her own determination.[109] The judicial bypass process must be made available to any minor unwilling to involve her parents in the abortion decision. This mandatory access to a neutral decision maker who is required to follow the minor's best interests is aimed at safeguarding the minor's liberty interest in deciding whether to terminate a pregnancy. But the mandatory access is not confined to mature minors who are capable of some measure of self-determination about an abortion decision; immature minors are also entitled to pursue a judicial bypass that entails a careful consideration of the minor's various interests.[110]

These abortion cases involving minors provide an analogy to the broader issue of medical decision making for the profoundly disabled. In both settings, a fundamental liberty interest is at stake—in one, a choice about continuing a pregnancy; in the other, a choice about receiving life-sustaining medical intervention (or sterilization or any other serious medical intervention). In both settings, state failure to allow surrogate choice relegates the incapacitated patient to a status quo (without access to a possibly desirable medical option) in a way that offends human well-being and sometimes human dignity by precluding consideration of that person's various interests. In both settings, I suggest, an incapacitated person's liberty interest triggers a requirement that a surrogate be allowed to choose among medical options according to the dependent person's interests. The abortion cases support the argument here that constitutional liberty ought ordinarily be deemed to include surrogate choice when the mentally incapacitated rights bearer cannot exercise the medical choice at stake.

The constitutional principle for which I am arguing would be limited in ways I sketch here. First, the contemplated decision-making authority that is lodged in a surrogate must be constrained in a manner consistent with the helpless ward's interests. Unbridled authority in the hands of a surrogate would raise the specter of arbitrary decision making and unconscionable exploitation of the vulnerable person. An integral part of the traditional relationship between government and citizens is the state's *parens patriae* obligation to protect helpless populations against abuse. This means that a surrogate's decision-making prerogative must be limited—bound by standards such as substituted judgment (where the now incompetent person was formerly competent) and best interests (where the person was never competent or, if formerly competent, never provided meaningful guidance about the decision at hand). This lesson about standards that limit surrogate discretion can be gleaned from older cases dealing with the sterilization of profoundly disabled persons.[111] Those cases struck down statutory schemes that gave parents or guardians unlimited discretion to secure sterilization for profoundly disabled wards. The judicial message was that any decisions about sterilization must be grounded in the best interests of the ward. A similar message emanated from numerous decisions in the 1980s that upheld a surrogate's authority to seek sterilization *in the best interests* of a child or ward.[112]

In the contemplated constitutional framework, the state would have to do more than simply articulate a limiting standard, such as best interests, to protect the disabled person from abuse by surrogates. A state would be required to allow surrogate choice on behalf of a profoundly disabled person but would have a concomitant obligation to protect the dependent person against surrogate abuse. Pursuant to *parens patriae* authority, a state customarily enforces the fiduciary standards that bind a parent or guardian in charge of decisions on behalf of a mentally disabled individual.[113] The enforcement responsibility that would be incorporated into the constitutional framework would include criminal machinery to punish serious deviation from acceptable guardianship standards and civil machinery to actively intervene and supplant surrogate decisions that are inconsistent with the well-being of the ward. I have in mind the kinds of child-protection and adult-guardianship agencies found in most states.[114]

What about state prophylactic rules—efforts to bar entire subject areas from surrogate choice to preclude mistreatment of vulnerable disabled populations?[115] This was Missouri's rationale in *Cruzan* in barring surrogate end-of-life decisions in the absence of clear and convincing evidence of the patient's explicit wishes. While the state's protective concern is entirely legitimate, its sweeping means to accomplish its object are unacceptable. At least in the context of a fundamental-liberty interest, such as choice about life-sustaining medical intervention, Missouri should be required to make a stronger showing than it did in two ways. A state ought to be able to exclude an entire area of potentially beneficial medical decisions from surrogate choice only on a showing of substantial abuse—or the threat of such abuse—by surrogates. Missouri made no showing that helpless patients had been exploited in a manner that warranted a virtually wholesale exclusion of surrogate choice in the area of end-of-life decision making. Moreover, even if there appeared to be a substantial threat of abuse of surrogate authority, a state should have to consider less drastic alternatives—means of protecting helpless populations short of excluding all surrogate choice—before excluding an entire subject matter from surrogate control.[116]

A variety of alternative safeguards are available to make sure that surrogate decisions affecting the disabled are not abusive. One technique is to refine the best-interests standard by spelling out the factors that are supposed to govern a surrogate's decision. For example, in the context of sterilization, best interests could be broken down to include focus on the physical and mental needs of the disabled patient (as opposed to the convenience of surrounding family or caretakers), as well as on the availability of alternative contraceptive techniques.[117] An additional protective step is to explicitly warn surrogates and medical personnel against allowing common prejudices or stereotypical misconceptions to play a role in surrogate decision making.[118] Medical personnel should also be reminded of their duty to seek review (from an ethics committee or a court) when a surrogate medical decision seems inconsistent with acceptable standards of patient care.[119]

Besides carefully articulating a standard for surrogate decision making, a state can build in procedural safeguards to ensure that the standards are adhered to. If a parent or guardian is accorded decision-making authority, that surrogate's decision can be subjected to mandatory independent review, such as by an institutional ethics committee. That review can scrutinize both the underlying facts and the surrogate's application of the relevant decision-making standard to those facts.[120] Or, as in the case of sterilization decisions, decision-making authority can be relegated exclusively to a judge who is charged with deciding after fair-hearing processes. (In chapter 3, I further consider existing decision-making frameworks for critical medical decisions and desirable alterations. There, I express my opposition to systematic judicial involvement in medical decisions for profoundly disabled persons.) Typical hearing requirements regarding a sterilization decision include appointment of a guardian ad litem to represent the incapacitated person's interests and appointment of medical experts.[121] Another possible safeguard is to adjust the standard of proof to be utilized by the surrogate decision maker. For example, many decision-making frameworks that are applicable either to end-of-life or sterilization determinations have insisted on "clear and convincing" evidence that the incapacitated patient's interests dictate a particular medical course.[122] These various safeguards could provide alternative means to curb abusive treatment of disabled persons short of preventing all access to a possibly beneficial medical decision.

This sketch of the constitutional approach that should have been applied in *Cruzan* leaves unresolved issues. As to who decides on behalf of a disabled person, could a state require *judicial* determination of all critical medical issues that affect a profoundly disabled person, including end-of-life determinations? Parents and guardians who seek to act as surrogates would certainly argue that a requirement of judicial authorization is unduly burdensome, entailing too much expense and delay. Justice Stevens in his *Cruzan* dissent commented that it is "debatable" whether judicial process could be imposed as a prerequisite to a withdrawal of life support.[123] (Chapter 3 further discusses the question of who should be surrogates for profoundly disabled patients with regard to various types of medical decisions. While I argue here that Fourteenth Amendment liberty should be deemed to require giving a mentally disabled person access to a surrogate's decision regarding potentially beneficial medical issues, I do not contend that the Constitution dictates who that surrogate decision maker must be. In other words, allocation of serious medical decisions to judges would be constitutional, even though it would not be sound public policy.)

The applicable standard of proof that binds the surrogate could also be controversial. Many sources would argue that a conscientious surrogate ought to have discretion to make a judgment about a ward's best interests without a requirement that the judgment be grounded on clear and convincing evidence. However, as already noted, many states have imposed a requirement of clear and convincing evidence of best interests. That standard is probably constitutionally acceptable (even if imprudent). The Supreme Court upheld a state provision that required a pregnant minor who was seeking a judicial bypass of a parental notification requirement to show by "clear and convincing evidence" that notification would not be in her best interests.[124] While a clear-and-convincing-evidence standard is constitutionally tolerable, any higher standard would probably be unconstitutional. For example, setting proof beyond a reasonable doubt as a prerequisite to surrogate action is probably an unconstitutional barrier to surrogate choice.[125]

A requirement that a surrogate medical decision be grounded on clear and convincing evidence of best interests may be constitutionally tolerable, but that doesn't mean that it is wise policy. Recall that most medical decisions involve fundamental-liberty interests on both sides of the choice. A decision in favor of sterilization impacts a disabled person's right to procreate and right to bodily integrity, but a decision against sterilization can affect a right not to procreate. A decision to institute chemotherapy for a fatally stricken cancer patient affects the patient's rights to bodily integrity and to reject life-sustaining medical intervention, but a decision against chemotherapy preserves bodily integrity and fundamental interests in continued life. Given that the surrogate medical choice affects important personal interests no matter what the option chosen, a case can be made for allowing the surrogate to act on a preponderance of the evidence in either direction.[126] Medical uncertainty may too often inhibit a clear-and-convincing conclusion one way or the other, even though the surrogate determines that the incapacitated person's best interests *probably* lie in a particular direction. Some medical issues are so tied up with uncertain variables and professional judgment that they are not readily susceptible to a clear-and-convincing standard of proof.

On the other hand, even when important constitutional interests lie on either side of a decision, the potential harm may appear greater on one side than the other. A decision in favor of sterilization entails a significant bodily invasion and severe impact on procreation prospects, while a decision against sterilization leaves the disabled person alone. This fact, coupled with a history of mistreatment of profoundly disabled persons, accounts for the common legal requirement that a surrogate's consent to a ward's sterilization be based on clear and convincing evidence. Nonetheless, if failure to perform a sterilization would pose a serious risk of medical trauma for the patient, the balance of harms is not so clear. The same is true where a contemplated surgery (such as heart-bypass surgery) involves a serious bodily intrusion and some mortal risk, but failure to perform the surgery seriously endangers the patient's life. A preponderance-of-the-evidence standard is therefore defensible[127] and perhaps even wise.

My suggested constitutional approach—recognizing a right to have a surrogate weigh important medical options—would also cast doubt on some limitations on surrogate choice that are found in some state advance-directive legislation. One common statutory limitation confines withholding of treatment decisions (pursuant to previously issued instructions) to a point where the now incompetent patient is "terminal," which is variously defined. Sometimes, *terminal* is defined to mean that death is unavoidable within a short period. For example, *terminal* may be defined as an unavoidable death within six months (or some other period).[128] A terminal-patient limitation excludes surrogate decisions (despite their conformity to patient wishes or well-being) to end dialysis or other interventions that are capable of sustaining the life of a dying patient for a period longer than the statutory definition of terminal. Yet a competent patient's right to decline treatment is not confined to the terminal stages of an illness, and it is doubtful whether there is a constitutionally sustainable justification for so confining a surrogate. The same constitutional infirmity affects some state surrogacy laws that designate next of kin (in descending order) as the authorized decision makers for incapacitated patients.[129] Some of these statutes empowering next of kin to act as medical decision makers confine the decision makers' authority regarding end-of-life decisions to circumstances where the ward is terminal. Similar constitutional doubt hangs over advance-directive legislation that purports to exclude the withdrawal of artificial nutrition and hydration (ANH) as a surrogate option. No persuasive government interest warrants treating artificial nutrition and hydration differently from other forms of medical intervention, the Pope's opinion to the contrary notwithstanding.

The elements that can constitutionally be considered as part of a best-interests-of-the-patient decision-making standard are also disputed. Can the interests of others—such as caregivers—be included within a surrogate's decision-making calculus, or must the disabled person's interest be the exclusive focus? Can a surrogate's decision to authorize an "altruistic" course—such as tissue donation or participation in nontherapeutic medical research—be reconciled with the best-interests limitation? Can the patient's dignity be a legitimate consideration, or must the surrogate focus on the physical and mental well-being of the now incompetent patient? (I suggest that the answer to these questions is yes. Chapter 4 continues discussion of the bounds of a best-interests formula as a matter of public policy, though it does not pursue the constitutional aspects of that matter, and chapter 5 considers the tension between best interests of the incapacitated person and medical decisions, such as tissue donation and participation in nontherapeutic medical research, that primarily benefit others.)

My basic point here is that *Cruzan* was wrongly decided. Constitutional-liberty dictates, in most contexts affecting an incapacitated person's critical interests, that the incapacitated person is entitled to a surrogate's determination grounded in that incapacitated person's interests. (I say in *most* contexts because, as noted in the introduction, a few exclusions of surrogate choice for profoundly disabled persons—such as those regarding marriage and voting—can be sustained as necessary to the integrity of the institution involved.) The proposed constitutional right to a surrogate's determination applies at least to the important, potentially beneficial medical decisions at the heart of this book.

To this point, the constitutional analysis has centered on the *Cruzan* case, which involved a previously competent person who had permanently lost cognitive capacity. The subject of this book is lifelong profoundly disabled persons. Does the constitutional analysis change when the medical fate of a never competent person is in issue? There are some distinctions between the case of a previously competent person and that of a never competent person, but they probably do not change the bottom-line argument in favor of a liberty right to have critical medical determinations made by a surrogate who is bound to respect the incapacitated person's interests. In fact, some distinctions between the typical case of a conscious, never competent person and that of a permanently unconscious being like Nancy Beth Cruzan make the former's case even stronger than Ms. Cruzan's.

One distinction between the previously competent and never competent patient relates to the personal interests that are affected if a state excludes surrogate decisions on behalf of a now incompetent patient. A previously competent patient's self-determination interest may be at stake, while that is not so for a never competent person. The previously competent patient has had an opportunity to exercise personal choice—that is, self-determination—via prior expressions, so that state constraints on surrogate choice may impede implementation of the dependent person's constitutional liberty in the sense of autonomous choice. For example, Ms. Cruzan by age twenty-seven had had an opportunity to form personal values and preferences—and even express specific choices—that would inform how she would want to resolve the issue of life support in case of permanent unconsciousness. A profoundly disabled person never has the capacity for this level of self-determination, so that exclusion of surrogate choice on an issue like end-of-life care does not violate that disabled person's liberty in the sense of personal choice. To that extent, the constitutional claim of a profoundly disabled person is weaker than that of a previously competent person.

On the other hand, the negative consequences of an approach like Missouri's are even more severe on a lifelong profoundly disabled person than they were on Nancy Beth Cruzan. As a formerly competent person, Ms. Cruzan had some opportunity to speak to the matter of end-of-life medical treatment in a fashion that would meet Missouri's clear-and-convincing-evidence standard. (Indeed, her representatives eventually satisfied a Missouri court that Ms. Cruzan had previously expressed enough about her preferences to show clearly that she would prefer death to permanent unconsciousness.) A lifelong profoundly disabled person has no opportunity to meet the Missouri standard.

Another contrast between Ms. Cruzan and the typical profoundly disabled patient is that Ms. Cruzan, as a permanently insensate person, could not consciously experience the consequences of Missouri's insistence that she be kept alive in her gravely debilitated status. Most profoundly disabled persons are well aware of their surroundings and quite capable of experiencing acute suffering or affronts to dignity from intrusive medical technology. Recall the Massachusetts court's determination that Joseph Saikewicz would suffer so much in terms of pain, anxiety, and frustration from the uncomprehending receipt of intrusive chemotherapy that he would be better off forgoing possibly life-sustaining medical intervention. Recall Sheilah Pouliot, who lay moaning for two months as edema swelled her body and broke down her skin. Avoidance of unnecessary suffering has even been recognized by a number of Supreme Court justices as an interest of constitutional dimension safeguarded by Fourteenth Amendment liberty.[130]

A state's policy of excluding surrogate choice could have severe negative consequences for profoundly disabled persons in contexts beyond end-of-life treatment decisions. Once a profoundly disabled woman becomes pregnant, her medical circumstances and her incomprehension of the events taking place may make an abortion the only way to avoid torturous consequences.[131] State exclusion of such an option would be cruel and inhumane. Angela Holder explains: "The plight of a severely retarded woman who cannot understand that she is having a baby and why it hurts so much is a situation where any discussion of her right to procreate makes a mockery of her humanity and her dignity."[132] The medical circumstances of a profoundly disabled person might also make sterilization a needed process to avoid severe physical or mental harm. Severe mental distress from menstruation or severe hazards from pregnancy can even prompt a conclusion that, absent sterilization, a profoundly disabled person will undergo "devastating and perhaps fatal" consequences.[133] (In that instance, the disabled woman had a seizure condition that would be exacerbated by pregnancy. The California court ruled that she had a right to have a sterilization decision made on her behalf in order to enjoy the same benefits as a nondisabled person.)[134] Again, categorical exclusion of surrogate choice of sterilization might be cruel and inhumane.

Even in the absence of medical necessity, sterilization can be in the best interests of a profoundly disabled person, at least if the alternative is isolation in social relations or intrusive monitoring of behavior to avoid pregnancy. The New Jersey Supreme Court commented in the previously discussed *Grady* case: "Lee Ann should have the opportunity to lead a life as rewarding as her condition will permit. Courts should cautiously but resolutely help her achieve the fullness of that opportunity. If she can have a richer and more active life only if the risk of pregnancy is permanently eliminated, then sterilization may be in her best interests."[135] When Justice Rose Bird dissented from the California Supreme Court's authorization of a sterilization for Valerie N., lamenting the prospective deprivation of Valerie's right to procreate, Roger Dworkin responded: "What are we doing for Valerie by respecting her primal right to procreate if we then lock her away to be sure she does not procreate, or if the procreation experience is a frightening and awful one for her? How can we justify making Valerie suffer for Justice Bird's ideals?"[136] Professor Dworkin's point is well taken, even if couched in hyperbole. Access to sterilization can, at least in some instances, promote a disabled person's long-range happiness, dignity, and a fuller life.

I suggested in chapter 1 that intrinsic human dignity has an important role to play in shaping the medical handling of profoundly disabled persons. This context is one example. A dignitary harm occurs to profoundly disabled persons when a state categorically excludes a potentially beneficial class of medical decisions from the range of surrogate decision-making authority. It is dehumanizing to the affected disabled person when surrogates are required to preserve the medical status quo rather than weigh the potential benefits and detriments associated with possible medical responses. This is so whether the medical option in question relates to abortion, sterilization,[137] or life support. The disabled individual is treated like an inanimate object in contrast to the competent patient who would be entitled, in comparable medical circumstances, to exercise the potentially beneficial option.[138] The inhumane impact of excluding potentially beneficial options from profoundly disabled persons helps account for the slavery imagery that some commentators evoked in the wake of *Cruzan*. According to that commentary, Missouri made Nancy Beth Cruzan a slave of medical technology. Alex Capron viewed Ms. Cruzan as "enslaved by the extraordinary and evergrowing ability of medicine to sustain vital functions."[139] Giles Scofield called *Cruzan* the twentieth century's equivalent of *Dred Scott* in its failure to "treat Nancy Cruzan as a person instead of a slave."[140]

The dehumanizing effect of excluding surrogate choice also accounts for the previously mentioned state cases like *Saikewicz, Drabick, Grady,* and *Valerie N.*, all of which cited the dignity of the profoundly disabled person as a basis for according surrogates a prerogative to exercise choice regarding either end-of-life treatment or sterilization. Courts have also begun to recognize the indignity of excluding surrogate choice in another, unusual context—that of the customary rule that divorce is so personal a choice that a surrogate can never initiate a divorce on behalf of a now incompetent spouse. The traditional rule barring a surrogate petition for divorce is grounded on the principle that a person's degree of tolerance of spousal mistreatment is so subjective that no surrogate decision maker can effectively replicate what the now incompetent spouse would want. Yet as recognized in several recent decisions,[141] the categorical exclusion of a surrogate petition for divorce tends to treat the now incompetent spouse as an object locked into the status quo no matter how abusive or degrading the other spouse has been. These decisions see the incapacitated spouse as a "prisoner" who can be "captive to the whims of the competent spouse."[142] They therefore deviate from the traditional approach and allow surrogates to initiate divorce proceedings to allow full consideration of the incapacitated spouse's interests and to ensure dignified treatment for the incapacitated spouse.

I have argued to this point that *Cruzan* was wrongly decided and that the U.S. Supreme Court should have ruled that states cannot, constitutionally, circumscribe surrogate choice on behalf of incapacitated persons in the way that Missouri did. John Garvey was right, and Chief Justice Rehnquist was wrong. At the same time, I concede that the result in *Cruzan* was not terribly surprising. The Court was being asked to constitutionalize the handling of incapacitated, dying patients less than fifteen years after *Quinlan* ruled for the first time that a surrogate might legally be permitted to decline further life support for a helpless patient. The Court was faced with a state restriction on surrogate choice that was purportedly aimed at protecting vulnerable persons against exploitation. Protecting vulnerable populations against exploitation is a hallmark of the Supreme Court, a fact that was demonstrated not only in *Cruzan* in 1990 but in the physician-assisted-suicide cases seven years later where the Court cited apprehension about undue pressure on dying persons as one basis for upholding state bans on assistance to suicide. Moreover, the Court in *Cruzan* was confronting not a suffering person but rather the permanently insensate Nancy Beth Cruzan. All this helps explain the reticence behind the five to four vote to uphold Missouri's law.

In any event, *Cruzan* is not necessarily dispositive of the focal point of this chapter—the rights of profoundly disabled persons. At least those instances where the exclusion of surrogate choice forces a profoundly disabled person to experience suffering or degradation are conceivably distinguishable from *Cruzan*. I contend that it is an impermissible infringement of constitutional liberty (though not liberty in the sense of autonomy) when states categorically exclude surrogates from making potentially beneficial choices that are consistent with the best interests of the profoundly disabled person. This analysis applies to any state that precludes an end-of-life decision absent clear prior expressions (an approach that entirely forecloses a terminal choice for a profoundly disabled person) as well as any state that bars the possibility of a sterilization procedure. My analysis would also invalidate the federal regulations that seek to prevent parental choice of nontreatment for infants who are born with multiple deficits likely to cause them unremitting suffering.

Of course, my suggested constitutional analysis may not prevail.[143] The Court is naturally hesitant to constitutionalize legal doctrine about surrogate choice in the face of continuing concerns about surrogate exploitation of vulnerable populations. As noted, acknowledgment of a liberty interest in having a surrogate decide on behalf of a disabled patient entails subsidiary constitutional questions about who can serve as surrogate, the procedures to be followed by the surrogate, and the permissible scope of surrogate discretion. The Supreme Court may prefer to leave these matters to what Justice O'Connor dubbed "the laboratory of the states"[144] without federal judicial intrusion. On the constitutional plane, that would still leave state courts free to apply state constitutional provisions that protect liberty along the lines I have urged.

Even if the issue of surrogate decision making is left to public policy in the states (that is, to the state legislative laboratories), profoundly disabled persons should be given a right to have critical medical decisions made by conscientious surrogates acting according to the interests of the disabled person. This approach ought to apply at least in the contexts of end-of-life decisions, abortion, and sterilization. (The appropriate approach to surrogate decision making relating to organ or tissue donation and participation in medical research is discussed in chapter 5.) I have tried to show how it is inhumane and a denial of respect for persons to exclude the profoundly disabled from potentially beneficial surrogate decisions. A legal approach allowing conscientious surrogate decision making yields "a more just and compassionate result," to use the words of the New Jersey Supreme Court in *Grady*.[145] The objectives of justice and compassion surely underlie the elaborate guardianship structures that every jurisdiction now supplies on behalf of profoundly disabled persons.[146] Those structures are consistent with the ancient *parens patriae* principle that seeks to protect the interests of profoundly disabled persons. Legislatures should therefore "promote the human dignity of never competent patients by affording access to beneficial results which competent patients could, and likely would, choose under similar circumstances."[147] Even staunch advocates on behalf of disabled persons' rights sometimes acknowledge that preclusion of surrogate choice can single out and disadvantage the disabled.[148]

The central message of this chapter, then, is that the profoundly disabled have some rights, though not identical with the rights of competent persons. One of those rights—to be established by either constitutional law or public policy—should be a prerogative to have a conscientious surrogate make critical medical decisions according to the best interests of the disabled patient. The next two chapters consider who those surrogates should be and what the "best interests" concept embodies.

3

Who Decides for the Profoundly Disabled?

This book is about persons whose mental capacity is so limited that they cannot make important medical decisions on their own. Yet, as I argue in chapter 2, profoundly disabled persons ought to be accorded access to a full range of potentially beneficial medical interventions. If that strong patient interest is to be fulfilled, someone (a surrogate) must decide on behalf of the incapacitated patient whether to institute any medical intervention in issue. The candidates for surrogate decision maker are several—parents or other close relatives, court-appointed guardians, medical practitioners, institutional ethics committees (within the health-care institutions where the contemplated medical interventions would be carried out), regional ethics bodies, administrative tribunals, or courts. The profoundly disabled person is obviously vulnerable in the surrogate's hands—unable to assert independent judgment or to effectively protest against any ill-considered surrogate decisions.

The two overriding concerns, then, become ensuring access to appropriate medical procedures and protecting against abusive decision making. As is shown in chapter 4, these two concerns help shape the substantive decision-making standards that bind any surrogate decision maker. But these concerns also have to be accommodated in determining who decides on behalf of the profoundly disabled person. For the dependability of a surrogate and the degree of scrutiny given to the surrogate's decision-making process are highly relevant to allaying fears of abuse. The allocation of decision-making authority may therefore depend in part on the setting in which the prospective patient is located and the seriousness of the consequences that could possibly ensue from the contemplated medical procedures.

Minors Living with Their Parents

According to law, medical ethics, and custom, parents are generally entitled to make medical decisions on behalf of their children.[1] The common law traditionally regarded parents as the "natural guardians" of their children. They had the prerogative to control medical decisions for their offspring, unless their "unfitness by reason of moral depravity"[2] was demonstrated or unless they made a decision that seriously and imprudently jeopardized the child's life or health. Under this standard, even a parental medical strategy subjecting a child to an increased risk of death or harm could be upheld if based on reasonable considerations. For example, parents were deemed entitled to reject a potentially life-saving (40 percent chance of cure) chemotherapy regimen for their three-year-old where the proposed treatment for cancer would be painful, cause distasteful side effects, and itself risk causing death.[3]

Although common-law tradition accords considerable leeway to parents in making medical decisions for their children, I doubt that the federal Constitution entrenches parents as exclusive decision makers where the contemplated procedure may entail serious consequences for the child. (And serious consequences are clearly involved when the medical issues are abortion, sterilization, tissue donation, or end-of-life decisions.) While child rearing is indeed a fundamental aspect of liberty under the Fourteenth Amendment,[4] the constitutionally protected child-rearing prerogative probably does not include exclusive control of any and all medical decisions.[5] In the 1990 decision in *Cruzan v. Missouri Department of Health* (as described in chapter 2), the U.S. Supreme Court rejected an incapacitated patient's claim of a constitutional right to have the issue of life-sustaining medical intervention resolved by her loving family, which was seeking to implement the patient's projected wishes. Because the underlying issue was the life and death of a helpless being attached to life support, the Court indicated that a state could, constitutionally, set up protective decision-making machinery and restrictive standards. A few state courts also have ruled that parents have no authority to order the cessation of life support from a fatally afflicted infant. And state statutes often allow minors—even without parental authorization—to obtain medical intervention regarding sexually transmitted diseases. These measures undercut any constitutional claim for parents that is grounded in practice and tradition.

Beyond rejecting the constitutional claim in *Cruzan,* the Supreme Court has given oblique signals that the Constitution does not require that parents always control their children's medical fates. In *Hodgson v. Minnesota,* the Supreme Court upheld a system of abortion regulation that accorded control of some minors' abortion decisions to courts making determinations in conjunction with the minors' health-care providers.[6] The delicacy and intrinsic hazards of some kinds of medical decisions that affect minors leave constitutional leeway for states to take such decision making out of the exclusive hands of parents.[7] (This is not to say that supplanting parental authority over delicate medical issues is good public policy, only that such a step would probably be constitutional.)

So common law rather than the Constitution is the primary source of a parental prerogative to make medical decisions on behalf of their children. Does the broad common-law authority to control children's medical handling extend to parents of profoundly disabled offspring? Even when the child is a neonate? Even when the child is living in an institution rather than at home? Even when a medical procedure poses a significant risk to the child's well-being?

Some commentators are wary about allowing the parents of mentally retarded children to serve as surrogates in serious medical decisions. They fear that parents may share common social prejudices against the retarded and common misconceptions about retarded children's potential for successful adjustment to their circumstances.[8] Hesitations about parental decision-making authority are particularly acute when the sick child is a newborn.[9] A parent at that point may be unbonded with the infant and emotionally overwrought—mired in ambivalence, angst, and fear. Medical uncertainty also handicaps parents of newborns in their projecting of what the child's life with disability will be like. Commentators also fear the effects of conflicts of interest when parents make important medical decisions about their mentally disabled offspring. The apprehension is that because a family's lifestyle and resources may be intertwined with a disabled child's medical fate, the parental conflict of interest will distort sound decision making.

The apprehensions about parental conflict of interests are understandable in some contexts. If the issue is life-sustaining treatment for a profoundly disabled infant, a parent is likely to be conflicted by concerns about the financial and emotional well-being of the family as a whole if considerable resources and attention must be devoted to the raising of a child with multiple deficits. If the issue is organ donation by a profoundly disabled child, the prospective recipient is almost always a sibling or other close relative. A parent as surrogate decision maker is then inevitably faced with the tension between a strong incentive to salvage the donee's life (thus preserving family integrity) and a dedication to the interests and well-being of the incapacitated potential donor. If the issue is sterilization, a parent may be concerned about the supervisory load involved in monitoring the disabled child's activity (if sterilization is not employed) or even the potential responsibility for rearing a grandchild whom the profoundly disabled child is incapable of parenting.[10]

In short, the specter of confused and conflicting parental interests impels concern about the ability of parents to make objective, balanced medical determinations on behalf of their mentally retarded children. Almost everyone concedes that parents must be allocated responsibility for routine medical decisions. It would be impossibly cumbersome to disrupt parental control of the myriad minor medical treatment decisions that constantly arise. But for certain critical medical issues—including sterilization, organ donation, and end-of-life determinations—some sources urge a mandatory resort to the protective mantle of the courts as a safeguard against arbitrary parental determinations. The argument is that the adversarial format—in which lawyers (including a judicially appointed representative for the mentally disabled patient) present all perspectives and a judge acts as a neutral arbiter—makes judicial proceedings the best forum when a disabled person's vital interests are at stake.[11]

A contrary perspective holds that parents who act in conjunction with medical personnel should be the prime locus of decision making, even when serious consequences will flow from a medical decision made on behalf of a profoundly disabled person. Under this framework, courts would become involved only if objections to a parental decision are made by an interested party, such as a close relative or an involved health-care provider, and only if discussions and ethics consultations then fail to resolve the dispute. Part of the underlying hesitation about invoking the courts as primary decision maker relates to certain negative characteristics of the judicial process. Delay, expense, burdensome court proceedings, and public exposure of private matters are all negative features.[12] Moreover, the supposed neutrality of judges does not ensure the best decision on the merits.

Judges have no special competence regarding medical decisions, and judges may even be subject to the same preconceptions and prejudices as other segments of the population.[13]

In addition to the negative aspects of the judicial process, other arguments favor parental retention of a primary decision-making role. Some commentators see parental closeness to the family-member patient not as a disqualification because of conflict of interest but as a positive factor that helps to justify a reliance on parental decisions. Parents are seen by these observers as the people who best know the incapacitated patient and his or her needs.[14] The 1983 President's Commission for the Study of Ethical Problems in Medicine supported family responsibility for end-of-life decision making in part because close relatives are presumed to be the most caring, concerned, and knowledgeable about incapacitated patients.[15] Courts also have sometimes expressed confidence that family are generally loving and supportive and therefore the appropriate surrogate for an incapacitated loved one. Finally, the family is a vital social unit in American culture (as reflected in part by recognition of child rearing as a fundamental aspect of liberty), so that families should arguably be accorded the maximum decision-making responsibility regarding matters that have a clear impact on the family unit as a whole.[16] A few sources view the potential impact on the family unit as creating a fairness interest that justifies allowing parents to make important medical decisions on behalf of incapacitated offspring. Under this view, because parental and general family interests are intimately affected by the decision, "justice" supposedly requires that parents have a key role in the relevant decision making.[17]

Of course, some of the support for family as surrogate decision makers relies on arguments that are particularly applicable to previously competent, rather than never competent, patients. One notion is that most now incompetent persons would, if miraculously competent, prefer that a family member rather than a court or some other surrogate be responsible for critical medical decisions. That rationale fits previously competent patients both because a preexisting intimate relationship to the prospective family-member surrogate is often present and because we know from surveys that adults generally want their loved ones to be responsible for any critical medical decisions in the event of future incompetency. Similar preferences cannot readily be attributed to never competent, profoundly disabled persons. Such persons have never been able to deliberate about desirable surrogates or express their preferences about who should decide their medical fate. Another notion behind family decision making is that family members will best know and understand the values and preferences of the now incompetent patient. Again, that rationale is most relevant to previously competent patients where the central object of medical decision making is to replicate what the patient would have wanted. A never competent patient has not formed the kinds of values and preferences that might shape prospective medical handling.

All this does not mean that serious medical decisions affecting never competent, profoundly disabled persons should be removed from parents. There is still a strong argument that parents best know and understand the physical and emotional needs and interests of their profoundly disabled children. And understanding the feelings, emotions, and well-being of those children is indeed integral to medical decisions on the children's behalf. Moreover, the notion of the family as an institution that is entitled to reconcile its own internal tensions and frictions according to pluralistic value systems is a venerable part of American culture. I am simply noting that *some* of the arguments commonly used to support family members as surrogate decision makers have less force in the context of profoundly disabled patients (as opposed to previously competent patients).

Having set out the conflicting positions regarding judicial involvement in efforts of parents or other next of kin to control the medical handling of incapacitated family members, I turn to the resolution of that basic conflict in the context of the critical medical issues that occupy this book. I sketch the decision-making frameworks that have emerged in law and practice respecting serious medical decisions, including decisions about organ donation, reproduction (including abortion and sterilization), the end of life, and participation in nontherapeutic medical research.

As noted, the traditional common-law approach was that parents—and not health-care providers or courts—were entitled to control the medical fates of their dependent children. This approach applied to parents of profoundly disabled children living at home and to parents acting on behalf of their adult mentally disabled children.[18] The presumption of emancipation at the age of majority did not apply to a severely mentally disabled person. For such a person, parents continued to be legally responsible both for care and medical decision making.[19] Moreover, health-care providers developed a widespread practice of looking to close family for consent to perform medical procedures on incapacitated patients. Even in jurisdictions where only a judicially appointed guardian might have official authority to act as a surrogate (for example, for a postmajority incapacitated adult), few mentally incapacitated persons had such guardians, and health-care providers preferred to rely on conscientious next of kin rather than turn to courts for the appointment of a guardian. When there was unanimity among providers and relatives, the mutually favored course of medical treatment or nontreatment would be followed.[20] This pattern prevailed both as to routine and serious medical interventions so long as the primary object of the prospective intervention was the promotion of the incapacitated patient's well-being.

In the second half of the twentieth century, unconventional medical issues arose in which much more was at stake than preservation of the incapacitated patient's general health and well-being. Among the medical issues then confronting physicians and surrogate decision makers were tissue donation, abortion, therapeutic (as opposed to eugenic) sterilization, and withdrawal of life-sustaining medical intervention. Because the contemplated medical procedures carried unusual risks to the incapacitated patient, because unconventional bodily intrusions were in issue, or because involved parties seemed to have conflicting interests in the relevant decisions, physicians were uncomfortable with simply acquiescing in parental or family choice. Physicians or medical institutions then turned to the courts for guidance about who was authorized to decide for the incapacitated patient, what decision-making procedures had to be followed, and what decision-making standards or criteria had to be used. What emerged was a patchwork of decision-making frameworks that varies from jurisdiction to jurisdiction and even from one type of medical issue to another.

The dilemma of whether to accept parental determinations about problematic medical issues surfaced early on in the context of organ donations. Massachusetts in the mid-1950s served as the first testing ground. In 1956 and 1957, parents sought to secure kidney transplants from a healthy, nondisabled fourteen-year-old and a healthy, nondisabled nineteen-year-old to the young people's critically ill siblings. The hospitals involved were aware that the transplants were primarily intended to benefit the young prospective donors' siblings rather than the donors, were aware of significant risks and discomforts to the donor, and were reluctant to perform the operations based solely on parental authorization. A kidney transplant

was a far cry from the routine interventions—tonsillectomies, appendec-
tomies, and the like—that hospitals customarily performed in reliance on
parental authorization. The hospitals therefore turned to the courts for
confirmation that the kidney transplants could legally be performed. In unreported opinions, the Massachusetts Supreme Judicial Court endorsed
both the resort to a judicial forum and the appropriateness of the kidney
transplants in the circumstances. The circumstances deemed relevant were
not just that the kidney recipient would receive a life-saving gift, but that
the donor sibling's future well-being would be promoted (by the continued
presence of the beloved donee), and that the teenage donors consented to
the intrusive medical procedure.[21]

In 1969, Ava Strunk sought to direct a kidney transplant from her
twenty-seven-year-old son Jerry, physically healthy but mentally impaired
(with an I.Q. of 35 and the mental capacity of a six-year-old), to her twenty-
eight-year-old son Tommy, who was stricken with chronic nephritis.[22]
Again, the hospital hesitated to act solely on parental instructions. The
mother therefore sought judicial approval of her proposed course of action. By a four to three margin, the Kentucky Supreme Court ruled that an
equity court could properly authorize the kidney transplant so long as the
transplant was consistent with the interests of the incapacitated donor. The
majority approved the transplant from Jerry on the basis that he was so
emotionally attached to Tommy that preserving Tommy would serve Jerry's
interests. The dissent questioned whether the transplant could be deemed
a significant benefit to someone like Jerry, whose appreciation of sibling
loss might well be limited.

Some commentators in the wake of *Strunk v. Strunk* questioned the
propriety of using severely incapacitated persons as organ donors.[23] Their
apprehension was that such helpless individuals would be exploited—
without appropriate attention to their own interests—under the impetus
of saving the lives of siblings or others. Commentators contended that parents would be terribly conflicted at the prospect of harvesting an organ
from one child, especially an intellectually limited child, to salvage another
child. And like the dissenters in *Strunk,* some observers questioned the extent of any psychological benefit to the donor sibling. The bottom line was
that physicians and hospitals continued to hesitate about relying exclusively on parental consent to organ donation. They demanded judicial approval of any prospective organ transplant from an incapacitated donor.[24]

Since *Strunk* in 1969, parents or other guardians of minors or mentally disabled adults have periodically sought judicial authorization of organ donation.[25] Resort to court authorization has often occurred in instances of bone-marrow transplants despite the lesser burden on the prospective donor.[26] The courts have continued to articulate a test geared to the best interests of the donor-patient, and the judicial application of that standard has resulted in rulings both for and against donation. Judges have generally approved the proposed kidney or bone-marrow transplant when the donee had previously maintained a close relationship with the donor— thus accepting as plausible the parental claim that avoidance of the donee's death would significantly advance the donor's interests.[27] However, courts on several occasions have rejected surrogate requests for authorization of organ donation on behalf of mentally disabled persons.[28] In each instance of rejection, the potential donor had not previously had much contact with the prospective donee, so that the donor's potential benefit from the life-saving donation was deemed speculative or insubstantial.

Surrogate decisions involving organ or tissue donation from incapacitated donors remain problematic because the primary beneficiary is a sibling (any benefit to the donor being derivative) and parents have a considerable incentive to save the donee sibling. The involved physicians or health-care institutions also have a strong incentive to save the donee sibling, and so allocating decision making to the setting of the hospital—that is, to the hands of surrogates acting together with involved physicians— also seems problematic. As long as the applicable decision-making standard is best interests of the incapacitated donor, there appear to be strong reasons to invoke the judiciary to resolve whether to use the incapacitated person as an organ donor. (In chapter 5, in a discussion of "forced altruism," I examine the rationale for permitting nontherapeutic medical procedures to be performed on profoundly disabled persons. There I address not only tissue donation but also enrollment in nontherapeutic medical research. As part of that inquiry, I suggest that instead of the best interests of the donor, in some instances where surrogates act on behalf of incapacitated persons the decision-making standard might be relaxed to permit more leeway to a surrogate. If so, decision-making authority might be more readily accorded to parents acting under the scrutiny of institutional ethics committees.)

There are indications that decisions about bone-marrow transplants in some locales are being made within health-care institutions and without resort to the courts.[29] And statutes in a few jurisdictions permit bone-marrow transplants to be authorized by parents without judicial proceedings. Presumably, the rationale for this practice is the diminished risk and inconvenience to the incapacitated donor stemming from bone-marrow donation as opposed to kidney donation. Nonetheless, a bone-marrow transplant is a medical procedure that is undertaken primarily for the benefit of the recipient rather than the donor. And there are significant questions about any anticipated benefits for the bone-marrow donor—in part because the chances of success in bone-marrow transplants may be lower than those in kidney transplants.[30] Again, so long as the governing decision-making standard is the best interests of the incapacitated donor, judicial oversight of organ and tissue transplants might be expected.[31] (However, I argue in chapter 5 that the best interests of the donor ought not be the determinative standard.)

Regarding reproduction-related decisions by surrogates on behalf of profoundly disabled persons, the picture of parental authority is somewhat muddled. Contraception services are probably considered routine medical care, and for these decisions physicians look to the custodial parents for consent on behalf of the disabled patient. Abortion involves more serious consequences in terms both of the bodily invasion and the potential impact on the pregnant patient's life. The few cases on point are mixed. Most indicate that a court must resolve whether to authorize an abortion for a profoundly disabled woman, but the cases are not unanimous.[32] In practice, many physicians apparently are willing to implement—without seeking judicial intervention—parental requests for abortion on behalf of profoundly disabled pregnant women.[33] This medical willingness to act without judicial approval might be explainable on a couple of grounds. In some instances, the underlying medical issue might be easy because the trauma and stress associated with pregnancy and childbirth would clearly be counter to the disabled person's well-being. In some instances, the disabled woman might be so clearly incapable of child rearing that the physician might regard the woman's interest in carrying a child to term as negligible. Also, the profoundly disabled woman would not have any religious or conscience-related scruples about abortion. The bottom line is that parents as surrogates do make some abortion decisions on behalf of profoundly disabled women without judicial involvement.

The picture is much more uniform (and restrictive about parental authority) when the medical procedure is the sterilization of a mentally incapacitated person. The widely prevailing legal approach is that only a court can lawfully authorize the performance of that medical procedure, whether the impetus for its performance comes from a parent who is caring for a disabled child or from the administration of an institution that is housing the disabled person. The requirement of judicial authorization stems in large part from the history of the abusive use of sterilization as a eugenic tool to prevent procreation by those deemed socially unfit. During the first half of the twentieth century, tens of thousands of persons, many of them only slightly or moderately retarded, if retarded at all, were victimized by operations that wrongfully precluded them from becoming parents.[34]

By the 1960s and 1970s, the issue had shifted from sterilization compelled by state laws or impelled by state institutional administrators to sterilization undertaken at the initiative of a parent or other guardian. During that period, several state courts, acutely aware of the history of abuse and wary about the motives of parents seeking authorization, ruled that they had no jurisdiction to approve petitions for sterilization.[35] In those instances, the petitioning parents were not alleging that their children's medical interests dictated sterilization; rather, they relied either on discredited eugenic concerns or on their own interests in convenience and peace of mind. (Sterilization of an incapacitated child might relieve the supervisory responsibilities of parents and foreclose the possibility that the parents would end up raising an unwanted grandchild.) The courts were also sensitive to the fact that procreation had recently been deemed to be a fundamental-liberty interest under the federal Constitution, so that any proposed sterilization entailed not just a significant bodily invasion but also the potential deprivation of a constitutional prerogative.

Starting in 1980, state courts shifted markedly in their willingness to entertain petitions by parents who were seeking sterilization of profoundly disabled children.[36] These courts recognized that sterilization would, in some instances, promote the physical or emotional well-being of a profoundly disabled child. This might be the case, for example, where pregnancy would precipitate severe physical or emotional consequences and alternative means of contraception were contraindicated. This perception of a possible benefit to the child translated into seeing sterilization as implementation of a possible "right" to choose not to procreate. (As I observe in chapter 2, medical decisions that affect profoundly disabled persons do not reflect autonomous choice by the patient, so that the right in question cannot be personally exercised. But surrogate choice on behalf of a disabled person can still advance the important well-being and dignitary interests of that person.) Accordingly, judicial authorization of sterilization after 1980 was found to be within the inherent authority of equity courts to protect the interests of incapacitated persons as well as a means to preserve a right not to procreate.

At the same time, the courts required a judicial inquiry regarding each proposed sterilization and set down careful procedures and criteria that were designed to safeguard the well-being of the disabled individuals. Typically, a guardian ad litem would have to be appointed to represent the disabled person's interests, an independent medical assessment would be required, and no sterilization would be ordered without clear and convincing proof that such a procedure would be in the disabled person's best interests. Certain factors would have to be examined during the judicial inquiry into best interests. These factors included assessment of whether the disabled person was indeed in danger of becoming pregnant, whether the person was permanently incapable of child rearing, whether pregnancy and childbirth would be harmful experiences, and whether alternative means of contraception might be available.[37]

All these procedural and substantive protections were designed to protect vulnerable disabled persons against abusive sterilizations. While the practice of mass eugenic sterilization had long ceased, unnecessary sterilization of disabled persons was still a specter.[38] The courts therefore showed no inclination to forgo judicial administration of the applicable standards and to rely on parents acting in conjunction with medical personnel as surrogate decision makers. For example, the New Jersey Supreme Court declared in 1981 that "individual judicial decision making is the best way to protect the rights and interests of the incompetent and to avoid abuses of the decision to sterilize."[39] Many courts in the 1980s endorsed that position, exhibiting acute sensitivity to the procreative rights in issue, to the parents' conflicting interest in avoiding supervisory burdens, to the vulnerability of severely disabled persons, and to the dark history of eugenic sterilizations. Legislatures have also tended to dictate judicial scrutiny as a prerequisite to sterilization of incapacitated persons. Numerous states have statutes requiring judicial hearings and mandating careful attention to patient best interests before any nonvoluntary sterilization can be performed.[40] These measures require even court-appointed guardians to secure explicit judicial approval prior to any sterilization of a ward.[41]

Requiring judicial scrutiny of sterilization seems salutary, at least where the patient's mental impairment is mild or moderate and future child rearing would be a real possibility. A question arises whether courts should be invoked as surrogate decision makers when the patient is profoundly disabled and will never be capable of child rearing.[42] In that instance, a procreation interest is not genuinely at stake. I am suggesting that a profoundly disabled person does not have an independent interest in pregnancy and childbirth in the absence of a capacity to raise a child. Sterilization of such a person indeed entails a bodily invasion, but the impingement of bodily integrity is no greater than that involved in a variety of routine medical decisions that are normally left in the hands of parents (such as an appendectomy). Couldn't medical personnel be expected to scrutinize whether there's a serious medical need for sterilization just as they would do in the case of other medical decisions by the parents? Moreover, the patient's interest in having a sterilization is greater and more easily discernible in the case of a profoundly disabled woman than in the case of a moderately incapacitated woman. Consider the massive physical and psychological burden of pregnancy, labor, and delivery on a person who cannot comprehend why those phenomena are occurring. As I suggest below, ways exist to safeguard against abusive decision making without automatic judicial involvement.

A counterargument—one favoring judicial involvement—is that the factors determining the need for sterilization include some that are beyond medical expertise and more suited to judicial assessment. These include the likelihood that the disabled person will have sexual interactions as well as the practicality of alternative means of contraception. Resolution of the ultimate issue—whether to leave sterilization issues in the hands of judges and not parents and physicians—turns in part on an assessment of whether medical attitudes toward mentally disabled persons have shifted sufficiently since the mid-twentieth century (when prejudice against the disabled was more widespread). Arguably, a recognition of the rights and interests of the mentally impaired has become part of the prevailing medical ethic. Indeed, in some instances physicians might be more sensitive than judges to the mandate of following the disabled patient's interests. Martha Field and Valerie Sanchez contend that judicial proceedings regarding sterilization tend to be perfunctory and often ignore the exacting criteria that are supposed to govern a surrogate decision on this issue.[43] In the meantime, the prevailing pattern is that surrogate decisions regarding sterilization remain in judges' hands even where the patient is so profoundly disabled as to be incapable of child rearing.

In the same period that courts began to wrestle with the question of what surrogate decision maker may act on behalf of a mentally incapacitated person regarding tissue-donation and sterilization issues, a similar question arose in the context of end-of-life decisions. Judicial precedent had established by the 1950s and 1960s that parents generally control the medical handling of their minor children but cannot ordinarily reject medical care that is necessary to preserve the life of a child.[44] Those precedents addressed sick children who were presumed to be able to enjoy long and healthy lives, so that parental failure to utilize critical medical treatment could easily be deemed a form of parental neglect warranting judicial intervention. In the 1970s, the courts began to confront situations in which incapacitated patients were unavoidably dying and some surrogate had to determine whether to withhold or withdraw life-sustaining medical intervention from the fatally stricken patient.

The stakes were high. Fatally afflicted persons have an incalculable interest in avoiding premature death. Yet medical science had developed the capacity to prolong the dying process beyond the bounds that many people would find acceptable. In the words of one judge, "[T]o condemn persons to lives from which they cry out for release is nothing short of barbaric."[45] Even if the incompetent patient is not "crying out," denial of a surrogate's ability to choose to withdraw life support could easily relegate the patient to a grueling or demeaning dying process. As another judge commented: "To presume that the incompetent person must always be subjected to what many rational and intelligent persons may decline is to downgrade the status of the incompetent person by placing a lesser value on his intrinsic human worth."[46] Thus, it is respectful of a profoundly disabled person to have a surrogate evaluate the propriety of medical intervention rather than follow a technological imperative.[47]

Medical personnel who were caring for dying, incapacitated patients wondered in the 1970s whether the traditional resort to families as surrogate decision makers on behalf of incapacitated medical patients should extend to the context of the termination of life support. Families acting in this context clearly have potential conflicts of interest. Families deciding the fate of a fatally stricken loved one might be influenced by a desire to avoid financial and emotional burdens on themselves. Or families might be so stricken by grief or guilt that they are unable to make a wrenching decision to let the gravely deteriorated dying patient go. In all these instances, an impetus exists for family members to deviate from the strict best interests of the incapacitated patient. And physicians, fearing criminal liability for causing death by the removal of life support, were hesitant to remove life support from a helpless patient. Thus, in 1975, when Karen Ann Quinlan's father sought the removal of a respirator from his permanently unconscious twenty-one-year-old daughter, the attending physician feared that the detachment of the respirator would constitute homicide; he favored maintenance of life support and refused to implement Mr. Quinlan's wishes. Karen Ann Quinlan's father turned to the courts for authorization to dictate the removal of his daughter's life support.

The New Jersey Supreme Court unanimously ruled that the conscientious father could decide on behalf of his daughter even if the decision might prompt her death.[48] The court set down a tight decision-making standard. The father could end life support only if medical sources established that there was no hope that his daughter would return to a sapient state and only if the father projected that his daughter would want life support to be withdrawn in the dismal circumstances at hand. But the court refused to require that the father as guardian get judicial endorsement of his decision on behalf of his daughter. According to the court, judicial intervention would be "impossibly cumbersome" and "a gratuitous encroachment upon the medical profession's field of competence."[49] Sound decision making could be adequately ensured by scrutiny on the part of the attending physicians and by involvement of a "prognosis committee" to confirm the patient's permanently unconscious state.

Within a year of *Quinlan*, Massachusetts's highest court addressed the medical fate of Joseph Saikewicz, a sixty-seven-year-old, profoundly disabled resident of a state institution. Mr. Saikewicz was stricken with terminal leukemia, and the substantive issue became whether to initiate chemotherapy, which would yield a 30 to 50 percent chance of a significant period of remission—at a cost of discomforting and possibly terrifying side effects for the uncomprehending patient. The threshold question was who should decide the treatment issue on Mr. Saikewicz's behalf. He had no relatives willing to take decision-making responsibility. The superintendent of Saikewicz's state residential facility petitioned for judicial guidance. The Massachusetts Supreme Judicial Court did not share the *Quinlan* court's willingness to rely on private end-of-life decision making among family and health-care providers. The *Saikewicz* court insisted that judicial involvement should be a prerequisite to any determination to withhold life support from an incompetent person (even if a close relative were available to serve as decision maker). According to the court, life and death questions for an incompetent patient "require the process of detached but passionate investigation and decision" that characterizes judicial proceedings.[50] (The court went on to conclude that withholding chemotherapy from Joseph Saikewicz was the appropriate course to follow. That substantive result is discussed further in chapter 4. The focus here is on the procedural question of who should make end-of-life medical decisions for an incapacitated patient.)

Quinlan and *Saikewicz* offered divergent models for surrogate decision making in the end-of-life context—private determinations by family members acting in conjunction with health-care providers (subject to judicial recourse by any observer who claimed inappropriate conduct) versus mandatory judicial involvement. Since those cases were decided in the mid-1970s, there has been no uniform legal approach to this thorny issue of which surrogate should determine the medical course of a fatally stricken, incapacitated patient. A few jurisdictions have followed the Massachusetts lead and required judicial resolution of end-of-life decisions on behalf of incapacitated persons.[51] A few other jurisdictions demand judicial appointment of a guardian but then allow the guardian to act in conjunction with medical personnel—without further judicial involvement—in making the critical decisions in issue.[52] The bulk of jurisdictions appear willing to allow families, in conjunction with medical personnel, to make end-of-life medical decisions without any routine judicial involvement either in the form of judicial appointment of a guardian or judicial participation in the actual medical decision.[53] (Many but by no means all of the relevant cases involve permanently unconscious patients.) In delegating authority to the family and doctor framework, the relevant cases also make clear that other forums would be available if dissenting family members or

medical personnel objected to a surrogate's choice on behalf of an incapacitated patient. For example, medical personnel troubled by a surrogate's decision would be expected to seek consultation from a hospital
ethics committee and ultimately to resort to judicial intervention where a
surrogate continued to take an inappropriate stance.[54]

Beyond the court cases favoring private decision making, a clear legislative trend supports allocating end-of-life decision making to the private
family and doctor realm. A majority of states now have "surrogacy statutes" that set up a hierarchy of family members who are authorized to make
important medical decisions on behalf of an incapacitated relative in the absence of any agent previously designated by the now incapacitated person.[55]
These statutes sometimes confine the circumstances under which surrogates may withdraw life support, usually by demanding either a terminal
condition or permanent unconsciousness. While a terminal condition is not
uniformly defined, it usually means an unavoidable death within a brief
time—a situation that fits some decisions on behalf of dying, profoundly
disabled persons.[56] Moreover, these statutes leave the common-law authority of surrogates in place. In sum, these surrogacy statutes reinforce
the judicial inclination to leave end-of-life medical decisions to private
decision makers.

Willingness to authorize close family members to serve as surrogates in
end-of-life decisions is perhaps most understandable with regard to formerly competent patients—those whose mental deficits postdate a period
of mental capacity. Two factors then enhance the attractiveness of family
members as surrogate decision makers. In many instances, the surrogate
has bonded with the now incompetent patient, thus increasing the probability that the surrogate possesses a loving attitude toward the helpless patient. And the previously competent patient is more likely than a never
competent person to have adopted personal values and preferences that
could help a surrogate seeking to implement the incapacitated patient's
wishes. A bonded, family-member surrogate is more likely than any other
source to understand the now incompetent patient's putative wishes.[57]

Some willingness to rely on parental decision making—without routine
judicial involvement—can be observed even in the context of never competent patients who are facing critical end-of-life issues. This was the case,
for example, in *Jane Doe*,[58] where the parents of a thirteen-year-old who
was suffering from a degenerative neurological condition were allowed to

decide the medical fate of their semiconscious child. The Georgia court invoked the traditional common-law presumption that parents are the appropriate decision makers for their children and employed it even in the context of a life-and-death determination. A similar position has been adopted in other cases involving fatally stricken children. This was so for an eleven-year-old mired in a permanently unconscious state,[59] a ten-month-old who lacked 90 percent of brain function,[60] a twenty-year-old chronically suffering from Batten's disease and therefore reduced to the mental function of an infant,[61] and a three-year-old afflicted with terminal cancer.[62] In addition, there are indications that a parental prerogative to decide the medical fate of gravely ill children extends to parents of adult children who have always been profoundly disabled.[63] This is consistent with the approach, previously described, that holds that never competent persons are not emancipated from the care and control of their parents. Even in a jurisdiction where a parent must petition to become guardian for an adult child, the prevailing custom and practice are to acquiesce in the decisions of a parent who is the sole caretaker of the disabled adult child. That is, as long as the parent appears to be acting in a responsible manner as surrogate decision maker, physicians are likely to implement the parental decision. This tendency toward medical acquiescence in parental decision making stands in marked contrast to the practice regarding tissue donation and sterilization (where judicial involvement is customary).

The issue of surrogate authority to permit nontherapeutic medical research on profoundly disabled persons presents a muddled picture. Caution is aroused by a number of historic abuses—such as the medical researchers who secured parental consent to inject live hepatitis virus into children living at the Willowbrook State School in New York in the mid-1960s and the University of Iowa researchers who in 1939 induced stuttering in children at the Iowa Soldier's Orphans' Home.[64] Further concerns exist because the physician's role of researcher is not congruent with the role of healer, so that a conflict of interest can arise. Surrogate consent from parents—the minimum safeguard required—may be suspect if the attitudes of parents of profoundly disabled children are, as sometimes claimed, "quite ambivalent, a mixture of love, pity, and anger"[65] or if parents feel that care for their child is contingent on their participation in a research experiment. Nonetheless, parents or other close family are generally authorized to submit mentally incapacitated wards to limited kinds of research.

Various safeguards have been adopted or proposed for nontherapeutic research on disabled persons. The primary safeguard in place is that institutional review boards (IRBs) must review every research protocol for scientific, legal, and ethical flaws. The most prominent of the constraints on researchers is a universal understanding that a surrogate's consent must be obtained for any research that is conducted on a mentally incapacitated subject. In addition, limits exist on any surrogate's authority to subject an incapacitated person to risk. As chapter 5 indicates in more detail, a surrogate can subject an incapacitated ward to nontherapeutic research involving only minimal risk or a minor increase over minimal risk.

Numerous proposals have sought to reinforce the process by which surrogate (usually parental) decision making is made. In 1978, in the wake of the Belmont Report, the U.S. Department of Health, Education, and Welfare (HEW) issued proposed rules that covered research on mentally disabled, institutionalized persons. For research subjects who were incapable of giving assent to a proposed action, HEW considered requiring approval by a patient's advocate or by a court in addition to parental consent. (Indeed, HEW gave thought to banning any involvement of such patients in nontherapeutic research.) The HEW proposals were never adopted, but some commentators have suggested similar decision-making frameworks (such as requiring special patient advocates or, in their absence, judicial approval).[66] In 1986, the National Institutes of Health (NIH) recommended that for any research involving greater than minimal risk, the surrogate (usually a parent) should have to seek prior judicial appointment as a guardian before being able to consent to nontherapeutic research.[67] That recommendation has been widely condemned as too burdensome for researchers.[68]

Current federal policy does little to resolve the mélange of approaches to surrogate authority over nontherapeutic medical research. Federal policy does dictate that institutional review boards for the protection of human subjects examine the ethics of every research proposal, but that policy says little about who can make surrogate decisions regarding nontherapeutic research. The Common Rule (the short name for the Federal Policy for the Protection of Human Subjects, adopted in 1991) covers the regulations adhered to by most federal agencies that fund medical research. It allows consent by "a legally authorized representative," thus relegating the issue of surrogate decision-making authority to state law. State law takes no uniform position. Indeed, relatively little state law speaks directly to the issue of nontherapeutic research. A few states have statutes that rank parents as the appropriate decision makers for incapacitated subjects.[69] A few states, by judicial decision or statute, bar nontherapeutic research involving any more than minimal risk.[70] A number of states have statutes or regulations that insulate institutionalized disabled persons against nontherapeutic research unless either judicial approval is secured or the surrogate (usually a parent) is court appointed as guardian. The law of most states remains murky, and debate continues about whether parents or other close relatives of disabled persons have the authority to consent to nontherapeutic research without first being judicially appointed as guardian.[71] Numerous states have surrogacy laws that provide a hierarchy of health-care decision makers for incapacitated persons, but those laws don't speak directly to medical research. Those surrogacy laws might be interpreted to allow close family members to give surrogate consent for medical research—a result that would be likely for therapeutic research aimed at furthering the best interests of the incapacitated subject but less likely for nontherapeutic research.

While state law in many states remains murky about surrogate authority over medical research, practice seems to be fairly uniform. Researchers (as well as institutional review boards) commonly rely on informal family consent to low-risk nontherapeutic research. From the perspective of researchers, resorting to courts for the appointment of a formal guardian would be too time consuming and cumbersome. Researchers therefore rely on the traditional laws and customs under which health-care providers often turn to next of kin for consent to perform medical procedures on incapacitated patients.[72] This prevalent reliance on next of kin is probably less troubling in the medical-research context because of the widespread understanding that there are tight limits on the degree of risk to which surrogates can consent on behalf of their wards. The harder questions about surrogate authority relate to medical issues where more is at stake—tissue donation, abortion, sterilization, and end-of-life decisions. In those contexts, it is important to address the apparent anomaly that requires judicial intervention for sterilization and tissue donation but gives next of kin the authority to make decisions about life-sustaining medical intervention.

Does all of this make sense? Or is it anomalous to uniformly resort to courts for surrogate decisions about sterilization and organ donation while commonly relying on parents for determinations regarding nontherapeutic research and life-sustaining medical intervention? Aren't the consequences of decision making even more momentous in the death-and-dying context than in these other medical settings?

In part, the explanation may lie in practical constraints. Perhaps it would always be desirable to employ the kind of adversary process and impartial arbiter that characterizes judicial proceedings. But the inescapable fact is that court proceedings are cumbersome, prolonged, and expensive. Surrogate requests to harvest an organ from a profoundly disabled person are relatively rare, so that the cumbersome judicial process need seldom be invoked in that context. Similarly, surrogate requests for the performance of sterilization are relatively rare and should become even rarer as modern contraceptive techniques (like the Norplant implants) become more and more available. Fatal afflictions, by contrast, are more common, and surrogate decisions regarding the maintenance of life support are a relatively common phenomenon facing health-care providers. In other words, the prospective volume of expensive and cumbersome judicial proceedings may have deterred health-care providers from seeking, and lawmakers from demanding, resort to the judiciary to resolve end-of-life issues on behalf of incapacitated patients. Also, exigencies of time may be less for sterilization decision making than for end-of-life decision making, so the delay that is entailed by judicial proceedings might be more tolerable in the sterilization context.

Courts and legislatures also might be more confident of the reliability of health-care providers in scrutinizing end-of-life surrogate decisions than some other serious medical decisions. Health-care professions have a venerable tradition of preserving life. To the extent that professional distortions have occurred in the end-of-life context, they have tended toward overaggressive life-sustaining intervention rather than premature termination of life. This life-affirming medical orientation—combined with a clear ethical obligation to scrutinize surrogate end-of-life decisions in order to safeguard the best interests of an incapacitated patient[73]—may have impelled reliance on health-care providers rather than courts as a check on abuse in the end-of-life context.

Courts that allocate end-of-life decision-making authority to families commonly dictate certain procedural protections for the helpless patient. They usually require the attending physician to consult with at least one other, independent physician—both to verify the medical prognosis and to ensure that the course desired by the surrogate decision maker is consistent with ethical bounds.[74] In instances when the profoundly disabled, critically ill patient is hospitalized, an ethics committee is available for consultation and scrutiny.[75] In many states, a public advocate for the developmentally disabled can also scrutinize the decision making. And these courts further make clear that judicial recourse is available at the initiative of any surrounding health-care provider or family member who questions a surrogate's decision to withdraw life support from an incapacitated patient.[76]

Some observers are skeptical about reliance on family decision making rather than regularized judicial participation in end-of-life decision making. These observers view scrutiny by medical personnel as an inadequate safeguard against arbitrary or abusive surrogate decision making.[77] The main concern is that medical personnel are typically overburdened and highly reluctant to challenge surrogate decisions, especially by resorting to a potentially expensive judicial forum. The perceived hazard is too ready medical acquiescence in the wishes of the squeaky wheel—the surrounding family members who are seeking withdrawal of life support from a helpless patient. Even the mandatory involvement of institutional ethics committees would not placate these skeptics. They would be fearful about the varying capabilities of ethics committees and about possible conflicting interests of ethics committee members. According to this view, committee members might be swayed by their interests in institutional reputation, in professional convenience, and in avoiding litigation rather than by steadfast dedication to patient interests.

These concerns are understandable but not convincing. Parental decision making is appropriate for profoundly disabled persons—both because parents are more attuned than strangers to assessing the genuine feelings and well-being of their disabled offspring and because parents are still presumed to be caring and loving toward their offspring. Surrounding medical personnel and family can scrutinize a surrogate's proposed medical course to ensure that the suppositions about parental conduct coincide with reality in particular cases. Health-care providers are unlikely to be railroaded into too readily relinquishing a patient's life. The long medical tradition of preserving life has already been mentioned. Medical personnel in acute-care hospitals have extensive experience in assessing the propriety of allowing a person to die and can be expected to be alert and careful when a surrogate seeks to dispatch a patient whose life can be significantly extended.

No untoward burden exists for the physician or nurse who wants to resist a surrogate's premature push to end medical intervention. Health-care providers need not initiate judicial proceedings to thwart an erring surrogate. The typical situation is that the incapacitated patient is on life support, so any change in status quo requires medical cooperation (withdrawing life support). Nor is a surrogate's threat of litigation likely to impel a physician to capitulate and implement an improper surrogate decision. There is no serious chance of monetary or disciplinary liability, or even adverse publicity, when a physician makes a good-faith judgment that withdrawal of life support would be counter to the best interests of an incapacitated patient. Further, an attending physician need not stand alone in opposing improper surrogate requests. Resort to an institutional ethics committee (IEC) is available without excessive burden or expense. A multidisciplinary ethics committee—even one with only modest training—is likely to be sensitive to the interests of the incapacitated, dying patient. In short, continued reliance on private surrogate decision making seems entirely appropriate in the end-of-life context, at least where the process includes ready availability of scrutiny by a proper institutional ethics committee. A final precaution for profoundly disabled patients could be mandatory scrutiny by a special advocate for the mentally disabled, a procedure that is available in some states.

An ostensible anomaly remains in the prevailing pattern that upholds private end-of-life decision making and yet requires judicial participation in sterilization and organ-donation decisions. As mentioned above, numerical differences among these various medical interventions (surrogates typically face many more end-of-life issues than sterilization or organ donation matters) partially account for the anomaly. The question in my mind, though, is whether the anomaly should be resolved by less rather than more judicial involvement. That is, perhaps a uniform decision-making framework—one that relies on close family members to be the primary surrogate decision makers in consultation with attending physicians and subject to mandatory scrutiny by a multidisciplinary review committee on behalf of mentally disabled persons—ought to prevail for all critical medical decisions, such as abortion, sterilization, organ donation, and end-of-life determinations. A multidisciplinary institutional ethics committee includes a physician, a nurse, a social worker, an ethicist, a community representative, and someone experienced in issues that involve mentally disabled persons.

A model for decision making along these lines has been suggested by the New York State Task Force on Life and the Law.[78] Under such a model, an internal, multidisciplinary committee would review all critical decisions by surrogates, consult with the surrogates and their medical advisors, and seek judicial intervention in the event that the surrogate insisted on a course inconsistent with the applicable decision-making standards. (Chapter 4 addresses the substance of those standards—the criteria that govern surrogate medical decision making.) A uniform framework that relies on an internal institutional review might be justified on the basis that professional attitudes toward the mentally disabled and professional understanding of surrogate decision-making roles have substantially progressed over the last thirty years. Today, unlike in the 1950s and 1960s, prevailing medical ethics establish a patient-centered orientation that acknowledges the interests of even the most profoundly disabled individual as the principal focus of surrogate decision making.

An alternative approach is to accept the current decision-making framework—to use parents or close family members as primary surrogates for routine medical issues and for end-of-life issues while still using the courts for sterilization and organ-donation matters. A couple of rationales might support the current framework and explain any ostensible anomaly. One rationale would be that the history of abuse of vulnerable disabled populations is much more pronounced with sterilization (and to a lesser extent organ donation and nontherapeutic research) than with end-of-life decision making. This was part of the explanation that the New Jersey Supreme Court provided when it mandated judicial scrutiny of all surrogate sterilization decisions while allowing for private end-of-life determinations.[79] The history of sterilization abuse is well documented. And the relatively few cases that involve organ donation demonstrate that in several instances parents sought to derogate the interests of incapacitated persons in order to preserve close relatives.[80] While perceptible abuses have also occurred in the context of surrogate end-of-life decisions, they do not seem as prevalent. In the 1970s and early 1980s, there were notorious instances when parents sought to withhold life support from mentally disabled newborns in a fashion that was inconsistent with the children's best interests. (Such instances prompted the adoption of federal regulations—discussed below—that were aimed at limiting parental authority to withhold life support from newborns.) Yet as a whole, the area of surrogate end-of-life decision making has been remarkably free of documented abuse. Indeed, to this day overaggressive medical intervention that needlessly prolongs a dying process looms as a more common hazard than premature termination of life support.

Another rationale for differential decision-making frameworks might be that an antagonism of interests between parents and profoundly disabled children is more pronounced in the cases of sterilization and organ donation than in removal of life support. That is, even loving and devoted parents of a profoundly disabled person have strong interests in avoiding unwanted grandchildren or in saving a dying sibling. The incentive to allow a profoundly disabled child to die is less evident, at least for the category of cases under discussion. The focus of inquiry at the moment is who decides on behalf of profoundly disabled children (including adult children) who have been cared for at home. By undertaking the responsibility of home care, the parents have demonstrated some dedication to the interests and well-being of their profoundly disabled offspring.[81] While parents who act as surrogates in an end-of-life decision-making context might have some interest in avoiding a continued financial and emotional burden, concerns about that interest do not seem strong enough to oust the parents from primary decision-making authority. Keep in mind that surrounding health-care providers and family members typically serve as a check on abusive parental conduct. And a mandatory resort to the expensive and burdensome courts would serve to distort sound decision making by creating an incentive (avoidance of the burdensome judicial process) to prolong even a torturous or undignified dying process. For these reasons, it would at least be tolerable to maintain the status quo—a private forum for end-of-life issues and a judicial forum for sterilization and organ-donation decisions by surrogates.

Maintenance of the status quo regarding decision-making authority is arguably consistent with the legislative will as expressed in many states. Most states have statutes governing the authority of guardians who are formally appointed by courts to act on behalf of mentally disabled persons. In a number of jurisdictions, these statutes provide that a guardian is entitled to make medical decisions for an incapacitated ward but that certain extraordinary medical procedures require judicial approval. The extraordinary procedures that are covered are usually abortion, sterilization, electroconvulsive therapy, psychosurgery, and sometimes removal of an organ or amputation of a limb.[82] It is noteworthy that these statutes do not generally apply to the withholding or removal of life support. In some instances, statutes explicitly allow guardians to make end-of-life treatment decisions but provide limiting criteria (such as a requirement that the patient be in a terminal condition) that bind the surrogate.[83] A possible inference is that these legislatures did not view end-of-life decision making as being particularly prone to abuse, as contrasted with sterilization, psychosurgery, and the like. While these statutes requiring judicial scrutiny speak only to appointed guardians (and most parents of profoundly disabled children are acting as natural guardians without formal judicial appointment), the possible message is that certain medical interventions warrant more judicial scrutiny than others. End-of-life decisions apparently are not deemed to be as problematic or extraordinary as certain other types of surrogate decisions.

It might be possible to extend the impact of these statutory limitations on guardians by interpreting them as being applicable to any hazardous medical decision or any decision that carries a momentous consequence such as death. This has occurred in at least one instance.[84] There, an elderly, incapacitated woman stricken with throat cancer was facing a medical issue of whether to undergo surgery (to remove the cancerous vocal cords) or to begin chemotherapy as an alternative treatment. The court deemed the prospective vocal-cord surgery to be an "amputation" that triggered a statutory requirement of judicial resolution of the medical issue. That court saw the statutory requirement of judicial resolution as applicable whenever a surrogate medical decision involves an irreversible, intrusive, and momentous procedure.[85] But such expansive interpretations of guardianship statutes have not commonly occurred. The trend in statutory treatment of end-of-life matters, as described above, is toward reliance on close family members as surrogate decision makers.

Disabled Persons Living in Institutions

Some people with disabilities live in large state facilities with either dormitory or cottage sleeping arrangements, and others live in group arrangements—apartments or houses—within the broader community. The common element is government or government-financed supervision and control of the disabled person's daily living conditions. In these residential settings, professional staff members as a practical matter control the everyday medical treatment of residents, and parents impliedly consent to that arrangement when they place their disabled children in such facilities.

No such implied delegation of responsibility prevails with respect to the serious medical issues—including abortion, sterilization, organ donation, and end-of-life decisions—with which this book is concerned. A long-standing distrust of state institutional providers of residential services to the mentally disabled precludes any such implied authority. That distrust developed over the many decades during which many such institutions served merely as indifferent or hostile warehouses for the mentally disabled. It is currently fueled by the tendency of public institutions to be derelict in how they handle mentally disabled persons. Common concerns include the uneven quality of professional supervisory staff, the inadequate training of daily caregivers, and the inadequate presence and skill of medical personnel. For all these reasons, the control of serious medical issues is not ordinarily lodged in the hands of institutional staff.

The original approach was that the common law lodged all decision-making authority over critical medical decisions in the hands of the parents of institutionalized, disabled people.[86] This included institutionalized children. The right to determine an incompetent adult child's medical course resided "in the parent who has the legal responsibility to maintain such children."[87] (Many states assign to parents the responsibility for maintaining mentally disabled, adult children.) Even though the customary bonds associated with the daily interactions that accompany child rearing might be absent, the presumption was that parents were caring and conscientious and would be solicitous of their children's interests even in an institutional setting. This presumption applied initially even to serious medical interventions including abortion[88] and electric shock treatment.[89] (Of course, decision-making authority would rest in the hands of a judicially appointed guardian if such a person existed. But many institutionalized disabled persons have never been through a judicial process that results in the formal appointment of a guardian. And where such a process has transpired, the court usually designates a conscientious parent as formal guardian.) In the absence of an available parent, the institution would have to turn to a court for authorization regarding any serious medical intervention affecting a disabled resident.[90]

By the 1970s, though, with heightened public concern for the well-being and rights of disabled persons, challenges ensued to the prevailing pattern of reliance on parents for the critical medical decisions that affect their institutionalized offspring. When questions arose about the noneugenic sterilization of mentally disabled persons, the common response was that only courts—not parents, physicians, or institutional administrators—could authorize such a medical procedure.[91] The courts recalled that administrators of institutions had often played a central role in the sorry history of eugenic sterilizations. A similar reaction occurred in the context of the administration of antipsychotic medications and other forms of "extraordinary medical treatment."[92] As to antipsychotic medication, most courts rejected a medical model that would have permitted parents and institutional personnel to make the medical-treatment decision without judicial scrutiny. The judges apparently were suspicious of institutional interests in maintaining internal order and were sensitive to past abuses in the administration of antipsychotic drugs. They therefore demanded judicial participation in any initiation of antipsychotic treatment that was contrary to a disabled patient's wishes, except in exigent circumstances.[93]

Some other forms of medical intervention have been shifted from parental to judicial control. As previously noted, statutes in a number of states restrict the authority of guardians who are acting on the behalf of incapacitated persons and require the judicial authorization of certain critical medical matters, usually including sterilization, abortion, electroconvulsive treatment, and psychosurgery.[94] In those states, the restrictions imposed on guardians almost surely apply to the critical medical decisions that are contemplated for institutionalized disabled persons, whether the guardians have been formally appointed or not. That is, the same kinds of concerns about the conduct of formal guardians would extend to parental decisions that affect institutionalized persons. New Jersey legislation applies explicitly to institutionalized disabled persons and provides that no source—parent, guardian, or state protective service—other than a court can resolve medical issues relating to psychosurgery, electroconvulsive therapy, sterilization, or behavioral pharmacological research.[95] Similar constraints in other jurisdictions apply to decision making on behalf of profoundly disabled institutionalized persons.[96] The tendency of common-law courts to resolve issues of tissue donation (even without explicit statutory authorization) reinforces the tendency to shift certain critical decisions away from parents.

The allocation of decision-making responsibility for abortions appears to be quite uneven. In Massachusetts, where *Saikewicz* fixed a pattern of judicial involvement in medical decision making on behalf of the profoundly disabled, a court must authorize any abortion on an institutionalized, incapacitated person.[97] A similar approach seems to prevail in Rhode Island,[98] though the determinative case involved judicial intervention where the parent of the institutionalized pregnant woman had previously been found to neglect her daughter. In New York, by contrast, conscientious parents were deemed to be entitled to make an abortion decision for their profoundly disabled, institutionalized daughter.[99] And in New Jersey, regulations require the administrators of institutions for the developmentally disabled to conduct internal administrative proceedings—a trial-type hearing conducted by an administrative officer—on critical medical matters such as abortion, amputation, organ removal, or any medical procedure entailing "major irrevocable consequences."[100]

Practice also seems to be uneven regarding end-of-life decisions that affect disabled, institutionalized persons. As described earlier, *Saikewicz* established in 1977 that Massachusetts would require judicial participation in any decision to withhold or withdraw a life-sustaining medical intervention for a profoundly disabled resident of a state facility. There is also some evidence that, as a matter of practice in a number of states, institutional administrators often demand a court order before allowing the removal of life support from an institutionalized person.[101] By contrast, a New Mexico court recently ruled that the mother of a fifty-one-year-old retarded man, a long-time resident of a state training facility, could make a critical decision regarding artificial nutrition for her son without judicial intervention.[102] (The court there was willing to apply the Uniform Health Care Decisions Act—a surrogacy statute promoting family decision making—to the institutionalized patient. Similar surrogacy laws in other jurisdictions might also be read to allow family members to make end-of-life decisions—without judicial intervention—for institutionalized disabled persons.)[103] A couple of jurisdictions would apparently permit family members to make end-of-life determinations for disabled, institutionalized persons at least where the patient is permanently unconscious.[104] In some jurisdictions, statutes permit any court-appointed guardian to make end-of-life decisions pursuant to specified criteria.[105] That means that a parent could control an institutionalized child's medical fate regarding life-sustaining medical intervention so long as the parent first secured an appointment as guardian.

The above descriptions show that a dichotomy exists regarding medical decision making for profoundly disabled institutionalized persons, just as it does for those who live at home. Almost universally, matters of psychosurgery, electric shock treatment, sterilization, and tissue donation are reserved for a judicial forum. By contrast, the tendency is to allocate to parents (acting in conjunction with medical personnel) other important medical issues including life-sustaining medical intervention. Some sources would argue that the consequences of all these medical decisions are so critical to the life and well-being of a disabled person as to warrant judicial proceedings. Yet as noted, the judicial process often entails an onerous, costly, and protracted proceeding.[106] The clear trend—at least in end-of-life decision making—is to rely on administrative proceedings (rather than courts) with accompanying procedural protections. Both New York and New Jersey have recently moved toward informal administrative proceedings to resolve end-of-life issues for profoundly disabled, institutionalized persons.[107]

If the dichotomy in decision-making fora is to be eliminated, the question becomes in which direction to move—toward more reliance on the judiciary, more reliance on administrative proceedings, or more reliance on internal institutional channels? First, consider the kinds of procedural protections that would accompany nonjudicial proceedings. Taking an administrative hearing as the first model, the hearing officer would be someone independent of the institution. An advocacy service for the developmentally disabled would participate on behalf of the profoundly disabled person. A multidisciplinary medical-review panel (composed of people not involved in direct care to the patient) could provide medical and ethical input. The burden of proof on any parental decision maker seeking to fix a medical course that is normally deemed inconsistent with an incapacitated person's well-being might well be clear and convincing evidence. (I don't necessarily endorse the clear-and-convincing standard,[108] but it might well prevail in practice.) Under this framework, an informal administrative process that is less burdensome, protracted, and expensive than courts would exist for all serious medical decisions such as sterilization, abortion, and tissue donation.

An alternative model would use internal institutional proceedings rather than a quasi-judicial administrative forum. Deborah McKnight and Maureen Bellis propose such a model for end-of-life surrogate decision making within institutions.[109] While their model does accord many end-of-life decisions to family members who act in conjunction with medical staff, it also provides a number of safeguards.[110] Authoritative institutional proceedings are confined to certain medical circumstances—permanent unconsciousness or an advanced stage of terminal illness (meaning unavoidable death within a brief period and a condition that is accompanied by severe and permanent deterioration). The responsible surrogate must be a bonded family member (that is, someone with regular contact with the patient). To make a binding internal decision, the surrogate decision maker must gain the unanimous concurrence of the attending physician and a prognosis committee (independent medical personnel) for any judgment that the burdens of continued existence with medical intervention outweigh the benefits. (This framework could be altered by replacing a prognosis committee with a requirement of concurrence by an independent physician and by a multidisciplinary ethics committee.) Representatives of a state agency protective of the developmentally disabled must be permitted to advocate for the disabled patient. When the circumstances don't conform to all the above criteria, the removal of life support could occur only when some interested party seeks judicial intervention and a court finds that the burdens of continued existence on the patient outweigh the benefits.

The McKnight/Bellis framework would go far toward shaping sound surrogate decision making for profoundly disabled, institutionalized persons while avoiding the cumbersome judicial process. Their proposal—geared to end-of-life decision making—could be adapted to fit other serious medical decisions such as sterilization, abortion, and tissue donation. That is, a bonded surrogate such as a parent could make a binding decision on behalf of the disabled patient so long as the surrogate secured the concurrence of an attending physician, an independent physician, and an institutional ethics committee. The prevailing standard for decision making would still be the best interests of the patient, but bests interests, I suggest, should be adjusted along the lines I present in chapters 4 and 5. I shift now from the question of who decides to the issue or what decision-making standards apply to surrogate decision makers in any forum.

4

Defining the Best Interests of Profoundly Disabled Persons

Anglo-American law has traditionally recognized a sovereign's authority to protect helpless populations. This state authority, known as the *parens patriae* power, is expressed in several different ways relevant to profoundly disabled persons. In some cases, government takes over the daily care and management of severely dependent persons, as when it operates institutions or residential facilities for the mentally disabled.[1] In other instances, government merely safeguards the well-being of helpless persons who are under the control of natural guardians, as when government intervenes to protect children from neglect or abuse by their parents or when courts resolve disputes between divorced or estranged parents concerning the custody and well-being of their children. In the case of profoundly disabled adults, some parents may continue to act as natural guardians while caring for their offspring at home. Government then stands ready to intervene in the event of perceived neglect or abuse.

Not all disabled adults remain subject to the control of a natural guardian. Government sometimes assigns control of the disabled person to a court-appointed guardian (sometimes a parent, sometimes not) who is charged with protecting the interests and well-being of the disabled ward. Government then continues to protect the helpless ward by imposing fiduciary responsibilities on the guardian and by judicially supervising the guardian's performance of those responsibilities. Finally, some classes of medical decisions are so risky or otherwise problematic that they are excluded from a guardian's personal control. Courts then decide whether to authorize certain medical processes—such as sterilization or organ donation—that involve significant risks to the well-being of a disabled patient but that still hold out prospective benefits to the disabled person. In those instances, some petitioner to the court on behalf of the disabled patient seeks to invoke "the inherent equitable authority of the sovereign to protect those persons within the state who cannot protect themselves because of an innate legal disability."[2]

In all these contexts, the watchword for *parens patriae* jurisdiction is the best interests of the disabled person. That is, whenever government intervenes to scrutinize a surrogate's medical determination on behalf of a helpless person and whenever a problematic medical issue is reserved for judicial resolution, that helpless person's interests are ostensibly the key factor. Because the rationale for the various forms of governmental oversight at stake is protection of the ward, it is natural that the concept of best interests of the ward should dominate.[3] Not surprisingly, then, the best interests of the profoundly disabled patient has emerged as the common guideline for surrogate decision making in disparate medicolegal areas including end-of-life decisions, abortion, sterilization, and organ donation. (Best interests has not been the prevailing standard with regard to disabled persons' participation in nontherapeutic medical experimentation. Chapter 5 examines, under the heading of Forced Altruism, the legal and ethical status of medical research on disabled subjects.)

Identifying the best interests of the patient as the prevailing standard for surrogate decision making leaves many questions unresolved. What are the components of the best-interests formula—that is, what kinds of benefits and burdens can be considered by a conscientious surrogate? How are the interests and well-being of a profoundly disabled and barely communicative person assessed and measured? To what extent does quality of life play a role in decision making for the profoundly disabled? Whose perspective on quality of life governs—that of the guardian, the ward, or some hypothetical reasonable person? What is the role of human dignity within a best-interests-of-the-patient formula? Is it permissible for a surrogate decision maker to consider the interests of other persons, such as surrounding family and caregivers? How about the interests of society in avoiding extraordinary expense or in allocating scarce medical resources in a sound fashion? Must a surrogate decision maker seek to advance the *best* interests of the ward, or is it sufficient to act in a manner generally consistent with the ward's interests? What standard of proof of best interests should the surrogate employ—a preponderance of the evidence, clear and convincing evidence, or some other standard of inquiry? And if the surrogate decision maker is a private source such as a parent or a court-appointed guardian, what scope of judicial review is used to test the surrogate's adherence to best interests? These questions are addressed in this chapter, primarily in the settings of end-of-life decision making and sterilization, as the jurisprudence around these two situations is relatively well developed.

The Focus on a Never Competent Patient's Well-Being

Most jurisprudence relating to end-of-life medical decisions by surrogates focuses on the fulfillment of the self-determination interest of formerly competent patients. (I am referring here to the medical handling of the full range of mentally incapacitated patients, not just never competent, profoundly disabled persons.) I describe in chapter 2 how the earliest decisions regarding end-of-life care (*Quinlan* and some succeeding cases) articulated a substituted-judgment standard to preserve the now incompetent patient's liberty interest in choosing whether to accept or refuse life-sustaining medical intervention. That early effort to honor the self-determination of formerly competent persons has been reinforced by subsequent developments. Every jurisdiction that has spoken to end-of-life surrogate decision making has upheld a formerly competent patient's prerogative to shape postcompetence care either by advance medical directive or by other prior expressions. In most jurisdictions, the formerly competent patient's values and preferences—even if not explicitly directed toward end-of-life choices—are also deemed relevant to surrogate decision making. This is so under a substituted-judgment formula, where a patient's religious values or philosophical preferences can be determinative of postcompetence care.[4] And it is often the case under a best-interests-of-the-patient formula, at least in the many jurisdictions where the formerly competent patient's wishes, values, and preferences are considered part of the now incompetent patient's interests to be implemented by a surrogate. All this reliance on prior expressions and previously formed values seeks to honor the previously competent patient's autonomy or self-determination.

Even if the patient's previous values and expressed preferences don't furnish clear guidelines, the surrogate decision maker can still draw guidance from a projection of what most people would want done for themselves in the circumstances of the particular case. Again, this is so under both a substituted-judgment standard and a best-interests formula. Under the former, a surrogate may assume that a now incompetent person (who has not provided contrary indications) would want what a strong majority of people would want done in the circumstances.[5] Under a best-interests approach, the factors to be considered by a surrogate—including physical and mental suffering, chances of recovery, the nature of the patient's interactions with his or her environment, the potential for a regaining of function, and indignity—are drawn from what most people consider to be the critical factors in shaping postcompetence decision making. The overall object of the surrogate becomes to replicate the now incompetent patient's *likely* choices as determined by what most people would want done for themselves. Now incompetent patients are assumed to want their interests furthered and to have those interests defined according to majority preferences—absent personal indications to the contrary.[6] I call this *constructive* preference as opposed to *actual* preference because the approach governs formerly competent persons who have not left clear indications of their own end-of-life medical choices.[7] But the approach still seeks to honor a form of self-determination by implementing the now incompetent patient's likely, albeit putative, wishes.[8]

This book focuses on the profoundly disabled. Profoundly disabled persons, by definition, have never had the capacity for autonomy—have never had the ability to issue instructions concerning end-of-life treatment (or other serious medical matters) or to form values and preferences that would guide surrogate decision makers. And it is a lot more logical to attribute majoritarian values to formerly competent persons, who have once had the perspective of a competent person, than to attribute them to profoundly disabled persons whose values are either nonexistent or opaque. Neither actual preference nor constructive preference would therefore seem to provide a determinative guide for this never competent population.[9]

Not surprisingly, then, most commentators and courts have rejected the application of a substituted-judgment standard—a standard that seeks to replicate the patient's own likely decision—in the context of a never competent person. According to one early commentator, it is "nonsensical" to ask what a person with the mental age of a small child would choose.[10] And an Illinois court was similarly disparaging of the substituted-judgment standard in the context of three-and-one-half-year-old twins, one of whose parents was hoping to use the twins as bone-marrow donors to rescue the twins' dying half brother. In finding substituted judgment irrelevant to the children's situation, the court remarked: "[I]t is not possible to discover the child's likely treatment/nontreatment preferences by examining the child's philosophy, religion and moral views, life goals, values about the purpose of life and the way it should be lived."[11] Another court recently noted the "limited relevance" of substituted judgment because children (and never competent persons) have "no articulable judgment to be substituted."[12]

A few sources nonetheless insist on talking about substituted judgment even in the context of never competent persons. Massachusetts, for example, has clung to substituted judgment for the profoundly disabled ever since that standard was applied to Joseph Saikewicz in 1976. A few cases and a few commentators about decision making for profoundly disabled newborns recommend that surrogates put themselves in the place of the newborns and impute a judgment to the infant as though it were a moral agent. According to this commentary, the surrogate should ask: "Would the infant wish to lead such a life if it had the capacity of choosing for himself or herself?"[13] This transposition of a judgment to a profoundly disabled infant is grounded in a commendable motive—reminding the surrogate and all involved individuals about the human stature and personhood of the infant. But most commentators understandably deride the notion of attributing judgments or preferences to profoundly disabled persons as being muddled and nonsensical.[14] A strong majority of courts have refused to apply a substituted judgment standard in the context of never competent patients.

Even in the few judicial decisions that nominally apply a substituted-judgment standard to a never competent patient, the standards of substituted judgment and best interests often meld, and the court ends up relying on the patient's best interests. Because there is no basis for ascribing a personal choice—in the sense of personal preference among competing values and interests—to a profoundly disabled person, the courts purporting to apply a substituted-judgment standard end up resolving the disabled patient's medical fate according to a projected weighing of the patient's future pleasure and pain. In other words, they end up applying a best-interests-of-the-patient standard. That was true in *Strunk v. Strunk,* the 1969 case involving a kidney donation from a profoundly disabled sibling and in the 1976 *Superintendent of Belchertown v. Saikewicz* case involving treatment decisions for a sixty-seven-year-old, profoundly disabled, terminal cancer patient. In each instance, the court selected a medical course for the never competent person that the court believed would best promote the disabled person's interests in avoiding suffering (from the loss of a beloved sibling in one case or from the rigors of a chemotherapy regimen in the other) and in deriving satisfaction or pleasure from existence.

The commonly articulated standard for the never competent person is the same standard that has guided *parens patriae* jurisdiction for centuries—the best interests of the patient. A strong majority of the courts that have addressed surrogate medical decisions on behalf of profoundly disabled persons—whether in the context of sterilization, organ donation, or the cessation of life support—have prescribed a best-interests test. Most protocols governing clinical practice also prescribe that best interests should determine the medical fate of now incompetent persons who have never provided definitive guidance on their own.[15] As applied to the end-of-life setting, this means that life support should be maintained unless the patient would be better off dead than alive—that is, unless the burdens of further existence would outweigh the benefits.[16] As applied to other medical issues such as sterilization, the issue becomes whether the benefits of the contemplated medical intervention would outweigh the detriments—that is, whether the net welfare of the profoundly disabled patient would be advanced by the performance of the contemplated procedure.

The Problematic of Assessing Well-Being

The application of a best-interests standard to profoundly disabled, dying patients presents special challenges. Determining whether the patient is better off dead than alive provides an illustration. One underlying assumption in the context of end-of-life medical decisions is that a person's suffering can be so severe and unremitting that it outweighs the benefits—the pleasures and satisfactions—of further existence. In such instances, a best-interests standard dictates the cessation of life-sustaining medical intervention. That approach to end-of-life decisions seems valid as applied to never competent as well as previously competent beings. The devastating impact of intense pain on the patient and on interpersonal relations would seem as great for profoundly disabled persons as for others. While the avoidance of unremitting suffering is not a self-determined value for a profoundly disabled person, our understanding of human nature and the horror of extreme, unremitting suffering[17] warrant injecting that value into the standards that govern medical decisions for the never competent patient.

How much suffering, though, is so intolerable that it makes nonexistence the right choice? And how can a surrogate make that assessment for a profoundly disabled person? There are special difficulties that handicap that task.

For starters, what perspective does a surrogate assume when assessing the best interests of a never competent person in the context of serious medical issues? The common wisdom concerning best interests says that the judgment of "a reasonable person" about the net well-being of an incapacitated person must be determinative.[18] This makes sense because a profoundly disabled being cannot be expected to make or have a considered judgment about best interests when completely unable to grasp its component elements, like nonexistence or net welfare. Only a mentally competent person can make a considered judgment about whether the burdens of continued existence outweigh the benefits or whether the detriments of sterilization outweigh the benefits. The question is "what a reasonable person with the characteristics of the incompetent would [do] under similar circumstances."[19] And it is not far-fetched to suppose that if a never competent patient were to become miraculously competent, then he or she would want medical decisions to be based on the patient's interests as assessed by a reasonable person.

At the same time that a conscientious surrogate must use the reasonable-person perspective in fixing the level of suffering that should be deemed intolerable, the surrogate must scrupulously adhere to the disabled person's perspective in discerning the levels of suffering and gratification actually present (or foreseeable) in any individual case. The object is to discern the benefits and burdens from the point of view of the profoundly disabled patient rather than the point of view of a competent person (such as the surrogate) who has experienced the benefits and developed the expectations of a fully able existence. The question is whether the particular patient would be better off dead than alive in the circumstances facing the patient,[20] not whether the surrogate (or even the average-capacitated person) would want to live in those circumstances.

It is inherently difficult for a fully capacitated surrogate to assume the point of view of a person who has always been profoundly debilitated. The competent surrogate's frame of reference is vastly different from that of a never competent patient. It may be hard "for the fully competent person to have the sympathetic insight . . . into what it is like" to experience the world with gravely diminished mental function.[21] A strong temptation exists to transpose or project the fully capacitated surrogate's feelings onto the in-capacitated patient.[22] For example, it is common to ascribe hunger to a gravely debilitated, dying patient who is refusing nutrition when the reality is that the patient is not hungry.[23] And while there is no reason to think that a profoundly disabled person suffers from the mere status of being extremely cognitively disabled, the capacitated observer may attribute feelings of frustration or anxiety that the capacitated person thinks he or she would feel in comparable circumstances. One commentator laments a "grave danger of injecting our own values onto the child who has absolutely no basis for the fears and horrors we might have for ourselves in a similar state."[24] The hazard also exists that the competent surrogate will undervalue the simple benefits that the disabled patient derives from existence and project negative feelings (such as frustration at being incapacitated or embarrassment at posing a burden on others) onto the disabled patient based on a competent person's assumptions or prejudices about a profoundly disabled existence.[25]

A similar hazard is that the competent surrogate will inject personal values into the best-interests determination. (This happens, for example, when parents who are Christian Scientists or Jehovah's Witnesses use their own religious beliefs in forgoing important medical intervention for small children or other profoundly disabled charges.) Or a competent surrogate's personal perspective on quality of life can distort an assessment of a profoundly disabled patient's well-being and best interests. A distorted, stereotyped view of the impact of Down's syndrome led one set of parents in 1982 to inappropriately withhold life-preserving surgery for their newborn infant.[26] This is not to say that the requisite surrogate judgments are impossible, only that there are reasons for scrutiny of such judgments.

While the burdens of a profoundly disabled person's existence may in some instances outweigh the benefits so that cessation of life-sustaining medical intervention becomes consistent with that patient's best interests, a surrogate decision maker's determination of that status faces another major hurdle in assessing the experiential reality of a profoundly disabled person—a person whose cognitive understanding and communicative ability are likely to be extremely limited. To determine the best interests of a profoundly disabled person, a surrogate must be sensitive to "noncognitive notions of well-being" that are grounded in "emotional and relational well being."[27] Yet assessing the subjective reality behind the disabled person's sounds and gestures is a daunting task.[28] At the extremes, this assessment or measurement barrier may be surmountable by an attentive surrogate. Susan Martyn exhorts "caring interpreters" to determine what the profoundly disabled patient "finds meaningful in life" and "how that person experiences life."[29] The behavior and expressions of some persons may reflect a level of extreme and unmitigated suffering that readily prompts a conclusion that nonexistence is preferable to life. Or, by contrast, a profoundly disabled person's continued participation in, and response to, ostensibly enjoyable activity may make a life-affirming conclusion easy.[30] Putting those extremes aside, discernment of the profoundly disabled patient's experiential reality may depend on surrogate interpretation of signals and expressions—including enigmatic verbal expressions as well as nonverbal communication such as grimaces, moans, screams, smiles, and gestures—that are difficult to decipher. The difficulty of discerning the true feelings of the disabled person is compounded by the previously mentioned temptation of a fully capacitated surrogate to project certain feelings onto an incapacitated ward.[31]

The problematic of assessing the best interests of profoundly disabled beings is illustrated in the context of infants or young children born with grave afflictions that are certain to shorten their lives.[32] In some instances, their abbreviated lives will be accompanied by extreme dysfunction, considerable pain and suffering, and fairly continuous and intrusive medical interventions. State law generally accepts the principle that the best interests of at least some afflicted children would be served by withholding or withdrawing life-sustaining medical intervention.[33] Yet parents and healthcare providers who seek to apply this principle must cope with various uncertainties—uncertainty in measuring degree of pain, uncertainty in projecting the precise level of mental dysfunction, uncertainty in estimating the duration of potential survival, and uncertainty in determining whether the suffering outweighs any potential satisfactions from interactions with people and the environment.[34]

Take Baby Rena as an example.[35] She was an eighteen-month-old infant dying of acquired immune deficiency syndrome (AIDS). She had become ventilator dependent, was constantly sedated to relieve pain, but retained some awareness of her environment. Every time she was handled in any fashion, her blood pressure shot up and tears streamed from her eyes. Was it in her best interests to have the ventilator withdrawn so that she could die? Was her suffering so extreme and unremitting that she would be better off dead than alive? Baby Rena was already eighteen months old, and her condition and prognosis were well established. The difficulty of surrogate decision making is compounded in the case of newborns whose prognoses are ultimately dismal but whose precise levels of pain and cognitive dysfunction cannot yet be fixed.

Opposition has always existed to any parental prerogative to withhold or withdraw life support from an infant, even where that decision purports to be in the infant's best interests. Part of that opposition stems from a fear of parental (or professional) prejudice or ignorance about life as a disabled person, as occurred in the 1982 Indiana case that allowed the withholding of critical medical treatment from an infant born with Down's syndrome. There, the parents determined to withhold lifesaving treatment on the basis that children with Down's syndrome "don't do very well" and cannot be happy.[36] In the wake of that 1982 incident, the federal government sought to curb all decisions allowing newborns to die. An initial federal attempt to attack such decisions as unlawful discrimination against disabled persons failed. The courts ruled that the federal regulations exceeded the scope of authority that Congress had conferred.[37] Congress responded in 1984 by adopting the Child Abuse Amendments to a statute that dealt with federal grants to states for the operation of child-protection programs. Those amendments conditioned the grant of federal funds on the state's establishment of procedures to ensure that "medically indicated treatment" would always be provided to infants. Narrow statutory exclusions from required treatment applied only for comatose infants, for infants unavoidably dying so that treatment would be futile, and for infants in other situations where treatment would be "virtually futile" and "inhumane."[38] Federal interpretive guidelines indicated that the last-mentioned exclusion covered only treatment "highly unlikely to prevent death in the near future" and did not cover nontreatment "based on subjective opinions about future quality of life of a disabled person."[39]

The impact of these federal efforts on neonatal care practices is unknown, but it may well be "quite small."[40] The federal regulations themselves don't apply directly to health-care providers. The only sanction for "noncompliance" would be withdrawal of federal funding for certain state child-abuse-prevention programs (as opposed to any direct penalty on a health-care provider).[41] The federal impact is also likely to be small because of the compelling need to make some decisions not to treat newborns with certain severe deficits. Some congenital anomalies entail a foreshortened lifespan, as well as severe neurological impairment, physical incapacity, repeated bodily invasions, and suffering so acute that the affected infant is likely tortured by continued treatment. Examples include infants with trisomy 13 or 18.[42] Also, some children with Tay-Sachs disease face the prospect of dying in early childhood after inexorably declining via mental retardation, convulsions, blindness, and considerable pain.[43] These situations involving irremediable suffering and continuous bodily intrusions can make the withholding of life support consistent with a child's best interests, even if a precise measurement of suffering is not possible.

Extreme difficulties in assessing best interests also are encountered in the context of profoundly disabled adults. Physicians and surrogates must sometimes determine the medical fates of adults whose grave mental disability leaves them aware but uncomprehending, permanently immobile, totally helpless, and communicative only by grunts, cries, or smiles and whose fatal affliction leaves them dependent on constant medical intervention.[44]

British courts faced such a case in 1996.[45] R. was a twenty-three-year-old who was so profoundly disabled that her cognitive function was at the level of a newborn child. She was unable to communicate verbally but responded to stimuli with grimaces, cries, or smiles. She was incontinent. Because R. had recently lost the ability to chew, one medical issue became whether to install a gastrostomy tube. Her parents, who had devotedly cared for R. for twenty-three years, also wondered whether antibiotics should be used to fight recurrent infections that had begun to plague R. When physicians petitioned for judicial guidance, the court responded that the relevant decision-making standard is best interests of the patient. That meant a determination of whether, judging from the perspective of R., her future life would be so afflicted as to be unbearable. Using that best-interests standard, the British court ruled that a gastrostomy tube should be installed (that is, R.'s current level of suffering did not outweigh the benefits of her existence), that cardiopulmonary respiration (CPR) should not be instituted in the event of cardiac arrest (perhaps on the assumption that any cardiac arrest would mark a further decline in R.'s condition so that the burdens of CPR would exceed the benefit of life extension), and that antibiotics could be withheld during some future infection episode if the parents and physician then agreed that such withholding would be in R.'s best interests (that is, R.'s condition might deteriorate to the point when even a simple life-sustaining intervention would be contrary to her best interests). R.'s story helps show the delicacy of a best-interests determination in the context of some profoundly disabled and gravely physically afflicted persons.

Another uncertainty complicates the application of a best-interests standard to a profoundly disabled, fatally stricken person who is facing prospective pain and suffering during a contemplated treatment process. It is commonly asserted that the disabled person's incomprehension of the reasons for instituting painful medical interventions—that is, his or her failure to understand the curative or restorative hope behind a contemplated medical intervention—will heighten the anxiety and distress to be experienced by that person. The National Conference of Catholic Bishops admonishes physicians that a demented patient may find treatment "more frightening and burdensome" than other patients.[46] The specter of heightened suffering by an uncomprehending patient was part of the rationale of the Massachusetts court that concluded that sixty-seven-year-old Joseph Saikewicz should not receive chemotherapy for leukemia even though most competent patients would opt for chemo in the circumstances. Saikewicz's incomprehension about the reasons for the needles to be used in administering chemotherapy would supposedly cause him extreme distress and agitation and would necessitate his being restrained for extended periods of time. He might also be distressed by side effects whose origins he would not understand. (Commentators have wondered, though, whether Joseph Saikewicz's best interests would have been better served by a trial run of chemotherapy to see whether the feared consequences really ensued and, if so, whether sedatives succeeded in palliating his suffering.[47]) Another Massachusetts court cited the heightened burdens that a profoundly disabled woman would experience if she were denied an abortion. According to the judicial finding: "Normal discomforts of pregnancy such as bladder pressure, an increasingly bulky body, and backache would be felt as unendurable by Jane because she would not fully understand their cause."[48] These projections of heightened suffering flowing from the incomprehension of profoundly disabled persons might be accurate, but they might also be the product of speculation fueled by a surrogate's projection of imagined feelings or by negative assumptions about the patient's state of mind. In short, while a best-interests standard for surrogate medical decision making makes considerable sense, its application to profoundly disabled patients is complicated by the difficulties of assessing and measuring patients' feelings and emotions. And the problem of applying a best-interests standard is compounded if the patient's intrinsic human dignity becomes part of a best-interests calculus.

Quality of Life, Dignity, and Never Competent Persons

The 1983 President's Commission for the Study of Ethical Problems in Medicine listed "quality as well as the extent of the life sustained" as an element within a best-interests-of-the-patient standard.[49] Following that lead, a number of court opinions mention quality of life (or human dignity) as a relevant factor to be used by a surrogate in assessing an incapacitated patient's best interests when making end-of-life treatment determinations.[50] A few state statutes explicitly mention dignity in the same context.[51] I submit that quality of life entails more than weighing benefits and burdens—the delicate task of measuring and balancing the feelings and emotions that are described in the previous section—in severely debilitated patients. It includes a determination of whether the patient's deterioration is so extreme that life has become intrinsically undignified.

The importance of quality of life and avoidance of extreme indignity is easily understandable with regard to formerly competent persons. Most competent people care mightily about quality of life within the dying process. That concern was a major force behind the death-with-dignity movement that has been active in the United States for more than thirty years. People commonly fear that grave debilitation—particularly, severe dementia—will entail embarrassment and frustration stemming from helplessness, dependence, and incapacity. Even if these distasteful feelings might not materialize, people care about the image and memories that they will leave behind—images in the minds of loved ones that may be soiled by the patient's extreme mental and physical deterioration during the dying process. These common preoccupations with indignity in the dying process are readily observable in the context of competent patients contemplating their prospective medical fates—in decisions to reject life-sustaining medical interventions, in advance medical directives, and in attitudinal surveys showing the "paramount importance [attached to] . . . functional independence and the maintenance of mental faculties."[52] Afflicted patients seeking access to assisted suicide are often motivated by a desire to avoid helplessness and indignity rather than a need to avoid pain. Justice Souter in *Glucksberg v. Washington* portrayed the petitioning dying patients as seeking "an end to their short remaining lives with a dignity that they believed would be denied them by powerful pain medication, as well as by their consciousness of dependency and helplessness as they approached death."[53] Justice Stevens in *Glucksberg* accepted the notion that a person's interests in dignity in the dying process and in shaping the legacy of memories that survive might well qualify as a fundamental aspect of liberty.[54]

Some commentators question the relevance of the concept of indignity to the handling of profoundly disabled persons. One objection is that any indignity—in the form of embarrassment or humiliation—will not actually be experienced by a gravely incapacitated patient and that it cannot be demeaning or degrading to suffer debilitation, especially if others are providing loving, life-supporting care to a human being.[55] That objection seems shortsighted to me. Unsensed invasions of personal interests, including affronts to dignity, may be terribly offensive even if unsensed. What about the performance of unconsented medical experiments, harvesting of non-vital tissue, or sexual molestation with regard to even insensate, dying patients? Wouldn't those actions be deemed clearly violative of important dignity interests? What would we think about administering medical care that violates a now incompetent (and insensate) patient's religious precepts? Joel Feinberg correctly notes that incapacitated beings can be victimized by "harms" to their interests (even if unsensed) as well as by "hurts" that are experienced.[56] In short, a profoundly disabled person has important dignity interests whether or not the person actually senses invasions of those interests.

A stronger objection to use of the concept of indignity in the death-and-dying context is that the concept's imprecision and subjectivity would engender arbitrariness and abuse by surrogates making end-of-life decisions for the profoundly disabled. These concerns about the exploitation of vulnerable persons led to the policy described in chapter 2 prompting a few states to bar terminal surrogate decisions absent clear prior instructions. Recall Judge Wachtler's admonition in a 1988 case involving the continuation of life support for an elderly woman left barely conscious by a series of strokes: "No person or court should substitute its judgment as to what would be an acceptable quality of life for another."[57] Recall also the previously mentioned problem of perspective—the concern that able-bodied surrogates might project distorted visions of intolerable quality of life (grounded on their own base-line notions of the level of function necessary to a dignified existence) onto their incapacitated wards. Surrogates might be subject to the ignorance and prejudice that frequently characterize public attitudes toward gravely incapacitated persons. That certainly occurred in the previously mentioned 1982 Indiana case in which an Indiana couple determined to withhold life-saving treatment from their infant who had Down's syndrome. Another fear is that judgments about intolerable quality of life would mask social-worth assessments along the lines employed by the Nazis in their euthanasia program. A surrogate's quality-of-life judgment evokes in some people the fearful notion that some lives are not worth living—a notion that would supposedly jeopardize the well-being of helpless persons and undermine respect for the sanctity of life.[58]

The specter of abuse of quality-of-life judgments seems easy enough to curb in the context of previously competent persons. First, some people provide living wills or other prior expressions that articulate their personal vision of an intolerable quality of life—a level of deterioration that they would deem intolerably undignified. Implementation of a person's expressed value preferences may not always be easy—given the frequent imprecision of advance directives—but surrounding medical personnel can at least use the prior expressions in monitoring surrogate decisions to ensure that a surrogate is acting consistently with the now incompetent patient's expressed values. Second, even without advance expressions, we know a lot about how competent people regard an intolerable quality of life for themselves, at least in certain familiar postcompetence scenarios. For example, polls and surveys consistently show that at least 90 percent of people would not want to be given life-sustaining medical intervention if mired in a permanently unconscious state. Similarly, most people recoil at the prospect of lingering in a barely conscious state in which they no longer recognize or interact in a meaningful fashion with their loved ones or surrounding caregivers.[59] And gravely debilitated patients may begin to act in ways so antithetical to their previous values and character that the surrogate can make a judgment that the previously competent patient would deem the deteriorated status intolerably undignified.[60]

The point is that surrogate decision makers have some foundation—grounded either in the now incompetent patient's personal preferences and values or in consensus preferences that people have toward their own prospective end-of-life treatment—for making some judgments about an intolerable quality of life with regard to previously competent persons. Understandings about common preferences toward indignity in the dying process enable medical personnel to monitor the behavior of surrogate decision makers. Health-care providers can refuse to cooperate with surrogate decisions that deviate either from the patient's demonstrated values or from common attitudes about indignity. Part of professional responsibility is to show fidelity to the patient's vision of a humane and dignified dying process.

The harder issue is whether sufficient understandings exist about the concept of intolerable indignity as applied to profoundly disabled persons—never competent beings. Certainly, dignity cannot mean the same thing for a never competent, profoundly disabled person as for a previously competent person.[61] Take incontinence as an example. That condition might represent utter humiliation for a competent or previously competent person, yet not embarrass or particularly trouble a profoundly disabled person. The same goes for extreme dementia. While a previously acute person might experience frustration, anxiety, and embarrassment from a precipitous decline in mental faculties, the lifelong profoundly disabled person might have no similar feelings.[62] Meaningful emotional relationships can exist for a person without even near-normal intelligence so long as some ability to interact with others is present.

Every person's concept of personal dignity is shaped in part by his or her circumstances and experiences. The New York State Task Force on Life and the Law comments in this vein: "While some adults who were once fully capable might not want to live with severe mental handicaps, adults who are profoundly retarded have never known or aspired to a different kind of life."[63] A person who has always had extremely limited cognitive function thus may have modest expectations about quality of life. Existence as a locus of pleasure and pain may fulfill their interest in dignity. Indeed, the concept of a minimally acceptable quality of life is entirely beyond the ken of a profoundly disabled person. In the absence of notions of intolerable indignity that have been formed by the affected individuals themselves or by people similarly situated, how can surrogate decision makers apply the concept of indignity to profoundly disabled persons?

My response is that intrinsic human dignity can be sufficiently defined to play a legitimate, if limited, role in end-of-life decision making on behalf of the profoundly disabled. Respect for all persons (and chapter 1 establishes that profoundly disabled beings are persons) includes upholding their intrinsic or basic human dignity. The critical task is to give content to the notion of intrinsic human dignity, in the sense of a minimally acceptable quality of life, without jeopardizing the well-being of helpless human beings. Bruce Jennings suggests that any "dying person has a right to a certain quality of living while dying."[64] I concur in his notion that certain dying conditions can be so inhumane as to constitute "a moral trespass upon personhood."[65] And I agree that pain, suffering, intrusive bodily invasions, protracted physical restraint, and mental deterioration to a point of nonrecognition of the surrounding environment are relevant indices in assessing intolerable trespasses on human integrity.

A recent case illustrates the relevance of extreme indignity to a determination of best interests. Nicholas Truselo, a three-month-old child, had suffered extensive brain trauma from an adult's shaking (shaken-baby syndrome). According to the physicians' assessment, Nicholas would never be able to walk, speak, see, or communicate. He would be dependent on constant medical intervention. In deciding that Nicholas's best interests dictated the removal of life support (a ventilator and nasogastric tube), the court relied heavily on the child's dismal quality of life. Judge Ableman explained:

Nicholas will never stand, sit, eat, walk, speak, read, write, think, or exist without constant care for even the most basic of life's functions. He will be confined to his bed and will suffer constant lung infections because of his virtually non-existent gag reflex. He will never be able to communicate joy, fear, happiness, or sadness, will never be able to form relationships with others, and will live with tubes, machines, and other specialized medical care. He will never react to his surrounding environment, will never give or receive love, and may be subjected to substantial pain and discomfort. The physicians have evaluated the child's condition and have concluded that a future sustained by radical medical treatment, and entailing virtually no quality of life, is not a valued alternative, despite its effectiveness in extending life or delaying death.[66]

While Judge Ableman mentioned pain, his best-interests determination seemed to be prompted by his concerns for indignity and quality of life. The most obvious element of indignity was Nicholas's total inability to relate to his environment.

The understandable apprehension—already mentioned—is that human dignity is too imprecise a concept to be useful,[67] especially in the setting of end-of-life decision making for a vulnerable population like the lifelong profoundly disabled. As noted in chapter 1, the concept of human dignity is used in diverse ways and in a variety of contexts. Some jurists, for example, see human dignity as a concept helping to shape several aspects of fundamental liberty—for example, protection against excessively harsh punishment or against intolerable invasions of physical and emotional privacy. Justices William Douglas, William Brennan, and Thurgood Marshall often invoked human dignity as a basis for recognizing the civil and political rights for which they were advocating, including freedom of expression and freedom of conscience. Other social observers use the concept of human dignity to evoke a utopian notion of affirmative social obligations toward disadvantaged communities, including the provision of sufficient resources to allow maximum development of individual capacities.[68] Another vision of human dignity (considered in chapter 5 under the heading of The Kantian Imperative)—precludes using a person solely as a means to advance the well-being of others. These diverse perspectives on human dignity confirm the elusiveness of the concept. Yet that doesn't mean that the concept is inherently any more unmanageable than other important but elusive notions, such as liberty, justice, fairness, and equality. (Indeed, concepts of liberty, fairness, and equality have considerable utility and application in American jurisprudence.)

One mark of the imprecision of the concept of human dignity is that in the context of end-of-life decision making for incapacitated persons, human dignity is sometimes used to support diametrically opposed approaches. Take, for example, the handling of a patient who has permanently deteriorated to a point of semiconsciousness, is no longer aware of or interacting with his or her environment, and is dependent on artificial nutrition and hydration (ANH) for subsistence. One perspective is that this formally vital individual is being denied basic human dignity by the continuation of life support and the prolongation of a degrading dying process. The contrary perspective is that respect for human dignity—the intrinsic worth and equality of every human being—demands that nurturing in the form of artificial nutrition and hydration be continued for the helpless being. Given such disparate views of human dignity and given the pluralistic nature of American society, how can intrinsic human dignity be meaningfully used in end-of-life surrogate decisionmaking?

One useful source of content for intrinsic human dignity is constitutional jurisprudence. While the federal Constitution does not explicitly mention human dignity, the concept of human dignity provides an important "background norm" and aid in the interpretation of various constitutional rights.[69] An example is found in the jurisprudence surrounding the Eighth Amendment's prohibition of cruel and unusual punishment. In 1958, Chief Justice Warren called human dignity the "foundation" of the Eighth Amendment and insisted that the amendment's meaning must be drawn from "the evolving standards of decency that mark the progress of a maturing society."[70] (Warren then ruled that government imposition of statelessness as a punishment involves such psychic torture as to be constitutionally impermissible.) In 1976, the U.S. Supreme Court employed the human-dignity norm in finding that a correctional institution's deliberate indifference to a prisoner's serious medical needs is violative of the Eighth Amendment.[71] These cases illustrate the close connection between human dignity and evolving constitutional norms shaped by decent and humane social treatment—a theme repeated beyond the Eighth Amendment context.

The link between intrinsic human dignity and constitutional jurisprudence appears in the application of other parts of the Constitution. The Fourth Amendment's ban on unreasonable searches and seizures evinces a concern with dignity that is reflected by the amendment's restriction of government access to personal space and information. That dignity concern emerges particularly sharply in cases involving bodily integrity. In rejecting some government efforts to penetrate the body to secure criminal evidence, the Justices have expressed strong solicitude for personal control over the private space that is the human body.[72] The Supreme Court "sees human dignity implicated in government appropriation of the body by touching, undressing, or penetrating the body."[73] This is not to say that all government invasions of the body are constitutionally prohibited; cases upholding government intrusions such as vaccination and collection of blood samples (from drivers involved in accidents) contradict that notion. Yet even the cases upholding such intrusions recognize a close tie between human dignity and bodily integrity and therefore demand strong governmental justification before allowing bodily invasions.

A classic case, *Rochin v. California*,[74] illustrates that the judicial distaste for bodily searches is grounded on a dignity-based revulsion toward forced bodily invasions. In *Rochin*, police forcibly pumped the stomach of a suspected narcotics dealer in order to preserve evidence. The U.S. Supreme

Court threw out the evidence—not because of police disregard for the niceties of the Fourth Amendment warrant requirement but because the police conduct "shocked the conscience." The forced stomach pumping was too revolting to the Justices' sense of dignity. The Court's solicitude for bodily integrity (and associated dignity) as an element of liberty also surfaced in cases in the 1990s. As noted, *Cruzan* in 1990 and *Glucksberg* in 1997 together established that a competent person has a right to reject even life-sustaining medical intervention. Part of the basis for that liberty is a traditional respect for bodily integrity and an accompanying revulsion toward the spectacle of forcing an unwilling person to receive treatment. Justice O'Connor explicitly commented on the human degradation associated with forced treatment in her concurring opinion in *Cruzan,* and several other courts have noted how forced medical treatment offends basic human dignity.[75] The intolerable degradation stems from several elements— the overriding of the patient's will, the unwanted bodily invasion, and the distasteful restraints necessary to overcome a resisting patient's will.

Of course, acknowledgment of an important interest in bodily integrity as an aspect of human dignity does not resolve the scope of a profoundly disabled person's intrinsic human dignity. In the first place, no person's right to preserve bodily integrity is absolute. The same constitutional jurisprudence that recognizes an important interest in bodily integrity also recognizes that various competing interests can sometimes prevail in a balancing process. For example, public health can justify compulsory vaccination, public safety can warrant blood alcohol tests, and well-founded needs of law enforcement can sometimes justify searches of bodily cavities or even surgical intrusions. In those instances, competing interests override the normal revulsion toward forced bodily intrusions.

More important, the well-being interests of an incapacitated person often provide a legitimate basis for overriding that person's will, even if this entails what would otherwise be deemed an undignified and repulsive bodily invasion. Forced medication of mentally incapacitated persons whose conduct endangers themselves or others provides one illustration.[76] Another example is the common medical practice of providing critical treatment for a small child or a mentally disabled adult—where such treatment strongly advances the interests of the patient—despite the patient's objections and even resistance. In short, while a profoundly disabled person has a strong dignity-based interest in bodily integrity, the preservation of that person's life or the promotion of that person's well-being will often provide a sufficient justification for a forced bodily invasion. Again, the problem often boils down to the measurement and weighing of the profoundly disabled person's various interests—that is, determining whether the burdens of continued existence (including the undignified effects of the contemplated medical intervention) outweigh the benefits.

Another link between human dignity and the Constitution emerges in the jurisprudence that has interpreted the meaning of Fourteenth Amendment liberty. In elevating certain personal prerogatives to "fundamental" liberty status, the U.S. Supreme Court has stressed constitutional respect for intimate choices "central to dignity and autonomy."[77] This theme has surfaced in the reproductive-rights context (with its link to control over the human body) and in the right to reject life-sustaining medical intervention (with another link to bodily integrity).[78] In short, establishing that any particular aspect of self-determination or personal status is integral to human dignity provides a strong impetus for ranking that element high within the jurisprudence of constitutional liberty.[79]

All this testifies to a strong connection between human dignity and constitutional jurisprudence implementing certain constitutional provisions. Is that jurisprudence, in turn, translatable into norms that could shape or inform a concept of intrinsic human dignity applicable to profoundly disabled persons whose medical fates are being determined by surrogates? To some extent, the constitutional treatment of dignity merely reinforces norms that already prevail in the medical decision-making context (as discussed above in the section on measuring the patient's well-being). One norm established there—that persistent and unremitting suffering saps human dignity and can serve as an important guide to surrogate decision making pursuant to a best-interests standard—is amply reinforced in constitutional jurisprudence. The Supreme Court has relied in several contexts on the notion that extreme suffering intolerably degrades persons. For example, the unnecessary infliction of pain that is associated with failure to meet prison inmates' serious medical needs was a key element in the Court's determination that such failure could violate the Eighth Amendment.[80] Concerns about unnecessary suffering also prompted the comments by five Justices in *Glucksberg* in 1997 that any state barriers to effective pain relief would impinge on a dying patient's fundamental-liberty interests and might even prompt a reconsideration of the Court's position that state bans on assisted suicide were constitutional.[81] Some commentators have suggested that the concurring Justices in *Glucksberg* were implicitly announcing a constitutional "right to be free of unnecessary pain and suffering at the end of life."[82] All this judicial sensitivity to extreme suffering confirms that best-interests doctrine—in allowing the withdrawal of life support from persons suffering irremediably—draws on and is fully consistent with intrinsic human dignity. (The problem, as noted earlier, comes more in applying the doctrine—that is, in assessing when suffering outweighs any pleasures and satisfactions in a profoundly disabled person's existence.)

The incapacitated patient's dignity interest complicates the balancing process that is entailed in the best-interests formula. If a profoundly disabled patient is stricken with life-threatening cancer and will have to be physically or chemically restrained during the administration of chemotherapy, how much should the offense to dignity count in the surrogate's decision whether to initiate treatment? Presumably, it should not count very much if the forced restraint will be temporary or sporadic and should count much more if the restraint will be prolonged. Presumably, the offense to dignity should count more if the patient will experience frustration and anxiety from his or her struggle against the restraints. The percentage chance of significant remission and the potential duration of remission are relevant variables as well. We know that the degradation of a forced bodily invasion does not always violate intrinsic human dignity, but sometimes it does.

So far, I have suggested that dignity matters for a profoundly disabled person even when that person cannot appreciate any affront to dignity. At the same time, I concede that the dignity interest is ordinarily so hard to quantify and to factor into the best-interests formula that it would seldom be determinative of a dying person's fate. Are there circumstances where a never competent person's status is so intrinsically demeaning that the dignity interest alone—separate from any interest in avoidance of suffering—would justify removal of artificial life support? I think that permanent unconsciousness represents one such circumstance. Permanent insentience—the permanent inability to relate to a person's environment, to interact with fellow humans, or to experience any of the pleasures associated with human existence—constitutes an intrinsically undignified status for a human being. This is so whether the permanent unconsciousness comes about at the beginning of life, as when an anencephalic infant is born, or at its conclusion, as when a formerly conscious person deteriorates to a permanently vegetative state. In both instances, a surrogate decision to maintain artificial life support ought not be permissible because of the affront to intrinsic human dignity.

Some support exists for this notion of permanent unconsciousness as intrinsically undignified. Certainly, numerous cases—starting in 1976 with the *Quinlan* case in New Jersey—uphold surrogate determinations to end life support for permanently unconscious persons.[83] Sometimes, the articulated judicial rationale is that allowing the permanently insensate patient to die promotes that patient's best interests. Is that surrogate prerogative to end the permanently unconscious person's existence consistent with the customary legal requirement that surrogate action be confined to a person's best interests? Superficially, the answer would appear to be no, for a permanently unconscious person's interests, albeit extremely limited, would still seem to be in continued life. There is always some infinitesmal chance that a misdiagnosis has occurred or that a miracle will happen and the person will regain consciousness. The insensate person is not in pain (so far as is known).[84] Moreover, while we assume that the person lacking neocortical function is experiencing no positive feelings, we cannot know that. Withdrawal of life support does not seem to advance the tangible best interests of a permanently unconscious person. If not best interests, what accounts for a surrogate decision maker's legal prerogative to let the permanently unconscious person die?

The justification for surrogate decisions to remove life support from formerly competent persons now mired in permanent unconsciousness can be found in an effort to honor the patient's likely preferences. Numerous surveys and advance medical directives establish that the vast majority of competent persons would not want to be maintained in a permanently unconscious state. A decision to remove life support from a permanently unconscious, previously competent person therefore accomplishes what that person would very likely have wanted to be done in the circumstances. In effect, the surrogate is effectuating the previously competent patient's autonomy interest as best that can be done—by making a judgment about what the now incompetent patient would want done if able to choose. In the absence of explicit instructions or other indicia of the now incompetent patient's actual wishes, the best way to honor self-determination is by constructing the patient's likely preferences based on knowledge of what most people would want in the circumstances.[85]

An alternative explanation for removing life support from a permanently unconscious person might be that the interests of loved ones in avoiding the emotional and financial costs of a protracted death watch justify the decision to terminate care. Some commentators assert that the interests of others, such as surrounding family and care givers, account for judicial willingness to endorse removal of life support from permanently unconscious persons. No court articulates that rationale, though it would be consistent with my suggestion later in this chapter that the interests of third parties influence surrogate best-interests determinations at the margins. The margin here is permanent unconsciousness, a point where the patient's actual interests (including a tiny chance of regaining consciousness) are problematic at best. For previously competent persons, this marginal consideration of loved ones' interests is also consistent with the patients' likely wishes. (Most people don't want their loved ones to be subjected to heavy burdens during a protracted death watch while the dying person is in a permanently unconscious state.)

I have another explanation for the wide acceptance of surrogate decisions to remove life support from permanently unconscious persons, even from persons such as children or profoundly disabled beings who have never been competent. My view is that permanent unconsciousness is an intrinsically undignified state for any human being, so that being allowed to die is respectful of the unconscious patient's human dignity. Judges understand the intrinsic indignity of a permanently unconscious status and are therefore willing to uphold surrogate decisions to withdraw further treatment in that circumstance. Some cases that involve permanent unconsciousness explicitly cite quality of life and human dignity while endorsing the removal of life support.[86] I also suggest that surrogate respect for intrinsic human dignity is part of a never competent patient's interests, even if the patient can no longer experience the consequences of demeaning treatment. Indeed, respect for human dignity is what insulates the never competent patient from regularly being subjected to bodily invasions such as tissue harvesting or hazardous medical experimentation that would benefit others.[87]

I have argued that profoundly disabled persons are entitled to full moral status, including respect for their human dignity. The legal handling of end-of-life decisions on behalf of permanently unconscious patients accords those patients full moral status (by implementing intrinsic human dignity), even though the surrogate is permitted to let the patient die. A judgment of intrinsic indignity does not constitute a judgment about social worth or utility or the value of a life to others. A person who is moribund might be worth more to society alive as a subject for medical research. The recognition of a person's full moral status entails a consideration of that person's gravely deteriorated quality of life.

If a permanently unconscious status is intrinsically undignified, is a surrogate obligated to opt for the removal of life support from such an incapacitated ward? The answer under prevailing law and custom is clearly no. The *Cruzan* case, discussed earlier, upheld Missouri's insistence that Nancy Beth Cruzan's permanently unconscious life be preserved (absent clear evidence of her contrary wishes).[88] And the *Baby K* case[89] upheld a mother's determination to continue life support to her anencephalic infant. While numerous cases and statutes uphold a surrogate decision to remove life support from a patient who is in a permanent vegetative state, none declare that a surrogate *must* follow that course. Estimates are that thousands of such patients are regularly maintained in the United States by continued medical intervention. All this confirms that current law does not regard a surrogate's conduct as abusive if the surrogate chooses to preserve a permanently unconscious patient's existence.

My own position diverges from the prevailing law. Because I regard permanent unconsciousness as intrinsically undignified, I would make the removal of life support from a permanently unconscious person mandatory unless a previously competent patient had indicated a wish to be preserved in such a demeaning status. My exception for the expressed will of a previously competent person is debatable. Sometimes society allows no exceptions for consent (as when it outlaws an inherently inhumane practice such as slavery). On the other hand, we sometimes allow people to choose conditions that most other people would regard as intrinsically demeaning. Lois Shepherd points out that people can choose to be undignified—for example, by groveling[90] or by self-submitting to horribly inhumane relationships. And people whose religion or philosophy values all human life, no matter how degrading, ought probably to be able to choose preservation in a permanently unconscious state. (This is so as long as their resources last; I am not suggesting that public funds must be devoted to preserving a permanently unconscious state.) In the absence of such personal choices to accept what is generally regarded as an intrinsically undignified status, I would require that a surrogate respect intrinsic human dignity by allowing a permanently unconscious person to die.

My suggested framework would make the controversial *In re Wanglie* case[91] correctly decided. There, a husband as guardian successfully fought to maintain artificial nutrition and hydration for his permanently unconscious eighty-six-year-old wife. The wife's hospital had sought a court order to remove the husband as guardian on the basis that he was improperly insisting on "futile" care for his wife. The judge upheld the husband's guardianship because the husband purported to be implementing his wife's articulated religious beliefs that all life is sacred and ought to be preserved. Under my suggested framework, the wife's religiously based preference was properly upheld even though it involved submission to an intrinsically undignified status. If Ms. Wanglie never made such a choice or never embraced such values, then her husband should indeed have been removed as guardian and she should have been relieved from her intrinsically undignified state by removal of life support.

Notice that the option to extend a permanently unconscious existence would not apply to a never competent person. Denying a lifelong profoundly disabled person's surrogate an option to choose an intrinsically undignified existence for the ward does not seem to me to be a serious disadvantage or harm. The denial reflects a notion that no one ought to be subjected to an intrinsically undignified status without explicit consent. A choice of degradation can only be made volitionally (just as a choice of marital partner can only be made volitionally and is therefore excluded from surrogate control).

Generally, the difficulty of defining intrinsic indignity for a never competent person protects that person against premature termination of life support. The profoundly disabled person "benefits" from a tighter standard of indignity than that applied to a previously competent person. That is, a possibly degrading condition—like extreme dementia or total helplessness—is more likely to be deemed intolerably undignified when the actual values of a previously competent patient are known or when a constructive choice is imputed to a previously competent person than when notions of intrinsic indignity come into play. Intrinsic indignity as applied to a never competent person would be narrow. So far, only a few conditions—permanent unconsciousness, mental decline to a semiconscious state where the person can no longer recognize and relate to others, and serious irremediable suffering—might be classified by reference to contemporary norms as an intrinsically undignified status. And current law and practice have not yet reached a consensus even about permanent unconsciousness.

Admittedly, my approach to intrinsic indignity—making the removal of a permanently unconscious patient's life support mandatory (absent contrary preferences by a previously competent person)—is contrary to prevailing practice. Perhaps it is unrealistic to expect society to label the artificial preservation of life support as an inhumane, intrinsically demeaning practice—at least in any circumstance other than extreme, unremitting suffering. Government is understandably hesitant to impose its views of intrinsic indignity when the consequence is to force the death of live beings (by the removal of life support). This is especially so in a pluralistic society where cultural and religious attitudes toward permanently unconscious beings may vary. But perhaps it is a only a matter of time. The concept of intrinsic human dignity is "neither static nor universal" and evolves according to cultural conditions; the transformation of slavery between the sixteenth and nineteenth centuries provides an example.[92] A societal consensus has been reached that a human being is dead when all brain function has ceased, even though nails and hair continue to grow, hormonal secretions take place, and the heart and lungs could continue to function for months or years via artificial maintenance. A similar consensus may evolve that permanent unconsciousness (with no upper-brain function), while not identical to death, constitutes an intrinsically undignified existence that ought not be artificially extended.[93]

Must Medical Decisions Be in the *Best* Interests of a Profoundly Disabled Person?

The typical understanding is that a best-interests judgment requires maximizing the helpless ward's interest or determining "the highest benefit [for the ward] among available options."[94] I suggest that this definition is not always accurate. Although "best interests" is the common watchword when government intervenes pursuant to its *parens patriae* authority to supervise the handling of helpless populations, a surrogate decision on behalf of a profoundly disabled person does not always have to be the *best* choice for the disabled person.[95] Sometimes a surrogate's determination need only be reasonably consistent with the interests of the disabled person—an appropriate choice within several acceptable options. And sometimes a surrogate's determination need meet an even less restrictive standard—that the determination not be abusive in the sense of subjecting the dependent person to serious risk of harm. The most obvious situation where a less restrictive standard than "best" interests applies is where a profoundly disabled person is being cared for at home—that is, is being raised as part of a family unit by a parent or parents.

American custom and law give parents considerable dominion over their children. In part, this tradition is grounded on the assumption that parents will generally act benevolently toward their children:

The law's concept of the family rests on a presumption that parents possess what a child lacks in maturity, experience, and capacity for judgment required for making life's difficult decisions. More importantly, historically it [the law] has recognized that natural bonds of affection lead parents to act in the best interests of their children.[96]

But neither law nor tradition compels parents to adhere to a child's best interests. In myriad circumstances, parents are free to disadvantage or even harm a child without violating legal bounds.

One area in which parents are free to deviate from their children's best interests relates to child custody itself. Numerous decisions confirm that natural parents are entitled to custody, even where their children's interests would be better served by remaining with foster parents or with aspiring adoptive parents.[97] A similar parental prerogative to deviate from best interests (in a fashion short of serious neglect or abuse) applies to a multitude of child-rearing decisions. This principle covers formal and informal education, social interactions, the allocation of household responsibilities, and the distribution of rewards, benefits, and sanctions within the family: "Even though we often talk about doing what is *best,* it is clear that the courts and the American public do not really believe that such a high standard is necessary or even appropriate."[98] Parental autonomy allows the subordination of the best interests of a child to family well-being, to sibling well-being, to religious dictates, or to philosophical preferences that guide parental dominion (again, short of serious neglect or abuse). The Supreme Court has acknowledged this societal deference to parental control:

[T]he best interests of the child is not the legal standard that governs parents' or guardians' exercise of their custody: so long as certain minimum requirements of child care are met, the interests of the child may be subordinated to the interests of other children or indeed even to the interests of the parents or guardians themselves.[99]

Many rationales support the social policy of broad deference to parents in child rearing. As noted, there is an underlying assumption that parents will generally act in a benevolent fashion toward their offspring. At the same time, parental control of child rearing advances a social interest in pluralism—an interest in cultivating a diverse range of cultural and ideological perspectives.[100] Parental control is also perceived as an efficient mechanism for raising children. The practical reality is that government would not have the resources to control child-rearing decisions, even if it were thought to be able to do a better job than many parents. And there is considerable doubt whether government could or would do a sounder job of child rearing (or of close supervision of child rearing), even if it possessed the resources for such an undertaking.[101] In short, parental autonomy serves a useful social function in facilitating the upbringing and socialization of successive generations of citizens.

The U.S. Constitution also insulates parental decision making in some measure from governmental interference. Parental autonomy in child rearing is recognized by the U.S. Supreme Court as a fundamental aspect of liberty under the Fourteenth Amendment. The Court's solicitude for the parental role dates back to its 1923 decision in *Meyer v. Nebraska*,[102] striking down a state law that prohibited both the teaching of a subject in a foreign language and the teaching of a foreign language and acknowledging the important parental liberty interest in raising children. Although *Meyer* was a product of an era of aggressive judicial intervention limiting governmental management of economic and social affairs generally, its solicitude for parental autonomy has endured. Supreme Court opinions continue to acknowledge "a fundamental liberty interest of natural parents in the care, custody, and management of their children."[103]

The most recent confirmation of parents' fundamental right "to make decisions concerning the care, custody, and control of their children" came in April 2000 in *Troxel v. Granville*.[104] There, the Court considered a parent's substantive due-process challenge to a Washington statute permitting "any person" to petition for a visitation order (in the face of parental opposition to such visitation) and authorizing a judge to grant visitation if the court determined that the visitation would serve the best interests of the child in issue. The Washington state courts had struck down the statute as an impermissible interference with parental liberty both because it allowed any person to petition (not just an especially bonded or connected person) and because it supplanted parental judgment without any prerequisite finding of significant harm to the child flowing from the parental decision regarding visitation. By a six to three margin, the U.S. Supreme Court ruled that the Washington statute was unconstitutional, at least as it had been interpreted and applied in the case at hand.

Justice O'Connor spoke for a four-Justice plurality in *Troxel*. She declined to decide whether the due-process clause requires a threshold showing of substantial harm before a court can constitutionally interfere with a parental decision regarding visitation. She did find a constitutional defect in the statute's failure to give any "special weight" to the parental determination about the advisability of visitation.[105] Justice O'Connor declared that the due-process clause precludes state interference with child rearing simply because a judge believes that a better decision than the parent's could have been made. In other words, the Washington statute's deficiency was its failure to accord any deference to the parental judgment regarding grandparents' visitation to children.[106]

Constitutional jurisprudence regarding parental decision making is somewhat in disarray.[107] In theory, parental autonomy, as a fundamental liberty, is insulated against government interference unless government meets a strict-scrutiny standard of judicial review—a standard that requires government to demonstrate a compelling interest in the particular interference and that the government intervention is carefully tailored to accomplish its object. Yet in application of constitutional doctrine, the Court has sustained a wide variety of state impingements on parental autonomy that are aimed at promoting children's welfare or public health. A constant tension exists between judicial concern for parental liberty to control the family and judicial respect for various other interests, including the state's *parens patriae* role as protector of children's welfare. Judicial respect for government's *parens patriae* role has contributed to the Supreme Court's upholding of compulsory education, compulsory inoculations, and prohibition of child labor, to cite a few interferences with parental control that have withstood constitutional challenge. In such instances, the Court seems to resolve the tension between parental autonomy and children's welfare with an ad hoc balancing approach rather than a careful application of strict-scrutiny doctrine.

Another interest that justifies interference with parental dominion is the promotion of older children's self-determination. Some states have sought to promote the self-determination interests of adolescents and teenagers by creating a "mature-minor" exception to the normal parental prerogative to control health decisions on behalf of children.[108] Some states have also encouraged physicians to provide certain sensitive treatments, such as for venereal disease and substance abuse, without parental authorization.[109] And the Supreme Court has given mature minors a constitutional right to control their own fates regarding abortion.[110]

The bottom line appears to be that government may interfere with parental dominion to advance a variety of significant interests, especially children's welfare. To answer the question posed but left unanswered by Justice O'Connor in *Troxel,* states are probably not constitutionally required to demonstrate particularized, substantial harm to children as a prerequisite to their interference in the parental control of child rearing. The state may make categorical interventions to protect children's well-being, as in the case of child-labor laws and as in the case of a ban on parental consent to nontherapeutic medical experimentation carrying more than minimal risk for never competent patients.

What implications flow from this constitutional jurisprudence on parental control of medical decisions for children who are clearly incapable of making their own medical decisions? In large part, states conform to the constitutional framework by recognizing a fundamental liberty interest in child rearing and leaving medical decisions in the hands of parents. Absent an emergency situation, medical personnel commit a battery (a tortious touching) by performing medical procedures without parental consent. This principle applies to a wide range of medical interventions—from medication for small problems to surgical invasions for serious conditions (subject to the previously mentioned exceptions for mature minors and for certain sensitive medical issues, such as abortion).

Note that the parental prerogative to control medical decisions for minors (as recognized in state jurisprudence) does not ordinarily confine parents to choosing treatments that are in the *best* interests of the child—that is, the objectively best medical course. As many commentators have recognized, medical circumstances often yield a range of plausible approaches;[111] parents are certainly entitled to select from this range of reasonable medical responses. But the deference toward parental choice goes further than this in many jurisdictions. Some courts uphold parental choice among alternative approaches so long as the chosen course is "not totally rejected by responsible medical authority."[112] This means, for example, that a parent of a profoundly disabled child can opt for a more dangerous, professionally disfavored course of medical intervention because it would be more palatable to the child (more sensitive to the child's emotional well-being).[113] Other jurisdictions express their deference to parental medical decisions by refusing to intervene unless a decision is "clearly contrary" to the child's best interests.[114] Most jurisdictions make government interference with parental medical decisions contingent on a showing of serious harm to the child,[115] meaning a harm serious enough to constitute child neglect or abuse. This approach recognizes "the paramount right of parents to decide questions affecting the welfare of their children until such right is forfeited by neglect."[116] (I also show, in chapter 5, that a best-interests standard does not really apply as to decisions regarding participation in nontherapeutic medical research and, sometimes, not as to tissue donation.)

This state deference to parental decision making leaves some room, albeit limited, for parents to interpose religious and cultural beliefs (and perhaps familial interests) into medical decisions on behalf of their children. For example, a Jehovah's Witness parent who opts for bloodless surgery (meaning no transfusion of blood products) may be selecting a medically disfavored course but obeying what the parent perceives as a divine injunction to save the child patient's soul. States tolerate such an option so long as the choice does not seriously threaten the child's life or well-being to the point of constituting child neglect. Many states explicitly provide some sort of exemption from child-abuse prosecution for parents who opt for spiritual-healing techniques.[117] Parents who opt for circumcision of their infants provide another illustration of tolerable parental choices that are influenced by religious or cultural values that deviate from a child's best medical interests.[118] Again, so long as serious harm to the child is not threatened, parents are generally allowed flexibility in making medical choices for their offspring, even if the choices deviate from the child's best interests.

In contrast to this deference to parental choice in a wide range of medical decisions, states commonly identify certain classes of "critical" medical decisions where a strict best-interests standard is judicially enforced. These critical determinations include abortion, sterilization, organ or tissue donation, and (in most instances) withholding or withdrawal of life support. These areas are singled out as problematic because of their intrinsic danger (withdrawal of life support and electroconvulsive therapy), judicial concern about conflicts of loyalties (organ donations to siblings), a history of exploitation surrounding the medical procedure (sterilization), or the critical constitutional interest at stake (abortion and sterilization). As chapter 3 discusses, parental control is displaced in these areas (with the exception of end-of-life decisions in many jurisdictions), and the critical medical decision is assigned to the courts. Judges, in turn, are supposed to make an independent determination of the child-patient's best interests—meaning selection of the *best* course for the child—before authorizing one of these controversial medical interventions. Even when a critical medical issue is left to parents rather than a court—as is the case with end-of-life decision making in many jurisdictions—the articulated standard is usually declared to be best interests of the patient.

Sterilization decisions on behalf of disabled persons provide an illustration of judicial application of a strict best-interests standard. The dark history of eugenic sterilization, with the senseless sterilization of thousands of Americans between 1907 and 1950, has already been noted here.[119] That history explains the judicial rejections of nonvoluntary sterilization that prevailed in the 1960s and 1970s. Judicial attitudes subsequently changed in response to petitions by parents seeking authorization for sterilization that was not for eugenic reasons but supposedly would serve the mentally disabled person's own interests. And when judicial receptiveness to surrogate petitions for authorization of sterilization emerged after 1980, it was accompanied by strict procedural and substantive safeguards aimed at ensuring that sterilization would be authorized only when the disabled patient's interests so dictated.[120] Under this post-1980 jurisprudence, sterilization could be authorized only after a judicial hearing at which the disabled person was represented by counsel and after expert medical input that assessed the patient's welfare with and without sterilization.

Courts articulated various areas of inquiry to guide judicial determinations, including the probability of pregnancy and the availability of alternative contraceptive means. Most critically, the presiding judge could authorize sterilization only on finding clear and convincing evidence that sterilization would be in the disabled person's best interests.[121] A few jurisdictions went even further and insisted on a finding of "medical necessity" as a prerequisite to sterilization.[122] As is discussed in chapter 5, most courts have also articulated a strict best-interests-of-the-patient standard in determining whether to authorize organ and tissue donations from decisionally incapacitated patients. Even the few courts that have articulated a substituted-judgment standard for purposes of authorizing an organ donation have ended up applying a best-interests standard—a standard that purportedly requires a determination that the donating patient will incur a net benefit despite the risks involved.

Another area where courts have tended to articulate a strict best-interests standard to guide nonjudicial surrogate decision makers is the withdrawal of life-sustaining medical intervention. While most jurisdictions allow private decision making (usually by next of kin acting in conjunction with medical personnel) and do not insist on judicial determinations regarding end-of-life decisions, courts often impose a decision-making standard of clear and convincing evidence that cessation of life support is in the best interests of the patient.[123] This is applied to previously competent persons who have not left indicia of their postcompetence treatment preferences, and it is applicable for never competent persons (who could not have issued prior instructions). A best-interests standard fixes the requisite finding for the surrogate as clear and convincing evidence that the burdens of continued existence outweigh the benefits. A few sources see the clear-and-convincing standard as a constitutional requirement,[124] but most see that standard merely as an understandable (but not constitutionally required) precaution to safeguard the lives and well-being of vulnerable patients.[125]

While the clear-and convincing evidence standard is a well-intentioned device, its necessity or advisability in all end-of-life situations is debatable. As I have discussed earlier, discerning and measuring the actual burdens and benefits that are being experienced by profoundly disabled persons are daunting tasks. It is not clear that net suffering can be clearly and convincingly demonstrated in many situations.[126] A natural response to this fact might be, "If you can't confidently say that a person's suffering markedly outweighs his or her satisfactions, then keep that person alive." Yet keep in mind a point made earlier—that quality of life, in the sense of avoiding either irremediable suffering or an intolerably undignified status, is often the determinative factor shaping end-of-life treatment. Both of these elements arguably point toward some leeway in a bonded surrogate's decision. Perhaps, as some commentators have suggested, surrogates with close bonds to their wards have an instinctive sense of whether their loved ones are suffering irremediably or whether they have reached a point of such extreme deterioration and indignity that they are better off dead than alive. Perhaps a sufficient prerequisite to a surrogate's authorization of the removal of life support should be that the surrogate can reasonably say (subject to scrutiny by surrounding medical personnel and even an institutional ethics committee) that the dying patient has permanently declined to a point where continued medical intervention violates intrinsic human dignity. (Keep in mind the earlier point that the concept of intolerable indignity for a never competent person is not the same as that for a formerly competent person. The concept of intrinsic indignity for a never competent person is narrow and must be cautiously applied.)

Some relaxation of the strict requirement of clear and convincing evidence of net burdens seems to have occurred in many jurisdictions, at least with regard to the status of permanently unconscious persons. A surrogate is allowed to forgo life support for a permanently unconscious patient, even though there can be no pretense that the burdens of the patient's continued existence clearly outweigh the benefits.[127] The law accepts permanent unconsciousness as an area in which a surrogate is allowed to say that a person's deterioration is so extreme that medical intervention ought not prolong dying. (I have argued that offense to intrinsic human dignity explains the surrogate's conclusion.) Commentators like Nancy Rhoden have convincingly argued that there should be other gray areas in which a bonded surrogate's judgment to end life support ought to be upheld unless some challenger (family member, health-care provider, or member of a protective agency) shows that the surrogate judgment is unreasonable.[128] The point is that "clear and convincing evidence" that burdens exceed benefits may be an overly stringent standard when it is applied to gravely debilitated dying persons.

A similar point can be raised about the standard that guides sterilization decisions on behalf of profoundly disabled persons. Numerous cases dictate that the burden of proof on any surrogate who seeks sterilization is a showing of clear and convincing evidence of best interests.[129] The widespread judicial invocation of a "clear-and-convincing-evidence" requirement was based on the perception that sterilization entails a permanent impingement of a person's fundamental-liberty interest in procreation.[130] That perception is sound with regard to the range of mildly or moderately disabled people who may be capable of child rearing. But a profoundly disabled person—the subject matter of this book—is incapable of assuming the role of a parent and raising a child. Absent that child-rearing capacity, sterilization does not deprive a person of a fundamental interest in procreation.[131] For a profoundly disabled person, the decision regarding sterilization is like any serious medical decision. It involves a serious bodily invasion and carries certain risks, and a surrogate (a court, under prevailing practice) must make a judgment about whether the potential gains warrant those negative consequences. The potential gains for a profoundly disabled person may include freedom from an incomprehensible burden of gestation, labor, and childbirth and sometimes freedom from intrusive personal monitoring that interferes with sexual activity.[132] Arguably, a court (or other surrogate) ought to be able to decide by a preponderance of the evidence (rather than clear and convincing evidence) that pregnancy and birth carry greater detriments for the profoundly disabled person than tubal ligation. The preponderance-of-the-evidence standard is employed by at least a few courts already.[133] Again, the idea is not to discard the best-interests standard as a determinative guideline but to employ a lesser requirement of proof than clear and convincing evidence in light of the unavoidable indeterminacy of some medical issues.

Can the Interests of Others Be Included within a Patient's Best Interests?

The previous section showed that critical medical decisions affecting profoundly disabled persons—including end-of-life decisions, sterilization, organ donation, and abortion—are supposed to be made according to a best-interests-of-the-patient standard. (This was so even though a surrogate is not always confined to the very best choice.) This section considers to what extent, if any, the interests of others, particularly a loving family, might enter into a calculus of the patient's interests.

Competing family interests arise and appeal to a surrogate decision maker in a variety of circumstances. For example, when the medical issue is maintenance of life-sustaining treatment for a profoundly disabled, dying patient, then the emotional trauma being experienced by surrounding loved ones is a potential consideration. The emotional stake of family members could potentially influence the surrogate's decision in either direction—toward premature termination of life support or toward unwarranted extension of life support. A desire to relieve extreme emotional, physical, or financial burdens on a family conducting an agonizing death watch might tempt a surrogate to withdraw life support earlier than would otherwise be the case. On the other hand, family guilt, grief, or unwillingness to come to terms with the impending death can provide an incentive for prolonging the patient's dying process beyond a humane point.

Competing family interests are apparent in other medical contexts as well. When a surrogate contemplates an organ or tissue donation from a healthy, profoundly disabled person to a critically ill sibling, the life of that sibling and the welfare of the family as a whole loom as factors that might influence a decision to impose risks and burdens on the disabled donor. (Note that both organ donation and participation in nontherapeutic medical research reappear as the focal point of chapter 5, titled Forced Altruism.) When a surrogate contemplates sterilization for a profoundly disabled person, potential family interests also arise—including the burden of monitoring the patient's behavior absent sterilization and even the possible burden of child rearing should the disabled patient ultimately become a parent. One question, then, is what role, if any, these understandable and pressing family interests can legitimately play in deciding the medical fate of a profoundly disabled patient.

Family interests are not the only possible distractions from focus on a mentally disabled person's best interests in the context of medical decision making. When the issue is sterilization or abortion, for example, social interests are arguably implicated.

As recounted in the introduction to this book, public concerns about reproduction by mentally disabled persons affected public policy in the United States for many years. A eugenic rationale was the impetus for the state statutes that in the first half of the twentieth century impelled sterilization of many thousands of institutionalized disabled persons. That is, the object was to protect and improve society by preventing reproduction on the part of those persons deemed likely to produce mentally disabled offspring. Recall Justice Holmes's famous 1927 comment in *Buck v. Bell* that three generations of imbeciles were enough.[134] As late as 1962, a court authorized sterilization of a retarded person on the basis that the welfare of society would be promoted by the avoidance of more retarded children.[135] In short, social welfare, not the welfare of the affected individual, accounted for the original utilization of nonvoluntary sterilization.

The eugenic rationale for sterilization is now a thoroughly discredited relic. While *Buck v. Bell* has never been explicitly overruled, the widespread understanding among legal scholars is that sweeping laws targeting the mentally disabled for sterilization—as employed during the first half of the twentieth century—are surely unconstitutional.[136] Focus has shifted from laws that mandate sterilization to improve the gene pool to individualized judicial decisions that determine whether a sterilization procedure promotes the best interests of a disabled person. Petitions for judicial authorization of sterilization came to be brought by parents or other guardians asserting that sterilization would be in the best interests of their disabled wards. The earliest judicial appraisals of best interests tended to be skeptical about the motives for petitions, and in the late 1960s and 1970s a number of state courts refused to authorize sterilization of retarded persons in response to petitions by parents.[137] Several factors influenced these decisions—revulsion at the sorry history of eugenic sterilization, concern for protecting the emerging constitutional liberty interest in procreation, and fear that common prejudices about disabled persons would prompt abusive sterilization decisions.[138]

In the 1980s, the common judicial attitude shifted perceptibly. More and more state courts ruled that judges had *parens patriae* power (grounded in their intrinsic equity jurisdiction) to authorize sterilization so long as such a surgical procedure was found to be in the best interests of a profoundly disabled person.[139] And while the courts didn't always grant a parental petition, they did recognize that certain factors sometimes make sterilization consistent with the disabled person's own interests. A disabled person might have a medical condition that would make pregnancy or childbirth either a hazardous or torturous process. Or pregnancy, labor, and delivery might have grave emotional consequences for a profoundly disabled woman who has no grasp of the concept of pregnancy and its natural outcome. Or a profoundly disabled person may have an interest in sexual interactions that are free from the intrusive monitoring that would be necessary if effective contraception were not in place. Depending on the circumstances, such factors might justify a sterilization procedure despite the attendant bodily invasion, pain, medical risks, and effect on future procreation. Moreover, the public has a pecuniary interest in all forms of contraceptive decisions where the medical procedure will be financed by public funds or where any offspring will become public charges. While a person's liberty interest in procreation is constitutionally protected, it is surely less robust where the potential parent is clearly incapable of raising a child. To safeguard against biased or exploitative sterilization decisions, the courts prescribed careful procedures for determining the potential patient's best interests, including a full hearing, legal representation for the disabled person, a full medical investigation, and a requirement that clear and convincing evidence show that sterilization would indeed be in the patient's interests because less invasive contraceptive alternatives were absent.

These precedents demonstrate a judicial recognition that a disabled person's own interests can sometimes dictate sterilization. They also state that the interests of third parties—parents, institutional personnel, or society as a whole—cannot properly enter into a best-interests calculus. But they do not address whether there is a valid theoretical justification for injecting third-party interests into surrogate medical decision making on behalf of never competent persons. I briefly consider whether such a theoretical underpinning exists.

One claim for the inclusion of third-party interests is that justice or fairness requires it. John Hardwig is the principal advocate for that proposition.[140] Hardwig argues that where families have struggled and sacrificed for the incapacitated patient (and where a medical decision entails burdens on the surrounding family), fairness and equity demand consideration of the family's interests along with those of the patient. For him, the surrogate decision maker should "harmonize and balance" family interests to avoid the "injustice" of an exclusively patient-centered ethic. Such consideration of family interests would have an impact in many circumstances, including a situation where caring for an infant born with multiple deficits would impose considerable emotional and economic costs on parents and siblings.[141]

A similar argument (that considerations of fairness or justice warrant attention to third-party interests) can be constructed when a surrogate is contemplating sterilization for a profoundly disabled person. For example, when a disabled person is living at home, the absence of effective contraception may significantly increase the supervision or monitoring burden on devoted caretakers who are already expending considerable efforts on behalf of the disabled person.[142] Or when a disabled person is incapable of child rearing—so that any child born to that person will end up being the responsibility either of the disabled person's parents or state social-service agencies—there's room for a claim that fairness dictates attention to third-party interests (including the well-being of the helpless prospective child) in weighing the possibility of sterilization.

A justice rationale for injecting other parties' interests into the determination of an innocent and helpless person's medical fate is questionable. Justice does not demand that a caretaker be free of all onerous burdens.

The potential for "unfair" burden is implicit whenever a person assumes a relation that entails responsibility for another person. This is so for a guardian, a spouse, a parent, or even a teacher. In all these situations, the burdens of caretaking sometimes turn out to be disproportionate to the benefits. A once satisfying marital relationship may be rendered torturous as a result of an accident that makes one spouse totally dependent on the other. This may be unlucky for the person suddenly saddled by caretaking, but perhaps it's not unjust for a spouse or parent to be saddled with unexpected burdens. Justice cannot mean that burdens within a relationship must mesh perfectly with deserts. Persons entering into these fiduciary relationships understand at the outset that burdens may turn out to exceed any anticipated rewards. Also, the person whose serious medical fate is being determined is usually an innocent victim of some serious affliction (as opposed to someone who is simply being self-indulgent).

Another concern about achieving justice under John Hardwig's approach is that it ostensibly would entail a difficult and unseemly calculus by any surrogate decision maker. Hardwig's fairness calculation involves a case-by-case assessment of the degree of burden and sacrifice previously or prospectively invested by the third party (the family member) whose interests are to be considered.[143] For Hardwig, a parent who has previously been inattentive toward a child does not deserve much solicitude in determining whether the burdens of future care might be "unfair." Yet this kind of inquiry into relational history is arguably unseemly and not well suited to the surrogate or to the medical personnel attending the incapacitated patient whose fate is being determined.

There is also the problem of incommensurability. In the end-of-life decision-making context, for example, how much do physical and emotional tolls on surrounding family members count when weighed against a period of debilitated but tolerable existence for the dying patient? It is hard enough to determine the net interests of the patient without bringing third-party burdens into the best-interests formula.[144] (Comparable qualms about a justice rationale for consideration of third-party interests apply also in the context of organ or tissue donation, a matter discussed in chapter 5.)

An alternative rationale for consideration of third-party interests is fulfillment of the putative wishes of the disabled patient. Both the President's Commission for the Study of Ethical Problems in Medicine and the New York Task Force on Life and the Law—two of the most distinguished bodies that have analyzed end-of-life decision making—have suggested that a best-interests decision-making formula might accommodate third-party interests on the theory that the now incapacitated patient would want burdens on loved ones to come into play.[145] This approach certainly makes sense where the patient was previously competent and articulated his or her concern for loved ones when contemplating a future dying process. The patient's prior attitude toward familial interests counts—either because a substituted-judgment approach is being implemented (trying to replicate the patient's wishes) or because the patient's articulated values and preferences help to shape the content of that patient's best interests.[146] For previously competent patients, it might also make sense to consider family interests even if the patient has not previously expressed that wish, on the theory suggested by the New York State Task Force that most people have such strong solicitude for their immediate families that they would want such interests to be considered.[147] Some surveys about seriously ill people's preferences for their own end-of-life handling do show strong concern for the physical and emotional burdens that might be experienced by surrounding loved ones.[148] Thus, there is some empirical support for the Task Force's rationale.

Whatever the appeal of using family interests as a decision-making factor with regard to previously competent patients, it's problematic to ascribe to lifelong profoundly disabled persons an altruistic wish to have the interests of loved ones considered in critical medical decisions. I have already rejected a substituted-judgment formula in this decision-making context because profoundly disabled persons never had the capacity to form determinative wishes on complex issues of medical decision making. That incapacity applies to the task of weighing third-party interests against the patient's own well-being. As Margaret Battin has noted,[149] altruism that deserves respect is the product of deliberation about the positives and negatives of self-sacrifice. In the context of never competent persons, the attribution of a wish to show consideration for the interests of others is a convenient fiction.[150] There may be good reasons to consider third-party interests along with the profoundly disabled patient's interests, but the fulfillment of putative wishes is not one of them. (I further consider the attribution of altruistic sentiments to profoundly disabled persons in chapter 5's discussion of so called "forced altruism.")

Third-party interests may incidentally enter the picture of surrogate decision making when they happen to coincide with an incapacitated patient's own interests. In a few situations, the interests of a profoundly disabled person can be materially advanced by an action that immediately benefits a surrounding family member. This is sometimes the claim, for example, where parents seek to harvest a nonvital organ from a profoundly disabled person. The disabled person would supposedly be harmed by the failure to donate the organ because that person would lose a devoted caregiver (the organ donee) or because the family would be so devastated by the loss of a family member that the disabled donor would suffer. Or a family might claim that sterilization is in the best interests of a disabled person because otherwise the family unit would be severely disrupted by the burden of supervising the disabled person's sexual behavior. Family peace of mind then supposedly furnishes a benefit to the person slated for sterilization.[151] These claims warrant consideration by a surrogate decision maker because in some instances the interests of the incapacitated patient and the affected family members do coincide. But in the absence of circumstances where the disabled person benefits derivatively from an accommodation of loved ones' needs, the attribution of altruistic wishes to the profoundly disabled patient or the inclusion of third-party interests within the patient's interests rings hollow.

What do the cases and commentators say about the relation between a mentally incapacitated patient's medical fate and third-party interests? The issue has perhaps received the most attention in cases that address surrogate decision making on behalf of previously competent persons. In that context, some courts do suggest that the interests of a now incapacitated patient's family are an appropriate part of the surrogate's decision-making calculus. This approach is most common in jurisdictions that use a substituted-judgment standard—that is, when the surrogate is supposed to follow the patient's actual or likely wishes. Some courts using a substituted-judgment approach are willing to employ a premise that most competent people care considerably about the physical, emotional, and financial well-being of loved ones. As long as the now incapacitated patient was previously intimately connected with family, these courts allow a surrogate to project that the patient would want burdens on the family to be a relevant factor in medical decisions that are on the now incompetent patient's behalf. One court commented: "An individual who is part of a closely knit family would doubtless take into account the impact his acceptance or refusal of treatment would likely have on his family."[152]

Where the ward is a never competent person, there appears to be much less judicial willingness to permit third-party interests—including burdens on family or caretakers—to play a role in surrogate medical decision making. This is especially so where the ward is institutionalized (and therefore is not part of an intact family unit) or is an infant who has never been part of a family unit. For example, in one case involving life support for a permanently unconscious child and in another case involving dialysis for an institutionalized, mentally disabled person, the courts determined to ignore burdens on family or institutions as a relevant consideration.[153] In the latter instance, when the trial court mentioned the potential burden that would be placed on the patient's family from a dialysis regimen as a relevant decision-making factor, the appellate court admonished that the interests of persons other than the patient must be ignored in fixing the patient's medical course.

Nonjudicial commentary within the field of death and dying is more divided, particularly about the moral relevance of third-party interests in deciding the fate of a mentally incapacitated patient. Some commentators, like Yale Kamisar, insist that so long as an incapacitated patient has even the slightest interest in continued existence, burdens on others have no appropriate role in a decision-making calculus.[154] Other commentators see the interests of third parties as an appropriate or even necessary factor in surrogate decision making.[155]

All ambivalence about the role of third-party interests is absent from the judicial expressions in the post-1980 cases regarding sterilization in the best interests of a mentally incapacitated ward. This line of cases is acutely sensitive to the fact that earlier generations of mentally disabled persons had been exploited by nonvoluntary eugenic sterilization. (Keep in mind also that sterilization decisions generally involve never competent rather than formerly competent patients—thus making it harder to attribute altruism or solicitude for the interests of others to the incapacitated patient.) The cases uniformly and unequivocally stress that any surrogate authorization of sterilization for an incapacitated person must be grounded on the ward's own interests. The following quotations are typical in their insistence on exclusive focus on the ward's interests: "[T]he court considers only the best interests of the incompetent, not the interests or convenience of parents, guardians, or society."[156] "The fundamental right involved must be safeguarded to assure that sterilization is not a subterfuge for convenience and relief from the responsibility of supervision."[157] "[In considering the ward's best interests], the welfare of society or the convenience or peace of mind of the ward's parents or guardian plays no part."[158] The post-1980 opinions not only disclaim any reliance on family or social interests in making best-interests determinations, they constantly emphasize the importance of protecting the health and procreative interests of the disabled person for whom sterilization is being contemplated.

In sum, the current doctrinal framework of best interests leaves little room for surrogate consideration of third-party interests in the settings of sterilization or end-of-life medical decisions on behalf of never competent persons. The whole best-interests formula is geared to protecting the interests of helpless persons, without consideration of the incommensurate interests of the helpless person's family or caretakers. Law is understandably reluctant to openly encourage the balancing of a helpless person's life or procreative capacity against the comfort, convenience, and well-being of others. The main exception (in the context of end-of-life decision making) is for previously competent persons who may have defined their personal interests as embracing the well-being of others—an exception that cannot apply to lifelong disabled persons.

From my perspective, all this judicial emphasis on patients' well-being does not mean that third-party interests are in fact irrelevant to surrogate decision making on behalf of profoundly disabled persons. The reality is that third-party interests constitute a "looming omnipresence" that influences surrogate decision making in subtle and not so subtle ways.[159] And at least at the margins—circumstances where the burdens on third parties are extreme and the net interests of an incapacitated ward are very much in doubt—the impact of third-party interests seems inevitable and legitimate.

A number of situations reflect the almost unavoidable impact of third-party interests. One such situation is where a critically ill, incapacitated person is experiencing a difficult dying process that is causing emotional anguish to surrounding family members. This emotional burden on the family might impel the family, acting as surrogate decision maker, in either of two directions—unwarranted extension of artificial life support or premature termination of such support. An example of the former is a situation where a family insists that a gravely debilitated, dying patient be maintained on life support despite the health-care providers' perception that the unconscious, semiconscious, or conscious and suffering patient is deriving no benefit from the continued care. The family members may be motivated by their grief, by their guilt at being the agents of the termination of a loved one's life, or by their religious conviction that all life is precious.

Or the family may seek a delay in removing life support to accommodate a relative who wishes to make a last farewell to the moribund, stuporous patient. Many health-care providers will defer to the family's wishes—not because the patient's best interests dictate continued medical intervention but because the providers are either solicitous of the family's discomfort or fearful of antagonizing the family. The surrounding family members are in a position to make a fuss and assert their interests while the patient is oblivious or at least helpless. Rather than create friction and controversy and possible bad publicity, the health-care providers acquiesce in this derogation of the patient's interests.[160]

Sometimes, the impetus stemming from a consideration of family interests moves in the opposite direction—toward termination of life support. This is almost certainly the case when an infant is born with multiple, severe deficits. While the medical personnel may not yet be able to assess the precise long-term fate of the infant, they may already know that the parents will be facing enormous hardship and stress and that the infant's eventual quality of life will be problematic at best. A strong temptation then exists for the attending physician to acknowledge the parental (and familial) ordeal ahead and to influence the parents to consent to the withholding of life-sustaining medical intervention—not because of the infant's best interests but because of the family interests at stake.[161] That consideration of family interests was overt in the 1970s, when physicians started writing about selective nontreatment of newborns.[162] Raymond Duff, a well-known neonatologist of the time, operated on the premise that "families need to be spared the chronic sorrow of caring for infants with little or no possibility of meaningful lives." A similar attitude continues today among some physicians, albeit in more covert fashion.

A comparable phenomenon likely takes place where an adult patient has deteriorated to a point at which there is little chance that the patient can derive benefit from continued medical intervention. When the patient has reached this gray area in which any benefit (other than biological existence) is dubious, there's a strong impetus for the surrogate decision maker and attending medical personnel to bring the interests of the patient's loved ones into consideration.[163] This is one of the margins at which third-party interests almost inevitably come into play.

The marginal influence of third-party interests is perceptible in other medical contexts as well. As is analyzed further in chapter 5, the phenomenon seems to occur when the medical issue is organ or tissue donation from a mentally disabled person to a critically ill sibling or other close relative. While the cases articulate a strict standard of best interests of the donor patient, the surrogate decision makers who apply that standard appear to be influenced by the critical needs of the sick relative. That is, tissue donation sometimes is authorized when the donee relative's survival will help the donor patient in some measure (such as by allowing the relative to act as a caretaker), even though it is unclear whether donation will really further the donor's *best* interests. Also, when a mentally disabled person is living at home with siblings and parents, it is almost impossible for a surrogate decision maker to ignore those third-party interests. This fact was acknowledged in a case where the medical issue was whether to authorize antipsychotic medication for a mentally ill child who was living at home with his siblings.[164]

The dollar cost of end-of-life treatment is another part of the "looming omnipresence" of third-party interests. Treatment and nontreatment decisions are unquestionably influenced by cost factors, at least where the costs are considerable and where the patient's status is so debilitated that it is unclear where the patient's best interests lie—that is, whether the patient is better off dead than alive. While medical protocols and even state statutes may exclude cost as a relevant factor,[165] high costs are almost impossible to disregard. For example, if there is only a very slight chance that a medical intervention will be successful in extending life and if the proposed intervention is extremely expensive, then cost will likely impact on the medical decision.[166] Sometimes, the role of health-care cost is explicitly recognized. For example, society makes allowance for parents who are facing extraordinary financial burdens for their children's medical care. An explicit exemption under child-neglect statutes is provided for parental failure to provide medical care that would be beyond the family's financial capability. Nor is the influence of economics reserved to the setting of incapacitated patients. Society limits the funding of some expensive medical procedures on the basis of cost-worthiness even where competent patients are involved.[167]

As in the case of end-of-life surrogate decision making, it is impossible to entirely exclude the consideration of the prospective burdens on others when a surrogate is deciding whether to authorize a sterilization procedure. Those burdens act as a "looming omnipresence" over the surrogate's weighing of sterilization just as they do in the death-and-dying setting. For example, the burdens involved in the supervision of a disabled patient (to prevent unprotected sexual activity) unavoidably play a role when sterilization is in issue. While the judicial opinions constantly stress that close supervision of the disabled person should be considered as a less drastic alternative to sterilization, and they admonish that convenience to caregivers should not be a factor, they really mean that *reasonable* supervision efforts should be considered. At some point, the burden of constant supervision becomes an unreasonable burden on caretakers, a fact that ultimately gets noted.[168] (Of course, courts also recognize that constant supervision as an alternative to sterilization can be restrictive to the disabled person and counter to the maximal normalization that is an object of enlightened caregiving.)[169] And while it is unseemly for courts to mention the potential financial burden on the state in raising any offspring of a profoundly disabled person, that factor too looms over the sterilization determination.[170] Again, at the margins or extremes, the interests of third parties do inevitably influence surrogate determinations of whether to authorize sterilization for a profoundly disabled ward.

The lesson here is that a best-interests decision-making standard cannot be applied in a manner that entirely excludes third-party interests. The looming omnipresence of family emotional and financial interests inevitably materializes and influences decision making in extreme cases—especially where the pure best interests of the patient are difficult to determine and where the burdens on others are considerable. This is not shocking. While I previously noted that justice does not mean that caregivers must be freed from onerous burdens, it may be fair to consider the sacrifices that caretakers make, at least at the margins where the interests of the disabled wards are indeterminate, are in equipoise, or will be only modestly affected. Consideration of family interests at the margins recognizes that there are limits to the duty of sacrifice that even a fiduciary such as a parent or guardian owes to his or her ward. Some kinds of parental or family sacrifices are unreasonable. A parent shouldn't have to bankrupt a family to extend an unavoidably dying child's life. A parent shouldn't have to jeopardize the well-being of a sibling (by diverting important resources away from that healthy person), even to extend another child's life.

Consider the case of the conjoined twins that was litigated recently in Great Britain.[171] Both twins would have died absent separation. Physicians demanded that the parents authorize a separation operation that might preserve the healthier twin but would precipitate the prompt death of the feebler twin. When the parents refused to accelerate one child's death (even for the purpose of rescuing the other child), the British courts intervened and ordered the operation. To me, it seems wrong to call the parents' conduct child neglect.[172] Yes, the parents were failing to save their salvageable child's life, but their conduct was inspired by unwillingness to precipitate their other child's prompt death. To me, this is an illustration of the rare case where a consideration of a third-party's interest (the feebler twin) warranted a parental choice not to pursue the pure best interests of a dependent child (the stronger twin).

It is debatable whether the consideration of family and other third-party interests should be explicitly articulated as part of a best-interests formula.[173] The current framework is deceptive in ostensibly excluding third-party interests while actually tolerating them in certain circumstances. Yet arguably, third-party interests should be left as a looming omnipresence in the hope that they will be employed only at the margins where they almost unavoidably come into play. Open endorsement risks encouraging an extension of the consideration of third-party interests to a broad range of circumstances where the incommensurate nature of other people's interests might undermine sound surrogate decision making on the behalf of an incapacitated patient.

In sum, the commonly stated approach to surrogate decision making for profoundly disabled medical patients is best interests of the incapacitated ward. However, the literal best-interests standard gets applied primarily when a governmental agent—usually a court—is the responsible decision maker. When a parent is the surrogate decision maker, the medical course chosen need not be the *best* course, so long as it is a plausible medical option and is not so antithetical to the patient's interests that it constitutes neglect or abuse. And while third-party interests are not officially part of a never competent patient's interests, third-party interests constitute a looming omnipresence that inevitably influences surrogate decision making at the margins. That is so especially where the never competent patient's own interests are murky or in equipoise and the potential impact on third parties is extreme.

5

Forced Altruism

The Problematic of Surrogate Consent to Nontherapeutic Medical Procedures

As noted in chapters 3 and 4, parents are generally permitted to control medical procedures being performed on their children, including their profoundly disabled adult children. When parents consent to medical interventions on behalf of their children, though, they usually do so to preserve the children's lives or well-being. This is so when parents make routine medical decisions in response to a disease or pathology that is affecting a child, and it is so even when a medical procedure entails some risk of harm to the child. For example, sterilization risks harm by disabling a child's reproductive processes, yet parental consent to sterilization may be warranted where pregnancy or procreation would cause substantial harm to a child and where alternative means of preventing pregnancy are not usable. The same pattern of therapeutic interventions characterizes a parent or guardian's control over medical decisions for a mentally disabled adult. An abortion may interfere with the adult's right to carry a child to term, yet the adult's acute medical interests may justify terminating a pregnancy.

When a contemplated medical procedure involves the harvesting of an incapacitated person's bodily resource—whether blood, tissue, bone marrow, or an organ—to supply material to another individual, the medical conduct (and the surrogate's authorization of the medical procedure) are suspect. In the first place, a bodily invasion is being undertaken in which the primary beneficiary appears to be the needy transplant recipient rather than the donor patient. Second, the donor patient is subjected to some measure of burden and risk in the course of the transplant process. These elements of burden and risk vary according to the transplant procedure in issue, but consider a kidney transplant as one example. The donor patient undergoes the significant discomfort and inconvenience that are attendant to an invasive surgical procedure and to a hospitalization lasting days.[1] Anesthesia carries some minor risks of adverse reactions; the surgical procedure and accompanying hospitalization entail some minor risks of infection. Loss of one kidney means some life-style accommodations (such as avoidance of contact sports). In very rare instances, the remaining kidney fails, necessitating serious, unpleasant medical interventions.[2] And if the transplant recipient's body rejects the donated organ, the donor may ultimately experience guilt or other emotional trauma. For bone-marrow transplants, the accompanying burdens and risks are less significant than those in kidney transplants, but they are still significant.[3] Moreover, the failure rate—the percentage of cases in which the transplanted material fails to save the recipient—may be significantly greater regarding bone-marrow transplants.[4] That means a greater chance of guilt and psychological distress for the donor patient. Given these possible harms to a vulnerable ward, an important issue becomes whether adequate legal and moral justification exists for surrogate medical decisions to permit tissue transplantation.

The problem continues in the context of nontherapeutic medical research conducted on profoundly disabled (or other mentally incapacitated) persons. First, the central purpose of all medical research is "to advance knowledge for the benefit of future patients, not to provide what is best for individual study participants."[5] The potential derogation of research subjects' interests is particularly acute in the context of nontherapeutic research—meaning that the medical research is not only driven by the object of advancing knowledge but that there is no reasonable expectation that the research will improve the subject's health condition. (While some commentators disparage the categorization of medical research as therapeutic or nontherapeutic,[6] the fact remains that some research holds no prospect of direct benefit for the subject and is therefore distinctive. I continue to use the term *nontherapeutic medical research*.)[7] Competent persons may knowingly choose, for altruistic or other reasons, to participate in medical research involving significant risks and carrying no prospect of direct medical benefit to the research subject. But on what theory can a surrogate decision maker elect to submit a profoundly disabled person—someone who will not likely experience the satisfaction accompanying altruism— to nontherapeutic medical research?

It appears that at least in some instances the harvesting of body materials from a profoundly disabled donor or the performance of nontherapeutic medical research is not a positive or beneficial event for the donor. That possibility raises both legal and moral issues. On the legal front, if these forms of medical conduct involve some form of physical or emotional sacrifice by the profoundly disabled ward, can surrogate authorization of the conduct be reconciled with the customary expectation that a surrogate medical decision maker will act in the best interests of a ward? What legal standard prevails, if not best interests? And how much sacrifice (pursuant to a surrogate's authorization) is permissible?

Similar questions arise on a moral plane. What is the moral justification for a surrogate's imposition of sacrifice on a ward? Some commentators assert that there can be no moral justification for nontherapeutic bodily invasions of a helpless human.[8] According to this view, "utter helplessness demands utter protection,"[9] so that the exploitation of a profoundly disabled person's body for the primary benefit of someone else constitutes a form of disrespect for human beings—a violation of human dignity.

Reliance on the Best Interests of the Profoundly Disabled Patient

There would be no deviation from surrogate decision-making norms if the contested medical decisions were actually in the incapacitated ward's best interests. A best-interests claim is sometimes made in the contexts of both tissue donation and nontherapeutic medical research.

One rationale for authorizing organ or tissue donation on the part of an incapacitated patient relates to the best interests of the donor patient. The notion is that the donor patient will ultimately benefit in a meaningful way from the donation—perhaps by experiencing satisfaction from an altruistic act, by learning a valuable moral lesson, by preserving a supportive family unit, or by receiving continuing care and support from the salvaged donee. These arguments apply most readily to minor children, especially adolescents, who are asked to donate to an afflicted sibling. Beyond a certain age (which I do not purport to pinpoint), a child can indeed experience the satisfaction of salvaging human life or can absorb a valuable moral lesson about altruism. The picture becomes more complicated when the donor patient is profoundly mentally disabled. Any prospective benefit in the form of either experienced self-satisfaction from altruism or an absorbed moral lesson becomes problematic. Pleasure from the gratitude of family members or from the attention of the grateful recipient are conceivable, but the extent of any such benefit is difficult to assess. And levels of anxiety and stress may increase for a mentally disabled donor who does not comprehend the reasons for the bodily invasions in question. In short, prospective benefits to the profoundly disabled donor are more difficult to discern, and the hazards of donation may be greater than in the case of a competent living donor. My analysis of the cases—to be detailed below—suggests that some surrogate authorizations of tissue or organ donations from a mentally disabled donor deviate from a strict best-interests-of-the-patient approach.

A claim can also be made that nontherapeutic medical research is consistent with the interests of incapacitated wards. Such a claim seems implicit in the common requirement that any more than minimal-risk research performed on a disabled subject be aimed at understanding the same disease or condition as the one that afflicts the disabled research subject.[10]

The "same-disease" restriction is apparently aimed at justifying the imposition of risk on incapacitated subjects by finding some benefit to the patient. If the research has a significant prospect of finding a timely cure for the "same disease" that afflicts the subject, then the benefit is obvious. But such research could be classified as therapeutic, or at least as being for the direct benefit of the subject in some measure. Yet there are lots of nontherapeutic research protocols where no such salutary prospect exists. Some research aims to achieve a better understanding of the research subject's affliction but has no realistic chance of personally benefitting that subject. In those instances, what is the connection between research on a disabled subject and the fact that the research benefits some future persons who suffer from the same disease as the incapacitated subject? Charles Fried mentions "a community of interests" between the present research subject and the future beneficiaries—sufferers of the same affliction.[11] Peter Rabins cites "a special affinity" among people who have the same disorder and concludes that the incapacitated potential research subject, if miraculously competent, would want to make a modest sacrifice (such as incurring a minor increase over minimal risk) for the sake of helping future sufferers of the disorder.[12] However, in the absence of a significant prospect of direct benefits to the subject, this justification imputes a highly individualized sentiment like altruism (or perhaps even a sentiment of vengeance toward the affliction) to never competent persons. That attribution of sentiments seems problematic.

One possibility for finding a benefit from nontherapeutic research is that such research, while not aimed at ameliorating the subject's medical afflictions, can nonetheless have indirect benefits for the incapacitated subject. Indirect benefits of participation in medical research might include social interactions, positive feelings about contributing to medical science (where the subject's cognitive capacity permits), or increased medical attention pursuant to a research protocol.[13] Commentators are understandably skeptical about using indirect benefits as a justification for nontherapeutic medical research.[14] For one thing, these indirect benefits may be absent under some research protocols. Even if indirect benefits are present, they may be overvalued because of zeal to advance other persons' interests—whether those of researchers or those of future patients who will ultimately benefit from the scientific knowledge gleaned. Indirect benefits may serve as a fig leaf that screens research that is basically aimed at benefitting persons other than the subject. Observers perceive "a steely utilitarian calculus" as the real explanation for the conduct of nontherapeutic research on incapacitated persons.[15] (The utilitarian rationale is examined below.)

Another explanation for allowing surrogate consent for nontherapeutic research relies less on the benefit to the research subject's interests and more on the absence of any real imposition on the subject. It is commonly accepted that nontherapeutic research on never competent persons is appropriate so long as only "minimal risk" is entailed. The idea is apparently that subjection to minimal risk—meaning medical procedures that are no more risky than common daily activities or routine medical interventions—does not constitute a significant burden or hazard for the disabled research subject.[16] The concept of minimal risk supposedly "conveys a defensible normative judgment that the sorts of risks society deems acceptable in other contexts may be acceptable in research as well."[17] The premise is that if a parent or guardian is entitled to subject a ward to the risks that accompany a spectrum of daily activities, then that entitlement should extend to imposing similar risks on a ward even when done for the benefit of others.

One immediate problem with this explanation is that not all nontherapeutic research on disabled persons is confined to minimal risk; research sometimes involves a minor increase over minimal risk or even greater risk. Another problem is that even minimal-risk nontherapeutic research constitutes an imposition on the helpless research subject that necessitates some moral justification. Minimal-risk medical research can still involve some invasion of bodily integrity, some disorienting disruption of routine, some discomfort, or some anxiety on the part of an uncomprehending research subject—all for the benefit of persons other than the incapacitated ward. The surrogate's conduct then raises the specter of treating the profoundly disabled subject as an object of exploitation.[18] *Some* moral justification seems necessary even for very modest physical impositions on a helpless subject.

Discrimination against the Disabled

Another possible moral objection is that nontherapeutic research or tissue removal from an incapacitated person constitutes a form of unfair discrimination against helpless beings. This claim starts with the accurate proposition that competent adults cannot be compelled to sacrifice bodily parts for others, even others who are in critical need.[19] The argument is then that extracting an organ or some tissue from an incapacitated person involves a form of compulsion or an imposition of an altruistic act that unfairly treats the helpless donor as compared with a competent potential donor.[20] Quoting one example: "A child [or incapacitated adult] should not be required to come to the rescue by providing a critically needed organ since there is no general obligation to rescue. It would seem unfair to impose this burden on children [or incapacitated adults] when the same burden is not imposed on [competent] adults."[21] This is the "forced altruism" claim—that a capacitated person cannot be forced to sacrifice a body part to save another's life, and neither should an incapacitated person.

This unequal exploitation claim does not seem convincing. While a competent adult cannot be forced to donate bodily tissue, neither can a disabled person. It is not at all clear that a surrogate's choice to donate a disabled person's tissue entails compulsion of the donor. Where the donor is an adolescent, for example, courts make it clear that no donation can occur without assent from the potential donor. The potential donor's will (or lack of assent) is respected. A profoundly disabled potential donor might also be able to express firm opposition to the bodily invasion in issue and thus successfully resist donation. A surrogate decision maker and the medical staff would not override that resistance unless the proposed bodily invasion was clearly in the potential donor's own interests. As is shown below, similar respect for the objecting will of a profoundly disabled person attaches in the context of nontherapeutic medical research. (More is said on incapacitated persons' objections to medical procedures later in this chapter, and more is presented on the "voice" of the profoundly disabled patient in the next chapter.) So long as medical decision makers respect the resistance or objections of profoundly disabled persons, no forced sacrifice or compulsion exists.

Even if the surrogate and medical staff would override a profoundly incapacitated patient's opposition to donation, the claim of unfair exploitation would not necessarily be convincing. A policy of allowing surrogate decisions to donate tissue (or make other physical sacrifices) can be viewed as helping to equalize the situations of competent and incapacitated persons. A competent adult can choose to make a physical sacrifice by donating an organ or tissue or by participating in nontherapeutic medical research. While the competent person's prerogative is predicated on informed consent and while there may be ethical limits on the degree of risk to which the person may consent, competent patients are generally entitled to make nonbeneficial medical choices (such as tissue donation or participation in nontherapeutic research). By means of a surrogate's decision, a disabled person is afforded a similar opportunity to make a physical sacrifice. Chapter 2 points out that preclusion of surrogate medical choice—especially where the medical procedure has the potential to benefit the disabled patient in some measure—can single out and disadvantage disabled persons.[22] So total exclusion of organ donation by profoundly disabled individuals would itself raise a claim of unequal treatment. This would certainly be so if the consequences of organ donation by an incapacitated individual can be viewed as beneficial in some measure to the donor as well as to the recipient—a possibility to be examined below when I turn to the existing cases on point.

The "inequality" involved between competent and incapacitated donors is attributable to the absence of autonomous choice in the latter instance. While a competent patient can choose to be altruistic by donating a bodily resource, a profoundly disabled person cannot exercise autonomous choice to donate. As chapter 2 notes, the absence of autonomous choice does not foreclose giving a profoundly disabled person access to certain medical options by means of a bonded surrogate's decision. Indeed, I argue there that a profoundly disabled person should always have a right to surrogate decision making when a prospective medical intervention will further the net interests of the disabled person.

The critical question in this chapter is whether a surrogate should be allowed to make a choice on behalf of the nonautonomous individual to sacrifice a bodily resource, even if such a choice does not advance the net interests of the ward. The answer (for me) is easy, at least when a contemplated medical procedure will likely benefit the profoundly disabled donor in some measure. If an organ or tissue donation will clearly benefit the donor in some measure—via receipt of care and support from the saved donee—a surrogate decision to donate ought to be permissible. As is suggested in chapter 4, a surrogate is not really bound to make the *best* decision for an incapacitated ward or to exclude all considerations of third-party interests. Existence of some reasonable return for the disabled donor should suffice to warrant a surrogate's authorization. The surrogate is then making a good-faith judgment about the ward's interests. A competent patient can opt for a risky heart surgery that offers the potential for substantial improvement in lifestyle—even if the surgery's benefits do not clearly outweigh the risks or discomforts involved. A surrogate also ought to be able to make some choices for a disabled person that don't necessarily advance the ward's net interests.

The question of a surrogate's prerogative is harder if the contemplated medical procedure is clearly nontherapeutic and its consequences are clearly negative (in terms of net burdens and benefits) to the helpless ward. That would be the case where the donee who is to be salvaged by a transplant would not really supply a significant return to the donor in the form of care and support. In such a situation, a likely impetus for a competent patient's autonomous choice to donate organs is personal satisfaction from the performance of an altruistic act. (Let's put aside the possibility that relatives' pressure to donate is the prime impetus.) Assume that a profoundly disabled person cannot experience the sense of gratification that a self-determining donor can. Absent experienced gratification on the donor's part, what rationale, if any, supports allowing a surrogate to authorize a purely altruistic (meaning purely for the benefit of others) act of tissue donation?

The Kantian Imperative

All nontherapeutic medical handling of a profoundly disabled person, whether involving tissue donation or medical research, must confront a moral hurdle in the form of a Kantian aversion to using helpless people solely as a means to advance the interests of others. The original Kantian imperative reads: "Act in such a way that you always treat humanity, whether in your own person or in the person of any other, never simply as a means, but always at the same time as an end."[23] This moral injunction is grounded in respect for human dignity because treating helpless humans solely as a tool of others appears to treat them as an object or a thing rather than as valuable persons.[24] People like Paul Ramsey regarded use of children or profoundly disabled adults as either tissue donors or participants in nontherapeutic research as a violation of the Kantian imperative.[25] Their argument would be that tissue harvesting (as well as nontherapeutic medical research) treats profoundly disabled persons only as useful instruments.

The key to applying the Kantian imperative is to decide what it means to treat a person as an end (and hence not solely as a means). Considerable philosophers' ink has been spilt on that issue. One view—embraced by Ronald Dworkin and Martha Nussbaum, among others—is that the imperative does not categorically exclude instrumentalization of one human by another "but rather [requires] that people never be treated in a way that denies the distinct importance of their own lives."[26] Martha Nussbaum suggests that "what is problematic is not instrumentalization per se, but treating someone *primarily* or *merely* as an instrument."[27] Nussbaum goes on to show how the morality of an act of using one person as an instrument for another's object must be assessed in light of the context of the underlying human relationship and the act's regard for the humanity of the "exploited" being. For her, objectionable objectification usually takes the form of not just using another human as a tool but disregarding autonomy, disregarding subjectivity (the feelings and emotions of the exploited being), or disregarding certain boundaries that safeguard humans.[28] In other words, using another as an instrument—as when a parent imposes sacrifices on one sibling for the benefit of another—is not necessarily a moral wrong. It may be fully consistent with intrinsic human dignity to interpret the Kantian imperative to permit some instrumental use of a fellow human being. The context—including the will of the child, the feelings of the child, the relation between the child and the primary beneficiaries, and the nature of the sacrifice (in terms of degree of risk and bodily imposition)—affects the moral assessment.

I subscribe to the Dworkin/Nussbaum assessment of instrumentalization. How do tissue donation and nontherapeutic medical research fare from the Nussbaum perspective? Not too badly, I would say. Using Nussbaum's criteria for objectification, I do not think that a surrogate's choice of either of the two disputed medical procedures necessarily fails to treat the profoundly disabled subject as an end. Consider the context of the surrogate and ward relationship. It is mandatory that the surrogate acknowledge and respect, to the extent possible, the autonomy of the profoundly disabled ward. The surrogate defers to the will of the profoundly disabled ward as to simple daily choices (such as dress, eating, and recreation). The surrogate will consult with the ward about the contemplated medical procedure and even seek the ward's assent where mental capacity permits. If the ward objects to the procedure, that opposition will be respected by a conscientious surrogate. The surrogate will also take full account of what Nussbaum calls the person's subjectivity—his or her personal feelings, needs, and emotions. If, in light of the ward's subjective reactions, the disabled person's well-being or dignity is jeopardized by the contemplated medical procedure, then the conscientious surrogate must forgo the procedure. The physical integrity of the disabled person is also considered. The nature of the contemplated physical intrusion is important to the surrogate's determination of whether to proceed with the contemplated medical procedure. (Keep in mind that a disabled person's physical integrity is not entirely inviolable, as vaccinations and therapeutic medical interventions demonstrate.) Finally, the surrogate must carefully consider the degree of risk involved.

Any specter of complete objectification is also mitigated by respecting limits on a surrogate's authority that intrinsic human dignity imposes. A parent may be allowed to impose chores or even labor on a child, but that imposed labor cannot include prostitution or begging. Respect for persons still allows the extraction of a modicum of sacrifice from any human, including a profoundly disabled person. A surrogate's decision to initiate a nontherapeutic medical intervention can still show sensitivity to the agency (will), feelings, physical integrity, and humanity of the mentally disabled ward, even if the intervention's primary object is to advance someone else's well-being. Especially when viewed in the context of the surrogate's overall relationship with the mentally disabled ward, a surrogate's choice to permit a nontherapeutic intervention may still be respectful of the ward's intrinsic human dignity. (More is presented later in this chapter about the limits that intrinsic human dignity imposes on a surrogate's imposition of sacrifice on a ward.)

Even if a surrogate's choice of a nontherapeutic medical intervention does not treat the disabled ward "solely" as a means in violation of Kant's injunction, it is problematic. One person is still exploiting the control of another person to use that dependent person as a tool to advance others' interests. What moral justification is there for allocating that degree of control to a surrogate decision maker? Why shouldn't a surrogate be required to adhere strictly to a disabled ward's best interests, at least where bodily intrusions are in issue? I examine the possible moral rationales for a surrogate's consent to nontherapeutic medical procedures after examining the legal frameworks that surround both tissue donation and nontherapeutic medical research.

Existing Jurisprudence

The Decided Cases on the Donation of Bodily Resources

The earliest judicial treatments of the organ-donation issue came in unreported Massachusetts cases of the late 1950s.[29] In those instances, parents sought to authorize kidney transplants from healthy adolescent or post-adolescent children to siblings who were afflicted with renal disease. When hospitals refused to cooperate without judicial approval, the parents invoked the courts. The Massachusetts judges did not articulate a clear legal standard, but they did approve the transplants. They noted psychiatric testimony that the loss of a sibling would cause grave emotional harm to the potential donor (so that the donation would promote the donor's well-being in some measure) and that the donor in each instance had expressed willingness to make the donation.

The first reported case was decided in 1969 by the Kentucky Supreme Court. *Strunk v. Strunk*[30] involved parents seeking to authorize a kidney transplant from their twenty-seven-year-old mentally retarded son (with the mental capacity of a six-year-old) to his twenty-eight-year-old brother (stricken with kidney disease). The Kentucky court, by a four to three margin, found legal authority to authorize the transplant by invoking the inherent jurisdiction of equity courts. The majority looked at the traditional role that courts play in the handling of incapacitated wards and found two doctrinal threads suggesting judicial authority to authorize a kidney donation—substituted judgment to accomplish what an incapacitated person would want done, if he or she were capable of deciding, and *parens patriae* power to protect the interests of helpless citizens within the state. The majority placed primary emphasis on the *parens patriae* rationale, arguing that the contemplated transplant would actually serve the interests of the donor. Their opinion noted psychiatric testimony that the mentally disabled potential donor would suffer emotional trauma from the loss of a sibling who had been loving and supportive of the donor. (The dissent, though, questioned how devastating loss of a sibling would be to a person with the mental capacity of a six-year-old.)[31]

Cases subsequent to *Strunk* generally adopted that court's focus on the *parens patriae* rationale—the promotion of the best interests of the incapacitated ward.[32] These cases usually authorized a transplant where the incapacitated potential donor had an established relationship with the donee so that the transplant (and avoidance of emotional trauma accompanying loss of a loved one) would benefit the donor in significant measure. That analysis was applied not just in cases of healthy minors as donors but in some cases of mentally disabled children and adults as well. A 1979 Texas case is illustrative. In *Little v. Little*,[33] a Texas court applied a best-interests analysis to authorize a kidney transplant from a fourteen-year-old girl with Down's syndrome to her younger brother who was suffering from end-stage renal disease. The judges—noting the close relationship between the donor and donee, the donor's "genuine concern" for her sibling's welfare, and the possibility of her increased self-esteem stemming from the donation—found that the evidence of "substantial psychological benefits" to the donor was enough to justify the transplant.[34] In *In re Doe*,[35] a New York court found that a bone-marrow transplant from an institutionalized forty-three-year-old with the mental capacity of a two-year-old to his stricken thirty-six-year-old brother would be in the best interests of the disabled donor. According to the court, the benefit to the donor (survival of his brother who had been the exclusive family participant in treatment decisions on behalf of the donor) would outweigh any discomforts or risks associated with the tissue donation.

A 1972 Connecticut case diverged somewhat from this pattern while still approving a kidney transplant from a minor donor. The case, *Hart v. Brown*,[36] involved a donation from a healthy seven-year-old twin to her stricken twin sister. The lower-court judge (the case never went beyond that level) did not speak strictly in best-interests terms. He noted that "some benefit" to the donor would flow from avoidance of an emotional loss as well as from preservation of a happy, less stressed family unit. He then ruled that "justice" would be accomplished by approving the parental decision in light of the modest risks and burdens associated with the kidney donation. Yet the judge did not spell out why justice would be promoted.

Three cases applied the best-interests standard in common with the majority of courts but diverged by disapproving a proposed transplant as not being in the best interests of the incapacitated donor. In a 1973 Louisiana case,[37] a father sought judicial authorization for a kidney transplant from his seventeen-year-old son (a child with Down's syndrome and the mental function of a four-year-old) to his thirty-two-year-old daughter suffering from chronic kidney disease. Apparently the daughter had not been involved in caring for her disabled brother. The court ruled that the only prospective benefit to the donor—future care and support from his donee sister—was purely speculative and unlikely, so that the prospective donation could not be deemed to be in the interests of the profoundly disabled donor. In a 1975 Wisconsin case,[38] one sister, as guardian, sought to secure a kidney transplant from her thirty-nine-year-old catatonic schizophrenic brother (with a mental age of twelve) to a thirty-eight-year-old, critically ill sister. The Wisconsin court, applying a best-interests-of-the-ward approach, could perceive no significant benefit to the disabled potential donor and refused to authorize a transplant. Finally, a 1990 Illinois decision[39] took an approach similar to that of the Wisconsin court. The court ruled that a bone-marrow transplant could not be in the best interests of three-and-one-half-year-old twin potential donors where the prospective recipient was a half-brother with whom the twins had no substantial interaction.[40]

In sum, most of the courts that have spoken to the issue of organ and tissue transplants from mentally incapacitated donors have purported to apply a best-interests-of-the-donor standard—one requiring that the net benefits to the donor exceed the detriments (risks and impositions). That standard has considerable doctrinal support. As chapter 4 indicates, courts generally articulate a best-interests standard as governing surrogate medical decisions on behalf of profoundly disabled persons. (There, the focus was on sterilization, abortion, and end-of-life decisions.) The best-interests standard is consistent with the *parens patriae* rationale—government protection of helpless beings—that serves as the primary justification for judicial involvement in the handling of incapacitated persons. A best-interests approach can also fit an alternative rationale—implementing what the now incapacitated patient would want if somehow capable of self-determination—when used in the context of never competent persons. While a substituted-judgment approach is generally unsuited to a never competent person, it is at least plausible to project that an always incapacitated person—never having developed any idiosyncratic values—would want to have his or her personal well-being or net interests advanced.[41] A conceptual basis, then, exists for using the best interests of the patient as the appropriate legal boundary governing the profoundly disabled patient's medical fate. This is especially so because decisions regarding organ transplants are (as chapter 3 clarifies) usually placed in judicial rather than parental hands.

There is considerable doubt about whether the best-interests standard gets conscientiously applied in practice. A number of commentators suggest that the courts commonly engage in distortions or "mental gymnastics" when they find that an organ donation is in the net interests of a profoundly disabled donor.[42] David Price calls the psychiatric evidence in many cases "dubious and contrived."[43] The thrust of this criticism is that courts (and perhaps the psychologists who offer expert testimony) both overstate the benefits (to the donor) and underplay the risks of organ transplantation in their zeal to salvage a human life. The saga of Tommy Strunk provides an example. Commentators question (as did the dissent in *Strunk v. Strunk*) whether loss of a sibling would really have a severe negative impact on the mentally incapacitated donor (who had the mental function of a six-year-old). That same question can be posed in the case of any profoundly disabled potential donor. Indeed, in both *In re Richardson* and *In re Pescinski*, mentioned above, courts did not credit claims that a proposed kidney donation would ultimately benefit the disabled donor (by the avoidance of a traumatic loss).

Other claimed benefits may be contrived or exaggerated. In *In re Doe*,[44] which involved an institutionalized, profoundly disabled potential donor, the court speculated that the institutionalized donor would be severely harmed by loss of the organ donee who had been the lone family member participating in decision making for the donor. This gave the benefit of all doubt to a protransplantation decision by assuming that no conscientious guardian would fill any void left by the donee's demise and that subsequent staff decisions might well be contrary to the donor's interests. Similar speculation clouds other courts' assessments of a prospective benefit to the organ or tissue donor in the form of pride or self-satisfaction from an altruistic act. The earliest cases of minors' organ donation involved adolescents who could definitely grasp and experience the psychological benefits of altruism. However, the likelihood of psychological benefit in the form of enhanced self-esteem is more doubtful in the case of small children or profoundly mentally disabled individuals. It seems speculative to claim in such instances that the good feelings associated with being a samaritan will materialize and will outweigh the discomforts and anxieties that accompany the surgical procedures. And yet that element sometimes appears as a justification in such cases.

The decided cases also exhibit a tendency to minimize certain risks that accompany organ and tissue donation. For instance, there is some risk of psychological harm to the donor if the donated tissue is rejected.[45] This factor ought to play some role in bone-marrow donation, where the ultimate failure rate is significant, yet it appears to get little attention. Perhaps overlooking this risk factor is problematic only in cases that involve older children or adolescents (rather than profoundly disabled donors), but perhaps the phenomenon reflects a broad tendency of courts to strain to reach a result favoring transplantation. Such a broad tendency would account for distortions in the application of the best-interests standard. Another risk is that a profoundly disabled donor will have a particularly traumatic reaction to the transplant process because of a lack of understanding about the reasons for the bodily invasion. That possibility is either ignored or afforded lip service in the cases.[46]

Another questionable practice is apparent in the cases that purport to apply a best-interests-of-the-patient standard to organ and tissue donation. These courts concede that incapacitated patients ought not be utilized as donors unless alternative solutions are unavailable to the stricken potential donee. Yet for the most part, the courts dismiss the alternatives of dialysis or donation from other family members as unacceptable. In these instances, the incapacitated potential donor is a better match, with tissue more compatible and less likely than other donors' to prompt rejection by the donee's immune system.[47] Perhaps it is self-evident that the greater immunological compatibility of the incapacitated donor warrants putting aside the alternative solutions.[48] (It did not seem so self-evident, though, to the *Richardson* court, which ruled against using a disabled potential donor in favor of another relative who had a greater chance of causing organ rejection.) Perhaps courts are, in practice, slanting decisions toward authorizing transplantation not because such a result represents the net best interests of the disabled donor but because the impetus to try and save the donee's life is so strong.[49]

The reported cases at least present a distinct possibility, if not probability, that surrogate decisions to harvest organs and tissue from disabled donors are not really promoting the net interests of the donors. Does that phenomenon represent a shocking exploitation of helpless beings? Is this simply utilitarianism with an undercurrent of bias toward disabled persons who are deemed less valuable than other human beings? Or is there a principled basis to permit some imposition of sacrifice on a profoundly disabled person's bodily resources to promote the welfare of others? I turn to that issue after examining the regulatory framework that governs medical research on mentally incapacitated subjects.

The Legal and Moral Frameworks Governing Nontherapeutic Medical Research

No central authority controls medical research in the United States, and no uniform legal boundaries exist. Medical research is governed by a variety of legal sources, including federal regulations applicable to federally funded research and state law drawn both from statutes and judicially formulated tort law.[50] However, state law on medical research is fairly sparse, especially law relating to research on mentally incapacitated subjects. And as is discussed below, the federal regulations dealing with nontherapeutic research on incapacitated subjects do not provide definitive guidance.

Some principles and established practices do exist that shape the evolving regulatory framework for medical research. The origins of the principles go back to the Nuremburg Code, which was formulated by judges at the trials of German doctors who had conducted unconscionable experiments on nonconsenting people during World War II. In the United States, the development of principles has been influenced by diverse sources—by national commissions, by guidelines adopted by professional bodies, and by study panels at the state level. (For example, the American Medical Association and the American College of Physicians have, over the years, suggested ethical guidelines for medical research.)

Modern American focus on the legal and ethical boundaries of medical research can be dated to 1974, when Congress reacted to publicity about the U.S. Public Health Service's infamous syphilis experiments in Tuskegee, Alabama, by establishing a National Commission for the Protection of

Human Subjects of Biomedical and Behavioral Research (hereinafter, the National Commission). Over the next five years, the National Commission issued several reports, including one report dealing with the institutionalized mentally disabled, that were accompanied by proposed regulations. Its final report, known as the Belmont Report, was published in 1979 and strongly influenced the subsequent issuance of federal regulations.[51] The Belmont Report articulated several principles applicable to medical research, including respect for persons (dictating respect for autonomous choice and protection for persons not capable of autonomous choice), beneficence (dictating minimization of research risks and attention to risk/benefit ratios), and justice (dictating fair distribution of the burdens of undergoing research). While the Belmont Report talked about institutional review boards (IRBs) and legally authorized representatives (LARs) as protective devices, it did not spell out a standard (such as best interests of the patient) to govern surrogate decisions on behalf of incapacitated potential research subjects.

For purposes of this chapter, the key question is whether it is legally and morally permissible for a surrogate decision maker to submit a profoundly disabled person to medical research that has no reasonable prospect of benefit to that disabled person. The previous chapter establishes that American jurisprudence purports to impose a *parens patriae* approach to the medical handling of never competent persons. That paternalistic approach focuses on the personal interests of the mentally incapacitated person—usually demanding that surrogate efforts benefit that person in some measure, if not to promote that person's net best interests. In the context of medical research, surrogate consent to nontherapeutic medical research would seem incompatible with adherence to a standard focusing on the research subject's interests.[52] Contemporary commentators wonder regularly whether there is any justification for subjecting profoundly disabled people to nontherapeutic research, at least where the research carries more than minimal risk of harm to the helpless subject.[53] (While these commentators seem to assume the moral acceptability of nontherapeutic research carrying minimal risk, I have already argued that even minimal-risk research on never competent subjects needs some moral rationale.) Both the legality and morality of nontherapeutic medical research on profoundly disabled persons deserve examination.

As early as 1970, Paul Ramsey argued that only therapeutic medical research—research carrying a reasonable prospect of ameliorating a patient's condition—could morally be conducted on incapacitated subjects (such as children). He asserted that nontherapeutic research yielding benefits for other stricken children or future generations of children could not be moral because from his perspective it would treat the helpless human subject as only a means or an object.[54] That stance rejecting the validity of nontherapeutic research on never competent persons subsequently struck a responsive chord in some circles. In 1978, the U.S. Department of Health, Education, and Welfare (HEW) expressed uneasiness about such research and indicated that it was considering a ban (which never materialized).[55] Some state laws do ban nontherapeutic research on mentally incapacitated subjects. The Council of Europe confines research on incapacitated subjects to that carrying a prospect of a significant direct benefit to the subjects' health.[56] In the 1990s, three expert study panels—the National Bioethics Advisory Commission, a New York task force, and a Maryland working group—all concluded that a surrogate who is deciding about medical research on a never competent person should be bound by the best interests of the incapacitated person.[57] Adherence to a best-interests standard would seem to preclude nontherapeutic research, at least where the research involves more than minimal risk of harm or discomfort.[58]

That thesis is supported by a recent Maryland case called *Grimes v. Kennedy Krieger Institute*.[59] *Grimes* involved research concerning the effectiveness of various modes of lead-paint abatement. The research protocol anticipated that some children who lived in the rehabilitated housing would experience elevated blood lead levels (which would be monitored and treated). Although parents had consented to family participation in the research, some parents later sued, claiming tortious conduct in the researchers' slow or inaccurate reporting of blood lead levels and in a research protocol that knowingly exposed children to lead paint. Maryland's highest court ruled that the suit raised legitimate legal claims and could proceed to trial. As to the parental consent to children's participation, the court stated that it was inherently inappropriate and wrong to use healthy children in nontherapeutic research carrying a risk of harm (possible elevated blood lead levels).[60] The court repudiated any surrogate authority to subject children to nontherapeutic research aimed at benefitting children generally.[61]

Despite this skepticism about a surrogate's authorization of nontherapeutic research, the prevailing view in American jurisprudence is that surrogates may legally consent to at least some forms of nontherapeutic research. As early as 1966, American Medical Association guidelines allowed surrogate consent to nontherapeutic research where competent subjects were not suitable and "under circumstances in which an informed and prudent adult would reasonably be expected to volunteer himself or his child as a subject."[62] This presumably meant at least that a parent could submit a child to nontherapeutic research in order to convey a lesson about altruism so long as risks of harm or discomfort were modest. Also in the mid-1960s, institutional protocols apparently provided that consent for medical research on mentally incapacitated persons could be obtained either from appointed guardians or next of kin.[63] In 1978, the Department of Health, Education, and Welfare published proposed regulations to govern medical research on institutionalized, mentally infirm persons. Those regulations would have allowed surrogate consent to nontherapeutic, minimal-risk research so long as the potential subject did not object.[64] Moreover, HEW would have authorized nontherapeutic research that carried a minor increase over minimal risk if the anticipated scientific knowledge were of vital importance, if the patient's surrogate consented, and if a court gave authorization.[65] The proposed regulations were unclear about the fate of extremely incapacitated potential research subjects. HEW indicated that it was considering a ban on use of profoundly disabled residents (incapable of assent) in more than minimal-risk research.[66] Also, proposed section 46.409 indicated that for research on institutionalized children, a special advocate would be responsible for safeguarding each child's best interests. That seemed to leave the possibility of nontherapeutic research on institutionalized children in some doubt, as nontherapeutic research is hard to reconcile with a best-interests standard. Perhaps the proposed regulations intended to permit more than minimal-risk, nontherapeutic research if approved by a court, but to require a special advocate to intervene and withdraw a subject from a research project if significant harm or discomfort materialized. The proposed regulations were never adopted because they were deemed to be too restrictive on researchers.

The Belmont Report in 1979 and the federal regulations that were adopted in its wake both accepted, in principle, nontherapeutic research on mentally incapacitated persons. The Belmont Report, in speaking to risk/benefit determinations to be made by institutional review boards in approving research protocols, stated that "interests other than those of the subject may on some occasions be sufficient by themselves to justify the risks involved."[67] In short, the National Commission that issued the report felt that benefit to society in the form of increased scientific knowledge could outweigh some risks or inconveniences to incapacitated research subjects. According to the Commission, nontherapeutic research on children could be justified by the need to find effective ways to treat childhood diseases. While acknowledging that research going beyond minimal risks raises "a difficult ethical problem," the Commission noted that the wholesale exclusion of such research "would rule out much research promising great benefit to children in the future."[68] Similarly, the prohibition of nontherapeutic research on mentally incapacitated adults would impair development of important knowledge about neurological or psychiatric disorders. While the Commission did expect surrogates to safeguard the interests of incapacitated subjects, it did not preclude surrogate consent to nontherapeutic research.

The current federal regulations (known as the Common Rule) essentially adopt the Belmont Report's position regarding nontherapeutic research on incapacitated persons. In speaking to an institutional review board's consideration of risk/benefit ratios, the regulations demand that risks be reasonable "in relation to anticipated benefits, *if any*, to subjects, and the importance of the knowledge that may reasonably be expected to result."[69] This language is commonly regarded as indicating that prospective gains in scientific knowledge can, by themselves, warrant exposure of incapacitated persons to some research risks. The authorization of nontherapeutic research is even more explicit in the regulations that speak to research on children. There, research involving a minor increase over minimal risk is accepted, in principle, where the research can ultimately lead to the cure of the same disease as the one that afflicts the research subject.[70] The Common Rule acknowledges the vulnerability of incapacitated subjects and gives discretion to institutional review boards to impose "additional safeguards." But the primary protections against unconscionable exploitation in the research setting are supposed to come from the institutional review board's scrutiny of protocols and informed consent by a surrogate authorized by state law to make medical decisions on behalf of an incapacitated person. The question remains whether there is any convincing moral rationale for surrogates to subject incapacitated persons to medical-research procedures calculated to benefit persons other than the incapacitated person. I turn to that issue.

Justifications for Seeking Sacrifice from Profoundly Disabled Persons

Utilitarianism as a Rationale for Exploitation

A possible justification for allowing the harvesting of nonvital tissue from a never competent person, or for using such a being in the conduct of non-therapeutic research, is to accomplish the greatest good for the greatest number. If a mentally incapacitated donor will undergo only modest inconvenience and risk, and if the donee will likely receive a life-extending benefit, then the authorization of a kidney transplant promotes the net human welfare of the involved parties. Some commentators on organ donation perceive disguised utilitarianism as the actual explanation for the cases authorizing a surrogate's decision to allow an organ or a tissue transplant from an incapacitated patient. They see the putative psychological benefits to the donor as speculative and contrived, and they view benefit to the donee as the primary factor moving the surrogate decision makers.[71]

A similar utilitarian calculus might explain the use of a mentally incapacitated person as a subject in medical research that poses little risk to the subject but promises to yield significant knowledge likely to advance medical science and ultimately benefit other people. Unless never competent persons can be used in some nontherapeutic medical research, future generations of similarly situated persons will be deprived of important medical advances. This would represent a considerable social loss that might outweigh modest risks and discomforts to never competent research subjects. Some commentators on nontherapeutic medical research accordingly perceive net social benefit as the main justification for using mentally incapacitated persons as research subjects.[72] John Harris, noting the importance of some research that can be done only on incapacitated persons, argues that the social gain warrants minor impositions on a disabled subject. He contends that "a just and ethical society" must deem a technical battery on an incapacitated research subject to be "less of an evil than injury to the future beneficiaries of the research."[73] He gives no reason why it's ethical to perform any bodily imposition on a never competent person other than the enormous social gains over time.

The application of a utilitarian rationale to justify medical interventions that are aimed at promoting the well-being of others poses serious moral and ethical concerns. It is one thing to allow a competent person to make medical sacrifices in order to benefit others. Fully informed adults may agree to donate tissue to a needy donee, to participate in nontherapeutic medical research, or to forgo life-extending care in consideration of the emotional or financial burdens being imposed on loved ones. Autonomous choices that are based on altruistic values, personal satisfactions, or perceived moral obligations justify any burdens entailed. It is quite another thing to impose comparable sacrifices on profoundly disabled persons who have never developed altruistic values and who will never grasp or appreciate the virtue that is displayed in undergoing the medical procedures.

One hurdle to using a utilitarian rationale to justify the nontherapeutic exploitation of mentally incapacitated patients flows from the incommensurability of the various burdens and benefits entailed. How can the physical inconvenience or pain of the incapacitated patient be weighed against the extension of a family member's life (in the case of an organ transplant) or against the future welfare of other patients (in the case of nontherapeutic medical research)? How much burden on the incapacitated patient is warranted, for example, by a 35 percent chance of extending another person's life for one year? How much risk of infection or of other adverse consequences is warranted? This concern about the incommensurability in weighing one person's medical interests against the interests of a related donee, against the overall family's welfare, or against the interests of future medical patients is exacerbated when the patient to be exploited is profoundly disabled. The patient may be so cognitively impaired and so noncommunicative that assessment of the patient's feelings and emotions is extremely difficult, yet those feelings and emotions form a critical element in any utilitarian balancing process. Moreover, the hazard of a surrogate decision maker's prejudice or undervaluing of the disabled patient's personal stature may be lurking in some measure.

While there's a strong practical impetus to exploit never competent persons as research subjects, a utilitarian justification seems unacceptable. Under simple utilitarianism, important potential gains in medical knowledge might justify repulsive exploitation of profoundly disabled persons. The greater the potential research gains, the greater the sacrifice that can be imposed. Moreover, to the extent that utilitarianism would justify overriding the objecting will of profoundly disabled persons for the primary benefit of others, it threatens to relegate disabled persons to a secondary moral status. Respect for persons does not normally allow nonthreatening citizens to be bodily exploited against their will in order to benefit other citizens. Simple utilitarianism would thus contradict a central premise of American jurisprudence—that profoundly disabled persons have full moral status despite their intellectual deficits.

A utilitarian justification thus seems inconsistent with American jurisprudence. The prevailing legal framework clearly disfavors imposed sacrifice in the form of unconsented bodily invasions geared to benefitting others. As noted, a competent person can choose to donate a nonvital organ, but that person cannot be compelled to donate bodily tissue even to satisfy the critical needs of others or to advance scientific progress.[74] This does not mean that bodily integrity is so sacrosanct that it is immune from nonconsensual invasion. A child attending school may be compulsorily vaccinated or a driver involved in an automobile accident may be compelled to undergo a blood test. And it is conceivable that a court would compel a person to submit to life-sustaining medical intervention to preserve the well-being of that person's dependent.[75] But all of these bodily invasions involve circumstances where the person to be intruded on poses some kind of threat to the welfare of others—not a situation where an entirely innocuous person is invaded to promote the interests of others. Similarly, as the cases that govern organ donation and sterilization proclaim, the emphasis of *parens patriae* on best interests normally prevents a surrogate from exploiting a profoundly disabled person's body, even for a great benefit to others.

The moral hurdle might be surmountable, so that a utilitarian calculus could be applied, if the profoundly disabled patient or research subject were not deemed a person or were deemed a person with greatly reduced moral stature. Chapter 1 notes the philosophical controversy about whether all live human beings qualify for full moral status and for accompanying entitlement to insulation from being exploited to further net human interests or well-being. A number of philosophers contend that only "persons" enjoy full moral status, and they define *persons* according to a requisite level of intellectual capacity.[76] A few, like Kant, demand moral agency—the capacity to reason and grasp moral principles—as a prerequisite to personhood. Others demand a lower but still significant level of mental capacity—sufficient intellectual function for reason, self-awareness, or capacity to value existence.[77] Under these approaches, conditioning personhood on a level of reasoning ability as opposed to mere sentience (capacity for pleasure and pain), some human beings, including some profoundly mentally disabled beings, would be excluded from personhood. A status of nonpersonhood might then provide a moral foundation for treating profoundly mentally disabled humans as exploitable to further the interests of other humans.

A variation on this theme appeared in a 1995 report by the American Medical Association's Council on Ethical and Judicial Affairs (CEJA) that dealt with the handling of anencephalic infants—infants born without the portion of the brain controlling consciousness or cognitive function.[78] Anencephalic infants are fated to die within a brief period. CEJA initially suggested (the report was later withdrawn) that organs could be harvested from these infants even if that medical intervention would accelerate the infant's deaths. The justification for the harvesting lay in the utilitarian interests of others. The parents could then derive some satisfaction from what otherwise might be an unmitigated horror (the birth and death of the anencephalic), and other infants might benefit from the harvested tissue or organs. CEJA regarded anencephalic infants as unique because they were never conscious humans and lacked normal interests in continued existence. In effect, CEJA proposed to treat anencephalics as nonpersons or as persons with diminished moral status who do not enjoy normal protection against being exploited via bodily invasions for the benefit of others.[79]

As chapters 1 and 2 note, neither the law nor social practice regards profoundly mentally disabled human beings, even permanently unconscious human beings, as nonpersons. The claim that anencephalics have such diminished human interests or status that their tissue or organs may be harvested to benefit others has never prevailed. The main judicial precedent on point, a Florida case, rejected a parental petition for judicial authorization of the harvesting of a vital organ from an anencephalic infant.[80] Likewise, no state has adopted the position that permanently unconscious humans may be deemed dead. Such humans are biologically alive, and death is understood to mean the end of biological life.

American law thus accords full personhood to profoundly disabled beings. Even the jurisprudence allowing surrogate decision makers to withdraw life support from permanently unconscious persons does not contradict that thesis. The surrogate's prerogative to withdraw such life support recognizes the full legal and moral status of a permanently unconscious being and is grounded on the intrinsically undignified status of a person who is mired in permanent unconsciousness. This contention finds support in a few of the cases that relate to the medical handling of permanently unconscious persons. Most judicial opinions on the subject are somewhat murky about why surrogates can legally dictate the removal of life support from permanently unconscious wards. Some opinions refer to best interests without spelling out how death promotes those interests; others simply note that the patient has no positive experiential interests to preserve. But a few opinions do refer to the unconscious patient's dignity interest as a critical part of the surrogate's considerations in deciding to remove life support.[81]

The bottom line is that our culture does not treat profoundly disabled persons (even permanently unconscious ones) as nonpersons or as persons with diminished moral status.[82] Diminished moral status, then, cannot justify the application of a utilitarian calculus to profoundly disabled persons. Nor can it account for law's willingness to allow profoundly disabled persons to be subject to some nontherapeutic medical research and to be the source of tissue donations even where those donations will not likely promote the disabled patient's own interests. Some other rationale must account for the currently prevailing practices if they are to be upheld as moral.

Ascribing Altruism to Never Competent Persons

As noted in chapters 2 and 4, one approach to surrogate decision making for incompetent medical patients is to employ a substituted-judgment standard. Under that approach, the surrogate decision maker is supposed to construct the same decision that the now incompetent patient would make if the patient were somehow miraculously competent and aware of all the circumstances at hand, including the patient's diminished capacity. The object of using substituted judgment is to respect the now incompetent patient's dignity and humanity in two ways—by honoring self-determination (to the extent that the patient's actual preferences can be discerned) and by providing the patient with the same range of potentially beneficial medical options that a competent patient would have in the medical circumstances facing the patient. While the now incompetent patient is incapable of personally choosing among medical options, a surrogate can still seek to make the same choice that the patient would have made.

The substituted-judgment standard works well enough in handling previously competent persons. In that setting, inquiry can be made into the patient's competently expressed wishes, values, and preferences in order to project what the patient would want done in the circumstances. Even in the absence of previously expressed wishes or a well-developed value system, some medical decisions can be attributed to previously competent patients based on knowledge about what the vast majority of persons would want done in the circumstances facing the patient. If we know what the strong majority of persons would choose for themselves (based on common understandings about best interests, including dignity), then it makes sense to attribute a similar choice to the formerly competent patient unless that person's background or history indicates deviation from the common preferences. For example, because the vast majority of people do not want themselves to be medically sustained in a permanently unconscious state, a choice to reject life support in such a state can fairly be attributed to a formerly competent patient absent any indicia that the patient would choose otherwise.

We have no similar foundation on which to base medical decisions concerning never competent persons, especially medical decisions where the primary beneficiary is someone other than the patient. The never competent patient has always lacked the mental capacity to make informed judgments about the values and interests connected to any important medical decision. That patient has never been able to decide whether to take an antibiotic, let alone whether to donate tissue to a needy potential recipient or to participate in a nontherapeutic medical-research project. A profoundly disabled person typically has not developed a value system that favors altruistic behavior in general and medical sacrifice in particular.

Although a few courts talk about substituted judgment in the context of never competent patients, they don't really apply that standard. Rather, they end up weighing the various interests of the helpless never competent person.[83] This transformation of a substituted-judgment approach into a best-interests approach is not surprising in the context of never competent patients. A substituted-judgment approach seeks to honor the human status of a now incompetent person by striving to follow the medical course that the patient herself would want followed. Although we can't say much about what medical course a profoundly disabled person would actually choose, perhaps it is reasonable to assume that such a person, if miraculously competent, would act in accordance with the person's own best interests.[84] However, if the best interests of the patient is the applicable standard for never competent persons, it does not provide a rationale for subjecting a profoundly disabled patient to nontherapeutic research or for organ donation (other than to a donee who is intimately involved in caring for the disabled donor).

When the prospective organ or tissue donor is a child, a possible rationale in support of an altruistic medical choice is projection of the child's *future* preferences. The idea seems to be that it is moral to make surrogate decisions that affect a child according to values that the child will eventually embrace. The further argument is that the typical child will eventually adopt the values that most adults hold, such as a willingness to engage in at least modestly altruistic behavior. Since statistics show that the vast majority of adults would donate bone marrow to a critically needy sibling, we should assume (the argument goes) that a young child will eventually share the same willingness.[85] That rationale seems problematic even for children who have full developmental potential. Adults' decisions to engage in altruistic behavior such as organ or tissue donation are often partly grounded in contemporaneous experiential satisfactions accompanying the donation process. An adult may choose to be a donor because of personal values (a belief in the nobility of the act or in a moral obligation) or because of personal satisfactions including self-esteem or the gratitude of the donee and surrounding family members.[86] A small child cannot appreciate those contemporaneous experiential benefits, so the transposition of the adult preferences to the setting of the small child is a distortion; the adult choices reflect factors that cannot motivate the small child.[87]

Whatever the temptation to ascribe altruism to the future choices of children, that approach cannot be employed in the context of lifelong profoundly disabled persons. Profoundly disabled persons will never develop personal values concerning altruism or compassion for others and will never experience gratifications such as self-esteem and satisfaction that flow from the praise and gratitude of the beneficiaries of the altruistic behavior. It seems hollow, then, to connect never competent persons with the altruistic choices of competent persons when the latter choices are so tied up with values and experiences that the never competent patient cannot enjoy:[88] "[G]enerosity exercised for one who cannot speak for himself or herself is not, in fact, generosity, but imposition."[89]

Some commentators, though, regard unwillingness to ascribe altruism to mentally disabled persons as an affront to the dignity or humanity of those persons.[90] Their perspective is that because many competent persons perform altruistic acts (indeed, the vast majority of competent persons would donate tissue to a critically needy family member), to preclude all altruistic surrogate choice on behalf of an incompetent individual "is fundamentally to disrespect the incompetent and treat him as less than human."[91]

One judge, dissenting in a case in which the Wisconsin Supreme Court refused to authorize a kidney transplant from a profoundly disabled potential donor, deeply lamented the incompetent's fate as "always a receiver, a taker, but never a giver . . . , forever excluded from doing the decent thing, the charitable thing."[92] That judge would have assumed the goodness of the incompetent person's nature, thus endowing the potential donor "with the finest qualities of his humanity."[93] Others also consider a narrow judicial focus on an incompetent potential donor's best interests as projecting an impoverished view of the incompetent patient's nature.[94]

Respect for the intrinsic human dignity of a profoundly disabled person is indeed a critical object in shaping public policy concerning surrogate authority. And for some commentators, it seems disparaging of profoundly disabled persons' humanity to foreclose all surrogate choices benefitting persons other than the disabled person, especially where no significant risk is posed to the disabled being.[95] But I cannot view failure to ascribe altruistic choices to profoundly disabled persons as an impingement of intrinsic human dignity. While many people choose to be charitable and self-sacrificing, that route is a matter of individual choice. People's choices to act altruistically are grounded either on actual or anticipated benefits (personal satisfaction) or on the fulfillment of personal value choices. Both satisfaction from altruistic acts and formation of altruistic values seem beyond the capacity of profoundly disabled persons.

Failure to ascribe altruistic values to disabled persons does not label them as inhumane, undignified, selfish, or self-absorbed; it simply accepts some consequences of their limited intellectual function. Chapter 2 points out that respecting the dignity of profoundly disabled persons entails giving surrogate decision makers some, but not all, options that would be available to competent persons. Some kinds of decisions are so tied up with personal tastes and values that they cannot be assigned to surrogate choice. Marriage and voting are two examples. Excluding these kinds of surrogate choices does not reflect a social judgment that the profoundly disabled person is inhuman or undignified or has made a volitional decision to disparage these human institutions.

Ascription of "humane" values to profoundly disabled persons would pose serious questions about the nature and scope of the values to be ascribed. Many competent people are charitable. If benevolent inclinations were then attributed to profoundly disabled persons (and their personal estates), to what charities would contributions be made and in what measure? And which noble sentiments can be attributed to never competent persons? Consider the case of a moderately retarded, pregnant woman whose guardian applied for authorization to have an abortion performed. The lower court judge wanted to ascribe to the pregnant woman a humane concern for the fetus's potential life and therefore refused to authorize an abortion. An appellate court overturned the judge's decision and granted the abortion petition based on the pain and discomfort that childbirth would cause for the pregnant woman.[96] The lower-court judge's attribution of a prolife value to the incompetent patient illustrates the hazard of ascribing "humane values" to disabled persons.

Shannon Jordan suggests a different rationale for attributing values to never competent persons. She argues that decisions made on behalf of never competent persons can be grounded in part on the fact that each person is born into a particular family, faith community, or tradition with a set of beliefs that would likely influence the person's character (presumably meaning development of character consistent with the limited intellectual capacity of the person).[97] She is apparently willing, therefore, to ascribe certain beliefs or values of the surrounding family and community to the never competent person.

This attribution of values to a never competent person seems dubious to me. True, ascribing the family's values seems less officious or problematic than the judge's attempt to ascribe an extrinsic value (solicitude for fetal life) as described above. Yet if it's okay to circumcise or to baptize a profoundly disabled infant, I don't think it's because we can assume that the infant believes (or will believe) in the religious tradition involved. Society allows the parents to perform the religious rituals because society permits parents—as part of their child-rearing prerogative—to seek the spiritual well-being of their children short of practices that would entail serious negative consequences (such as parental failure to secure a critically needed blood transfusion). I don't think that societal acquiescence in parents' religious management of small children signifies a willingness to ascribe certain values, including altruism, to profoundly disabled persons. On the other hand, the existence of parental prerogatives does present another possible rationale for understanding why surrogates might be allowed to make decisions for disabled persons that don't principally advance the disabled persons' well-being. I turn to the question of parental prerogatives.

Parental Child-Rearing Prerogatives

Parental autonomy may account for some instances when a surrogate is permitted to demand a sacrifice from an incapacitated tissue donor or research subject.[98] This might be so, for example, where a parent is the surrogate decision maker behind a decision to have a profoundly disabled child donate tissue or an organ to a critically ill sibling. Similarly, parental autonomy may even encompass a parent's decision to involve a child in nontherapeutic medical research for the good of the general community. Thomas Murray suggests:

> [I]nvolving children in activities that impose no significant hazards on those children but that may contribute to other [social] goods and values even though the child may not benefit directly is well within the circle of morally permissible parental discretion. Non-therapeutic research, when the risks are truly minimal and the benefits to others potentially substantial, is just that kind of activity.[99]

Parents have long been entitled to make decisions for a child that may disadvantage or derogate the interests of that child in some measure. In the course of raising children and controlling the education, associations, recreation, duties, and responsibilities of children, parents can subordinate one child's interests for the benefit of siblings, parents, or the family as a whole. An imposed sacrifice on children can occur in myriad ways.[100] One sibling can be impelled to defer college or make other money-saving sacrifices to help finance another sibling's college education. An older sibling may have to babysit and supervise younger siblings despite the burden and inconvenience. A parent may decide to move a family unit (despite the trauma involved in uprooting a child from a comfortable environment), to dissolve an existing family unit (despite a child's distress at the prospective divorce), or to form a new family unit (despite a child's strong distaste for the prospective stepparent and stepsiblings). Parents are free to make such monumental family decisions notwithstanding any negative impacts on some children within the family.

The risks and impositions typically entailed in tissue or organ donation (or in low-risk nontherapeutic medical research) may well be within the limits that constrain parental autonomy. Indeed, several of the early cases that deal with organ donations from minors to siblings regarded the matter largely as involving limited judicial scrutiny of a parental right and responsibility to control children's medical fate.[101] One commentator describes these cases as reflecting judicial acceptance that "the family as a unit [controlled by parents] is permitted to use its resources and make reasonable sacrifices to save the life of a sick child."[102] Granted, parental demands on children do not commonly involve nontherapeutic bodily invasions. Yet circumcision and ear piercing are certainly permissible when in line with certain religious or cultural norms that are embraced by the parents rather than by the children involved.[103] The usual legal understanding is that parents may control their children's upbringing up to the point of parental abuse or neglect—that is, parental conduct that poses a serious threat to the health or well-being of the child.[104] The traditional parental prerogative includes parental control of medical decisions for an immature child so long as the parental choice falls somewhere within medically acceptable options.[105] The authorization of tissue or organ donation from a minor sibling to preserve the life of an integral family member probably does not pose the kind of unjustified threat to a child's health and well-being that would qualify as abusive or neglectful. Nor does it qualify as unacceptable according to medical ethics.

Deference to parental control of family decision making is not just an element of traditional family law. The U.S. Supreme Court has recognized a parental prerogative in child rearing as a fundamental aspect of the liberty protected by the Fourteenth Amendment. In the recent *Troxel v. Granville* case involving parental control over grandparent visitation, Justice O'Connor commented on behalf of a four-Justice plurality:

Our jurisprudence historically has reflected Western civilization concepts of the family as a unit with broad parental authority over minor children. . . . In light of this extensive precedent, it cannot now be doubted that the Due Process Clause of the Fourteenth Amendment protects the fundamental right of parents to make decisions concerning the care, custody, and control of their children.[106]

On occasion, parental child-rearing liberty can trump the best interests of children, as when religiously motivated Amish parents were deemed entitled to remove their children from mandatory schooling once a basic level of education had been achieved.[107] The Supreme Court ruled that parental control of children's education would yield when parental decisions jeopardize the children's health or safety or threaten to create significant social burdens.[108] Such harm was not shown in the case of the Amish. Their custom of providing formal education only through eighth grade was upheld even though it might well have been in the children's best interests to obtain a high school education.

This is not to say that a state must, as a matter of constitutional mandate, allow parents to make nontherapeutic medical decisions on behalf of their children.[109] While *Troxel* acknowledged a parent's fundamental-liberty interest in controlling a child's interactions with grandparents, the Court did not resolve at what point a state's interest in promoting the child's well-being (such as maintaining contact with grandparents or avoiding exposure to medical risks) could constitutionally justify overriding parental judgment.[110] The constitutional defect in *Troxel* was the state law's failure to give *any* deference to the parent's judgment about the child's contacts with grandparents. The *Troxel* decision specifically declined to rule on whether state interferences with parental discretion must be grounded on determinations of substantial harm to the child (as opposed to a finding that a parental choice deviates from the child's best interests).

As a matter of constitutional law, states are probably free to intervene in parental decision making even without a showing of substantial harm to the child. As noted in chapter 3, at least some states purport to oust parental discretion in the context of various serious medical decisions affecting disabled offspring. For example, courts in some jurisdictions purport to make independent assessments of the best interests of children whenever sterilization, civil commitment, or organ donation is in issue.[111] Also, it is understood in the context of medical research that government could constrain parents from subjecting a child to nontherapeutic medical experimentation. This history tends to show that states can, if they choose, intervene in some kinds of parental decisions affecting children's interests even without a showing of substantial harm to the child.

Even if the Constitution does not mandate state deference to parental decisions in the context of bodily resource donation and medical research, states can and often do choose to show deference to parental medical choices. States commonly accord parents considerable leeway in medical decision making, demanding that a parental course be within reasonable medical bounds and not necessarily that it be the *best* medical choice for the child.[112] This deferential approach is consistent with a public policy of not intervening in the vast bulk of parental child-rearing decisions in the absence of demonstrated child abuse or neglect. Social solicitude is customarily extended to parental control, including a decision-making prerogative in which "the interests of the child may be subordinated to the interests of other children, or indeed even to the interests of the parents or guardians themselves."[113]

Not everyone concedes that parental child-rearing prerogatives include authorization of medical procedures (such as tissue donation or nontherapeutic research) that don't primarily benefit the young child involved. Paul Ramsey, for example, has argued that a parental relationship carries a fiduciary duty of loyalty and protection that is inconsistent with permitting the bodily invasion of a child other than for the child's own benefit.[114] He claims that "no parent is morally competent to consent that his child shall be submitted to hazardous or other experimentation having no diagnostic or therapeutic benefit for the child himself."[115] Some commentators even contend that parents have no legal authority to deviate from their child's best interests in making medical decisions[116]—a claim that seems clearly erroneous to me. In fact, American law has consistently accorded significant leeway to parental child-rearing decisions, including medical decisions. And while the cases purport to preclude parental authorization of tissue donation other than in a minor donor's best interests, courts sometimes apply that principle in a flexible fashion. One recent state court decision rejects any parental prerogative to subject a child to nontherapeutic research involving more than minimal risks.[117] Yet the prevailing legal framework (already described) permits parents to subject their children to some nontherapeutic medical research, including research involving a minor increase over minimal risk.

On what conceptual or moral foundation does deference to parental autonomy lie? Does that foundation adequately support allowing parents to authorize organ and tissue transplants where the incapacitated donor's interests are not principally being advanced? Does that foundation support the subjection of helpless persons to nontherapeutic medical research?

One rationale for deferring to parental control in child rearing is to cultivate a range of values and virtues within a pluralistic society. Parents are the primary vehicle for developing children's values and virtues. While deference to parental control allows some unwholesome values (such as sexism and selfishness) to be promoted, the societal expectation is that a variety of philosophies is salutary and that the values inculcated by parents will generally be sound. Within the diverse values being inculcated, altruism—the willingness to sacrifice for the benefit of others—is certainly a useful value for the community at large. Some commentators therefore view a parental prerogative to authorize nontherapeutic medical interventions for minor children as part of a socially beneficial parental development of their children's values.[118] John Lantos goes further and calls the imposition of altruistic decisions—including sacrifice of bodily tissue to benefit a sibling—a part of parental *responsibility* in morally educating children.[119] While tissue harvesting usually takes place to benefit a disabled person's sibling, parental authority to educate their children is not confined to teaching sacrifice toward loved ones. Parents can encourage their children's contribution to the general welfare or the welfare of specific others (such as via a blood donation to benefit disaster victims).

Of course, the character-development rationale is not always available for parental medical choices that impose some measure of sacrifice on affected children. That rationale may account for parental decisions where the sacrificing children are at an age and mental capacity that permits the absorption of the moral lesson.[120] The educational rationale is more problematic in the context of lifelong, profoundly disabled persons whose absorption of the value lessons is dubious.

An alternative explanation for societal deference to nonbeneficial parental decisions lies in pragmatism. From this perspective, society would like all parental decisions to reflect the best interests of the children involved, but society simply lacks the resources to monitor parental decision making and to intervene whenever parents deviate from best interests.[121] This practical limitation confines social intervention in parental decision making to circumstances of abuse and neglect. While this explanation may account for deference to the vast majority of parental child-rearing decisions, it doesn't account for the leeway allowed to parents in opting for children's participation in nontherapeutic medical experimentation or donation of tissue or organs in circumstances where the best interests of the incapacitated donor are not being furthered. Mechanisms already exist for societal scrutiny of these sorts of medical decisions. As noted in chapter 3, decisions involving bodily invasions aimed at harvesting bodily material for the primary benefit of someone other than the donor-patient are commonly subject to judicial scrutiny. And in the case of medical research, institutional review boards serve as review mechanisms—not for an individual parental decision but for the research protocol that enables physicians to secure parental authorization to enroll children or mentally disabled persons in medical research. The impracticality of scrutinizing, then, does not account for allowing parents to make nontherapeutic medical decisions for their children. Nor does the parental prerogative to develop children's moral values account for decisions affecting profoundly disabled children. Another rationale must account for parental autonomy in these problematic instances of medical decision making.

For some commentators, a mutual moral responsibility associated with family relationships is the foundation of parental authority to demand some sacrifice from children for the benefit of the family as a whole.[122] Under this view, family members, including profoundly disabled family members, share a mutual interdependence and concomitant reciprocal obligation to promote the well-being of the family. Certainly, family members are interdependent in countless ways, and sometimes some members of a family must sacrifice for other members. This phenomenon is unavoidable in any family in which there are multiple participants and limited family resources. While the profoundly disabled child who serves as a tissue donor for a close relative may be sacrificing in some measure (i.e., the personal benefits that the donor will derive from salvaging the relative may not be equal to the impositions), the donor is not simply being exploited as a means to someone else's betterment. As long as a benefit accrues to a family unit that is nurturing the disabled person, the nurtured donor is benefitting in some measure and is serving both as a means and an end.[123]

The imposition of a return duty on a profoundly disabled child in exchange for parental or family care might be grounded on a debt of gratitude for benefits received.[124] However, the notion of a duty of gratitude grates in this context. Isn't gratitude, like altruism, grounded in subjective feelings that are beyond the reach of profoundly disabled persons?[125] Projecting fictitious feelings onto a profoundly disabled person seems as hollow here as in the context of altruism. Calling gratitude a duty here implies that a profoundly disabled person must perform a sacrifice for the family, even to the extent of having the person's violent opposition overridden.

A better explanation for the parental prerogative to demand some sacrifice from children is family justice. Parents raising children must make considerable sacrifices—in terms of time, money, and physical and emotional effort. Perhaps fairness requires that society accord some prerogatives in return, including a prerogative to make some surrogate decisions that don't principally advance a child's interests. Perhaps part of a fair return for parental effort is parental authority to demand some sacrifice from children to assist a close relative for the benefit of the family as a whole.[126]

It does not seem unjust for a surrogate decision maker to take account of the benefits that are bestowed by parents and other family members and the sacrifices that are made by them. Some commentators might object to rewarding parents for deeds performed pursuant to their social duties. For them, parental responsibility flows from the parental act of bringing a helpless child into existence and from social practice assigning duties of care. From that perspective, parents cannot expect reciprocal benefits from their children.[127] To me, parents deserve some consideration for their child-rearing efforts even if they are fulfilling a legal duty. I understand that children may not have a lifelong duty toward parents, but while parents are providing care to profoundly disabled children, those parents deserve recognition.

Not all parents deserve to be able to impose a sacrifice on their profoundly disabled children. Fairness might not demand that sacrifices extracted from children be perfectly commensurate with the benefits that parents have conferred. But it demands that in "pathological cases," where parents have exhibited extreme indifference or cruelty to their profoundly disabled children, parents be deprived of a prerogative to submit their children to bodily sacrifices.[128] This requirement is consistent with the principle of neglect that generally applies in the parent-child context.

Family justice as a rationale for the parental imposition of sacrifice most clearly covers profoundly disabled children who are living at home as part of an integral family unit. That supportive effort by parents and family normally benefits a profoundly disabled person. A family interdependence rationale cannot account for decisions that relate to profoundly disabled persons who are detached from any family unit. Nor can a family-interdependence rationale readily account for parental decisions to subject children to nontherapeutic medical research that is not likely to benefit any family member.

What about children who have been institutionalized and infants who will never leave the hospital where they were born? For example, the harvesting of organs from anencephalic infants cannot be governed by a family-interdependence or family-justice rationale.[129] Some commentators would insist that a close family unit be a precondition to any parental prerogative to exploit one child for the primary benefit of another family member.[130] They would permit a profoundly disabled person to be used as a tissue or organ donor only on behalf of a close family member and in circumstances where the disabled donor is an integral part of the family unit. Ordinarily, this would mean that the profoundly disabled person is living at home. There might, however, be situations where the family is so attentive to an institutionalized, disabled family member that family justice could come into play even in an institutional setting. As to nontherapeutic research, the parent would be making the community a sort of intended beneficiary of the sacrifice that a devoted parent can impose on a profoundly disabled person. Another possible explanation for broad parental prerogatives (to be considered in the next section) is that a social-justice rationale could warrant some imposition of sacrifice on a profoundly disabled person who is not living at home.

Under either aspect of the family-justice rationale—the mutual interdependence of family members or a fair return from parental investment of effort—important questions remain about the bounds of any parental prerogative to demand sacrifice from a profoundly disabled child. As noted, parental child-rearing decisions are usually not displaced unless the parental choice constitutes neglect or abuse. What constitutes abuse in the special context of invasion of bodily integrity and utilization of profoundly disabled children who don't have the intellectual capacity to learn from the bodily sacrifices being imposed? How much sacrifice can a parent opt to impose on such children? What is the source of the moral boundaries that prevent excessive instrumentalization of the profoundly disabled person? And what are those moral boundaries?

Lainie Friedman Ross looks to respect for persons—that is, respect for human dignity—as the principal limit on any parental prerogative to impose sacrifice on children.[131] She views this standard as requiring that medical procedures that are being imposed by parents be confined to circumstances of "no more than a minor increase over minimal risk."[132] For her, this means that a parent could authorize a bone-marrow transplantation but not a kidney donation. (The latter would involve more than a minor increase over minimal risk because anesthesia, surgery, and a hospital stay are required and morbidity is a possible outcome.) Other commentators would pose further constraints on parental authority to allow donation of bodily resources. For example, John Lantos argues that children or disabled persons should be used as tissue donors only if they are the only possible donors—that is, no other compatible donor is available.[133]

I strongly agree with Ross that human dignity—what she calls respect for persons—represents the primary determinant shaping the limits of sacrifice that parents may morally impose on their children. And I agree that the concept of dignity confines the type of bodily invasions and the degree of risk to which parents may subject their children. I am postponing my discussion of the precise limits that flow from the concept of human dignity to the next section, which deals with social justice as a rationale for subjecting profoundly disabled persons to medical procedures that are not strictly in their best interests.

Social Fairness as a Justification for Using the Profoundly Disabled

Commentators have cited a number of possible rationales for allowing surrogates to subject never competent persons to nontherapeutic medical research. Richard McCormick, for instance, relies on the precept that promoting health benefits for all persons is such a preeminent good that everyone *ought* to want to share in that task; he therefore is willing to imply a never competent person's consent to participation in some medical research.[134] My objection to this rationale is similar to my objection—given above—to ascribing altruism to never competent persons. Altruism is a matter of personal satisfaction or personal philosophy rather than a universally accepted moral injunction. So ascribing altruistic sentiments to profoundly disabled persons is an artificial distortion of reality. A surrogate who is seeking to hypothesize what a never competent person would embrace if miraculously competent is on much safer ground by hypothesizing a wish to promote the person's temporal well-being rather than the advancement of medical science.

A more promising rationale for nontherapeutic medical research relies on a concept of justice or fairness that is associated with mutual interdependence within communities. Robert Veatch argues that all members of a community owe some obligation to the common welfare. He comments: "If, in addition to being an end in himself with inalienable rights, the individual is seen as a member of a social community, then certain obligations to the common welfare may be presupposed even in cases where consent is not obtained."[135]

This communitarian perspective seems plausible to me if it is adjusted to require that some measure of benefits be provided by the community to the profoundly disabled person who is being imposed on. As long as the disabled person is receiving benefits—perhaps in the form of decent food, shelter, and care—then some notion of rough social justice may come into play.[136] A conscientious surrogate may justly impose some measure of sacrifice on the profoundly disabled person in return for the social or family child-rearing benefits being conferred on that person. When tissue is donated to a family member within an intact family, the incapacitated donor receives some return benefit in the context of the family itself—either from the grateful donee or from the preservation of a supportive family environment—as opposed to a more generalized social benefit. When an incapacitated person is used as a nontherapeutic research subject, no comparable direct benefit flows to that person from the sacrificial activity. Still, the incapacitated research subject is receiving a general social benefit if he or she is receiving humane care in a public institutional setting or publicly financed support services in a private setting. A conscientious guardian can then determine whether to authorize a nontherapeutic medical procedure as a fair return for social benevolence. Moreover, even if purely private supportive benefits are being provided to the incapacitated research subject, the subject may be receiving some return—in the form of private care and nurturing—for the bodily sacrifice extracted. Conscientious parents may be providing beneficial nurturing that warrants the imposition of some measure of sacrifice in return, and the parents may allow medical science to be their designated beneficiary when imposing sacrifice.[137]

Rough social justice is probably the most that can be achieved. Given the incommensurability of the elements in issue—the support and care received by the disabled person on the one hand and burden, risk, and inconvenience to the disabled research subject on the other—a precise balance or exchange cannot be ensured.[138] Weighing the public and private benefits that are extended to the patient against the burdens to be experienced as a research subject presents hard questions. Is it really fair and just to extract sacrifices from a never competent person—a person who has been nonvolitionally thrust into the circumstances at hand and who, unlike the competent citizen, cannot opt to leave the polity in objection to the sacrifices that a social-justice rationale permits? And how much sacrifice can be imposed by a surrogate?

The use of a social-justice rationale raises a specter of the past abusive exploitation of disabled populations. When Justice Holmes endorsed compulsory sterilization in *Buck v. Bell*,[139] he noted that society can extract considerable sacrifices from some citizens—such as service in war—thereby suggesting that minor surgery and the forgoing of parenthood was little enough to ask of the incompetent persons who were slated for sterilization and who were already burdening public social services. Yet our society has come to regret the abusive sterilization that was senselessly imposed on many thousands of mentally disabled persons.[140]

Other dubious historic practices have also been justified on social-justice grounds. In the 1940s, state institutions for the mentally disabled used moderately disabled residents as unpaid workers and justified the exploitation of their labor as a partial repayment of the costs of care being absorbed by the state.[141] In some past instances, American physicians have subjected disabled patients to quite risky, unconsented medical experiments in the pursuit of scientific advances.[142] The Nazis exterminated mentally disabled persons rather than continue absorbing the social expenditures required for their support. This history of abuse must give pause about using a social-justice rationale to justify sacrifices—such as participation in nontherapeutic medical research or extraction of bodily resources—from profoundly disabled persons. Keep in mind, though, that the issue here is not government-required sacrifices but rather sacrifices authorized by a close family member or other guardian who is bonded to the patient. Keep in mind also that important limitations exist on any "sacrificial" surrogate decisions because such decisions are subject to intrinsic human dignity, which—I suggest—entails serious constraints.

Is it inherently unfair to impose physical sacrifices on people who cannot consent (or perhaps even assent) and who will not themselves benefit from the physical intrusions? Never competent persons have never volitionally assumed any obligation toward their family or toward society. Some commentators would contend that there can be no reciprocity of claims, no quid pro quo, that can fairly be exacted from profoundly disabled beneficiaries of benevolence.[143] From their perspective, sacrifice in return for benefits cannot be imposed on profoundly disabled persons when the benefits are provided as part of a public or private duty to assist helpless persons. One observer labels as "repulsive" the notion that disabled persons should "pay their way through life."[144]

To me, it does not seem intrinsically unfair or inhumane to extract some return from a never competent person who is receiving social benefits. If a profoundly disabled person is resident in a public facility, it seems fair to require that person to keep his or her room neat and to abide by reasonable institutional rules (so long as the requirements are consistent with the person's mental and physical capabilities). If such an institutionalized person receives federal disability payments, states commonly collect a large portion of the payments as partial reimbursement for the costs of food, lodging, and care.[145] If a profoundly disabled person inherits financial assets, it seems fair to tax those assets (pursuant to uniform tax regulations), even if the asset holder gets no proportionate benefit from the government.

Extraction of some sacrifice—even from a profoundly disabled person—seems consistent with the treatment that people get in a representative democracy. Nonvolitional burdens are imposed on competent citizens who, as a practical matter, may not be free to avoid those burdens. This might be so either because the citizen has inadequate resources to move away or because similar burdens would be encountered in most destinations. In a democracy, people, whether or not disabled, are not entitled to an exactly proportionate return for the extractions that society may make. Collectivist impositions on citizens are commonly part of our governmental regulatory framework. A property owner may be injured both emotionally and financially when zoning regulations suddenly prevent the most desired uses of property.[146] Cruel mandatory sentences may be imposed without regard to the mitigating circumstances that surround the individual defendant.[147] And taxpayers pay many exactions without proportionate return. Childless persons are expected to pay taxes to support public school systems. A taxpayer is required to pay taxes to subsidize projects to which the taxpayer is ideologically opposed.

Taxpayers usually get some benefit in return for their money. Disabled residents of public facilities get some benefits in return for participation in research. Of course, fairness and decency demand that the public "return" benefits meet a reasonable quality level.[148] People who are warehoused in inhumane conditions cannot be expected to reciprocate with bodily invasions aimed at helping others. To be fair and humane, the level of sacrifice must be at least roughly commensurate with the benefits received and also suited to the person's mental and physical capabilities (so that the experience is not too burdensome). Perhaps the level of public provision of benefits must at least satisfy Rawlsian justice. That is, the public benefit being provided to the never competent person must be sufficiently large (and the bodily sacrifice sufficiently modest) so that a reasonable person regarding the system from a blind original position would find it acceptable.[149]

As noted earlier, some commentators reject the use of never competent persons in nontherapeutic medical research on the ground that the profoundly disabled subjects are unfairly treated in comparison to able persons. The claim is that never competent persons are forced to be research subjects whereas competent persons choose whether to participate in medical research and are never compelled to do so. Jonathan Moreno, for example, comments that incompetent persons are the only ones on whom a "duty of beneficence" is placed.[150]

This criticism seems misplaced. Properly confined participation in medical research does not entail compulsion of disabled persons—certainly not in the sense of a government that conscripts helpless persons against their will. The issue is surrogate decision making—a choice by a bonded surrogate to allow an incapacitated ward to participate in a research protocol. Some competent persons volunteer to be research subjects, and some never competent persons get volunteered after consideration of the interests and feelings of the vulnerable potential research subject. Disabled persons are not being forced to participate so long as their assent is secured (where they are capable of giving assent) and so long as their objection to participation, even if expressed only by physical resistance, is respected.[151] And as I shortly explain, deference to such resistance can be deemed a precondition of any acceptable framework for surrogate consent to nontherapeutic research or to tissue donation.

To be humane and consistent with full moral status for profoundly disabled persons, a fairness or justice rationale for extracting a sacrifice from profoundly disabled persons must meet other criteria besides the provision of a modicum of return social benefit. For example, government commissions addressing human subject research have long recognized that basic social justice means that disabled populations cannot be exploited—used needlessly or disproportionately in comparison to abled populations— just because of their availability.[152] Also, profoundly disabled persons, as bearers of full moral status, are entitled to have their intrinsic human dignity respected, thus placing further constraints and preconditions on medical research.[153] These constraints relate not just to necessity (the absence of nondisabled research subjects or donors) as a prerequisite to utilizing mentally disabled persons but also to the degree of risk involved, the degree and nature of the bodily invasions, and respect for the will of the disabled person via deference to any objections or opposition manifested by a profoundly disabled ward. I turn now to a consideration of the precise limitations that human dignity imposes on surrogates' extraction of sacrifice from profoundly disabled persons.

The Limits of a Surrogate's Imposition of Sacrifice

I argued earlier that U.S. law treats profoundly disabled humans as persons bearing full moral status despite their intellectual deficits. A central element of that moral stature is respect for intrinsic human dignity, sometimes called respect for persons. The concept of human dignity, in turn, can furnish important limitations on the nature and extent of sacrifices that surrogates can morally (and perhaps legally) impose on mentally incapacitated persons.[154] There must be limits to the possibility that justice within families might enable parents to extract tissue from a profoundly disabled child primarily to benefit others and limits to the possibility that social justice warrants allowing surrogates to consent to the participation of never competent persons in nontherapeutic medical research. Without such limits, increasingly good treatment of disabled persons could warrant surrogates' imposition of increasingly harsh or risky extractions from those disabled persons.

I examine here principally the limits that intrinsic human dignity imposes on nontherapeutic medical research. The context of medical research and experimentation is well suited to exploring the impact of human dignity. At least since the Nuremberg principles were articulated in the late 1940s, physicians have understood that research subjects are, as a matter of human dignity, entitled to protection against exploitation. A succession of commissions, professional organizations, regulatory bodies, and ethics commentators have wrestled with the question of what practices in medical research constitute an unconscionable exploitation of fellow human beings.

The precise bounds of what medical research conduct is unconscionable and hence violative of intrinsic human dignity are not definitively established, especially in the context of research subjects who are incapable of informed consent. There may also be cultural variations in the boundaries that ultimately are to be fixed.[155] Yet a succession of bodies that have examined the ethics of medical research over the last sixty years has produced a consensus about certain principles defining the unconscionable exploitation of fellow human beings. We can thus at least discern a set of emerging principles that respect the human dignity of mentally incapacitated subjects of medical research. For example, widely accepted principles demand that consent be obtained from the subject or an appropriate surrogate, that the research protocol minimize risks, discomforts, anxiety, and pain, and that disabled subjects be used only if necessary.

A centerpiece of the principles applicable to human research is a limit on the level of risks that can be imposed on a research subject. Limits on risk apply even if a research subject is competent and consents to nontherapeutic research with a full understanding of the research and its attendant hazards. Even for such competent subjects (or now incompetent subjects who consented in advance to be research subjects) the risk/benefit ratio must be judged "reasonable." The Nuremberg principles stated that subjects must give informed consent and that "degree of risk should never exceed that determined by the humanitarian importance of the problem to be solved by the experiment."[156] Current federal regulations require that an institutional review board (IRB) that is considering research proposals ensure that "risks to the subject [whether capable of consent or not] are reasonable in relation to anticipated benefits, if any, to subjects, and the importance of the knowledge that may reasonably be expected to result."[157] Where competent persons make informed decisions to participate in medical research, their autonomy may impel them to undertake quite significant risks, but researchers and the institutional review board are still charged with ensuring that the risks entailed are reasonable in relation to anticipated benefits.[158] (A regime could exist in which competent and informed adults were allowed to submit to any kinds of risks in order to further human knowledge and medical science. That approach has not prevailed in the context of medical research. Regulators and commentators have always maintained that some levels of risk or some excessive risk/benefit ratios would be intrinsically wrong or immoral and therefore unacceptable even for competent adults.)

Where surrogates are deciding about consenting to medical research on never competent persons, the absence of autonomous patient choice and the human-dignity concern about exploitation of helpless persons must further constrain the degree of risk allowed. Where nontherapeutic research is in issue, the basis for caution increases. In therapeutic research, a potential benefit to the patient—the promotion of the research subject's own interests—may warrant a considerable degree of risk even for an incapacitated patient.[159] In nontherapeutic research, benefit to others (in the form of advancing medical science) is the main object. Surrogate subjection of mentally incapacitated persons to risk for the purpose of benefitting others is, as previously described, problematic[160] and susceptible to abuse. Potential gains to medical science loom as attractive justifications for subjecting research subjects to risk. Yet those gains are speculative, unquantifiable, and difficult to place on commensurable scales to be weighed against the risk of harm or discomfort to an incapacitated research subject.[161] If large social gains can simply outweigh individual harms, the ultimate hazard is "a utilitarian subordination of the individual to the collectivity"[162] or an unconscionable exploitation of helpless persons in violation of human dignity.[163]

One possible position on the upper limit of risk is that nontherapeutic research on a never competent person can never entail more than a minimal risk.[164] Minimal risk means "those [risks] ordinarily encountered in daily life or during the performance of routine physical or psychological examinations or tests."[165] This standard leaves some room for interpretation, but its thrust is to confine the nontherapeutic medical procedures employed on helpless persons to low-risk interventions—such as physical examinations, changes in diet, or the collection of blood or urine samples.[166] Several sources have cited minimal risk as an ethically sound level of nontherapeutic medical research that can be performed on never competent persons. These include the American Academy of Pediatrics in its 1995 guidelines,[167] the American College of Physicians in a 1989 report,[168] and the American Bar Association Commission on the Mentally Disabled in a 1978 statement.[169] For these sources, minimal risk represents the limit of potential harm to which a never competent person may ethically be exposed under a justification of social benefit. The implicit judgment is that it is fair (for the purpose of advancing medical knowledge) to subject helpless persons to conditions that are no more hazardous or burdensome than their usual daily activities. This judgment seems compatible with the fairness rationale that I have advanced to justify, in principle, a surrogate's imposition of bodily sacrifice. A possible rule, then, would be that in return for the benefits that are conferred by society or families on profoundly disabled persons, a conscientious surrogate may choose a medical step primarily benefitting others but entailing no more than minimal risk of significant harm or discomfort to the ward.

It is not self-evident that even minimal-risk nontherapeutic research on a never competent person is morally justifiable. While a minimal-risk medical procedure may be no more burdensome or dangerous than a daily activity, the procedure involves some minor risk that would presumably not otherwise be incurred—that is, some minor chance of physical harm like infection, discomfort, or emotional distress. The justifying rationale might be that a minimal-risk research intervention is fungible with any other daily activity that the incapacitated person would otherwise be engaged in. That is, the incapacitated person is always subject to the minimal risks of daily living—whether he or she is operating in the context of research or not. This explanation is not fully convincing if the incapacitated research subject would normally be idle at the time that a research procedure is being performed. The research procedure would then be more risky than what the subject would otherwise be doing at that moment, though it would be no more risky than other daily activities. (And I have already noted the possibility of the special burdens of a bodily invasion on a never competent subject in the form of a disorienting disruption of routine, a bodily invasion, or an uncomprehending discomfort or anxiety.) Also, a parent or guardian normally has objects like education or recreation in mind—as opposed to sacrifice for others—when directing the daily activities of helpless wards. Arguably, then, subjection to even minimal-risk nontherapeutic research needs some moral justification beyond the fact that it involves nothing more dangerous than daily activity. As noted, the social benefits being received by the incapacitated person perhaps justify imposition of a burden attended by no more than minimal risk.

Some sources assert that the risk-related limit of permissible nontherapeutic research on never competent persons is the imposition of a "minor increase over minimal risk." This is the standard that is incorporated in U.S. Department of Health and Human Services regulations that govern federally funded research on children. Section 46.406 allows nontherapeutic research that involves a minor increase over minimal risk where the institutional review board finds that the research is "likely to yield generalizable knowledge about the subject's disorder or condition which is of vital importance" and the procedure is reasonably similar to experiences that the subject would normally encounter in medical situations.[170] A 1978 report on children's research by the National Commission endorsed the standard of "a minor increase over minimal risk" on the basis that it would not pose a significant risk of harm to any minor research subject.[171] That same year, the U.S. Department of Health, Education, and Welfare used that level of risk in proposed regulations regarding medical research on institutionalized persons.[172] A much more recent statute in Virginia, a recent report by a special New York State task force, and some commentators also adopt the "minor-increase" standard.[173]

The term "minor increase over minimal risk" has never been precisely defined. One authority, Rebecca Dresser, suggests that the term (as applied to mentally incapacitated persons) "covers interventions somewhat more risky than routine medical tests or procedures but no more risky than tests or procedures typically used in the case of dementia patients."[174] She sees magnetic resonance images (MRIs), positron emission tomography (PET scans), lumbar puncture, and the brief use of a catheter as among those interventions falling within a permissible range. A Yale University institutional review board saw bone-marrow aspiration and spinal taps as within the range of a minor increase over minimal risk—at least for people who had previously experienced some similar medical procedure.[175]

Not everyone agrees that it is morally permissible to go beyond minimal risk in the conduct of nontherapeutic research on mentally incapacitated subjects. A 1978 report by the National Commission (proposing policies relating to research on institutionalized, incapacitated persons) stated that research involving greater than minimal risks should be carried out only when the subject will derive direct benefit from the research.[176] ("Direct benefit" meant at least a reasonable chance that the research results would aid the incapacitated subject.) Similarly, a recent directive from the European Union confines medical research on incapacitated adults to either research that holds a prospect of a direct benefit or research that involves minimal risks.[177] The 1998 report of the National Bioethics Advisory Commission also suggests that nontherapeutic research that carries a greater than minimal risk is not permissible on never competent persons.[178]

At the same time, some sources suggest that nontherapeutic research that involves even more than a minor increase over minimal risk is permissible, at least if it is approved by special review. For example, the federal regulations governing federally funded research on children allow the

Secretary of Health and Human Services to approve research that goes beyond the bounds of a minor increase over minimal risk. The Secretary must
first determine that the proposed research provides a reasonable opportunity to alleviate "a serious problem affecting the health or welfare of children" and that the research will conform to "sound ethical principles."[179]
One commentator proposes that research involving greater than a minor
increase over minimal risk be allowed on children where the scientific
knowledge would be of vital importance and a special national board ap-
proves the protocol.[180]

This last position—authorizing nontherapeutic surrogate decisions that
involve a greater than minor increase over minimal risk—goes well beyond
the frequently expressed sentiment that only research carrying minimal
risk for incapacitated subjects is ethical and humane. A critical question
then is what, if any, rationale might justify nontherapeutic research bearing such a significant increase over minimal risk. The most obvious rationale would be utilitarian—the notion that medical research is critical to
progress in curing children's diseases and various disorders that affect the
mentally disabled. Research on mentally infirm persons is indeed essential
to understand and combat mental impairments and associated conditions.[181] That utilitarian fact seems to lie behind various authorizations of
nontherapeutic research on incapacitated persons despite more than minimal risks.[182] A purely utilitarian approach is, as previously noted, incompatible with the full moral status that is attached to profoundly disabled
persons. The well-being and bodily integrity of disabled humans cannot
simply be overcome by the interests of others.

Some further rationale is necessary for surrogate imposition of more
than minimal risk. One argument is that this degree of risk imposition is
consistent with the prerogatives of responsible parents in child-rearing situations.[183] It is probably true that parents expose their children to more
than minimal risks in the course of educating their children about various
subjects (such as in teaching survival skills and perhaps even in teaching
altruistic behavior). And we generally consider such exposure to be appropriate. However, a few obstacles are evident here. The normal parental prerogative seems to derive in part from the educational role that parents play.
When parents expose their children to hunting and other dangerous pur-
suits, the expectation is that the child will benefit either by enjoyment or
by learning. Yet as previously noted, profoundly disabled children may

not be able to absorb the lessons involved in making medical sacrifices for others. Moreover, the customary bounds of the parental decision-making prerogative may not be as flexible for parents who are functioning as court-appointed guardians or acting on behalf of institutionalized adults.[184] In theory, their fiduciary obligations may be more restrictive than those of parents acting as natural guardians at home.[185] When parents as surrogates seek to authorize nontherapeutic, noneducational bodily invasions that entail any significant risks, the normal range of parental discretion may shrink. The cases dealing with tissue donation, for example, prescribe a strict best-interests-of-the-patient formula that would not seem to authorize nontherapeutic research at all, let alone research involving more than minimal risk.

Is there a further rationale for a surrogate's imposition of more than minimal risk in the context of nontherapeutic research? The sources that endorse more than minimal risk in this context confine authorization to circumstances where the research is aimed at the same disease or disorder that afflicts the incapacitated research subject. The "same-disease" limitation apparently seeks to justify imposition of risk on incapacitated subjects by finding some benefit to the subject. As noted in this chapter, some benefit to an incapacitated patient can justify some surrogate decisions that primarily benefit third parties. However, the reality is that most "same-disease" research has no chance to help the incapacitated subject. In the absence of a significant prospect of direct benefit to the subject, any assumption that the incapacitated subject would have a special sympathy with same-disease research is effectively the attribution of an altruistic frame of mind to a never competent person. I have already expressed my discomfort with imputing a highly individualized sentiment like altruism (or perhaps even a sentiment of vengeance toward the affliction) to never competent persons.

Does a social-justice rationale account for the imposition of more than minimal risk on a never competent research subject? As noted, most profoundly disabled persons benefit from caretaking provided by family or by institutions. For me, this benefit (when the disabled person is being properly cared for) offers the best rationale for allowing nontherapeutic research at all. I previously argued that there can be rough justice in allowing conscientious surrogates to submit their loved ones to nontherapeutic research, though I did not fix a maximum-risk limitation. At some point, a surrogate's imposition of risk becomes unconscionable exploitation of another person in violation of intrinsic human dignity. American society has, for approximately thirty years, been struggling to define what degree of risk is consistent with human dignity. The ultimate American stopping point for tolerable risk might well be a minor increase over minimal risk. That standard has found considerable, though by no means universal, acceptance. This stopping point is both justifiable (given the social benefits conferred) and roughly consistent with the degree of control that caretakers are generally accorded over their never competent wards. As previously noted, even institutional caretakers may extract some concessions—such as adherence to schedules or performance of neatness tasks—that may not be strictly in the institutionalized persons' best interests. In other words, guardians may generally be able to impose burdens or tasks on wards that go somewhat beyond the minimal risks of daily living.

In sum, the appropriate guideline in fixing maximum permissible risk (for a surrogate's extraction of sacrifice) is intrinsic human dignity—meaning freedom from unconscionable exploitation. The boundary of that constraint has not definitively been established, but a minor increase over minimal risk has distinct promise. Some recent examinations of the ethical limits of medical research are comfortable with that risk limit.[186]

Besides a limit on degree of risk, there is another dignity-driven limitation on nontherapeutic research that uses never competent subjects—a requirement of absolute necessity of using this population. This necessity requirement flows from a precept of social justice that helpless persons should not be exploited solely for administrative convenience or because they are easily manipulable. The 1966 American Medical Association Guidelines for Medical Research[187] may have been the first source to articulate "necessity" as a principle of justice that should be applied to research on vulnerable humans, but the principle has found widespread support. A 1978 Report by the National Commission on the Protection of Human Subjects of Biomedical and Behavioral Research endorsed research on incapacitated persons only if no competent adults were suitable.[188] Many other sources suggest that no medical research should be conducted on incapacitated persons unless competent persons cannot be utilized.[189] (A similar principle appears in some of the cases dealing with organ donation. That is, courts will not authorize an organ donation from an incapacitated person if a competent donor is available who is also compatible with the potential donee.)[190] This necessity constraint is arguably grounded in the intrinsic human dignity—that is, respect for persons—that is owed to profoundly disabled persons. Human dignity precludes unconscionable exploitation. While social benefits accorded to a profoundly disabled person might justify a conscientious surrogate's choice to subject a profoundly disabled person to nontherapeutic research (involving minimal risk or a minor increase over minimal risk), *some* risks or discomforts are almost always present. That being the case, and given the always lurking hazard of a prejudice against profoundly disabled persons, it makes sense to be cautious and to require use of competent, consenting persons as research subjects (or tissue donors) whenever possible.

A final dignity-related condition applies to a surrogate's consent to nontherapeutic medical research—appropriate deference to the incapacitated person's objections. Respect for the objecting will of even profoundly disabled persons flows from their moral status as bearers of intrinsic human dignity. A person's objecting will can involve human dignity in a couple of ways. If a mentally incapacitated person can understand in some measure the nature and consequences of proposed medical research, the person's informed assent to nontherapeutic research is widely understood as a prerequisite to using that person as a research subject. In that instance, respect for human dignity dictates that mentally incapacitated persons be allowed to exercise choice to the extent that they are able, at least where the person's rudimentary expression of will is not inconsistent with that person's own interests.[191] A refusal of assent to nontherapeutic research is therefore relevant where the potential subject has sufficient mental capacity to understand and consider enough basic facts about the proposed research to make the refusal meaningful.[192]

For persons who are incapable of assent, including profoundly disabled persons, their expression of will cannot involve considered choice. Surrogates must make important decisions on behalf of these persons, and we have established that surrogates may consent to some nontherapeutic research. Yet a person who lacks sufficient understanding to assent can still express an objection to a painful or distressing medical intervention. Objections or resistance on the part of profoundly disabled, uncomprehending persons should be honored because it is unseemly and demeaning to override their will, especially if physical restraint is necessary. Many sources therefore require that researchers refrain from medical research in the face of a patient's objection, unless the incapacitated subject has a strong beneficial interest in the research procedure.[193] The National Bioethics Advisory Commission in 1998 went further and asserted that respect for persons precludes forcing an unwilling person to submit to a research procedure, even when that person is severely mentally impaired and even when the procedure might be beneficial to that person.[194] (The discussion on assent and dissent by profoundly disabled persons continues in the next chapter, which deals with the voice of incapacitated persons.)

I have suggested that a social-justice concept offers the best rationale for allowing surrogates to impose a modicum of sacrifice on profoundly disabled persons. At the same time, intrinsic human dignity imposes significant constraints on the surrogate. Principles of limited risk, necessity, and deference to objection confine the surrogate's moral authority. Still, what are the ultimate implications of the social-justice theory for profoundly disabled persons? When a profoundly disabled person donates tissue for a close relative, the donor at least receives some direct personal benefit—in the form of continued personal interactions—in addition to public benefits. If a profoundly disabled person receives public benefits in the form of caregiving and medical treatment, can a surrogate agree to the harvesting of nonvital bodily tissue for the benefit of strangers—that is, in circumstances where the potential donee is not a family member close to the donor (so that the procedure will be entirely nontherapeutic for the potential donor)? My response is yes—subject to the limitations previously discussed. A surrogate should not be able to consent to a donation from a profoundly disabled person if a competent donor or some other means of alleviating the donee's plight is available, if the risk is more than a minor increase over minimal, or if the disabled person objects to the procedure. Applying this framework to the context of tissue and organ donation, it is possible that the risk element would exclude organ donation but allow a surrogate the authority to donate tissue (such as bone marrow or blood). Lainie Friedman Ross argues that an organ donation would entail more than a minor increase over minimal risk but that tissue donation would not.[195] This position is subject to empirical confirmation but seems plausible.

Again, social justice can warrant a surrogate's imposition of a modicum of sacrifice on a profoundly disabled person. A surrogate may authorize a medical procedure—such as nontherapeutic research or tissue donation to a stranger—even though the profoundly disabled person gets no benefit from the particular medical procedure. That is not "forced altruism" because the impetus for the sacrifice has nothing to do with virtue or altruistic sentiment on the part of the disabled potential donor. The imposed sacrifice also deviates from the customary supposition that a surrogate decision maker must act in the best interests of a profoundly disabled ward. Yet chapter 4 has questioned the accuracy of that supposition. For reasons articulated earlier in this chapter, the use of persons as a means to promote others' interests is not always disrespectful of persons and immoral. When sufficient attention is paid to the human dignity of the sacrificing person, the disabled donor is not being treated *solely* as a means. The conditions noted ensure that intrinsic human dignity is respected—that is, that the profoundly disabled person is not unconscionably exploited.

6

The Voice of the Profoundly Disabled Person

The prevailing ethic in American bioethics is respect for autonomy—that is, deference to the personal choices of people who are capable of understanding the nature and consequences of particular medical decisions and who are capable of making a judgment in light of those considerations. Profoundly disabled persons are, by definition, intellectually incapable of deliberating about serious medical choices in this manner. For a patient who has always lacked the capacity for serious medical choices, the dominant ethic becomes protection of the patient's well-being. As chapter 4 has indicated, the watchword for courts and legislatures relating to the medical fates of profoundly disabled persons is "best interests" of the patient. In other words, in the absence of mental competence, the focus shifts from autonomy to the well-being of the vulnerable person as determined by a conscientious surrogate operating with the particular circumstances of the never competent person in mind.[1]

The courts and legislatures that stress the well-being of the never competent patient as the primary determinant in medical decision making also mandate attention to the incompetent voice of the patient. For example, in the numerous post-1980 cases that involve petitions to allow the sterilization of mentally disabled persons, courts almost invariably mention a surrogate decision maker's duty to elicit the view of the incompetent person, to take that view into account, and to weigh the view heavily (especially where the patient opposes performance of the contemplated medical procedure).[2] And where state statutes speak to the possibility of judicial authorization of sterilization, they often require consideration of the prospective patient's views toward the contemplated medical procedure.[3] A similar mandate to consult with an incapacitated ward appears in cases relating to other serious medical issues, including cases involving abortion and end-of-life decision making.[4]

This mandate to elicit and consider profoundly disabled wards' views and feelings raises questions. Why is it appropriate to consult with nonautonomous persons before making decisions on their behalf? Why, for example, would a surrogate decision maker who is contemplating sterilization or abortion for a ward discuss matters of reproduction and contraception with a person who is utterly incapable of comprehending such matters? And what force do the utterances of an uncomprehending person have?

The preferences and expressions of profoundly disabled persons are not ordinarily binding on a surrogate who is charged with decision making on behalf of a ward. The same courts that mandate consultation with a mentally disabled person indicate—either explicitly or by inference—that the voice elicited from the disabled person is not determinative by itself.[5] This judicial refusal to give binding effect to the expressions of profoundly disabled persons is unsurprising. A patient's right to choose among medical options—grounded on self-determination and informed consent—requires the mental capacity to understand and weigh the options at hand. In a framework that exalts autonomy, the preferences and expressions of mentally incompetent persons cannot be accorded uncritical acceptance.[6] H. Tristam Engelhardt explains: "the duty to respect freedom does not include a duty to respect the unfree choice [about death or other serious medical consequences] by mentally ill persons."[7] Yet while incompetent beings may not be entitled to act on ill-conceived plans, their "voice" has considerable importance in the context of surrogate medical decision making.

The Connection between Consultation and Well-Being

The clearest justification for seeking input from profoundly disabled persons whose medical fate is being determined by a surrogate decision maker is the promotion of the profoundly disabled person's interests or well-being. Even if "best interests" is a misnomer of sorts (as is suggested in chapter 4), the identification of a patient's interests is highly relevant to surrogate medical decision making. The expressions of a mentally disabled patient furnish insights into the emotional and physical status of the patient. Eliciting a profoundly disabled patient's feelings is thus important in the assessment of the patient's well-being (or lack thereof)—a critical factor in shaping the patient's medical care.

The best-interests formula is geared to a weighing of a patient's benefits and burdens. In major part, the formula counts pleasure or satisfaction as a prime benefit and counts pain or discomfort as a prime burden. In turn, assessment of pleasure and pain are dependent on an interpretation of the communications that are provided by the profoundly disabled patient. Expressed pain or discomfort by the disabled patient helps both in determining the need for treatment and in estimating the degree to which the profoundly disabled person will tolerate various medical procedures.

Communication with the profoundly disabled patient and a concomitant assessment of patient feelings can also help to predict the likely success of contemplated medical interventions. If a patient is instinctively adverse to a proposed treatment modality, that attitude may limit the patient's willingness to cooperate with a contemplated medical regimen.[8] Likely noncooperation with one mode of treatment might impel a decision to try a different, less threatening treatment modality. A nurse who is experienced in dealing with profoundly disabled persons recently provided an illustration of the importance of monitoring and understanding a patient's patterns and preferences. She noted that we wouldn't put a dying patient on a ventilator if that person has always reacted with persistent and strenuous distress to the sound of a vacuum cleaner. At the same time, communication that is aimed at discovering and calming the patient's anxiety or fears may ease what would otherwise be a highly traumatic medical procedure.

Consideration of a person's interests includes not just universally valued factors such as freedom from suffering but also self-defined elements that furnish special pleasure or pain to the incapacitated individual. Profoundly disabled persons may have personal wants or needs that are relevant to defining their interests in a particular medical situation and that can be discerned only via communication with the individual. That fact helps explain why courts often mandate consultation with the mentally disabled patient as part of a surrogate decision maker's task. By identifying what is important to the particular patient, the decision maker can better project whether the proposed medical intervention will advance that patient's interests. For example, if eating is a central pleasure in a profoundly disabled person's life, a treatment modality that necessitates permanent resort to artificial nutrition may be disfavored. Identifying and honoring a profoundly disabled person's wants is a critical part of a surrogate decision-making strategy called "best respect" suggested by Susan Martyn—one of the few commentators who has devoted special attention to decision making on behalf of profoundly disabled persons.[9]

Another reason for consulting with a mentally disabled patient is to assess prospective physical or emotional resistance to contemplated medical procedures. Patient resistance might even necessitate physical or chemical restraints. Beyond a concern (addressed below) about depriving a patient of human dignity, prospective restraints might increase the frustration, distress, and suffering associated with a particular treatment regimen. Or the forcible restraint might engender distrust and resentment toward care givers. Those possibilities create an additional reason for carefully communicating with a profoundly disabled patient prior to taking any medical course.

Dignity-Based Reasons for Soliciting Input

Important dignity-related reasons exist for seeking to inform and involve persons in decision making in whatever rudimentary way might be possible—even profoundly disabled persons who ostensibly can understand little or nothing about the medical decisions in issue. Respect for persons demands inquiry about the will or wishes of any person whose medical fate is in issue.[10] Seeking to explain a contemplated medical procedure is thus a gesture of respect for the human being whose will, bodily integrity, and well-being are at stake.[11] The gesture of providing information and seeking feedback is appropriate because it has symbolic significance and also because the psychic reality of a profoundly disabled person may sometimes be underestimated. It is at least possible that the affected person absorbs more of the message than is apparent. In short, it would be dehumanizing to ignore the will and feelings of a profoundly disabled person and to simply impose a surrogate's will. This would treat the prospective patient as if he or she were an inanimate object.

Another dignity-related reason exists for consulting with a severely demented person. Soliciting the feelings and predisposition of a mentally disabled person toward a contemplated medical procedure can provide an indication of whether that person will physically resist the medical intervention in a way that will necessitate chemical or physical restraints. Especially when the medical interventions will be frequent or prolonged,[12] the prospect of forcible restraint is in tension with common understandings about human dignity. Courts have frequently expressed revulsion at the prospect of physically restraining medical patients.[13] That revulsion is colloquially known as "the yuck factor" in conscientious decision making. Of course, the yuck factor does not always compel acquiescence in a mentally disabled patient's opposition to medical intervention. Where the potentially resisting patient's own interests strongly dictate a medical procedure, that benefit may warrant overcoming the patient's resistance. While the patient may then be temporarily placed in a position (forced restraint) that seems undignified and demeaning, intrinsic human dignity is not violated because a strong justification exists. This is consistent with Meir Dan-Cohen's observation that context can sometimes determine whether ostensibly demeaning practices are truly violative of human dignity.[14] To illustrate how indignity can depend on the social setting of a practice, he contrasts legalized boxing with wife beating. The use of restraints is also context sensitive. Temporary physical restraints don't violate intrinsic human dignity when adopted in order to render important benefits to the affected person.

Limited Self-Determination

A surrogate honors and respects the limited self-determination capacities of a ward by seeking to explain the pending medical issue and by engaging the ward's mental faculties. Even where a ward does not have the mental capacity to make a fully considered weighing of the pros and cons, that person may still have a "limited but real understanding" of the medical issues that is sufficient to express a judgment or preference.[15] In such instances, the assent (or dissent) of the incapacitated person can involve a meaningful application of personal judgment or self-determination. The President's Commission for the Study of Ethical Problems in Medicine called respect for this partially considered judgment "self-determination, though of an attenuated kind."[16]

A conscientious surrogate who feels that an incapacitated patient's condition either warrants or does not warrant medical intervention always seeks the input of the partially comprehending ward. The impetus for soliciting assent (or dissent) in these instances is respect for human dignity in the form of the patient's reflective character and capacity to understand the elements in issue. Consultation in that instance acknowledges the self-determination capacity of the patient (albeit limited) and presumably makes the patient feel more respected as a human being.[17] When the incapacitated patient's assent or dissent coincides with a surrogate's assessment of best interests, the patient's wish will almost certainly be followed.[18] Because the medical decision is initially grounded in a physician's and a surrogate's assessment of the incapacitated patient's welfare, Bruce Winick labels the decision-making process an exercise of beneficence. For him, the "watered down assent" represents "little genuine autonomy."[19] For me, much more is involved than just beneficence in the sense of promoting an incapacitated patient's medical welfare. The consultation between surrogate and incapacitated patient can generate a feeling and appearance of autonomy that respect the patient's human dignity.

When there is divergence between a patient's express wish and a surrogate's assessment of best interests, the results will vary. Often, the best-interests factor will override the mentally disabled patient's will. That is, where the interests and well-being of the disabled patient clearly dictate a particular medical path, opposition or even a contrary preference by the patient may well be overridden in order to achieve the beneficial result. That policy applies in many medical contexts. For example, a mentally disabled patient in great physical distress will likely be given a pain killer even if the disoriented patient seems highly resistant to the medication. Similarly, parents in conjunction with health-care providers might choose an experimental treatment regimen for a gravely ill, mentally disabled child even though the child is resistant to the medical procedures involved.[20] And where there are strong medical reasons for performing an abortion on a pregnant disabled woman, a surrogate may opt for abortion despite the woman's childlike wish to have a baby.[21] All this willingness to override the expressions of profoundly disabled persons makes sense where this course clearly promotes the disabled person's well-being.

An incapacitated patient's wish might be followed despite its noncongruence with a surrogate's assessment of best interests where the patient is ostensibly opting to reject a significant burden or imposition. The implicit judgment is that a person's "understanding will" (meaning a person's preference based on an understanding of the essence of the medical procedure contemplated, though without capacity to fully process the variables involved) warrants significant respect when the patient is objecting to a major bodily intervention or a major alteration of lifestyle. For example, California law precludes surrogate consent to sterilization when the person to be sterilized makes "a knowing objection."[22] This respect for the mentally disabled person's will is reinforced by respect for bodily integrity—a person's prerogative to resist bodily intrusions. (As noted, a patient's objection to prospective bodily invasion can also affect surrogate choice by signaling resistance to a medical regimen or a need to employ distasteful restraints.) Another hesitance to override an incapacitated patient's knowing would apply to a removal of life-sustaining medical intervention where the patient's expressed will is life affirming.

Note that this limited deference to an incapacitated patient's expressed preference would not govern when the patient is seeking to take on (as opposed to resisting) a significant burden in contravention of his or her best interests. This would be so as to organ donation or sterilization, for instance. When the mentally disabled person with limited understanding is ostensibly agreeing to a burdensome intervention, there is understandable concern about the person's well-being and about the potential manipulation of the expressions of a person who has only limited comprehension of the medical matters in issue.

In sum, efforts to involve an incapacitated patient in decision making make sense where the affected patient has at least partial understanding of the medical issue and its underlying components. Consultation provides important information about the patient's medical interests and acknowledges the patient's humanity. What about the profoundly disabled patient who has no understanding of the medical issue and its components? Does it make any sense to seek to discuss sterilization or abortion with a person who cannot fathom reproduction or contraception? Would a surrogate decision maker follow the wishes of a profoundly disabled pregnant woman who expresses a childlike wish to have a baby but who has no comprehension of the tasks and burdens involved in gestation, birthing, and child rearing?

In some situations, a surrogate may elect to implement a ward's preferences even though the ward lacks significant cognitive capacity. A profoundly disabled person's feelings or preferences should prevail when the substantive medical decision is essentially in equipoise—that is, in instances when the well-being of the person might lie in either of two directions. For example, where a disabled patient is clearly dying and has only a brief life expectancy, that patient's refusal of food and drink might be accepted as determinative—within a gray area in which the patient's own interests could lie in either of two directions. If we believe the observation of a friend of mine who has long worked with the developmentally disabled, wisdom is often reflected in the preferences of even profoundly disabled persons. She comments: "regardless of intellectual capacity, most people know what is right and good for themselves at any given moment."[23] Deference to the will of a profoundly disabled person is also appropriate when nonessential medical procedures are in issue. If the well-being of the patient would not be seriously compromised by waiting until the patient is more receptive (if ever), honoring the patient's uncomprehending will can be a gesture of respect. This is especially so where failure to follow the uncomprehending person's will would entail physical resistance and create a need for undignified restraints.

A surrogate decision maker may sometimes be expected to follow the unconsidered or irrational wishes of a profoundly disabled person where the contemplated medical intervention is not primarily for the patient's own benefit. For example, if a mentally incapacitated person resists, either physically or verbally, continued participation in a nontherapeutic research protocol, the appropriate response is to withdraw that person's participation. The federal regulations that govern medical research involving children dictate that result when a child is capable of assent (that is, has a basic understanding of the medical procedures but dissents from participation).[24] Commentators go further and favor that result whenever a person resists participation in nontherapeutic research, regardless of whether that person has the mental capacity to understand the procedure being resisted.[25]

What happens in a situation where a profoundly disabled potential tissue donor is adverse to cooperating with the harvesting of tissue? Overriding the donor's objections would certainly be warranted where the donation—by salvaging a person who is highly supportive of the potential tissue donor—would seem to promote the donor's own interests as well as those of the donee. Can the mentally disabled donor's objections be overridden if the tissue is critical to salvaging a sibling or other close relative (even if not particularly beneficial to the disabled donor)? I argue in chapter 5 that surrogates should sometimes have the authority to deviate from an incapacitated person's strict best interests so long as the surrogate is still respectful of the disabled person's intrinsic human dignity. And I note there that emerging standards reflected in recent regulations and commentary suggest that overriding an objecting person's will and thus invading bodily integrity would indeed be violative of intrinsic human dignity in the absence of compensating benefit to the profoundly disabled patient. This fact dictates that tissue removal not proceed where the prospective donor is actively resisting the proposed medical procedure.

Ambiguity of Expressions

Consultation with profoundly disabled persons does not always yield satisfying or clear results. Sometimes, the factors involved in a particular medical decision are beyond the ken of the affected person. Raising concepts like contraception or reproduction or transplantation may simply be futile in some instances.[26] Or the mentally disabled person's responses may be so inconsistent, vacillating, or incoherent that they defy sensible interpretation.[27] Or the ambiguity sometimes involved in the expressions of profoundly disabled persons may pose an obstacle to assessing the persons' preferences or feelings. One recent commentator describes the puzzlement sometimes encountered in seeking to understand the signs and gestures of a gravely debilitated person (in this instance her mother):

My mother's [frantically] pumping hand . . . seemed to us a clear sign of physical pain. But arguably she could be signaling frustration that she could not "say" anything anymore. . . . Maybe it was a reflex, devoid of meaning. Possibly, she was rowing herself across the river Styx. Who is to say?[28]

In some instances, surrogate decision makers and health-care providers must decypher puzzling signals and cues—gestures, grimaces, facial expressions, bodily spasms, moans, groans, and other patient sounds. The experiential reality of a profoundly disabled person may be difficult to fathom. There may be no way of knowing exactly how a particular profoundly disabled person thinks and feels.[29] And there may be some temptation to interpret the clues in a fashion that coincides with the observer's predispositions. One court interpreted a demented patient's pulling at a nasogastric tube as a plea to be allowed to die, terming the resistance to a feeding tube as "a plea for privacy and personal dignity."[30] That interpretation could be right, or the conduct could have reflected only transient irritation or reflexive behavior.[31] Similar uncertainty can also surround some oral expressions. In a deeply demented person, a moan can signal pain, mild discomfort, or just a reflexive response to some stimulus.[32]

The frequent ambiguity of expression creates a temptation to manipulate profoundly disabled patients. A high potential exists for eliciting expressions from the patient—however uncomprehending—that are favored by the surrogate decision maker or medical staff. If a caretaker knows that a profoundly disabled patient responds to all questions with a yes, then it is easy to shape the questions to get a desired result, and the caretaker can do the same when the consistent response is no.

All this potential for ambiguity in body language and verbal utterances prompts caution, but it does not undermine the importance of communication with a profoundly disabled person who is facing a serious medical procedure. Sometimes, the signals via sounds and gestures are unmistakable. For example, in the case of Sheila Pouliot (discussed earlier), no one contended that the profoundly disabled patient's moaning and writhing reflected anything other than extreme discomfort and unhappiness. By the same token, a profoundly disabled person's smiles and other behavior can unmistakably communicate pleasure or satisfaction. The interpretation of seemingly ambiguous communication can be facilitated when the interpreter is either a person who has known the disabled person well or a person who is skilled in communication with profoundly disabled persons. Those interpreters can often understand communications that otherwise seem puzzling.[33] And sometimes a rough understanding of a disabled person's feelings can suffice to prompt a surrogate's decision. For example, a disabled person's expression of significant distress should be enough for a surrogate to withdraw that person from further participation in a nontherapeutic research protocol. In short, even though a profoundly disabled patient is not competent to determine his or her own medical fate and the patient's will is subject to being overridden (in the best interests of the patient), respect for human dignity dictates consultation with the patient and careful attention to the expressions elicited.

Another factor that comes into play in medical decision making for profoundly disabled persons is the customary presumption in favor of preserving human life. For example, in interpreting a mentally incapacitated person's ambiguous or opaque communications, the natural tendency should be to attribute a life-affirming significance to them (or at least to refuse to view the communications as representing a choice to die). This approach has prevailed in a couple of instances where judges disregarded the expressions of unhappiness and annoyance made by dying persons and insisted that life must be preserved in the absence of a more clear and considered choice.[34]

A life-affirming bias on the part of surrogate decision makers is generally salutary but can sometimes extend too far. One example of excess is found in statutes providing that an effective revocation of an advance medical directive takes place when a now incompetent patient expresses any apparent intention to revoke—at any time, in any manner, and regardless of the patient's mental condition.[35] These statutes do not impact on never competent persons, but they do show how a prolife bias can, on occasion, negatively affect surrogate decision making. The impetus behind these statutes is apparently a legislative reluctance to have life support removed from a person who is expressing in some fashion a wish to continue living. (The implicit legislative assumption is that an advance medical directive generally seeks an end to life-sustaining medical intervention, so that revocation is viewed as a life-affirming gesture.) Such a prolife policy is appropriate where the now incompetent patient has some understanding of the matters of life and death in issue and is expressing a desire to live.[36] Yet it makes no sense to follow the completely deranged utterances of a person if and when those utterances conflict either with the patient's contemporaneous interests or (in the case of previously competent persons) with the person's prior competent wishes. The human dignity of a profoundly disabled person dictates inquiry into the feelings and wishes of that person, but it does not dictate an unquestioning adherence to that person's will.

That is an appropriate point at which to end this book—with one more illustration of how intrinsic human dignity plays a key role in shaping medical decision making on behalf of profoundly disabled persons. Throughout this work, I have tried to show how human dignity shapes the ways in which medical decisions can legally and morally be made for profoundly disabled persons. Intrinsic human dignity influences the kinds of decisions that are subject to surrogate control, the identity of appropriate surrogate decision makers, the standards applicable to surrogate decision making, and the extent to which surrogates may make nontherapeutic choices for profoundly disabled persons. Finally, human dignity shapes the response that surrogate decision makers provide to the voice of the profoundly disabled person.

Notes

Introduction

1. I use the term *persons* here advisedly. Some moral philosophers contend that human beings who are profoundly mentally disabled do not meet the minimum criteria for personhood. As is discussed in chapter 1, the law appropriately treats the profoundly disabled as persons, and I use that terminology throughout.

2. Throughout this book, I often use the terms *profoundly disabled, incapacitated,* and *disabled* without adding the word *mentally.* Unless otherwise noted, the reference is always to people with mental disabilities and not to people with physical disabilities.

3. Burton Blatt, *The Conquest of Mental Retardation* 68–69 (1987); James W. Ellis, *Decisions by and for People with Mental Retardation: Balancing Considerations of Autonomy and Protection,* 37 Vill. L. Rev. 1779, 1795 (1992).

4. *See* Thomas L. Whitman, Cynthia L. Miller & Deirdre Mylod, Mental Retardation, in *Encyclopedia of Disability and Rehabilitation* (1995).

5. James W. Trent, Jr., *Inventing the Feeble Mind: A History of Mental Retardation in the United States* 162 (1994).

6. This is not to say that laws that categorically exclude "mental defectives," the "feebleminded," those of "unsound mind," the "mentally incompetent," "imbeciles," or "idiots" from voting are defensible. Such statutory provisions may be vague and overly inclusive and may be arbitrarily applied to exclude people who could meet the modest intellectual capacities that are needed for the tasks in question. *See generally* Kay Schriner, Lisa Ochs & Todd Shields, *Democratic Dilemmas: Notes on the ADA and Voting Rights of People with Cognitive and Emotional Impairments,* 21 Berkeley J. Emp. & Lab. L. 437 (2000); Patricia Wald, Basic Personal and Civil Rights, in *The Mentally Retarded Citizen and the Law* 24–25 (Michael Kindred, ed., 1976).

7. *See, e.g.*, Ellis, *supra* note 3, at 1795; John H. Garvey, *Freedom and Choice in Constitutional Law,* 94 Harv. L. Rev. 1756, 1760–61 (1981).

8. Loren E. Lomasky, *Persons, Rights and the Moral Community* 207 (1987).

9. People's autonomous choices do not always prevail. For example, in the medical context, patients are not entitled to make choices that are medically inappropriate

in the sense that the patient's desired course would clearly be ineffectual or even contraindicated. A doctor need not furnish a medical intervention that would have no therapeutic or palliative utility. Similarly, limits apply to autonomous choice in a nonmedical context. Intrinsic human dignity may constrain self-determination: A person is not entitled to enter slavery. A dwarf might not be entitled to be bounced off walls as part of a public exhibition. And a person might not be entitled to engage in all forms of self-mutilation or sadomasochistic sexual behavior.

10. Alan Gewirth, Human Dignity as the Basis of Rights, in *The Constitution of Rights* 10, 15 (M. J. Meyer & W. A. Parent eds., 1992); Evelyn B. Pluhar, *Beyond Prejudice: The Moral Significance of Human and Nonhuman Animals* 269 (1995).

11. *E.g.*, David Feldman, *Human Dignity as a Legal Value:* Part I, Public Law 682, 685–86, 697–98 (1999); Ruth Macklin, *Dignity as a Useless Concept,* 327 BMJ (British Medical Journal) 1419 (2003).

12. *Id.*

13. Deryck Beyleveld & Roger Brownsword, *Human Dignity, Human Rights, and Human Genetics,* 61 Modern L. Rev. 661, 662 (1998). Human dignity is "a notoriously elusive concept" and "a highly abstract concept generating differences of opinion." Dierk Ullrich, *Concurring Visions: Human Dignity in the Canadian Charter of Rights and Freedoms and the Basic Law of the Federal Republic of Germany,* 3 Global Jurist (2003), <http://www.bepress.com/gj/frontiers/vol3/art>.

14. Leon Kass maintains that human dignity is reflected in a dignified attitude in the face of death regardless of how debilitated and helpless a person may be. Leon R. Kass, *Death with Dignity and the Sanctity of Life,* Commentary 33, 39 (March 1990). See also John Kavanaugh, *Who Counts as Persons?* 134–37 (2002).

15. *See Lawrence v. Texas,* 539 U.S. 558 (2003) for a recent affirmation of the importance and role of Fourteenth Amendment liberty.

16. *Cf.* Matthew O. Clifford & Thomas P. Huff, *Some Thoughts on the Meaning and Scope of the Montana Constitution's Dignity Clause,* 61 Montana L. Rev. 301, 326–27 (2000); Jamie Mayerfeld, *Suffering and Moral Responsibility* 5 (1999); Wojciech Sadurski, *Conventional Morality and Judicial Standards,* 73 Va. L. Rev. 339, 379–80 (1987).

17. But an individual may have some room to shape the concept of intrinsic human dignity as applied to his or her own medical handling. For example, a person is currently allowed to dictate that he or she will be medically maintained in a permanently unconscious state even though the vast majority of persons might deem permanent unconsciousness to be intrinsically undignified and surrogates might terminate life support for most wards who are permanently unconscious. Still, while people can choose to behave in ways that others deem undignified, their conduct may reach a level of degradation that is intolerably indignified according to a prevailing societal norm. Some day, then, the status of permanent unconsciousness might be deemed so intrinsically demeaning that no one will be permitted to be medically sustained in that condition.

18. This does not mean that it is easy to differentiate between popular conceptions that may be transient and fundamental tenets of decency. Controversy has swirled

around the intrinsic nature and importance of decisions about abortion, death with dignity, and cloning—to give a few examples of the difficulty of identifying intrinsic human dignity.

19. Ullrich, *supra* note 13, at 91–97.

20. *Id.* at 74–75.

21. Trent, *supra* note 5, at 16–20.

22. *Id.* at 57–66, 70–72, 75–91.

23. *Id.* at 136–42, 163; Blatt, *supra* note 3, at 320–21.

24. *See* Andre N. Sofair & Lewis C. Kaldjean, *Eugenic Sterilization and a Qualified Nazi Analogy: The U.S. and Germany,* 132 Ann. Internal Med. 312, 316–18 (2000).

25. Buck v. Bell, 274 U.S. 200, 207 (1927); *see* Paul A. Lombardo, Medicine, *Eugenics and the Supreme Court: From Coercive Sterilization to Reproductive Freedom,* 13 J. Contemp. Health L. & Pol'y 1, 6–9 (1996).

26. Martha A. Field & Valerie A. Sanchez, *Equal Treatment for People with Mental Retardation* 75–78 (1999).

27. Blatt, *supra* note 3, at 325; Foster Kennedy, *The Problem of Social Control of the Congenital Defective,* 99 Am. J. Psychiatry 13, 14–15 (1942).

28. Kennedy, *supra* note 27, at 15.

29. Trent, *supra* note 5, at 226–29, 238.

30. *See* Richard C. Allen, *Legal Rights of the Disabled and Disadvantaged* (1970); Blatt, *supra* note 3, at 226–28; Robert A. Burt, *Developing Constitutional Rights of, in, and for Children,* 39 J.L. & Contemp. Probs. 118, 140 (1975); Charles Murdock, *Civil Rights of the Mentally Retarded: Some Critical Issues,* 48 Notre Dame Law. 133, 146–53 (1972); Trent, *supra* note 5, at 257–61.

31. *See Youngberg v. Romeo,* 457 U.S. 307, 322–23 (1982); *Pennhurst v. Halderman,* 451 U.S. 1 (1981); *Society for Good Will to Retarded Children v. Cuomo,* 737 F.2d 1239 (2d Cir. 1984).

Chapter 1

1. Gilbert Meilaender, *Bioethics and the Character of Human Life,* 1 New Atlantis 67, 69 (Spring 2003).

2. *See* Eric Blumenson, *Who Counts Morally?,* 14 J.L. & Religion 1 (1999–2000). Strictly speaking, a prerogative must be legally enforceable to constitute a right. But philosophical reference to moral rights is common, as Blumenson explains. *See also* Mary Anne Warren, *Moral Status: Obligations to Persons and Other Living Things* 9–10 (2000).

3. Peter Byrne, *Philosophical and Ethical Problems in Mental Handicap* 57–58, 103, 120, 132–33 (2000); Ronald M. Green, Determining Moral Status, in *The Human Embryo Research Debate* 61–62 (Ronald M. Green ed., 2001).

4. I disclaim any intention to resolve whether nonhuman animals (or human embryos and fetuses) can qualify for personhood. I am aware that the cognitive capacities of some nonhuman animals surpass those of humans with severe cognitive deficits. *See* Adam Kolber, *Note, Standing Upright: The Moral and Legal Standing of Humans and Other Apes,* 54 Stanford L. Rev. 163, 166, 184 (2001). My focus is the legal and moral status of live human beings with severely impaired mental function. I reserve judgment on whether humans are "animals of special endowments that separate and valorize them above all other living organisms." John J. Kavanaugh, *Who Counts as Persons?* 9, 39–40 (2002).

5. *See* Peter Singer, *Rethinking Life and Death* 129–30 (1995). *See also* James W. Walters, *What Is a Person?* 3–4 (1997), arguing that a person's unique moral claim to life is dependent on higher mental capacities. Warren, *supra* note 2, at 90–95, presents various perspectives on the degree of mental function that is requisite for personhood.

6. Green, *supra* note 3, at 61.

7. A number of legal and philosophical commentators, most notably Robert Veatch, take the position that a permanently unconscious being is dead. Robert Veatch, *The Dead Donor Rule: True by Definition,* 3 Am. J. Bioethics 10 (Winter 2003). *See also* Ronald Cranford & David Smith, *Consciousness: The Most Critical Moral (Constitutional) Standard for Human Personhood,* 13 Am. J.L. & Med. 233 (1992); Raymond Devettere, *Neocortical Death and Human Death,* 18 Law, Med. & Health Care 96 (1990); John P. Lizza, *Persons and Death: What's Metaphysically Wrong with Our Current Statutory Definition of Death?* 18 J. Med. & Phil. 351 (1993).

8. *See* John Arras, *The Severely Demented, Minimally Functional Patient: An Ethical Analysis,* 36 J. Am. Geriatric Soc'y 938, 940 (1988), arguing that a patient who is in a permanently vegetative state has ceased to be a person and therefore that decision makers can consider the interests of others in deciding the patient's medical fate.

9. The removal of life support might be warranted to spare the unconscious being's loved ones the burden of a continued death watch or to avoid the economic burdens of continued life support.

10. Warren, *supra* note 2, at 8–9, 77.

11. Loren E. Lomasky, *Persons, Rights, and the Moral Community* 226 (1987): "One may not kill one person to confiscate organs that can be used to save three others even if the utilitarian calculus indicates that total utility is thereby increased."

12. Byrne, *supra* note 3, at 127–28, 132–33.

13. *See* Walters, *supra* note 5, at 151.

14. *Id.* at 143–49; AMA Council on Ethical and Judicial Affairs, *The Use of Anencephalic Neonates as Organ Donors,* 273 JAMA 1614 (1995).

15. The infliction of suffering is generally considered to be inhumane and morally bad. *See* Jamie Mayerfeld, *Suffering and Moral Responsibility* (1999); Peter Singer, *Writings on an Ethical Life* 34–35, 42 (2000).

16. Allen C. Buchanan & Dan W. Brock, *Deciding for Others: The Ethics of Surrogate Decision Making* 196–99 (1989).

17. R. S. Downie & K. C. Calman, *Healthy Respect: Ethics in Health Care* (2d ed. 1994), 71–75; Margaret A. Somerville, *Birth and Life: Establishing a Framework of Concepts,* 21 Conn. L. Rev. 667, 671–72 (1989); Warren, *supra* note 2, at 91–92.

18. Lainie Friedman Ross, *Children, Families, and Health Care Decision-Making* 18 n.26 (1998). *See also id.* at 45–46.

19. Derryck Beyleveld & Roger Brownsword, *Human Dignity in Bioethics and Biolaw* 112–13, 117, 130 (2001).

20. Wendy Anton Fitzgerald, *Engineering Perfect Offspring: Devaluing Children and Childhood,* 24 Hastings Const. L.Q. 833, 840–41 (1997).

21. Tom L. Beauchamp, *The Failure of Theories of Personhood,* 9 Kennedy Instit. Ethics J. 309, 310 (1999); John Harris, *The Concept of the Person and the Value of Life,* 9 Kennedy Instit. Ethics J. 293, 294 (1999).

22. Michael Freeden, *Rights* (1991), 58–59; Warren, *supra* note 2, at 90–95.

23. Beyleveld & Brownsword, *supra* note 19, at 22–23; H. Tristram Engelhardt, Jr., *The Foundations of Bioethics* 239 (2d ed. 1996); Lomasky, *supra* note 11, at 194–95; Carl E. Schneider, *Rights Discourse and Neonatal Euthanasia,* 76 Calif. L. Rev. 151, 165 (1988). For a discussion of moral agency, *see* Evelyn B. Pluhar, *Beyond Prejudice: The Moral Significance of Human and Nonhuman Animals* 3–4, 55 (1995). It is possible to be even more demanding in according rights-bearing status, such as by claiming that only humans who are capable of understanding and enforcing obligations can be rights bearers. *See* E. W. Kluge, *The Ethics of Deliberate Death* 118 (1981).

24. Beauchamp, *supra* note 21, at 314. Beauchamp, though, is willing to give respect as persons to beings who lack "moral personhood." *Id.* at 311.

25. *E.g.,* Douglas O. Linder, *The Other Right-to-Life Debate: When Does Fourteenth Amendment Life End?,* 37 Arizona L. Rev. 1182, 1198–99 (1995); Singer, *supra* note 15, at 191–92.

26. Walters, *supra* note 5, at 26. Walters argues that consciousness of self is "the distinctive characteristic that gives high moral standing." *Id.* at 155. *See also infra* note 27.

27. Carl Elliott comments that such beings "fail to meet the criteria by which we [the mentally able] count our own lives as meaningful." Carl Elliott, Attitudes, Souls, and Persons: Children with Severe Neurological Impairment, in *Slow Cures and Bad Philosophers* 99 (Carl Elliott ed., 2001). They "have an interest in avoiding pain and in things that give them pleasure, but we cannot say much more." *Id.* at 98.

28. Michael P. Ambrosio, *A Moral Appraisal of Legal Education: A Plea for a Return to Forgotten Truths,* 22 Seton Hall L. Rev. 1177, 1206 (1992). Any position that holds that only moral agents possess human dignity would exclude severely demented humans. *See* Beyleveld & Brownsword, *supra* note 19, at 112; Izhak

Englard, *Human Dignity*, 21 Cardozo L. Rev. 1903, 1918–19 (2002); R. George Wright, *Treating Persons as Ends in Themselves: The Legal Implications of a Kantian Principle*, 36 U. Richmond L. Rev. 271, 274–76 (2002).

29. *See* Dan W. Brock, *Justice and the Severely Demented Elderly*, 13 J. Med. & Phil. 73, 85–89 (1988).

30. John Kavanaugh talks about "reflexive consciousness"—meaning an "awareness of being aware of oneself"—as the key ingredient of personhood. Kavanaugh, *supra* note 4, at 39–40. However, he would not disqualify profoundly disabled beings, for he views humans as endowed persons who have the potential for reflexive consciousness from the time of conception. For him, a lack of actualization of human potential does not make human beings nonpersons. *Id.* at 67–68, 131.

31. Joseph Fletcher, *Four Indicators of Humanhood*, 6 Hastings Center Rep. 4–7 (December 1974).

32. See John Robertson, *Assessing Quality of Life: A Response to Professor Kamisar*, 25 Ga. L. Rev. 1243, 1247 (1991).

33. Many people have argued that a permanently unconscious being is a nonperson and that the definition of death ought to be altered to include such beings. *See supra* note 7.

34. Bruce Morton, *Right to Die*, 7 Touro L. Rev. 409, 421 (1991). A capacity for pain and suffering can be morally significant even if not sufficient to confer personhood. Gratuitous infliction of suffering is an evil whether the victim is human or not. Blumenson, *supra* note 2, at 26–33; Lomasky, *supra* note 11, at 224–25; Mayerfeld, *supra* note 15.

35. Blumenson, *supra* note 2, at 1; Edmund D. Pellegrino, *Patient and Physician Autonomy: Conflicting Rights and Obligations in the Physician-Patient Relationship*, 10 J. Contemp. Health L. & Pol'y 47, 49 (1994) ("Human beings who lack or have lost the capacity for autonomous actions are nonetheless humans who retain their inherent dignity"); Walters, *supra* note 5, at 19–20, 28–32.

36. *E.g.*, Ambrosio, *supra* note 28, at 1210; Leon R. Kass, *Life, Liberty and the Defense of Dignity* 241–42, 247 (2002).

37. Some philosophers attribute radical capacity to all humans by virtue of their species membership. *See* Beyleveld & Brownsword, *supra* note 19, at 262–63; Kavanaugh, *supra* note 4.

38. R. G. Frey, *Rights, Killing, and Suffering* 62 (1983); Robert Veatch, *The Foundations of Justice* 88–93 (1986).

39. Lois Shepherd, *Face to Face: A Call for Radical Responsibility in Place of Compassion*, Pub. L. & Legal Theory Working Paper #77, p. 36 n.87 (April 2003).

40. Byrne, *supra* note 3, at 55–58.

41. Jean Bethke Elshtain, *The Dignity of the Human Person and the Idea of Human Rights*, 14 J.L. & Religion 53, 65 (2000).

42. Hilde Lindemann Nelson, *What Child Is This?*, 32 Hastings Center Rep. 34–36 (2002). *See also* Beauchamp, *supra* note 21, at 309–11; Arthur Caplan, *Dignity Is a Social Construct*, 327 BMJ (British Medical Journal) 1419 (2003).

43. "Basing the intrinsic worth of all human beings on the fact that they all, qua human, share in rational nature entails no devaluation of other kinds of creatures." Byrne, *supra* note 3, at 57.

44. *Roe v. Wade*, 410 U.S. 113, 158 (1973).

45. This is not to say that it is always in a person's interests to be kept alive. Chapter 4 explores the content of a best-interests formula for surrogate end-of-life medical decision making. Legislators and policy makers sometimes go beyond the realm of born-alive humans to promote respect for human life. I am referring to protections for embryos and fetuses, a subject that is beyond the scope of this book.

46. *In re Hocker*, 791 N.E.2d 302 (Mass. 2003).

47. Linder, *supra* note 25, at 1195: "[T]he prevailing official view is that PVS patients are persons to whom care may or may not be given."

48. *In re T.A.C.P.*, 609 So. 2d 588 (Fla. 1992).

49. *In re Baby K*, 832 F. Supp. 1022 (E.D. Va. 1993), *aff'd on other grounds,* 16 F.3d 590 (4th Cir. 1994), *cert. denied,* 513 U.S. 825 (1994).

50. *Cruzan v. Director, Missouri Department of Health*, 497 U.S. 261 (1990). *Cruzan* is examined in more depth in chapter 2.

51. The treatment of profoundly disabled humans as rights-bearing persons is by no means limited to the United States. The United Nation's Universal Declaration of Human Rights proclaims: "All human beings are born free and equal in dignity and rights." The International Covenant on Civil and Political Rights likewise proclaims the inalienable rights of "all members of the human family." *See* David Feldman, *Human Dignity as a Legal Value: Public Law* 682, 686, 688–89 (1999); Dierck Ullrich, *Concurring Visions: Human Dignity in the Canadian Charter of Rights and Freedoms and the Basic Law of the Federal Republic of Germany,* 3 Global Jurist 12–13 (2003).

52. Lomasky, *supra* note 11, at 203.

53. Walters, *supra* note 5, at 52. *See also* Nancy S. Jecker, *Anencephalic Infants and Special Relationships,* 11 Theoretical Med. 333, 339 (1990).

54. As quoted in Pluhar, *supra* note 23, at 89.

55. The tendency to identify emotionally with all humanlike beings provided part of the impetus for state legislative efforts to ban partial-birth abortions. Although one such legislative effort was struck down in *Stenberg v. Carhart*, 530 U.S. 914 (2000), the legislative distaste for an abortion process that so resembles infanticide struck a responsive chord from Justice Kennedy in dissent. *Id.* at 963.

56. Lomasky, *supra* note 11, at 199–204; Pluhar, *supra* note 23, at 96–97.

57. Warren, *supra* note 2, at 88, 170–71.

58. Engelhardt, *supra* note 23, at 147–50; Walters, *supra* note 5, at 37–38, 70; Warren, *supra* note 2, at 164–66.

59. Engelhardt, *supra* note 23, at 147, 240; Walters, *supra* note 5, at 70.

60. Moreover, as Leon Kass points out, because we don't fully know the inner life and feelings of profoundly disabled humans, excluding them from personhood risks

denying some humans simple pleasure and interactions. *See also* Linder, *supra* note 25, at 1199: "Persons in persistent vegetative states could conceivably retain some form of primitive consciousness that resides in the reticular formation of the brain. Though we assume that they do not, we cannot know what we assume."

61. *See* Jennifer S. Bard, *The Diagnosis Is Anencephaly and the Parents Ask about Organ Donation: A Guide for Hospital Counsel and Ethics Committees,* 21 West. N. Eng. L. Rev. 49, 79–80 (1999), for a more detailed account of this episode.

62. Pluhar, *supra* note 23, at 267.

63. Alan Gewirth, *Human Dignity as the Basis of Rights,* in The Constitution of Rights 10, 24 (M. J. Meyer & W. A. Parent eds., 1992).

64. *See id.* at 25–26, suggesting a "principle of proportionality" that would give minimally rational people rights that are proportionate to their agency. *See also* Pluhar, *supra* note 23, at 249.

65. *Id.* at 240, 243–45, 248–51.

66. *Id.* at 250–51. Pluhar believes that some nonhuman animals also have moral status that is grounded on their purposiveness. As noted, a discussion about the moral status of nonhuman animals is beyond the scope of this book, as is a discussion about the capacity of non–human animals to have desires and purposes.

67. *Id.* at 259, saying that the key issue is "whether the being has the capacity to *care* about what happens to him or her."

68. Harris, *supra* note 21, at 293, 307.

69. Pluhar, *supra* note 23, at 293.

70. John Keown, *Euthanasia, Ethics, and Public Policy* 245 (2002).

71. Gewirth, *supra* note 63, at 15–17.

72. Feldman, *supra* note 51, at 700.

73. Matthew O. Clifford & Thomas P. Huff, *Some Thoughts on the Meaning and Scope of the Montana Constitution's Dignity Clause,* 61 Montana L. Rev. 301, 331–32 (2000); Paul R. Friedman, *The Rights of Mentally Retarded Persons* 94 (1976).

74. *See* Ullrich, *supra* note 51, at 26, 80, explaining how human dignity informs various rights that are protected by the German constitution. *See also* Doron Shultziner, *Human Dignity: Functions and Meanings,* 3 Global Jurist Topics 1–3 (2003) (describing how human dignity provides a foundational value that informs various rights that are protected in many international conventions and national constitutions).

75. Beyleveld & Brownsword, *supra* note 19, at 30.

76. Clifford & Huff, *supra* note 73, at 308–11; Englard, *supra* note 28, at 1913.

77. The quotation is from *Casey v. Planned Parenthood,* which dealt with a woman's decision whether to terminate a pregnancy. However, the U.S. Supreme Court has recognized the fundamental nature of medical decision making in other contexts as well, such as in decisions to reject life-sustaining medical intervention.

See Cruzan, 497 U.S. at 277–79, as reinforced by *Washington v. Glucksberg,* 521 U.S. 702, 719–20 (1990).

78. *E.g., Matter of Requena,* 517 A.2d 886, 891 (N.J. Chancery Div. 1986).

79. *See* Norman L. Cantor, *Prospective Autonomy: On the Limits of Shaping One's Post-Competence Medical Fate,* 8 J. Contemp. Health L. & Pol'y 13 (1992).

80. Norman L. Cantor, *Advance Directives and the Pursuit of Death with Dignity* (1993); Robert S. Olick, *Taking Advance Directives Seriously* (2001).

81. Some jurisdictions (including New York, California, Kentucky, Michigan, and Wisconsin) diverge from this model. They insist that a decision to end life-sustaining medical interventions must be grounded on clear and convincing evidence of the patient's prior wishes (or on a judgment by a surrogate previously designated by the now incompetent patient). *See* Mary Ann Buckley, *Comment, Matter of Wendland: Contradiction, Confusion, and Constitutionality,* 11 J.L. & Pol'y 255 (2002); Norman L. Cantor, *Twenty-five Years after* Quinlan: *A Review of the Jurisprudence of Death and Dying,* 29 J.L. Med. & Ethics, 182, 190 (2001).

82. *E.g., Matter of Wendland,* 28 P.3d 151 (Calif. 2001) (drawing a sharp distinction between autonomy-based decisions—for example, implementing an advance medical directive—and a guardian's *parens patriae* role of protecting a ward's interests); *Wentzel v. Montgomery General Hospital,* 447 A.2d 1244 (Md. App. 1982).

83. Application of a best-interests standard does not mean that the wishes of the never-competent patient are ignored. Chapter 6 addresses the impact of the utterances of profoundly disabled persons.

84. The notion of intrinsic human worth and concomitant dignity is widely accepted as a key element in defining the limits of civilized behavior. *See, e.g.,* Beyleveld & Brownsword, *supra* note 19 at 26–29, 42–45, 50–53; Deryck Beyleveld & Roger Brownsword, *Human Dignity, Human Rights, and Human Genetics,* 61 Mod. L. Rev. 661, 665–67 (1998); Meir Dan-Cohen, Defending Dignity, in *Harmful Thoughts: Essays on Law, Self, and Morality* (M. Dan-Cohen ed. 2002), 150–71; Elshtain, *supra* note 41, at 62–73; England, *supra* note 28, at 1906; Gewirth, *supra* note 63, at 12, 17; Lois Shepherd, *Dignity and Autonomy after* Washington v. Glucksberg: *An Essay about Abortion, Death, and Crime,* 7 Cornell J.L. & Pub. Pol'y 431, 456 (1998); Shultziner, *supra* note 74, at 12. Earlier in this chapter, I suggest that permanently unconscious humans do not have full moral status. For me, all other human beings do have full moral status and intrinsic human dignity, and even the permanently unconscious have full legal status and a measure of moral status.

85. Beyleveld & Brownsword, *Human Dignity, Human Rights, supra* note 84, at 662–63; Feldman, *supra* note 51, at 689–90, 696–700; Wright, *supra* note 28, at 295–96.

86. Ullrich, *supra* note 51, at 23.

87. Gewirth, *supra* note 63, at 15–17; William A. Parent, Constitutional Values and Human Dignity, in the *Constitution of Rights* 47, 62–63 (M. J. Meyer & W. A. Parent eds., 1992); Ullrich, *supra* note 51, at 74–75.

88. See Dan-Cohen, *supra* note 84, at 161; Clifford & Huff, *supra* note 73, at 326–27; Wright, *supra* note 28, at 295–96.

89. *Ribitsch v. Austria*, 236 *Judgments and Decisions of the Council of Europe* (vol. 236) 32–33, 38 (1996). *See* Feldman, *supra* note 51, at 690–93.

Chapter 2

1. 381 U.S. 479 (1965).

2. *See, e.g., In re Brook's Estate*, 205 N.E.2d 435, 442 (Ill. 1965); William P. Cannon, *The Right to Die*, 7 Hous. L. Rev. 654 (1970); Norman L. Cantor, *A Patient's Decision to Decline Life-Saving Medical Treatment: Bodily Integrity versus the Preservation of Life*, 26 Rutgers L. Rev. 228, 240–41 (1973); Dana J. Sharpe & Robert F. Hargest, *Lifesaving Treatment for Unwilling Patients*, 36 Ford. L. Rev. 695 (1968).

3. *Roe v. Wade*, 410 U.S. 113 (1973). *Lawrence v. Texas*, 539 U.S. 558 (2003), recently confirmed the principle that certain intimate personal choices are entitled to special constitutional protection.

4. *In re Quinlan*, 355 A.2d 647, 670 (N.J. 1976).

5. *Id.* at 664. *See* Donald Beschle, *Autonomous Decisionmaking and Social Choice: Examining the Right to Die*, 77 Ky. L. Rev. 319, 327 (1988–89).

6. *See Rasmussen v. Fleming*, 741 P.2d 674, 686 (Ariz. 1987); *In re Foody*, 482 A.2d 713, 718 (Conn. 1984); *Severns v. Wilmington Medical Center*, 421 A.2d 1334, 1347 (Del. 1980); *John F. Kennedy Memorial Hospital v. Bludworth*, 452 So. 2d 921, 924 (Fla. 1984); *Matter of Ingram*, 689 P.2d 1363, 1370–72 (Wash. 1984); *In re Colyer*, 660 P.2d 738, 746 (Wash. 1983).

7. "The right of incompetent individuals to refuse medical treatment is effectuated through the doctrine of substituted judgement." *Matter of R.H.*, 622 N.E.2d 1071, 1075 (Mass. App. 1993). *See also Bludworth*, 452 So. 2d at 923–24; *Brophy v. New England Sinai Hospital*, 497 N.E.2d 626, 635 (Mass. 1986); *In re Moe*, 432 N.E.2d 712, 719–20, 725–26 (Mass. 1982); *Rosebush v. Oakland City Prosecutor*, 491 N.W.2d 633 (Mich. App. 1992); *Ingram*, 689 P.2d at 1369.

8. *Bludworth*, 452 So. 2d at 926; *Superintendent of Belchertown State School v. Saikewicz*, 370 N.E.2d 417, 423 (Mass. 1977); *Colyer*, 660 P.2d at 744. Another court has commented: "The constitutional right to choose or refuse treatment extends to incompetent as well as competent individuals." *Guardianship of Ruth E.J.*, 514 N.W.2d 213, 217 (Wis. App. 1995). *See also Bush v. Schiavo*, 2004 Fla. LEXIS 1539 (Fla. 2004).

9. *See* Wentzel v. Montgomery General Hospital, 447 A.2d 1244, 1258 (Md. App. 1982), *quoting from In re Grady*, 426 A.2d 467, 482 (N.J. 1981); *Matter of Hayes*, 608 P.2d 635, 637 (Wash. 1980).

10. Sanford Kadish, *Letting Patients Die: Legal and Moral Reflections*, 80 Calif. L. Rev. 857, 870 (1992). *See also Developments in the Law, Medical Technology and the Law*, 103 Harv. L. Rev. 1519, 1664–65 (1990); Thomas Mayo, *Constitu-*

tionalizing the Right to Die, 49 Md. L. Rev. 103, 146 (1990) (arguing that irreversible incompetency is "incompatible with notions of autonomy and personal decision-making").

11. Allan Buchanan, *The Limits of Proxy Decision Making,* 29 UCLA L. Rev. 386, 407 (1981); Martha Minow, *Making All the Difference* 325 (1990).

12. For a detailed presentation of this argument, *see* Norman L. Cantor, *Discarding Substituted Judgment and Best Interests: Toward a Constructive Preference Standard for Dying, Previously Competent Patients without Advance Instructions,* 48 Rutgers L. Rev. 1193, 1241–67 (1996). If a patient's condition fits a scenario as to which we know people's overwhelming preference, following group preference makes sense, at least where the individual's actual personal preference is unknown. *See Rasmussen,* 741 P.2d at 686. And we do know strong majority preferences for certain end-of-life scenarios, such as a revulsion toward being mired in a permanently unconscious state.

13. Rebecca Dresser, *Confronting the Near Irrelevancy of Advance Directives,* 5 J. Clinical Ethics 55, 56 (1994); Rebecca Dresser & John A. Robertson, *Quality of Life and Non-Treatment for Incompetent Patients,* 17 J.L. Med. & Ethics 234 (1989).

14. *Superintendent of Belchertown State School v. Saikewicz,* 370 N.E.2d 417 (Mass. 1976). *See also Foody,* 482 A.2d at 718; *Bludworth,* 452 So. 2d at 921.

15. *Saikewicz* at 428, 434. The New Jersey Supreme Court has also suggested that incompetent patients have the "same right of self-determination" as competent patients. *In re Jobes,* 529 A.2d 434 (N.J. 1987). *See also In re Peter,* 529 A.2d 419, 423 (N.J. 1987); *Schiavo, supra* note 8.

16. *See In re L.H.R.,* 321 S.E.2d 716, 722 (Ga. 1984) (declaring that infants have a right to refuse treatment that can be exercised by their parents); *In re Torres,* 357 N.W.2d 332, 341 (Minn. 1984); *In re Hamlin,* 689 P.2d 1372, 1375 (Wash. 1984).

17. *In re Jane A.,* 629 N.E.2d 1337 (Mass. App. 1994); *In re Moe,* 579 N.E.2d 682, 685 (Mass. App. 1991); *In re Jane Doe,* 533 A.2d 523, 525–26 (R.I. 1987).

18. *Matter of Susan S.,* 1996 W.L. 75343 (Del. Ch. 1996) (recognizing that a surrogate's decision for a profoundly disabled woman is not a "personal choice" or "genuine choice," although the surrogate may still be entitled to choose on behalf of a ward).

19. *See, e.g.,* Buchanan, *supra* note 11, at 407; Mark Strasser, *Incompetents and the Right to Die: In Search of Consistent Meaningful Standards,* 83 Ky. L.J. 733, 738–40 (1994–95); Walter L. Webster, *"Right to Die" Cases: A Model for Judicial Decision-Making?,* 7 N.Y.L. Sch. J. Hum. Rts. 140, 147 (1990).

20. Peter G. Filene, *In the Arms of Others* 137 (1999); Susan R. Martyn, *Substituted Judgment, Best Interests, and the Need for Best Respect,* 3 Cambridge Q. Health Care Ethics 195, 198–99 (1994); Minow, *supra* note 11, at 325; Bernadette Tobin, *Did You Think about Buying Her a Cat? Some Reflections on the Concept of Autonomy,* 11 J. Contemp. Health L. & Pol'y 417, 422–23 (1995).

21. Louise Harmon, *Falling Off the Vine: Legal Fictions and the Doctrine of Substituted Judgment,* 100 Yale L.J. 1, 64–65 (1990); Tobin, *supra* note 20.

22. The majority in *Cruzan* noted that an incompetent person cannot "make an informed and voluntary choice to exercise" any right, including rejection of medical treatment, 497 U.S. at 280. *See In re L.W.*, 735 A.2d 448, 460 (D.C. 1999); *In re Storar*, 438 N.Y.S.2d 266, 275, 420 N.E.2d 64, 72 (N.Y. 1981); *In re L.W.*, 482 N.W.2d 60, 69–70 (Wis. 1992).

23. *Matter of Susan S.*, 1996 W.L. at 75343; commenting that a surrogate's choice is "not a personal choice, and no amount of legal legerdemain can make it so." *In re Moe*, 432 N.E.2d 712, 724 (Mass. 1982) (Nolan, J. dissenting); *In re Eberhardy*, 307 N.W.2d 881, 893 (Wis. 1981).

24. *Curran v. Bosze*, 566 N.E.2d 1319, 1326 (Ill. 1990).

25. Roger B. Dworkin, *Limits: The Role of the Law in Bioethical Decision Making* 117 (1996). *See also* Lynn E. Lebit, *Note, Compelled Medical Procedures Involving Minors and Incompetents and Misapplication of the Substituted Judgment Doctrine*, 7 J.L. & Health 107, 124–27 (1992–93).

26. *See* Robert Burt & Monroe Price, Nonconsensual Medical Procedures and the Right to Privacy, in *The Mentally Retarded Citizen and the Law* 95–96 (Michael Kindred ed., 1976); Harmon, *supra* note 21; Walter M. Weber, *Substituted Judgment Doctrine: A Critical Analysis*, 1 Issues L. & Med. 131, 152–53 (1985).

27. The status of a constitutional right to refuse treatment was assumed by the U.S. Supreme Court in 1990 and confirmed in 1997. *See Cruzan v. Missouri Department of Health*, 497 U.S. 261, 278 (1990), and *Washington v. Glucksberg*, 521 U.S. 702, 720 (1997). "[T]he right to self-determination in matters of personal health is deeply rooted in our constitutional tradition." *In re Cincinnati Radiation*, 874 F. Supp. 796, 815 (D. Ohio 1995).

28. Conservatorship of Valerie N., 707 P.2d 760, 772 (Cal. 1985); *Wentzel*, 447 A.2d at 1258.

29. *Saikewicz*, 370 N.E.2d at 435. *See also Brophy* 497 N.E.2d at 634–35.

30. *Bludworth*, 452 So. 2d at 923. *See also Bush v. Schiavo*, 2004 Fla. LEXIS 1539 (2004).

31. *Saikewicz*, 370 N.E.2d at 428.

32. *Moe*, 432 N.E.2d at 720.

33. *Blouin v. Spitzer*, 213 F. Supp. 2d 184 (N.D.N.Y. 2002), *aff'd*, 356 F.3d 348 (2d Cir. 2004). *See* Alicia R. Ouellette, *When Vitalism Is Dead Wrong: The Discrimination against Torture of Incompetent Patients*, 79 Ind. L.J. 1, 13–18 (2004).

34. This determination flows both from common sense and from the affidavit that was submitted by a palliative care expert, Dr. Kathleen McGrail, in litigation involving Pouliot's estate. *Id.* at 21–22.

35. *Thompson v. Oklahoma*, 487 U.S. 815, 824 n.23 (1988). *See also In re Hocker*, 791 N.E.2d 302 (Mass. 2003), acknowledging that a mentally disabled person may have rights and interests that can be vindicated by a surrogate.

36. *In re L.W.*, 482 N.W.2d 60, 68–69, 76 (Wis. 1992). *See also Gray v. Romeo*, 697 F. Supp. 580, 587 (D.R.I. 1988); *Eichner v. Dillon*, 426 N.Y.S.2d 517, 542–43 (N.Y. App. Div. 1980); Larwrence J. Nelson et al., *Forgoing Medically Provided*

Nutrition and Hydration in Pediatrics Care, 23 J.L. Med. & Ethics 33, 38 (1995); William A. Krais, *Note, The Incompetent Developmentally Disabled Person's Right of Self-Determination: Right to Die, Sterilization, and Institutionalization,* 15 Am. J.L. & Med. 333, 350 (1989).

37. *In re Jane Doe,* 583 N.E.2d 1263, 1267–68 (Mass. 1992).

38. *Custody of a Minor,* 393 N.E.2d 836, 844 (Mass. 1979). *See also* David S. Lockemeyer, *Note, At What Cost Will the Court Impose a Duty to Preserve the Life of a Child?,* 39 Cleveland St. L. Rev. 577, 586 (1991) (noting the judicial melding of substituted judgment and best interests in the context of decisions affecting small children).

39. *In re Grady,* 426 A.2d 467, 482 (N.J. 1981). *See In re P.S.,* 452 N.E.2d 969, 974 (Ind. 1982); Harmon, *supra* note 21, at 48–49.

40. Alan B. Handler, *Individual Worth,* 17 Hofstra L. Rev. 493, 513–14 (1989). *See also* Stewart Pollock, *Life and Death Decisions: Who Makes Them and by What Standard?,* 41 Rutgers L. Rev. 505, 525–30 (1988).

41. *Strunk v. Strunk,* 445 S.W.2d 145 (Ky. 1969).

42. Joel Feinberg, *Freedom and Fulfillment* 20–23 (1992).

43. John Garvey, *Freedom and Choice in Constitutional Law,* 94 Harv. L. Rev. 1756, 1777–78, 1782–83, 1791–94 (1981).

44. *See, e.g.,* Martha A. Field, *Killing "The Handicapped": Before and after Birth,* 16 Harvard Women's L.J. 79, 95 (1993); Martha Minow, *Interpreting Rights: An Essay for Robert Cover,* 96 Yale L.J. 1860, 1888–90 (1987); Carl E. Schneider, *Rights Discourse and Neonatal Euthanasia,* 76 Calif. L. Rev. 151, 175 (1988); Lois Shepherd, *Dignity and Autonomy after* Washington v. Glucksberg: *An Essay about Abortion, Death, and Crime,* 7 Cornell J.L. & Pub. Pol'y 431, 455 (1998).

45. *See Jane Doe,* 432 N.E.2d at 1272 (Nolan, J. dissenting); *Matter of Finn,* 625 N.Y.S.2d 809–11 (Sup. Ct. 1995).

46. Regarding sterilization, *see* Ohio Stat. §§ 5123.86(A) and 5123.86(B) (2004). For state cases that radically restrict surrogate removal of life support, *see infra* note 54. The federal government has also sought to limit end-of-life medical decision making for handicapped newborns. In 1984, the Department of Health and Human Services adopted the famous "Baby Doe" regulations, which sought to limit circumstances in which life support is withheld from severely stricken infants. The regulations required states to institute systems to respond to any reports of newborns who were being denied medical treatment. Those regulations were invalidated in *Bowen v. American Hospital Association,* 476 U.S. 610 (1986). The current regulations purport to limit the circumstances in which life support may be withheld from an infant, but the impact of those regulations is uncertain. *See infra* note 103.

47. Jonas Robitscher, *Eugenic Sterilization* 9–14 (1973).

48. Some state courts ruled that the statutes denied procedural due process in not providing sufficient notice or a sufficient opportunity to contest a petition for sterilization. A few state courts found that statutes denied equal protection by mandating sterilization only of institutionalized feebleminded persons (in contrast to noninstitutionalized feebleminded persons). *See generally* Elizabeth S. Scott, *Ster-*

ilization of Mentally Retarded Persons: Reproductive Rights and Family Privacy, 1986 Duke L.J. 806, 809–13 (1986).

49. Buck v. Bell, 274 U.S. 200 (1927).

50. *North Carolina Association for Retarded Children v. State of North Carolina,* 420 F. Supp. 451, 457–58 (M.D.N.C. 1976); *Cook v. Oregon,* 495 P.2d 768, 771–72 (Or. Ct. App. 1972); Erika T. Blum, *Note, When Terminating Parental Rights Is Not Enough: A New Look at Compulsory Sterilization,* 28 Ga. L. Rev. 977, 989, 1000–05 (1994). *See also In re Simpson,* 180 N.E.2d 206, 208 (Ohio Prob. 1962).

51. Burt & Price, *supra* note 26, at 97.

52. *See id.*

53. Donald Giannella, *Eugenic Sterilization and the Law, in Eugenic Sterilization* 74–75 (J. Robitscher ed., 1973).

54. *See Hudson v. Hudson,* 373 So. 2d 310, 312 (Ala. 1979); *A.L. v. G.R.H.,* 325 N.E.2d 501 (Ind. App. 1975); *Holmes v. Powers,* 439 S.W.2d 579 (Ky. 1968); *In re M.K.R.,* 515 S.W.2d 467, 471 (Mo. 1974); *In re D.D.,* 408 N.Y.S.2d 104 (App. Div. 1978); *Frazier v. Levi,* 440 S.W.2d 393 (Tex. Civ. App. 1969); Annotation, *Jurisdiction of Court to Permit Sterilization of Mentally Defective Person in Absence of Specific Statutory Authority,* 74 A.L.R.3d 1210, 1213 (1976). *But see Jessin v. County of Shasta,* 79 Cal. Rep. 359 (Cal. App. 1969); *In re Simpson,* 180 N.E.2d 206 (Ohio Prob. Ct. 1962).

55. Questions existed not only about the heredity of conditions but about whether the patients actually had the suspect conditions. For example, research indicates that Carrie Buck, the focus of *Buck v. Bell,* was not mentally handicapped. *See* Roberta M. Berry, *From Involuntary Sterilization to Genetic Enhancement: The Unsettled Legacy of* Buck v. Bell, 12 Notre Dame J.L. Ethics & Pub. Pol'y 401, 419–21 (1998).

56. *In re M.K.R.,* 515 S.W.2d 467 (Mo. 1974).

57. Martha A. Field & Valerie A. Sanchez, *Equal Treatment for People with Mental Retardation* 87 (1999). *See* Ohio Stat. § 5123.86(A) (2004).

58. *In re Storar,* 438 N.Y.S.2d 266, 420 N.E.2d 64 (N.Y. 1981), *cert. denied,* 454 U.S. 858 (1981).

59. *In re Westchester Medical Center* (O'Connor), 534 N.Y.S.2d 886, 521 N.E.2d 607 (N.Y. 1988).

60. *Id.,* 534 N.Y.S.2d at 892.

61. *Matter of Wendland,* 28 P.3d 152 (Calif. 2001); *DeGrella v. Elston,* 858 S.W.2d 698 (Ky. 1993); *Mack v. Mack,* 618 A.2d 744 (Md. 1993); *In re Martin,* 538 N.W.2d 399 (Mich. 1995); *Cruzan v. Harmon,* 760 S.W.2d 408 (Mo. 1989); *Spahn v. Eisenberg,* 543 N.W.2d 485 (Wis. 1997).

62. *Grady,* 426 A.2d at 467.

63. A few cases that were decided even before the 1980s upheld the jurisdiction of courts to authorize sterilizations that were sought by parents and guardians on behalf of their profoundly disabled charges. *See Ruby v. Massey,* 452 F. Supp. 361, 368 (D. Conn. 1978); *Jessin v. County of Shasta,* 79 Cal. Rep. 359 (1969); *In re Sallmaier,*

378 N.Y.S.2d 989 (N.Y. Sup. Ct. 1976); *In re Simpson,* 180 N.E.2d 206 (Ohio Prob. Ct. 1962). *In re Grady* in 1981 was a landmark case—in part because of the carefully considered judicial analysis that influenced almost all succeeding courts.

64. *Grady,* 426 A.2d at 469.

65. Sterilization is one instance where a medical choice affects fundamental constitutional interests, however the choice is exercised. Just as a decision to submit to sterilization promotes one constitutional interest (nonprocreation) while sacrificing another (procreation), a decision to choose heart surgery promotes one interest (life) while sacrificing another (the right to reject life-sustaining treatment and thus to preserve bodily integrity).

66. *Grady,* 426 A.2d at 474.

67. *Id.* at 475.

68. *Id.* at 481.

69. For a list of the relevant cases, *see* Edward J. Larson & Leonard J. Nelson, *Involuntary Sexual Sterilization of Incompetents in Alabama: Past, Present, and Future,* 43 Ala. L. Rev. 399, 431 n.188 (1992). *See also* John Hackett, *Note, Procreative Choice for the Incompetent Developmentally Disabled,* 36 DePaul L. Rev. 95, 102–03, 111 (1986). Not every judicial decision in the 1980s favored allowing surrogate consent to sterilization. *See Eberhardy,* 307 N.W.2d at 881 (finding no jurisdiction to authorize a guardian's choice of sterilization for a profoundly disabled ward).

70. *Moe,* 432 N.E.2d at 719. *See also Wentzel,* 447 A.2d at 1258.

71. *Conservatorship of Valerie N.,* 707 P.2d 760 (Calif. 1985).

72. *Id.* at 773.

73. *Matter of Drabick,* 200 Cal. App. 3d 185 (Cal. App. 1988). *But see Conservatorship of Wendland,* 28 P.3d 151 (Cal. 2001).

74. *Drabick,* 200 Cal. App. 3d at 208.

75. *Id.* at 205.

76. *Id.* at 208.

77. *See also Matter of L.W.,* 482 N.W.2d 60, 68–69 (Wis. 1992) (allowing a surrogate choice to end life support for a seventy-nine-year-old lifelong incompetent who had deteriorated to a permanently vegetative state). Unfortunately, both California and Wisconsin have retreated from this favorable disposition toward surrogate end-of-life decisions. Both states confine a surrogate prerogative to end life support to instances where the patient is permanently unconscious or where the still-conscious patient previously gave clear and convincing instructions declining treatment (or previously appointed a health-care agent). *See Wendland & Spahn, supra* note 61.

78. Mark Kuczewski, *Narrative Views of Personal Identity and Substituted Judgment in Surrogate Decision Making,* 27 J.L. Med. & Ethics 32, 34 (1999). *See also* Lawrence J. Nelson et al., *Forgoing Medically Provided Nutrition and Hydration in Pediatric Patients,* 23 J.L. Med. & Ethics 33, 38–39 (1995).

79. *Cruzan,* 497 U.S. at 261 (1990).

80. *Cruzan v. Harmon,* 760 S.W.2d 408, 426 (Mo. 1989).

81. Petitioners' Brief in *Cruzan,* 497 U.S. at 261.

82. See Brief of Society for the Right to Die, *amicus curiae* in *Cruzan.* Besides attacking Missouri's restrictive decision-making standard, the petitioners in *Cruzan* also argued for a recognition of the patient's constitutional interest in having medical decisions on her behalf made by her loving and devoted family. In effect, petitioners were asserting a constitutional claim on the part of a bonded surrogate decision maker. Attention to that constitutional claim is deferred to chapter 3, which deals with who decides for the profoundly disabled person.

83. *Cruzan,* 497 U.S. at 267–69.

84. *Id.* at 279–81.

85. *Id.* at 285–88. *See* Cathleen A. Roach, *Paradox and Pandora's Box: The Tragedy of Current Right-to-Die Jurisprudence,* 25 U. Mich. J.L. Reform 133, 144–45 (1991).

86. For a similar critique of the recent *Wendland* case from California, *see* Mary Ann Buckley, *Note,* In re Wendland: *Contradiction, Confusion and Constitutionality,* 11 J.L. & Pol'y 255, 299 (2002); Bernard Lo, Laune Dornbrand, Leslie E. Wolf, & Michelle Groman, *The* Wendland *Case—Withdrawing Life Support from Incompetent Patients Who are Not Terminally Ill,* 346 N. Eng. J. Med. 1489, 1492 (2002).

87. Citations to relevant surveys can be found in Norman L. Cantor, *The Perma nently Unconscious Patient, Nonfeeding, and Euthanasia,* 15 Am. J.L. & Med. 381 (1989). Since 1989, many additional surveys have confirmed the original findings about people's strong aversion to permanent unconsciousness. Robert A. Pearlman et al., *Insights Pertaining to Patient Assessments of States Worse Than Death,* 4 J. Clinical Ethics 35 (1993); Peter A. Singer, Douglas K. Martin & Merrijoy Kelner, *Quality End-of-Life Care: Patients' Perspectives,* 281 JAMA 163 (1999).

88. In her case, the chances were probably even more lopsided since she had uttered expressions that, while not definitive enough to satisfy the Missouri standard of clear and convincing evidence, still indicated a preference not to linger in a permanently unconscious status.

89. *Cruzan,* 497 U.S. at 283–84.

90. On the irony of protecting vulnerable patients by mandating life support contrary to what they would likely prefer, *see* Steven Miles & Allison August, *Courts, Gender, and the Right to Die,* 18 Law, Med. & Health Care 85, 92 (1990).

91. *Cruzan,* 497 U.S. at 283–84.

92. Laurence Tribe, *Constitutional Law* § 15-11, p. 1369 (2d ed. 1988). For other views that mistakenly preserving a person's life can have dire consequences, *see* Nancy Rhoden, *Litigating Life and Death,* 102 Harv. L. Rev. 375, 436 (1988); David J. Mays & Martin Gunderson, *Vitalism Revitalized,* 32 Hastings Center Report 14, 19 (July 2002).

93. *See In re A.C.,* 573 A.2d 1235 (D.C. App. 1990); *In re Bryant,* 542 A.2d 1216, 1220 (D.C. App. 1988); *Wentzel v. Montgomery General Hospital,* 447 A.2d 1244, 1258 (Md. App. 1982). There are various means of measuring majority sen-

timent toward medical handling in particular circumstances. *See* Cantor, *supra* note 12, at 1255–67. Of course, majority sentiment would be known only about certain common situations (such as permanent unconsciousness or extreme mental deterioration). In other situations—where no knowledge exists about strong majoritarian preferences—a life-preserving presumption would prevail.

94. *Cruzan*, 497 U.S. at 310–13.

95. *Id.* at 329–30.

96. *Id.* at 352–57.

97. Petitioner's Reply Brief in *Cruzan*. Cruzan's limbo did not endure thirty years. After the U.S. Supreme Court's decision, her parents presented "new" evidence about Cruzan's prior expressions. That evidence was enough to prompt a trial court to find "clear and convincing" proof of her wishes to have artificial nutrition and hydration removed. The gastrostomy tube was then removed, and Nancy Beth Cruzan was allowed to die. William A. Leschensky, *Note, Constitutional Protection of the Refusal of Treatment*, 14 Harv. J.L. & Pub. Pol'y 248, 259 (1990).

98. *Cruzan*, 497 U.S. at 352–54.

99. Justice Brennan also invoked *Drabick* and its notion that respect for persons demands that surrogates be allowed to take incapacitated persons' interests into account. *Cruzan*, 497 U.S. at 349–50. *See also Strasser, supra* note 19, at 756.

100. Philip Peters, *The State's Interest in the Preservation of Life: From* Quinlan *to* Cruzan, 50 Ohio St. L.J. 891, 943 (1989). Jonathan Moreno comments, in a similar vein: "[The *Cruzan* approach] prevents families from making humane, common sense decisions for their loved ones, prolongs pain, suffering, and frustration for all concerned, and exacerbates the fiscal realities that lurk in the background." Jonathan Moreno, *Who's to Choose? Surrogate Decisionmaking in New York State*, 23 Hastings Cent. Rep. 5, 6 (1993).

101. *See, e.g., Matter of Conroy* 486 A.2d 1209, 1242 (N.J. 1985); *Rasmussen*, 741 P.2d at 689; *In re Grant*, 747 P.2d 445, 457 (Wash. 1987).

102. *In re K.I.*, 735 A.2d 448 (D.C. 1999); *Newmark v. Williams*, 588 A.2d 1108 (Del. 1991); *Matter of A.M.B.*, 640 N.W.2d 262 (Mich. App. 2001); *In re Christopher I.*, 131 Cal. Rep. 122, 136 (Cal. App. 2003); *In re C.A.*, 603 N.E.2d 1171 (Ill. App. 1992). *See* Carol A. Heimer, *Competing Institutions: Law, Medicine, and Family in Neonatal Intensive Care*, 33 Law & Soc'y Rev. 17, 42–43 (1999). *But see Montalvo v. Borkevec*, 647 N.W.2d 413 (Wis. 2002).

103. Developments in the Law, supra note 10, at 1602–03, quoting from the Child Abuse Amendments of 1984. Those regulations are not directly applicable to health-care providers. *Miller v. H.C.A.*, 2003 W.L. 22232090 (Tex. 2003); Heimer, *supra* note 102, at 57–58; Tucker & Goldstein, *The Legal Rights of Persons with Disabilities* (1992), 19:26.

104. The Rehnquist opinion assumed arguendo that a competent patient would have such a right. Seven years later, Chief Justice Rehnquist acknowledged what had been implied in *Cruzan*—that a competent person has a constitutional right to reject life-sustaining medical intervention. *Washington v. Glucksberg*, 521 U.S. 702, 724–26 (1997).

105. *See Guardianship of Ruth E.J.*, 540 N.W.2d 213, 217 (Wis. App. 1995) (invalidating state efforts to exclude electroconvulsive treatment); Rebecca M. Keown, *A Case-Based Approach to Sterilization of Mentally Incompetent Women,* 1 Princeton J. Bioethics 94, 106 (1998); Ouellette, *supra* note 34, at 30–31.

106. *Cruzan*, 497 U.S. at 331–32. *See also* Deborah K. McKnight & Maureen Bellis, *Foregoing Life-Sustaining Treatment for Adult, Developmentally Disabled, Public Wards,* 18 Am. J.L. & Med. 203, 213 (1992) (urging incapacitated persons' "right to have appropriate medical decisions made on their behalf"); Michael T. Morley, *Note, Proxy Consent to Organ Donation by Incompetents,* 111 Yale L.J. 1215, 1218 (2002) (favoring a constitutional right to a surrogate's determination).

107. *See* John Robertson, *Cruzan and the Constitutional Status of Nontreatment Decisions for Incompetent Patients,* 25 Ga. L. Rev. 1139, 1187 (1991); Strasser, *supra* note 19, at 739. *Contra, Matter of Wendland,* 28 P.3d 181 (Calif. 2001); *In re Martin,* 538 N.W.2d 399 (Mich. 1995).

108. The fact that a profoundly disabled person cannot make autonomous choices does not mean that the person's preferences and expressions can be ignored. In Chapter 6, I speak to the importance of a profoundly disabled person's voice to a surrogate's assessment of a ward's feelings and interests.

109. *Lambert v. Wicklund,* 520 U.S. 292 (1997); *Ohio v. Akron,* 497 U.S. 502, 510–12 (1990); *Bellotti v. Beaird,* 443 U.S. 622, 642–50 (1979). *See generally* Martin Guggenheim, *Minor Rights: The Adolescent Abortion Cases,* 30 Hofstra L. Rev. 589 (2002); David D. Meyer, *Lochner Redeemed: Family Privacy after Troxel,* 48 UCLA L. Rev. 1125, 1165–66 (2001).

110. "[E]very minor must have the opportunity . . . to go directly to a court without first consulting or notifying her parents." Guggenheim, *supra* note 109 at 589.

111. *North Carolina Association for Retarded Children v. State of North Carolina,* 420 F. Supp. 451, 455–56 (M.D.N.C. 1976); *Wyatt v. Aderholt,* 368 F. Supp. 1383, 1385 (M.D. Ala. 1974). *See* Krais, *supra* note 36, at 342.

112. *See, e.g., In re A.W.,* 637 P.2d 366, 376 (Colo. 1981); *In re P.S.,* 452 N.E.2d 969 (Ind. 1982); *In re Debra B.,* 495 A.2d 781, 783 (Me. 1985).

113. *Grady,* 426 A.2d at 479. *See generally* Douglas R. Rendleman, *Parens Patriae from Chancery to the Juvenile Court,* 23 S.C. L. Rev. 204, 240 (1971).

114. For description of the kinds of agencies that protect developmentally disabled persons against abuse, *see* McKnight & Bellis, *supra* note 106, at 217–19.

115. Many states foreclose guardians' determinations on troublesome issues such as psychosurgery, electroconvulsive treatment, sterilization, or civil commitment. *See* Bruce Winick, *Advance Directive Instruments for Those with Mental Illness,* 51 U. Miami L. Rev. 57, 79 (1996). These state provisions do not, however, exclude all access by disabled persons to such controversial services. Judges can ordinarily authorize resort to the services in issue as part of equity courts' *parens patriae* authority to act in the best interests of helpless populations.

116. *See In re Valerie N.,* 707 P.2d 760, 775 (Calif. 1985) (striking down a statute that excessively impeded surrogate decision making regarding sterilization).

117. *See, e.g., In re A.W.,* 637 P.2d at 375; *Hayes,* 608 P.2d at 641.

118. The New Jersey Supreme Court was careful to issue such a warning when it articulated standards for judicial approval of sterilization applications that affect profoundly disabled persons. *Grady,* 426 A.2d at 472.

119. AMA Council on Ethical and Judicial Affairs, Policy E-2.20.

120. For a model framework designed to provide nonjudicial review of surrogate end-of-life decisions, *see* McKnight & Bellis, *supra* note 106, at 228–31. That model—applicable to surrogate end-of-life decisions regarding institutionalized patients—includes independent medical review and scrutiny by an institutional ethics committee as well as by an agency charged with protecting the developmentally disabled.

121. *See* Eric M. Jaegers, *Note, Modern Judicial Treatment of Procreative Rights of Developmentally Disabled Persons: Equal Rights to Procreation and Sterilization,* 31 U. Louisville J. Fam. L. 947, 962–63 (1992) (describing the procedural safeguards that are typically mandated for sterilization hearings).

122. *See, e.g., In re C.D.M.,* 627 P.2d 607, 612 (Alaska 1981); *In re Debra B.,* 495 A.2d 781, 783 (Me. 1985); *In re Hilstrom,* 363 N.W.2d 871, 877 (Minn. App. 1985); *Hayes,* 608 P.2d at 635.

123. *Cruzan,* 497 U.S. at 342.

124. *Lambert v. Wicklund,* 520 U.S. 292 (1997). For a case suggesting that clear and convincing evidence of the incapacitated patient's best interests is a constitutional prerequisite to invasion of bodily integrity, *see Matter of Shirley Hilstrom,* 363 N.W.2d 871, 877 (Minn. App. 1985).

125. *In re Angela D.,* 70 Cal. App. 4th 1410, 1418 (Cal. App. 1999).

126. See Buckley, *supra* note 86, at 303–04 (criticizing a clear-and-convincing-evidence standard in the context of refusal of medical intervention). *Cf.* Marybeth Herald, *Until Life Support Do Us Part: A Spouse's Limited Ability to Terminate Life Support for an Incompetent Spouse with No Hope of Recovery,* 24 Thomas Jefferson L. Rev. 207, 215 (2002).

127. *Cf. Addington v. Texas,* 441 U.S. 418, 430 (1979) (upholding a standard of proof that is lesser than clear and convincing for civil commitment), and *In re Wirsing,* 573 N.W.2d 51, 55 (Mich. 1998) (rejecting a clear-and-convincing-proof standard for sterilization).

128. *E.g.,* Cal. Health & Safety Code, § 1250(B) (2000). *Woods v. Kentucky,* 142 S.W. 3d 24 (Ky. 2004) uses an even shorter period.

129. Ore. Rev. Stat. § 97.083, 127.635 (1990); Va. Code § 54.1-2986 (2002); N.C. Gen. Stat. § 90-322 (2003).

130. That recognition came in several concurring opinions that were issued in the 1997 decisions that rejected constitutional challenges to state laws punishing physician assistance to suicide. *Vacco v. Quill,* 521 U.S. 793 (1997); *Washington v. Glucksberg,* 521 U.S. 702 (1997). Several justices indicated that they would perceive significant constitutional problems if a state banned effective pain relief to dying patients, even if the pain relief would hasten the patient's demise. Commen-

tators have suggested that these judicial expressions reflect an emerging constitutional "right to be free of unnecessary pain and suffering at the end of life." David A. Pratt, *Too Many Physicians: Physician-Assisted Suicide after* Glucksberg/Quill, 9 Alb. L.J. Sci. & Tech. 161, 223 (1999). See Robert A. Burt, *The Supreme Court Speaks: Not Assisted Suicide But a Constitutional Right to Palliative Care,* 337 N. Eng. J. Med. 1234 (1997); David J. Garrow, The Right to Die: Death with Dignity in America, 68 Miss. L.J. 407, 417–19 (1998); Ouellette, *supra* note 34, at 33–34.

131. *See In re Jane A.,* 629 N.E.2d 1337, 1340 (1994); *In re D.W.,* 481 N.E.2d 355 (Ill. App. 1985); *In re Jane Doe,* 533 A.2d 523, 526 (R.I. 1987).

132. Angela R. Holder, *Legal Issues in Pediatrics and Adolescent Medicine* 285 (1985).

133. *Angela D.,* 70 Cal. App. 4th at 1419. *See also Ruby v. Massey,* 452 F. Supp. 361, 363 (D. Conn. 1978); *Matter of Susan S.,* 1996 W.L. 75343 (Del. Ch. 1996); *Matter of E.J. Nilsson,* 122 Misc. 2d 458 (N.Y. Sup. Ct. 1983).

134. *Angela D.,* 70 Cal. App. 4th at 420.

135. *Grady,* 426 A.2d at 486.

136. Dworkin, *supra* note 25, at 59–60.

137. "To take away the right to obtain sterilization for persons who are incapable of exercising it personally is to degrade those whose disabilities make them wholly reliant on other, more fortunate, individuals." Jaegers, *supra* note 121, at 976.

138. *See* Peters, *supra* note 100, at 960–61.

139. Alex Capron, July 1990 presentation in Bellagio, Italy, at 23–24 (unpublished manuscript).

140. Giles R. Scofield, *Letters:* Dred Scott *Revisited,* 21 Hastings Center Rep. 41 (September 1991).

141. *Ruvalcalba v. Ruvalcalba,* 850 P.2d 674, 681 (Ariz. App. 1993); *Vaughan v. Vaughan,* 648 So. 2d 193, 195 (Fla. App. 1994); *Kronberg v. Kronberg,* 623 A.2d 806, 811–12 (N.J. Ch. Div. 1993); *Nelson v. Nelson,* 878 P.2d 335 (N.M. App. 1994). *Cf. Newman v. Newman,* 191 N.E. 2d 614, 619 (1963) (allowing a surrogate to elect between alimony and a property settlement).

142. *Ruvalcalba,* 850 P.2d at 681; *Nelson,* 878 P.2d at 339–40.

143. *See Blouin v. Spitzer,* 2004 W.L. 187146 (2d Cir. 2004) (refusing to distinguish between the case of a conscious, suffering patient and a permanently unconscious patient like Cruzan).

144. *Cruzan,* 497 U.S. at 425.

145. *Grady,* 426 A.2d at 481.

146. *E.g.,* Conn. Gen. Stat. Annot. § 45a-682 (1993); Mich. Comp. Laws § 700.5215 (2001); Neb. Rev. Stat. Annot. § 30-2627 (2001).

147. Strasser, *supra* note 19, at 771.

148. Burt & Price, *supra* note 26, at 102–03; Michael Kindred, Guardianship and Limitations upon Capacity, in *The Mentally Retarded Citizen and the Law* 79–80 (Michael Kindred ed., 1976).

Chapter 3

1. *See* American Medical Association, Treatment Decisions for Seriously Ill Newborns, <http://www.ama-assn.org/amal/upload/mm/369/43b.pdf>; *Grecco v. University of Medicine and Dentistry of New Jersey*, 783 A.2d 741, 743–44 (N.J. App. Div. 2001); *Rosebush v. Oakland County Prosecutor*, 491 N.W.2d 633, 636 (Mich. App. 1992). Exceptions exist for emergency situations, emancipated minors (those who have established independent living arrangements), and mature minors (in some jurisdictions).

2. *Bonner v. Moran*, 126 F.2d 121 (D.C. Cir. 1941); *Zaman v. Schultz*, 19 Pa. D. & C. 309, 312 (Cambria County 1933).

3. *Newmark v. Williams*, 588 A.2d 1108 (Del. 1991). *See generally* Lawrence J. Nelson et al., *Forgoing Medically Provided Nutrition and Hydration in Pediatric Patients*, 23 J.L. Med. & Ethics 33, 38–39 (1995); Jennifer Rosato, *Using Bioethics Discourse to Determine When Parents Should Make Health Care Decision for Their Children*, 73 Temple L. Rev. 1, 25–26 (2000).

4. *Troxell v. Granville*, 530 U.S. 57, 65–67 (2000).

5. Some kinds of parental medical determinations might be constitutionally protected. *See Bendiburg v. Dempsey*, 909 F.2d 463 (11th Cir. 1990) (indicating that a state child-protection service's approval of a Hickman catheter when a parent objects "might" be a constitutional violation). But this does not mean that medical issues involving grave consequences for children must be left in parental hands.

6. 497 U.S. 417, 427 (1990) (statute allows judicial bypass of a parental-notification requirement to any minor who is mature enough to consent on her own or whose best interests dictate no parental notification).

7. *But see* Stanley E. Cox, *Government as Arbiter, Not Custodian: Relational Privacy as Foundation for a Right to Refuse Medical Treatment Prolonging Incompetents' Lives*, 18 N.M. L. Rev. 131, 140–44 (1988) (arguing for a broad right of bonded surrogates to make decisions on behalf of incapacitated persons).

8. *See* Robert Burt & Monroe Price, Nonconsensual Medical Procedures and the Right to Privacy, in *The Mentally Retarded Citizen and the Law* 93, 104–07 (Michael Kindred et al. eds., 1976); Martha Minow, *Making All the Difference* 321–22, 326 (1990); Charles Murdock, *Civil Rights of the Mentally Retarded: Some Critical Issues*, 48 N.D. Law. 133, 137–39 (1972); Bonnie P. Tucker & Bruce A. Goldstein, *The Legal Rights of Persons with Disabilities* § 19:3 (1992).

9. *See* Martha A. Field, *Killing the Handicapped—Before and after Birth*, 16 Harv. Women's L.J. 79, 80 (1993) (arguing that parental authority to withdraw life support violates a newborn's right to be free of discrimination); Carl E. Schneider, *Rights Discourse and Neonatal Euthanasia*, 76 Calif. L. Rev. 151, 159 (1988).

10. Former California Supreme Court Justice Rose Bird commented about parental involvement in sterilization decisions: "[P]arents, at least in this limited context, cannot be presumed to have an identity of interests with their children. The inconvenience of caring for the incompetent child coupled with fears of sexual promiscuity or exploitation may lead parents to seek a solution which infringes their

offspring's fundamental procreational rights." *In re Valerie N.,* 707 P.2d 760, 783 n.5 (Calif. 1985).

11. For arguments that support judicial involvement in critical decisions for disabled persons, *see* Martha A. Field & Valerie A. Sanchez, *Equal Treatment for People with Mental Retardation* 100 (1999); Elaine Krasik, *Comment, The Role of the Family in Medical Decision Making for Incompetent Adult Patients: A Historical Perspective and Case Analysis,* 48 U. Pitts. L. Rev. 539, 562–63 (1986); Patricia Wald, Basic Personal and Civil Rights, in *The Mentally Retarded Citizen and the Law* 25–26; (Michael Kindred et al. eds., 1976); Walter L. Webster, *Right-to-Die Cases: A Model for Judicial Decision-Making?,* 7 N.Y.L. Sch. J. Hum. Rts. 140, 151–54 (1990).

12. For example, in the *Quinlan* case, decided in 1976, the New Jersey Supreme Court ruled that requiring judicial recourse as a prerequisite to removal of life support from the unconscious patient would be "impossibly cumbersome." 355 A.2d at 669. *See also In re Lawrance,* 579 N.E.2d 36, 42 (Ind. 1991) (calling reliance on courts "unduly burdensome"); *Woods v. Kentucky,* 142 S.W. 3d 24 (Ky. 2004).

13. Field & Sanchez, *supra* note 11, at 96, 168.

14. American Academy of Pediatrics Committee on Bioethics, *Ethics and the Care of Critically Ill Infants and Children,* 98 Pediatrics 149 (July 1996); Alan Meisel, Legal Issues in Decision Making for Incompetent Patients, in *Advance Directives and Surrogate Decision Making in Health Care* 56–57 (H. Sass, R. Veatch & R. Kinura eds., 1998).

15. President's Commission for the Study of Ethical Problems in Medicine and Biomedical and Behavioral Research, *Deciding to Forgo Life-Sustaining Treatment* 127 (1983). *See also* Nancy Rhoden, *How Should We View the Incompetent?,* 17 Law, Med. & Health Care 264, 266 (1989).

16. President's Commission, *supra* note 15, at 127, recognized the family as an important social unit as part of the Commission's rationale for allocating responsibility to family for end-of-life decisions. *See also* Lainie Friedman Ross, *Children, Families, and Health Care Decision-Making* 39–41 (1998), for another strong endorsement of the value of family autonomy in medical decision making.

17. Dan W. Brock, *What Is the Moral Authority of Family Members to Act as Surrogates of Incompetent Patients?,* 74 Milbank Q. (1996), 599; Ross, *supra* note 16, at 138. I don't have much sympathy with this justice argument. While a personal stake in the outcome does give a person an interest in making a decision, it does not seem "unjust" to avoid a conflict of interest and to seek a more neutral forum for decision making when a helpless person's critical interests are at stake. That does not mean, though, that circumventing parental decisions is good policy, only that "justice" doesn't compel giving affected parties decision-making authority over others.

18. *See Farber v. Olkon,* 254 P.2d 520, 524 (Cal. 1953); *Ritz v. Florida Patients' Compensation Fund,* 436 So. 2d 987, 989 (Fla. App. 1983).

19. *Stern v. Stern,* 473 A.2d 56, 62–63 (Md. App. 1984); *Riggs v. Riggs,* 578 S.E.2d 3, 5 (S.C. 2003).

20. *See generally* Daryl Paul Evans, The Lives of Mentally Retarded People 276 (1983); Krasik, *supra* note 11, at 448, 451; Paul B. Solnick, *Proxy Consent for Incompetent Non-Terminally Ill Adult Patients*, 6 J. Leg. Med. 1, 20–21 (1985). *See also In re Nemser*, 273 N.Y.S.2d 624 (Sup. Ct. 1966) (commenting on the propriety of medical reliance on family determinations in the absence of internal division within the family).

21. For description of the Massachusetts cases, *see* William J. Curran, *A Problem of Consent: Kidney Transplantation in Minors*, 34 N.Y.U.L. Rev. 891, 892–93 (1959); Rachel M. Dufault, *Bone Marrow Donations by Children: Rethinking the Legal Framework in Light of* Curran v. Bosze, 24 Conn. L. Rev. 211, 229 (1991); Janet B. Korins, *Toward a Clear Standard for Authorizing Kidney and Bone Marrow Transplants between Minor Siblings*, 16 Vt. L. Rev. 499, 509–14 (1992).

22. *Strunk v. Strunk*, 445 S.W.2d 145 (Ky. 1969).

23. *See, e.g.*, Dufault, *supra* note 21, at 222; Melvin Lewis, *Kidney Donation by a Seven-Year-Old Identical Twin Child: Psychological, Legal, and Ethical Considerations*, 13 J. Am. Acad. Psychiatry 221, 236–37 (1974).

24. Dorothy M. Bernstein & Roberta G. Simmons, *The Adolescent Kidney Donor: The Right to Give*, 131 Am. J. Psychiatry (1974), 1338, 1341; Thomas H. Murphy, Jr., *Minor Consent to Transplant Surgery: A Review of the Law*, 62 Marq. L. Rev. 149, 152–53 (1978).

25. *See generally* Lisa K. Gregory, *Annotation, Propriety of Surgically Invading Incompetent or Minor for Benefit of a Third Party*, 4 A.L.R.5th 1000 (1999).

26. *See* Melvin D. Levine, Bruce M. Camitta, David Nathan & William J. Curran, *The Medical Ethics of Bone Marrow Transplantation in Children*, 86 J. Pediatrics 145, 146–47 (1975).

27. *See Hart v. Brown*, 289 A.2d 386 (Conn. Super. 1972); *Howard v. Fulton*, 42 U.S.L.W. 2322 (Ga. 1973); *Matter of Doe*, 481 N.Y.S.2d 932 (App. Div. 1984); *Little v. Little*, 576 S.W.2d 493 (Tex. App. 1979); and cases cited in Annotation, *supra* note 25, at 1000 n.8.

28. *See In re Richardson*, 284 So. 2d 185 (La. App. 1973); *In re Pescinski*, 226 N.W.2d 180 (Wis. 1975); Gregory, *supra* note 25, at § 5.

29. *See* Bryan Shartle, *Comment, Proposed Legislation for Safely Regulating the Increasing Number of Living Organ and Tissue Donations by Minors*, 61 La. L. Rev. 433, 450 (2001); Victoria Weisz, *Psycholegal Issues in Sibling Bone Marrow Donation*, 2 Ethics & Behavior 185, 186 (1992).

30. *See* Cara Cheyette, *Note, Organ Harvests from the Legally Incompetent: An Argument against Compelled Altruism*, 41 B.C. L. Rev. 465, 477 (2000).

31. "Judicial oversight of all living organ and tissue donations by minors provides reassurance that the parties involved have carefully considered the relevant factors with central focus on the welfare of the potential donating minor." Shartle, *supra* note 29, at 462.

32. *Compare Lefebvre v. North Broward Hospital District*, 566 So. 2d 568 (Fla. App. 1990); and *Estate of D.W.*, 481 N.E.2d 355 (Ill. App. 1985); *Matter of Jane*

A., 629 N.E.2d 1337 (Mass. App. 1994) (all indicating that judicial approval of a surrogate's abortion decision must be obtained), with *Matter of Barbara C.,* 474 N.Y.S.2d 799 (N.Y. App. Div. 1984); *In re Doe,* 533 A.2d 523, 527 (R.I. 1987) (mother disqualified as surrogate for a disabled daughter only because of sparse contact).

33. Field & Sanchez, *supra* note 11, at 150–54.

34. *E.g.,* Jonas Robitscher, *Eugenic Sterilization* (1973); Edward J. Larson & Leonard J. Nelson, *Involuntary Sexual Sterilization of Incompetents in Alabama: Past, Present, and Future,* 43 Ala. L. Rev. 349 (1992); Elizabeth S. Scott, *Sterilization of Mentally Retarded Persons: Reproductive Rights and Family Privacy,* 1986 Duke L.J. 806, 808–10 (1986).

35. *See Hudson v. Hudson,* 373 So. 2d 310 (Ala. 1979); *In re M.K.R.,* 515 S.W.2d 467, 470–71 (Mo. 1974); *Frazier v. Levi,* 440 S.W.2d 393 (Tex. App. 1969); and cases cited in *In re Moe,* 432 N.E.2d 712 (Mass. 1982). Not every court rejected the parental petitions. *See In re Simpson, Stump v. Sparkman,* 435 U.S. 349 (1978); *Downs v. Sawtelle,* 574 F.2d 1 (1st Cir. 1978); *Matter of Sallmaier* 378 N.Y.S. 2d 989 (Sup. Ct. 1976); 180 N.E.2d 206 (Ohio Prob. Ct. 1962).

36. *See generally* Roger B. Dworkin, *Limits: The Role of the Law in Bioethical Decision Making* 58–60 (1996); Field & Sanchez, *supra* note 11, at 70–89; Scott, *supra* note 34.

37. For articulation of the relevant factors for judicial inquiry, *see Wentzel v. Montgomery General Hospital,* 447 A.2d 1244, 1253–54 (Md. App. 1982); *In re Grady,* 426 A.2d 464, 482–83 (N.J. 1981); *In re Hayes,* 608 P.2d 635, 641 (Wash. 1980).

38. *See Stump v. Sparkman,* 435 U.S. 349 (1978); *Lake v. Arnold,* 232 F.3d 360 (3d Cir. 2000) (involving a 1977 sterilization).

39. *Grady,* 426 A.2d at 474–75. The New Jersey court's 1981 requirement of judicial intervention regarding sterilization contrasted with its 1976 willingness to allocate certain end-of-life decisions to incapacitated patients' guardians who were acting in conjunction with medical personnel (but without judicial participation). I comment on this tension later in this chapter.

40. *See* Roberta Cepko, *Involuntary Sterilization of Mentally Disabled Women,* 8 Berkeley Women's L.J. 122, 145, 153–54 (1993). The California legislature even sought to make judicial findings that sterilization was "beyond a reasonable doubt" a benefit for the mentally disabled person a prerequisite to the procedure. That requirement was struck down as unconstitutional by the California Supreme Court. *Conservatorship of Angela D.,* 83 Cal. Rep. 2d 411, 416 (Cal. App. 1999).

41. *E.g.,* Fla. Stat. Annot. § 744.3215(4) (1997); Idaho Stat. § 66-405(10) (2000); Mich. Comp. L. § 330.1629(B) (2001); Minn. Stat. Annot. § 525.56 (2002); 20 Pa. Consolidated Stat. Annot. §§ 5521, 5155(d) (1975).

42. For a position favoring a parental decision-making prerogative in such a case, subject to judicial intervention only if some interested observer contests the parental determination, *see* Scott, *supra* note 34, at 854–56, 862–63.

43. Field & Sanchez, *supra* note 11, at 165–68, asserting that judicial hearings can be meaningless because in many locales "the request of a family member, accompanied by some evidence of retardation and no vocal opposition, is all that is necessary." *See also* Cepko, *supra* note 40, at 136.

44. *People* ex rel. *Wallace v. Labrenz,* 104 N.E.2d 769 (Ill. 1952); *State v. Perricone,* 181 A.2d 751 (N.J. 1961).

45. *In re Martin,* 538 N.W.2d 399, 401 (Mich. 1995).

46. *Superintendent of Belchertown State School v. Saikewicz,* 370 N.E.2d 417, 428 (Mass. 1977).

47. Nelson et al., *supra* note 3, at 38–39.

48. *In re Quinlan,* 355 A.2d 647 (N.J. 1976).

49. *Id.* at 665.

50. *Id.* at 435. Nor did the Massachusetts court confine its insistence on judicial scrutiny to cases like *Saikewicz,* where the patient was both institutionalized and without close family. However, the Massachusetts judges did subsequently indicate that judicial involvement would not be necessary in all cases involving end-of-life decision making. They tended to rely on bonded family, acting in conjunction with medical personnel, to make decisions for patients unavoidably dying (as opposed to patients with a reasonable chance to gain significant relief from their illness). *See Dinnerstein,* 380 N.E.2d 134, 137–38 (Mass. App. 1978).

51. *See Severns v. Wilmington Medical Center,* 421 A.2d 1334 (Del. 1980); *Estate of Longeway,* 549 N.E.2d 292 (Ill. 1989); *In re P.V.W.,* 424 So. 2d 1015 (La. 1982); *Estate of Leach v. Shapiro,* 13 Ohio App. 3d 393 (Ohio App. 1984).

52. *Warren v. Wheeler,* 858 S.W.2d 263 (Mo. App. 1993).

53. *Rasmussen v. Fleming,* 741 P.2d 674 (Ariz. 1987); *In re Drabick,* 245 Cal. Rep. 840, 852 (Cal. App. 1988); *John F. Kennedy Hospital v. Bludworth,* 452 So. 2d 921, 926 (Fla. 1984); *In re Jane Doe,* 418 S.E.2d 3, 6 (Ga. 1992); *In re Lawrance,* 579 N.E.2d 32, 39 (Ind. 1991); *Matter of Torres,* 357 N.W.2d 332, 341 n.4 (Minn. 1984) (judicial participation was required for a patient who lacked immediate family to act as surrogate, but no judicial intervention was necessary where close family and medical providers were in agreement about a course of treatment); *In re Hamlin,* 689 P.2d 1372, 1377 (Wash. 1984); *Woods v. Kentucky,* 142 S.W. 3d 24 (Ky. 2004); *Protection and Advocacy System v. Presbyterian Healthcare Services,* 989 P.2d 280, 894 (N.M. App. 1999). *See generally* Krasik, *supra* note 11, at 605–07; Alan Meisel, Legal Issues in Decision Making for Incompetent Patients, in *Advance Directives and Surrogate Decision Making in Health Care* (H. Sass, R. Veatch & R. Kamura eds., 1998), 52.

54. *See* American Medical Association Council on Ethical and Judicial Affairs, Opinion 2.20; *Lawrance,* 579 N.E.2d at 42; *Protection and Advocacy System,* 989 P.2d at 896. When health-care providers have qualms about surrogate motivations or about the propriety of the medical course sought by a surrogate, consultation with an institutional ethics committee is almost universally available. *See* Joseph E. Beltran, *Shared Decision Making: The Ethics of Caring and Best Respect,* Bioethics Forum 17, 21–22 (Fall 1996); Nelson et al., *supra* note 3, at 42.

55. *See generally* Ardath A. Hamann, *Family Surrogate Laws: A Necessary Supplement to Living Wills and Durable Powers of Attorney,* 38 Villanova L. Rev. 103 (1993); Adrienne E. Quinn, *Who Should Make Decisions for Incompetent Adults?,* 20 Seattle L. Rev. 573 (1997).

56. Conn. Gen. Stat. § 19a-570(3) (2001); 6 Del. Code § 2501(r)(1) (2003); Iowa Code § 144A.2 (1997); *Protection and Advocacy System,* 989 P.2d at 280. *But see First Healthcare Corp. v. Rettinger,* 467 S.E.2d 243 (N.C. 1996).

57. *See Jane Doe,* 418 S.E.2d at 6 (saying that medical decision making is "best left to the patient's family" and the medical community); *Lawrance,* 579 N.E.2d at 39; *In re Jobes,* 529 A.2d 434, 451 (N.J. 1987) (indicating that family members are generally the best surrogate decision makers because of their familiarity with the patient's values and beliefs).

58. *Jane Doe,* 418 S.E.2d at 3.

59. *In re Rosebush,* 491 N.W.2d 633 (Mich. App. 1992).

60. *In re Barry,* 445 So. 2d 365 (Fla. App. 1984).

61. *In re Grant,* 747 P.2d 445, 456 n.5 (Wash. 1987) (while the patient's mother had been formally appointed a legal guardian, the Washington court indicated that close family members would be accorded similar authority, even in the absence of a guardianship proceeding).

62. *Newmark v. Williams,* 588 A.2d 1108 (Del. 1991).

63. *See Ritz v. Florida Patients' Compensation Fund,* 436 So. 2d 987, 989 (Fla. App. 1983) (a father was allowed to consent to brain surgery for his thirty-two-year-old mentally retarded daughter); *Matter of Cartrette,* #90 SP 35 (N.C. Super. Ct. 2001) (a mother as guardian was allowed to cease artificial nutrition and hydration for a twenty-nine-year-old disabled daughter who was stricken with a fatal illness); *Matter of Hamlin,* 689 P.2d 1372, 1377 (Wash. 1984) (dictum). *See also* Krasik, *supra* note 11, at 556–57. At this point, we are dealing with profoundly disabled children who are living with their parents. Surrogate roles regarding institutionalized persons are discussed later in this chapter.

64. Philip M. Bein, *Surrogate Consent and the Incompetent Experimental Subject,* 46 Food, Drug & Cosmetic L.J. 739, 755–56 (1991). *See also* M. H. Pappworth, *Human Guinea Pigs* 31–43, 52–60 (1968).

65. John Fletcher, *Human Experimentation: Ethics in the Consent Situation,* 32 J.L. & Contemp. Probls. 620, 637 (1967).

66. Bein, *supra* note 64, at 747–48.

67. The National Institutes of Health policy, titled Research Involving Impaired Human Subjects, can be found in Baruch Brody, *The Ethics of Biomedical Research: An International Perspective* 300–03 (1998).

68. *Id.* at 132–33; Jessica Wilen Berg, *Legal and Ethical Complexities of Consent with Cognitively Impaired Research Subjects: Proposed Guidelines,* 24 J.L. Med. & Ethics 18, 21 (1996).

69. Cal. Health & Safety Code § 24178 (1992); Va. Code Annot. § 32.1-162.16 (2001).

70. *Grimes v. Kennedy Krieger Institute,* 782 A.2d 807 (Md. 2001); Bein, *supra* note 64, at 741–42; Diane E. Hoffmann & Jack Schwartz, *Proxy Consent to Participation of the Decisionally Impaired in Medical Research: Maryland's Policy Initiative,* 1 J. Health Care L. & Pol'y 123, 125–26 (1998).

71. *See* Bernadette Tansey, *UCSF Violated Patients' Rights,* San Francisco Chronicle, July 28, 2002, p. A-1 (noting divergent views on whether California law precludes surrogate consent by anyone other than a court-appointed conservator).

72. Rebecca Dresser, *Dementia Research: Ethics and Policy for the Twenty-first Century,* 35 Ga. L. Rev. 661, 675 (2001); Peter V. Rabins, *Issues Raised by Research Using Persons Suffering from Dementia Who Have Impaired Decisional Capacity,* 1 J. Health Care L. & Pol'y 22, 29–30 (1998).

73. *See* Bernard Lo, *Caring for Incompetent Patients: Is There a Physician on the Case?,* 17 Law, Med. & Health Care 214, 217–18 (1989).

74. *See, e.g., Lawrance,* 579 N.E.2d at 42; *In re Jobes,* 529 A.2d 434, 447 (N.J. 1987); *In re Colyer,* 660 P.2d 738, 747 (Wash. 1983); Mark Strasser, *Incompetents and the Right to Die: In Search of Consistent Meaningful Standards,* 83 Ky. L.J. 733, 787–88 (1994–95).

75. Nelson et al., *supra* note 3, at 42.

76. *E.g., Lawrance,* 579 N.E.2d at 42–43; *In re Clark,* 510 A.2d 136, 141–42 (N.J. Ch. Div. 1986).

77. *See* Rebecca Dresser, *Relitigating Life and Death,* 51 Ohio St. L.J. 425, 435 (1990); Minow, *supra* note 8, at 327; Susan Wolf, *Toward a Theory of Process,* 20 Law, Med. & Health Care 278, 286 (1992).

78. New York State Task Force on Life and the Law, *When Others Must Choose: Deciding for Patients without Capacity* 113, 137–47 (1992); *see also* Solnick, *supra* note 20, at 42.

79. *Grady,* 426 A.2d 467, 475 (N.J. 1981). The court also suggested that the criteria for making sterilization decisions were complex and require reasoned deliberation and that end-of-life decisions rely more on "instinct." *Id.*

80. *See* cases cited *supra* note 28.

81. This is not to deny the possibility that parents who care for their children at home might be moved by guilt, fatigue, or some emotion other than concern for the well-being of their offspring. Extreme burdens of care can furnish an incentive for a caretaker to end those burdens. As a general matter, though, a parent who undertakes the burden of home care is likely to be exhibiting devotion to the child's interests and is unlikely to seek premature death for the child.

82. See Fla. Stat. Annot. § 744.3215(4) (1997); Kansas Stat. Annot. § 59-3018(g) (1994); Ky. Stat. § 387.660 (1999); Mich. Comp. L. § 330.1629(B) (2001); 14.800(629)(B) Ill Mental Health & Disability Code § 2-110; Wash. RCW § 11.92.040(3) (1998). Cf. N.J.S.A. § 30:6D-5(a)(4).

83. Ala. Stat. § 22-8A-11 (1997); Idaho Code § 66-405 (2000). New Mexico Stat. § 24-7-6.1(B) (1978).

84. *Matter of Ingram,* 689 P.2d 1363 (Wash. 1984).

85. *Id.* at 1369.

86. *Fincham v. Levin,* 155 So. 2d 883 (Fla. App. 1963).

87. *Farber v. Olkon,* 254 P.2d 520, 524 (Calif. 1953).

88. *McCandless v. New York,* 162 N.Y.S.2d 570 (N.Y. App. Div. 1957).

89. *Farber v. Olkon,* 254 P.2d 520 (Calif. 1953).

90. *In re Foster,* 547 N.W.2d 81, 85 (Minn. 1996); *Price v. Sheppard,* 239 N.W.2d 905, 913 (Minn. 1976); *Matter of Aaron Strauss,* 391 N.Y.S.2d 168 (N.Y. App. Div. 1977). Institutional administrators would usually be accorded the authority to initiate medical treatment in an emergency situation. *See* N.J.S.A. § 30:4-7.2 (1997).

91. *See Michigan Protective Services v. Kirkendall,* 841 F. Supp. 796 (E.D. Mich. 1993), and cases cited *supra* note 37.

92. *Tolley v. Commonwealth of Kentucky,* 892 S.W.2d 580 (Ky. 1995); *Rogers v. Commissioner of Department of Mental Health,* 458 N.E.2d 308, 316 (Mass. 1983).

93. *Id.* at 321–22.

94. *See supra* notes 41 and 82.

95. *See* N.J.S.A. §§ 30:6D-5(a)(4), 30:4-24.2 (1997); Matter of J.M., 678 A.2d 751, 757 (N.J. Ch. Div. 1996); *In re* Promulgation of Guardianship Service Regulations, 512 A.2d 453, 464 (N.J. 1986).

96. *See* Ohio R.C. § 5123.86 (2004).

97. *Matter of Jane A.,* 629 N.E.2d 1337 (Mass. App. 1994).

98. *Matter of Jane Doe,* 533 A.2d 523, 525–26 (R.I. 1987).

99. *In re Barbara C.,* 474 N.Y.S.2d 799 (App. Div. 1984).

100. *In re Promulgation of Guardianship Services Regulations,* 512 A.2d 453, 464 (N.J. 1986) (interpreting New Jersey Administrative Code § 10:45-5.3(c)1) (2001).

101. *See* Deborah K. McKnight & Maureen Bellis, *Foregoing Life-Sustaining Treatment for Adult, Developmentally Disabled Public Wards: A Proposed Statute,* 18 Am. J.L. & Med. 215 n.1 (1992).

102. *Protection and Advocacy System v. Presbyterian Healthcare Services,* 989 P.2d 890 (N. Mex. App. 1999). New York also appears to allow parents to control end-of-life decision making on behalf of their profoundly disabled, institutionalized offspring. *Matter of Mathews,* 650 N.Y.S.2d 373 (N.Y. App. Div. 1996). However, New York courts will review a parental decision at the impetus of institutional administrators and will overrule a parental decision that is not deemed to be in the disabled child's best interests. *See Matter of Storar,* 438 N.Y.S.2d 266 (N.Y. 1981). And the New York attorney general contends that New York law precludes removing life support from any incompetent person without clear prior instructions from the patient. *See Blouin v. Spitzer,* 213 F. Supp. 2d 184 (N.D.N.Y. 2002).

103. *See* Ala. Stat. § 22-8A-11 (1997).

104. *See Matter of Moorhouse,* 593 A.2d 1256, 1262 (N.J. App. Div. 1991) (no judicial intervention where the family decides to withdraw life support from the now permanently unconscious long-term resident of a facility for the disabled, but

a public advocate must review the decision); *In re Hamlin,* 689 P.2d 1372, 1377–78 (Wash. 1984) (dictum saying that the family of a severely retarded man could act without judicial authorization if the family members were in agreement and if physicians and a medical-prognosis committee confirm the dismal medical prognosis). *See also In re Clark,* 510 A.2d 136 (N.J. Ch. Div. 1986) (judicial decision about life-sustaining care where the family of the disabled resident could not agree).

105. Idaho Stat., Tit. 66, § 66-405(8) (2000) (giving a guardian authority to remove life support where physicians certify that the patient is terminal and medical intervention "would only serve to prolong the moment of death for a period of hours, days, or weeks"). *Cf. Matter of Finn,* 634 N.Y.S.2d 262 (App. Div. 1995).

106. Even proceedings aimed at formal appointment of a guardian can be time-consuming, expensive, and difficult. *See Promulgation of Guardian Services Regulations,* 512 A.2d 453, 461 (N.J. 1986); Quinn, *supra* note 55, at 583.

107. New Jersey's scheme, aimed at institutionalized persons under the state Bureau of Guardianship control, provides for medical confirmation of a terminal prognosis, consultation with an institutional ethics committee, and notice to a protective agency before life support is withdrawn. N.J. Admin. Code tit. 48, § 10:48B (2003).

108. See discussion in chapter 4, *infra* at 176–77.

109. McKnight & Bellis, *supra* note 101, at 203.

110. *Id.* at 205–06, 215–19.

Chapter 4

1. State custody and daily responsibility for a profoundly disabled person do not necessarily entail state control of serious medical decisions. Chapter 3 speaks to medical decision-making authority.

2. *In re Grady,* 426 A.2d 467, 479 (N.J. 1981). *See also* Douglas R. Rendleman, Parens Patriae *from Chancery to the Juvenile Court,* 23 S.C. L. Rev. 205, 240 (1971).

3. Alan Handler, *Individual Worth,* 17 Hofstra L. Rev. 493, 528 (1989); Michael Kindred, Guardianships and Limitations upon Capacity, in *The Mentally Retarded Citizen and the Law* 85 n.109 (Michael Kindred et al. eds., 1976).

4. *See In re A.C.,* 573 A.2d 1235, 1247, 1249–50 (D.C. Ct. App. 1990); *In re Boyd,* 403 A.2d 744, 750 (D.C. Ct. App. 1979) (implementing the formerly competent patient's deeply felt religious preferences is the "only way to pay full respect to the individuality and dignity" of that person).

5. *A.C.,* 573 A.2d at 1249–50; *In re Bryant,* 542 A.2d 1216, 1220 (D.C. App. 1988); *Superintendent of Belchertown v. Saikewicz,* 370 N.E.2d 417, 430 n.15 (Mass. 1976).

6. Jonathan Moreno describes the best-interests standard as "intended to reproduce . . . decisions that we imagine the gravely ill patient would have made." Jonathan D. Moreno, *Who's to Choose? Surrogate Decisionmaking in New York State,* 23 Hastings Cent. Rep. 5 (1993).

7. For a further explanation of how people's common preferences can shape end-of-life decision making, *see* Norman L. Cantor, *Discarding Substituted Judgment and Best Interests: Toward a Constructive Preference Standard for Dying—Previously Competent Patients without Advance Instructions*, 48 Rutgers L. Rev. 1193 (1996). *See also* John Arras, *The Severely Demented, Minimally Functional Patient: An Ethical Analysis*, 36 J. Am. Geriatrics Soc'y 938, 943 (1988).

8. To honor self-determination, "we should try our honest best to do what we think [the formerly competent patient] would have chosen." Deryck Beyleveld & Roger Brownsword, *Human Dignity in Bioethics and Biolaw* 245 (2001).

9. This is not to say that the expressions of incapacitated persons are irrelevant to surrogate decision making. The appropriate role of such expressions is addressed later in this chapter and in chapter 6.

10. Allen Buchanan, *The Limits of Proxy Decision Making for Incompetents*, 29 UCLA L. Rev. 386, 397 (1981).

11. *Curran v. Bosze*, 566 N.E.2d 1320, 1326 (Ill. 1990). *See also Matter of Susan S.*, 1996 W.L. 75343 (Del. Ch. 1996); *In re Pescinski*, 226 N.W.2d 180, 181–82 (Wis. 1975).

12. *Truselo v. Carroll*, 846 A.2d 256 (Del. Fam. Ct. 2000). *See also In re Christopher I.*, 131 Cal. Rep. 2d 122, 133 (Calif. App. 2003); *In re K.I.* 735 A.2d 448, 455–56 (D.C. 1999).

13. Max Charlesworth, *Bioethics in a Liberal Society* 51–52 (1993); Max Charlesworth, *Disabled Newborn Infants and the Quality of Life*, 9 J. Contemp. Health L. & Pol'y 129, 136 (1993). *See also In re Barry*, 445 So. 2d 365 (Fla. Ct. App. 1984); *In re L.H.R.*, 321 S.E.2d 716 (Ga. 1984).

14. Joel Feinberg, *Freedom and Fulfillment* 20 (1992); James W. Walters, What Is a Person? An Ethical Exploration (1997).

15. American Medical Association Council on Ethical and Judicial Affairs, Ethical Standards Section 2.20; John M. Stanley et al., *The Appleton Consensus: Suggested International guidelines for Decisions to Forego Medical Treatment*, 15 J. Med. Ethics 129, 133 (1989) (the critical issue for surrogates is whether "continued treatment would lead to unacceptable burdens without sufficient compensating benefits").

16. *E.g., K.I.*, 735 A.2d 448; *In re C.A.*, 603 N.E.2d 1171, 1181 (Ill. App. 1992); *In re Conroy*, 486 A.2d 1209, 1231 (N.J. 1986); *Matter of L.W.*, 482 N.W.2d 60, 70 (Wis. 1992).

17. Johanna Meehan, *Plurality, Autonomy, and the Right to Take One's Life*, 47 Drake L. Rev. 87, 102–03 (1998) (relying on Elaine Scarry, *The Body in Pain* (1985)); Jamie Mayerfeld, *Suffering and Moral Responsibility* 24–27, 40–42 (1995).

18. *K.I.*, 735 A.2d at 464 (quoting Karen Rothenberg, "Foregoing Life-Sustaining Treatment: What Are the Legal Limits in an Aging Society?" 33 St. Louis U.L.J. 575 (1989); Wentzel v. Montgomery General Hospital, 447 A.2d 1244, 1258 (Md. App. 1982); Tom L. Beauchamp & James F. Childress, *Principles of Biomedical Ethics* (4th ed. 1994), 218; Dan W. Brock, *Ethical Issues in Exposing Children to*

Risks in Research, in *Children as Research Subjects* 85 (Michael A. Grodin & Leonard H. Glantz eds., 1994); President's Commission for the Study of Ethical Problems in Medicine, *Deciding to Forgo Life-Sustaining Treatment* (1983), 136.

19. Paul B. Solnick, *Proxy Consent for Incompetent Non-Terminally Ill Adult Patients,* 6 J. Legal Med. 1, 15 (1985).

20. *See* Susan R. Martyn, *Substituted Judgment, Best Interests, and the Need for Best Respect,* 3 Cambridge Q. Healthcare Ethics 195, 200 (1994) ("The central inquiry is whether continued life currently has value to [the never competent patient]"); Mark R. Wicclair, *Ethics and the Elderly* 58–60 (1993).

21. R. S. Downie & K. C. Calman, *Healthy Respect: Ethics in Health Care* 75 (2d ed. 1994). *See also* Martha Minow, *Making All the Difference: Inclusion, Exclusion, and American Law* 327–28 (1990); Daryl Paul Evans, The Lives of Mentally Retarded People 275 (1983).

22. Lois Shepherd ably describes the phenomenon of projecting the surrogate's own feelings in the course of imagining what life is like for a profoundly disabled person. Lois Shepherd, *Face to Face: A Call for Radical Responsibility in Place of Compassion,* 77 St. John's L. Rev. 445, 448 (2003).

23. Dena S. Davis, *Old and Thin,* 15 Second Opinion 26, 29–30 (November 1990).

24. Peter Riga, *Right to Die or Right to Live? Legal Aspects of Death and Dying* 155 (1981).

25. Nazi doctors perceived disabled lives as inherently stressful and claimed that ending those lives would relieve the unfit from their own misery. *See* Robert Proctor, Racial Hygiene: Medicine Under the Nazis (1988).

26. *Baby Doe v. Hancock County Board of Health,* 436 N.E.2d 791 (Ind. 1982).

27. Stephen G. Post, *Dementia in Our Midst: The Moral Community,* 4 Cambridge Q. Healthcare Ethics 142, 143–44 (1995).

28. Rebecca Dresser has written often and incisively about the difficulty of assessing the experiential reality of disabled persons who can supply little or no verbal input. Rebecca Dresser, *Missing Persons: Legal Perspectives of Incompetent Patients,* 46 Rutgers L. Rev. 609 (1994); Rebecca Dresser, *Relitigating Life and Death,* 51 Ohio State L.J. 425, 428 (1994); Rebecca Dresser & John Robertson, *Quality of Life and Non-treatment Decisions for Incompetent Patients: A Critique of the Orthodox Approach,* 17 J.L. Med. & Ethics 234, 241 (1989). On the difficulty of discerning the true feelings of aware but noncommunicative dying persons, *see* Michael H. Cohen, *Toward a Bioethics of Compassion,* 28 Ind. L. Rev. 667, 674–75 (1995).

29. Martyn, *supra* note 20, at 199–201.

30. For an example, *see Matter of R.H.,* 622 N.E.2d 1071, 1077 (Mass. App. 1993) (regarding initiation of kidney dialysis for a mentally retarded patient).

31. On the problematic of judging when a profoundly disabled person's existence is "too painful to be bearable," *see* Carl E. Schneider, *Hard Cases,* 28 Hastings Center Rep. 24 (March 1998), (recounting the story of Tracy Latimer, a thirteen-year-old girl who was rendered helpless by cerebral palsy and killed by her father to end her suffering).

32. *See generally* Nancy Rhoden, *Treatment Dilemmas for Imperiled Newborns: Why Quality of Life Counts,* 58 S. Cal. L. Rev. 1283 (1985); Robert Weir, *Selective Nontreatment of Handicapped Newborns: Moral Dilemmas in Neonatal Medicine* (1986).

33. *Truselo v. Carroll,* 846 A.2d 256 (Del. Fam. Ct. 2000); *Newmark v. Williams,* 588 A.2d 1108 (Del. 1991); *K.I.,* 735 A.2d at 460; *C.A.,* 603 N.E.2d at 1181–82; Tina Kelley, *Ruling Supports Parents' Rights to Decide on Child's Life Support,* New York Times, May 17, 2003, p. B1. *But see Miller v. Hospital Corporation of America,* 118 S.W.2d 758 (Tex. 2003); *Infant C.,* 1995 W.L. 1058596 (Va. Cir. Ct. 1995) (a lower court disclaiming authority to authorize a do-not-resuscitate order for a neurologically devastated one-year-old in the custody of the state department of social services); *Montalvo v. Borkovec,* 647 N.W.2d 413 (Wis. App. 2002).

34. On the disparate perspectives of competent adults and profoundly disabled infants, *see* John D. Arras, *Toward an Ethic of Ambiguity,* 14 Hastings Center Rep. 29–31 (April 1984).

35. Benjamin Weiser, *Child's Trauma Drives Doctors to Reexamine Ethical Role,* Washington Post, July 14, 1991, p. A-1. *See also* Kathleen Knepper, *Withholding Medical Treatment from Infants: When Is It Neglect?,* 33 U. of Louisville J. of Fam. L. 1, 21 (1994).

36. Peter G. Filene, *In the Arms of Others: A Cultural History of the Right to Die in America* 109–10 (1999) (Infant Doe's parents "necessarily projected their own values, feelings, and needs about whether extending his life would be worthwhile").

37. *Bowen v. American Hospital Association,* 476 U.S. 610 (1986). *See generally* Bonnie P. Tucker & Bruce A. Goldstein, *Legal Rights of Persons with Disabilities: An Analysis of Federal Law* 19:16 to 19:18 (1991).

38. *Id.* at 19:21, quoting from 42 U.S.C.A. § 5106(g)(10).

39. *Id.* at 19:22, citing 45 C.F.R. pt. 1340; Knepper, *supra* note 35, at 18–19.

40. Carol A. Heimer, *Competing Institutions: Law, Medicine and Family in Neonatal Intensive Care,* 33 Law & Soc'y Rev. 17, 57 (1999). But see Amer. Acad. Pediatrics Committee on Bioethics, 98 Pediatrics 149 (7/1/96).

41. *See* Miller, 118 S.W.3d at 758, 771. *But see Montalvo,* 647 N.W.2d at 418, contending that the federal regulations are directly applicable to clinical practice.

42. Tracy K. Koogler, Benjamin S. Wilfond & Lainie Friedman Ross, *Lethal Language, Lethal Decisions,* 33 Hastings Center Rep. 37, 38–39 (2003). *See also Truselo v. Carroll,* 2000 W.L. 33324536 (Del. Fam. Ct. 2000); Angie L. Guevara, Note, In re K.I.: *An Urgent Need for a Uniform System in the Treatment of the Critically Ill Infant—Recognizing the Sanctity of the Life of the Child,* 36 U. San Francisco L. Rev. 237, 247 (2001).

43. *See Curlender v. Bio-Science Laboratories,* 165 Cal. Rep. 477, 479–81 (Cal. App. 1980), described in Shepherd, *supra* note 22, at 481 n.102.

44. Betty Dew, *Do Those Who Cannot Speak Really Have a Voice?,* 20 Law, Med. & Healthcare 316 (1992) (recounting the case of Joseph Finelli, a fifty-seven-year-old brain-damaged patient).

45. *In re R.,* [1996] 3 Fam. C.R. 473, 31 B.M.L.R. 127, 2 Fam. L.R. 99.

46. National Conference of Catholic Bishops, *Nutrition and Hydration: Moral and Pastoral Reflections,* 15 J. Contemp. Health, L. & Pol'y 455, 469 (1999).

47. Teresa Harvey Paredes, *The Killing Words? How the New Quality of Life Ethic Affects People with Severe Disabilities,* 46 SMU L. Rev. 805, 829 (1992).

48. *Matter of Jane A.,* 629 N.E.2d 1337, 1340 (Mass. App. 1994). John Storar was a profoundly disabled adult who found cancer therapy (involving blood transfusions) to be disagreeable and distressing in part because of his noncomprehension of their purpose. Nonetheless, a New York court ruled that sedation would sufficiently mitigate John's apprehensions to make continued chemotherapy be in John's best interests. *In re Storar,* 420 N.E.2d 64 (N.Y. 1981).

49. President's Commission for the Study of Ethical Problems in Medicine, *supra* note 18, at 135. *See also* Guevara, *supra* note 42, at 247–48, citing studies showing physicians' use of quality-of-life factors in neonatal care.

50. *See Rasmussen v. Fleming,* 741 P.2d 674 (Ariz. 1987); *Foody v. Manchester Hospital,* 482 A.2d 713, 718–19 (Conn. Super. 1984); *Truselo v. Carroll,* 2000 W.L. 33324536 (Del. Fam. Ct. 2000); *Newmark v. Williams,* 588 A.2d 1108 (Del. 1991); *Care and Protection of Beth,* 587 N.E.2d 1377 (Mass. 1992); *Matter of A.M.B.,* 640 N.W.2d 262 (Mich. App. 2001); *In re Torres,* 357 N.W.2d 332 (Minn. 1984); *Guardianship of Myers,* 610 N.E.2d 663 (Ohio Common Pleas 1993); *In re Grant,* 747 P.2d 445, 451 (Wash. 1987); *In re Christopher I.,* 131 Cal. Rptr 122, 133–34 (Cal. App. 2003).

51. Md. Code Annot., Health § 5-601(e) (2000); N.Y. Surrogate Court Procedures Act § 1750-b(2) (1996).

52. Peter A. Singer, Douglas K. Martin & Merrijoy Kelner, Quality End of Life Care: Patients' Perspectives, 281 JAMA 163, 165 (1999). R. A. Pearlman et al., Insights Pertaining to Patient Assessments of States Worse Than Death, 4 J. Clinical Ethics 35 (1993).

53. *Glucksberg v. Washington,* 521 U.S. 702 (1997).

54. *Id.* at 742.

55. John Finnis, *Euthanasia, Morality, and Law,* 31 Loyola L.A. L. Rev. 1123, 1143 (1998). Leon Kass also contends that human life is inherently dignified regardless of how debilitated or full of suffering that life may be. Leon Kass, *Life, Liberty and the Defense of Dignity: The Challenge for Bioethics* 248 (2002). Kass asserts that dignity in dying means showing endurance and courage in the face of the fear and pain that are often part of the dying process. *Id.* at 248, 253. That whole concept of persevering in the face of death matters little for profoundly disabled persons who do not grasp that they are mortally ill.

56. Feinberg, *supra* note 14.

57. *Westchester Medical Center (O'Connor),* 72 N.Y.2d 517, 530, 531 N.E.2d 607 (N.Y. 1988).

58. *Matter of Finn,* 625 N.Y.S.2d 809, 813 (Sup. Ct. 1995); Peter Byrne, Philosophical and Ethical Problems in Mental Handicap 81 (2000); Carl E. Schneider,

Rights Discourse and Neonatal Euthanasia, 76 Calif. L. Rev. 151, 175 (1988); Lois Shepherd, *Dignity and Autonomy after* Washington v. Glucksberg: *An Essay about Abortion, Death, and Crime,* 7 Cornell J.L. & Pub. Pol'y 431, 448 (1998).

59. Many commentators regard deterioration to a point where the previously competent patient lacks capacity to interact with loved ones as a key guide for surrogates who are contemplating cessation of life support because of the incapacitated patient's quality of life. *See* Arras, *supra* note 7, at 938; Dan W. Brock, *Justice and the Severely Demented Elderly,* 13 J. Med. & Philosophy 73 (1988); Dresser, Relitigating, *supra* note 28, at 430; Ezekiel Emanuel, *The Promise of a Good Death,* 351 Lancet 4 (1998); Larry Gostin, *Family, Privacy, and Persistent Vegetative State,* 17 Law, Med. & Health Care 295, 296–97 (1989).

60. *In re Spring,* 399 N.E.2d 493, 496, 499–500 (Mass. App. 1979).

61. *See* Judith C. Ahronheim, Jonathan D. Moreno & Connie Zuckerman, *Ethics in Clinical Practice* 43 (2d ed. 2000); Downie & Calman, *supra* note 21, at 74.

62. Deborah K. McKnight & Maureen Bellis, *Foregoing Life-Sustaining Treatment for Adult, Developmentally Disabled Public Wards: A Proposed Statute,* 18 Am. J.L. & Med. 203, 213 (1992).

63. New York State Task Force on Life and the Law, *When Others Must Choose: Deciding for Patients without Capacity* 113 (1992); see Evans, supra note 21, at 275.

64. Bruce Jennings, *The Liberal Neutrality of Living and Dying: Bioethics, Constitutional Law, and Political Theory in the American Right-to-Die Debate,* 16 J. Contemp. Health L. & Pol'y 97, 119 (1999).

65. *Id.* at 126.

66. *Division of Family Services v. Truselo,* 846 A.2d 256, 273–74 (Del. Fam. Ct. 2000).

67. Ruth Macklin, *Dignity Is a Useless Concept,* 327 BMJ (British Medical Journal) 1419 (2003).

68. For some advocates for the developmentally disabled, human dignity demands the provision of sufficient resources to allow each handicapped person to achieve the maximum possible independence and "normalization." *E.g.,* Richard C. Allen, *Legal Rights of the Disabled and Disadvantaged* (1969); Deryck Beyleveld & Roger Brownsword, *Human Dignity, Human Rights, and Human Genetics,* 61 Mod. L. Rev. 661, 663 (1998).

69. Gerald L. Neumann, Human Dignity in U.S. Constitutional Law, in *Zur Autonomie des Individuums* 249, 270–71 (Dieter Simon & Manfred Weiss eds., 2000); Charles Tremper, *Respect for the Human Dignity of Minors: What the Constitution Requires,* 39 Syracuse L. Rev. 1293, 1305–07 (1988); Barbara Bennett Woodhouse, *The Dark Side of Family Privacy,* 67 Geo. Wash. L. Rev. 1247, 1261 (2000) (describing human dignity as an essential ingredient in the penumbras of several constitutional provisions). Some commentators call human dignity "a pervasive underlying value" within the Constitution. *Id.* at 1298–99. Jordan Paust, *Dignity as a Constitutional Right,* 27 Howard L.J. 145, 176–80 (1984).

70. *Trop v. Dulles,* 356 U.S. 86, 100–01 (1958). Justice Blackmun, in an early opinion written before his term on the U.S. Supreme Court, relied on concepts of human dignity and decency in declaring unconstitutional the whipping of prisoners. *Jackson v. Bishop,* 404 F.2d 571 (8th Cir. 1968).

71. *Estelle v. Gamble,* 429 U.S. 97, 102, 105–06 (1976). The subjectivity of the human-dignity concept is perhaps underlined by an ongoing dispute among U.S. Supreme Court justices about the relation between human dignity and the death penalty. While there was judicial consensus that respect for the humanity of criminals requires individualized consideration of an offender's character and record before imposing capital punishment, there was bitter dispute about whether capital punishment is an inherent violation of human dignity. *Compare Woodson v. North Carolina,* 428 U.S. 280 (1976) with *Furman v. Georgia,* 408 U.S. 238, 270 (1972).

72. *Winston v. Lee,* 470 U.S. 753 (1985); *Rochin v. California,* 342 U.S. 165 (1952).

73. Neumann, *supra* note 68, at 265.

74. 342 U.S. 165 (1952).

75. *A.C.,* 573 A.2d at 1244; *Louisiana v. Perry,* 610 So. 2d 746 (La. 1992).

76. *Washington v. Harper,* 494 U.S. 210 (1990).

77. *Planned Parenthood of Southeast Pennsylvania v. Casey,* 505 U.S. 833, 851 (1992); *Thornburg v. American College of Obstetricians,* 476 U.S. 747, 772 (1986).

78. Justice Stevens's opinion in *Washington v. Glucksberg,* 521 U.S. 702, 743 (1997), stressed a dying patient's liberty interest not just in controlling bodily invasions but "in dignity, and in determining the character of the memories that will survive long after her death." *But see* Shepherd, *supra* note 58, rejecting the concept of dignity in shaping liberty to control the time and manner of dying.

79. I suggest that the notion of basic human dignity helps explain why certain liberties that had not historically enjoyed widespread public acceptance or even government tolerance nonetheless were accorded the status of fundamental liberties by the Supreme Court. This is so with regard to interracial marriage and abortion. In both instances, the Court classified the liberty interests as fundamental according to "the traditions and collective conscience of the people," despite common legislative antipathy toward the conduct in issue.

80. *Estelle v. Gamble,* 429 U.S. 97, 104–05 (1976); Felicia Cohn, *The Ethics of End-of-Life Care for Prison Inmates,* 27 J.L. Med. & Ethics 252, 254–55 (1999).

81. *Glucksberg,* 521 U.S. at 745 (concurring justices). Note especially Justice Stevens's assertion that avoidance of pain and agony in the dying process is at the heart of fundamental liberty under the Fourteenth Amendment.

82. Susan Adler Channick, *The Myth of Autonomy at the End of Life: Questioning the Paradigm of Rights,* 44 Vill. L. Rev. 577, 602, 606 (1999); David J. Garrow, *The Right to Die: Death with Dignity in America,* 68 Miss. L.J. 407, 417–19 (1998); Alan Meisel, Legal Issues in Decision Making for Incompetent Patients, in *Advance Directives and Surrogate Decision Making in Health Care* (H. Sass, R. Veatch & R. Kamura eds., 1998); David A. Pratt, *Too Many Physicians: Physician-Assisted Suicide after* Glucksberg/Quill, 9 Alb. L.J. Sci. & Tech. 161, 223 (1999).

83. *E.g., Matter of Lawrance,* 579 N.E.2d 32 (Ind. 1991); *Care and Protection of Beth,* 587 N.E.2d 1377 (Mass. 1992); *In re Moorhouse,* 593 A.2d 1256 (N.J. App. Div. 1991); *Guardianship of L. W.,* 482 N.W.2d 60 (Wis. 1992).

84. "Pain cannot be experienced by brains that no longer retain the neural apparatus for suffering." American Medical Association Council on Ethical and Judicial Affairs, *Persistent Vegetative State and the Decision to Withdraw or Withhold Life Support,* 263 JAMA 426, 428 (1990).

85. *See* Cantor, *supra* note 7, at 1241–63.

86. *See In re Christopher I.,* 131 Cal. Rep. 2d 122, 134 (Cal. App. 2003); *Care and Protection of Beth,* 587 N.E.2d 1377, 1382 (Mass. 1992); *Matter of A.B.,* 2003 N.Y. Misc. LEXIS 878 (N.Y. Probate 2003); *In re Myers,* 610 N.E.2d 663 (Ohio 1993).

87. Ironically, some commentators use human dignity as a rationale for the contrary result—to justify allowing the exploitation of never competent persons' tissue. I address that rationale *infra* at pp. 175–76.

88. *Cruzan v. Director, Missouri Department of Health,* 497 U.S. 261 (1990).

89. *Matter of Baby K,* 832 F. Supp. 1022 (E.D. Va. 1993), *aff'd,* 16 F.3d 590 (4th Cir. 1994).

90. Shepherd, *supra* note 58, at 454.

91. *In re Wanglie,* Px-91-283 (4th Judicial Dist., Hennepin County, Minn., July 1991).

92. Doron Shultziner, *Human Dignity: Functions and Meanings,* 3 Global Jurist 5–8, 13 (2003).

93. *See* Rosamond Rhodes, *Futility and the Goals of Medicine,* 9 J. Clinical Ethics 194, 200 (1998) (asserting that no consensus yet exists about whether the goals of medicine include preservation of mere biological existence); Kristi E. Schrode, *Comment, Life in Limbo: Revising Policies for Permanently Unconscious Patients,* 32 Houston L. Rev. 1609 (1995).

94. Beauchamp & Childress, *supra* note 18, at 173.

95. Gregory A. Loken, *Gratitude and the Map of Moral Duties toward Children,* 31 Ariz. St. L.J. 1121, 1142 (1999).

96. *Parham v. J.R.,* 442 U.S. 584, 602 (1979), quoted in Rachel M. Dufault, *Bone Marrow Donations by Children: Rethinking the Legal Framework in Light of Curran v. Bosze* 24 Conn. L. Rev. 211, 235 n.120 (1991).

97. *E.g., Peterson v. Rogers,* 445 S.E.2d 901 (N.C. 1994); *In re Doe,* 638 N.E.2d 181 (Ill. 1994); *In re Baby Girl Clausen,* 502 N.W.2d 649 (Mich. 1993), *aff'd,* 509 U.S. 1301 (1993); *see* Gregory A. Kelson, *In the Best Interests of the Child: What Have We Learned from Baby Jessica and Baby Richard?,* 33 J. Marshall L. Rev. 353, 372 (2000).

98. Robert Veatch, Ethical Dimensions of Advance Directives and Surrogate Decisionmaking, in *Advance Directives on Surrogate Decision Making in Health Care: United States, Germany, and Japan* 66, 74 (Hans-Martin Sass et al. eds., 1998).

99. *Reno v. Flores,* 507 U.S. 292, 304 (1993). *See generally* Lainie Friedman Ross, *Children, Families, and Health Care Decision-Making* 10–12, 30, 42 (1998); Frederick Schoeman, *Parental Discretion and Children's Rights,* 10 J. Med. & Philosophy 48 (1985).

100. "A diverse array of conflicting claims about the good is both possible and desirable in a humane political order." Christopher C. Kutz, *Just Disagreement: Indeterminacy and Rationality in the Rule of Law,* 103 Yale L.J. 997, 1024 (1994). *See also* Jennifer L. Rosato, *Using Bioethics Discourse to Determine When Parents Should Make Health Care Decisions for Their Children: Is Deference Justified?,* 73 Temple L. Rev. 1, 6 (2000).

101. Robert A. Burt, *Developing Constitutional Rights of, in, and for Children,* 39 L. & Contemp. Probs. 118, 121 (1975).

102. 262 U.S. 390 (1923).

103. *Santosky v. Kramer,* 455 U.S. 745, 753 (1982), *quoted approvingly in Troxel v. Granville,* 530 U.S. 57 (2000).

104. 530 U.S. at 67.

105. *Id.* at 70.

106. Justice O'Connor noted that—in contrast to Washington state—some states in regulating visitation orders uphold parental decisions unless a petitioner rebuts a presumption that the parental decision is reasonable. *Id.* at 70.

107. For a lucid and convincing description of the doctrinal disarray surrounding parental decision making, *see* David D. Meyer, *The Paradox of Family Privacy,* 53 Vand. L. Rev. 527, 528–29, 545–46 (2000).

108. *E.g., In re E.G.,* 549 N.E.2d 322, 326–27 (Ill. 1989). *But see Novak v. Cobb County Hospital Authority,* 849 F. Supp. 1559 (D. Ga. 1994).

109. These statutes recognize that parental interests sometimes diverge from their children's interests and that public-health interests may override child-rearing interests when maintenance of parental control would discourage children's resort to important medical treatment.

110. *Planned Parenthood v. Danforth,* 428 U.S. 52, 74 (1976).

111. *E.g.,* New York State Task Force on Life and the Law, *supra* note 63, at 107; Alexander M. Capron, *Where Is the Sure Interpreter?,* 22 Hastings Center Rep. 26–27 (July 1992).

112. *In re Jane Doe,* 418 S.E.2d 3 (Ga. 1992); *Matter of Hofbauer,* 419 N.Y.S.2d 936 (N.Y. 1979); *In re Hudson,* 126 P.2d 765, 771 (Wash. 1992).

113. *Matter of Mathews,* 650 N.Y.S.2d 373, 377–78 (App. Div. 1996).

114. *Newmark v. Williams,* 588 A.2d 1108 (Del. 1991); *Grecco v. UMDNJ,* 783 A.2d 741, 744 (N.J. App. Div. 2001). *See generally* Heimer, *supra* note 40, at 51–52; Koogler et al., *supra* note 42, at 39–40.

115. *Custody of a Minor,* 393 N.E.2d 836, 841 (Mass. 1979); *Matter of Cabrera,* 552 A.2d 1114, 1118 (Pa. Super. 1989); *Matter of Hudson,* 126 P.2d 765, 771 (Wash. 1942); Knepper, *supra* note 35, at 3, 7–8; Laura M. Plastine, *"In God We*

Trust": When Parents Refuse Medical Treatment for Their Children Based upon Their Sincere Religious Beliefs, 3 Const. L.J. 123, 139–45 (1993).

116. *Hudson,* 126 P.2d at 778.

117. Jennifer Hartsell, *"Mother, May I . . . Live?" Parental Refusal of Life-Sustaining Medical Treatment for Children Based on Religious Objections,* 66 Tenn. L. Rev. 499, 509 (1999). The exemption does not cover instances when serious harm to the child is threatened or ensues. *Id.* at 518.

118. *See* Rebecca Dresser, *Standards for Family Decisions: Replacing Best Interests with Harm Prevention,* 3 Am. J. Bioethics 54 (2003). *But see* George Hill, *Can Anyone Authorize the Nontherapeutic Permanent Alteration of a Child's Body?* 3 Am. J. Bioethics 47 (2003).

119. *See* pp. 10–11, *supra.*

120. *E.g., Matter of C.D.M.,* 627 P.2d 607 (Alaska 1981); *Matter of Shirley Hilstrom,* 363 N.W.2d 871 (Minn. App. 1985); *Matter of Hayes,* 608 P.2d 635 (Wash. 1980).

121. *E.g., In re W.,* 637 P.2d 366 (Colo. 1981); *Motes v. Hall County Department of Family and Children's Services,* 306 S.E.2d 260, 262 (Ga. 1983). *See generally* Elizabeth S. Scott, *Sterilization of Mentally Retarded Persons: Reproductive Rights and Family Privacy,* 1986 Duke L.J. 806 (1986); Eric M. Jaegers, *Note, Modern Judicial Treatment of Procreative Rights of Developmentally Disabled Persons: Equal Rights to Procreation and Sterilization,* 31 U. Louisville J. Fam. L. 947 (1992).

122. *Matter of A.W.,* 637 P.2d 366 (Colo. 1981); *In re Debra B.,* 495 A.2d 781 (Me. 1985); *Wentzel v. Montgomery General Hospital,* 447 A.2d 1244 (Md. App. 1982).

123. *In re Conroy,* 486 A.2d 1209, 1233 (N.J. 1986); *Rasmussen v. Fleming,* 741 P.2d 674 (Ariz. 1987); *In re Beth Israel Medical Center for Weinstein,* 519 N.Y.S.2d 511 (Sup. Ct. 1987); *Grant,* 747 P.2d at 445.

124. *Knight v. Beverly Health Bay Manor Center,* 820 So. 2d 92, 100 (Ala. 2001); *Motes v. Hall County Department of Family Services,* 306 S.E.2d at 260 (Ga. 1983); James Bopp & Thomas Marzden, *Cruzan: Facing the Inevitable,* 19 Law, Med. & Health Care 37, 43 (1991).

125. Daniel B. Griffith, *The Best Interests Standard: A Comparison of the State's* Parens Patriae *Authority and Judicial Oversight in Best-Interests Determinations for Children and Incompetent Patients,* 7 Issues L. & Med. 283, 315–16 (1991); John Robertson, Cruzan *and the Constitutional Status of Nontreatment Decisions for Incompetent Patients,* 25 Ga. L. Rev. 1139, 1164–65 (1991); Michele Yuen, *Comment, Letting Daddy Die: Adopting New Standards for Surrogate Decision-making,* 39 UCLA L. Rev. 581, 631 (1992).

126. Nancy Rhoden, *Litigating Life and Death,* 102 Harv. L. Rev. 375, 379, 393, 419–20 (1988); Neal F. Splaine, *Note, The Incompetent Individual's Right to Refuse Life-Sustaining Medical Treatment,* 27 Suffolk U. L. Rev. 905, 939 (1993).

127. Dresser, *supra* note 117, at 55. A couple of jurisdictions ban the removal of life support absent proof that while the permanently unconscious patient was competent, he or she clearly indicated a preference not to be subjected to treatment in the circumstances at hand.

128. Nancy Rhoden, *supra* note 125, at 379, 393, 419–20; Arras, *supra* note 7, at 943; Ardath Hamann *Family Surrogate Laws: A Necessary Supplement to Living Wills and Durable Powers of Attorneys,* 38 Villanova L. Rev. 103, 159 (1993). *See also Conservatorship of Drabick,* 245 Cal. Rep. 840, 844 n.7 (Cal. App. 1988); Mary Ann Buckley, Note, *In re Wendland: Contradiction, Confusion, and Constitutionality,* 11 J.L. & Policy 255, 257 (2002).

129. *E.g., In re V.S.D.,* 660 N.E.2d 1064 (Ind. App. 1996); *In re Debra B.,* 495 A.2d 781 (Me. 1985).

130. However, a decision regarding sterilization involves a choice between two fundamental-liberty interests—a right to procreate and a right to refrain from procreation.

131. Scott, *supra* note 120, at 831–32.

132. "[I]f the woman truly can never parent, it probably is in her interests not to give birth to a child who will have to be removed." Martha Field & Valerie Sanchez, *Equal Treatment for People with Mental Retardation: Having and Raising Children* 106 (1999).

133. *In re Wirsing* 573 N.W.2d 51, 55 (Mich. 1998).

134. *Buck v. Bell,* 274 U.S. 200, 207 (1927).

135. *In re Simpson,* 180 N.E.2d 206 (Ohio Prob. Ct. 1962), noted in Donald Gianella, Eugenic Sterilization and the Law, in *Eugenic Sterilization* 64–65 (Jonas Robitscher ed., 1973).

136. *See, e.g.,* Roberta M. Berry, *From Involuntary Sterilization to Genetic Enhancement: The Unsettled Legacy of* Buck v. Bell, 12 Notre Dame J.L. Ethics & Pub. Pol'y 401, 428–30 (1998); Paul A. Lombardo, *Medicine, Eugenics, and the Supreme Court: From Coercive Sterilization to Reproductive Freedom,* 13 J. Contemp. Health L. & Pol'y 1, 19 (1996).

137. *Hudson v. Hudson,* 373 So. 2d 310 (Ala. 1979); *In re M.K.R.,* 515 S.W.2d 467 (Mo. 1974); *Frazier v. Levi,* 440 S.W.2d 393 (Tex. 1969); Annotation, *Jurisdiction of Court to Permit Sterilization of Mentally Defective Person,* 74 A.L.R.3d 1210, 1214 (1976). *But see Wyatt v. Aderholt,* 368 F. Supp. 1383, 1384 (D. Ala. 1974); *In re Sallmaier,* 378 N.Y.S.2d 989, 991 (N.Y. 1976).

138. Robert Burt & Monroe Price, Nonconsensual Medical Procedures and the Right to Privacy, in *The Mentally Retarded Citizen and the Law* (Michael Kindred et al. eds., 1976); Richard K. Sherlock & Robert D. Sherlock, *Sterilizing the Retarded: Constitutional, Statutory, and Policy Alternatives,* 60 N.C. L. Rev. 943 (1982). Instances of abusive decision making had, in fact, surfaced in this period. *See In re Stump v. Sparkman,* 435 U.S. 349 (1978); *Downs v. Sawtelle,* 574 F.2d 1 (1st Cir. 1978).

139. *Matter of Romero,* 790 P.2d 819 (Colo. 1990); *In re A.W.,* 637 P.2d 366, 376 (Colo. 1981); *P.S. v. W.S.,* 452 N.E.2d 969, 976 (Ind. 1982); *Wentzel v. Montgomery General Hospital,* 447 A.2d 1244 (Md. App. 1982); *In re Moe,* 432 N.E.2d 712, 718 (Mass. 1982); *In re Grady,* 426 A.2d 467, 481 (N.J. 1981); *Matter of Hayes,* 601 P.2d 635 (Wash. 1980); Scott, *supra* note 120, at 822–23. A few cases suggest that a showing of medical necessity—a standard even more demanding

than plain best interests—is a prerequisite to a surrogate's consent to sterilization for a disabled person.

140. John Hardwig, *The Problem of Proxies with Interests of Their Own,* 1992 Utah L. Rev. 803 (1992); John Hardwig, *The Problem of Proxies with Interests of Their Own: Toward a Better Theory of Proxy Decisions,* 4 J. Clinical Ethics 20 (1993). For another commentary that expresses some sympathy with the justice rationale, *see* Dan W. Brock, *What Is the Moral Authority of Family Members to Act as Surrogates of Incompetent Patients?,* 74 Milbank Q. 599 (1996).

141. George P. Smith, *"Death Be Not Proud": Medical, Ethical and Legal Dilemmas in Resource Allocation,* 3 J. Contemp. Health L. & Pol'y 47, 59 (1987).

142. *See Michigan Protection and Advocacy Service v. Kirkendall,* 863 F. Supp. 482 (E.D. Mich. 1994); William A. Krais, *Note, The Incompetent Developmentally Disabled Person's Right of Self-Determination: Right to Die, Sterilization, and Institutionalization,* 15 Am. J.L. & Med. 333, 357 (1989) (suggesting a legitimate parental interest in a daughter's sterilization).

143. Hardwig, *supra,* note 140, at 814–15.

144. The problem of commensurability is always present in the absence of explicit prior instructions from the now incapacitated patient. If the average patient wants the economic or emotional burden on surrounding family to be considered, questions still arise—about the debilitated circumstances in which the patient wants these extrinsic factors (economic and emotional burdens) to come into play and about how much weight these factors warrant. And if a now incompetent patient previously specified that the interests of family should be part of the surrogate's calculus, then the incommensurability problem is unavoidable. *See* Md. Code Annot., Health § 5-605(c)(2) (2003).

145. President's Commission for the Study of Ethical Problems in Medicine, *Making Health Care Decisions* 180 (1983). *See also* Brock, *supra* note 140.

146. *See* Md. Code Annot., Health § 5-605(c)(2) (2003).

147. New York State Task Force on Life and the Law, *supra* note 63, at 109. The Task Force suggests that it would be necessary to make a strong showing that the average person would want the interests of third parties to be considered in the circumstances at hand. And the Task Force gives a caveat that the boundary of consideration for others would be harm to the patient. This is somewhat puzzling. When third-party interests advance a termination of life support prior to the point when such a decision would otherwise have been made, that seems like a form of harm. Perhaps the Task Force meant *harm* in the sense of suffering experienced by the patient.

148. *E.g.,* Singer et al., *supra* note 52, at 166.

149. Margaret Battin, *The Least Worst Death* (1994).

150. Martha Field objects to ascribing consideration of others to newborns because it is "projecting upon the baby a personality that allows society to do what it wants for reasons other than the child's own interests." Martha Field, *Killing "the Handicapped"—Before and after Birth,* 16 Harv. Women's L.J. 79, 89 (1993). *See also* Schneider, *supra* note 58, at 165, 172.

151. For such an argument, *see* Scott, *supra* note 120, at 845.

152. *Guardianship of Roe,* 421 N.E.2d 40, 58 (Mass. 1981) (antipsychotic medication). *See also In re Torres,* 357 N.W.2d 332, 339 (Minn. 1984) (permanently unconscious patient); *In re Ingram,* 689 P.2d 1363, 1370 (Wash. 1984) (cancer treatment).

153. *See Matter of R.H.,* 622 N.E.2d 1071, 1078 (Mass. App. 1993); *Care and Protection of Beth,* 587 N.E.2d 1377, 1383 (Mass. 1992). *See also In re A.C.,* 573 A.2d 1235 (D.C. Ct. App. 1990) (emphasizing that a surrogate must focus on the patient's interests rather than those of others). *But see Guardianship of Jane Doe,* 583 N.E.2d 1263, 1268 (Mass. 1992).

154. Yale Kamisar, *When Is There a Constitutional "Right to Die"?,* 25 Ga. L. Rev. 1203, 1236–37 (1991). *See also* Shannon Jordan, *Decision Making for Incompetent Persons The Law and Morality of Who Shall Decide* 72–73 (1985); Schneider, *supra* note 58, at 175.

155. Baruch Brody, *Life and Death Decision Making* 31 (1988).

156. *Matter of Terwilliger,* 450 A.2d 1376 (Pa. 1982).

157. *Matter of Shirley Hilstrom,* 363 N.W.2d 871, 876 (Minn. App. 1985).

158. *Wentzel,* 447 A.2d at 1253–54.

159. Robert Veatch observes that third-party interests "unavoidably influence treatment decisions" on behalf of incapacitated persons. Robert M. Veatch, *The Patient-Physician Relation: The Patient as Partner,* pt. 2, 229 (1991). *See also Guardianship of Roe,* 421 N.E.2d 40, 55 (Mass. 1981), where the court considered whether to compel antipsychotic medication and noted the impossibility of ignoring the interests of siblings who lived with the ward.

160. The legitimacy of third-party interests surfaces even when the medical fate of a fully competent person is in issue. Consider, for example, a seriously ill Jehovah's Witness and parent who is refusing a critical blood transfusion on religious grounds. Courts that address whether to override the patient's objection to treatment often cite the interests of "innocent third parties" as a potential compelling justification for judicial intervention. *See, e.g., Public Health Trust v. Wons,* 541 So. 2d 96 (Fla. 1989); *Fosmire v. Nicoleau,* 551 N.Y.S.2d 876, 551 N.E.2d 77 (N.Y. 1990). The cases find either that the dependent child's interests are satisfied by the continued availability of the second parent or that the patient's fundamental-liberty interest outweighs the concerns about an "abandoned" child. The point is that the third-party interests—here the dependent children of a competent medical patient—are deemed legitimate and important. Of course, injecting third-party interests when the competent patient has assumed a fiduciary relationship to the third party is not the same as injecting third-party interests into medical decision making for a never competent person (who cannot have assumed a fiduciary role).

161. Robert N. Wennberg, *Terminal Choices: Euthanasia, Suicide, and the Right to Die* 200 (1989).

162. *See* Raymond S. Duff & A. G. M. Campbell, *Moral and Ethical Dilemmas in the Special Care Nursery,* 289 N. Eng. J. Med. 890, 891 (1973), as quoted in

Martha Minow, *supra* note 21, at 319 n.27. *See also* John A. Robertson, *Dilemma in Danville*, 11 Hastings Center Rep 5 (October 1981).

163. James Childress, *Dying Patients: Who's in Control?*, 17 J.L. Med. & Health Care 227, 229 (1989).

164. *Guardianship of Roe*, 421 N.E.2d 40, 55 (Mass. 1981).

165. *See, e.g.*, New York Surrogates Court Procedures Act § 1750-b(2) (2003).

166. Veatch, *supra* note 159, at 229. John Fader urges that costs of care be openly acknowledged as part of a best-interests formula. John Fader, *Trends in Health Care Decision Making: The Precarious Role of the Courts*, 53 Md. L. Rev. 1193, 1213 (1994).

167. Candace Cummins Gauthier, *Philosophical Foundations of Respect for Autonomy*, 3 Kennedy Inst. of Ethics J. 21, 35 (1993).

168. *Conservatorship of Angela D.*, 83 Cal. Rep. 411, 417 (Cal. App. 1999).

169. *Estate of C.W.*, 640 A.2d 427, 436 (Pa. Super. 1994).

170. *See North Carolina Association for Retarded Children v. North Carolina*, 420 F. Supp. 451, 455–56 (D.N.C. 1976).

171. *In re A (Conjoined Twins)*, [2000] H.R.L.R. 721 (Eng. C.A.); Rachel Donnelly, *Twin "Critical But Stable" as Sister Dies*, Irish Times, November 8, 2000.

172. *See also* Daniel Sulmasy, *Heart and Soul: The Case of the Conjoined Twins*, America (December 2, 2000).

173. *Compare* Robertson, *supra* note 124, at 1250–51, and Fader, *supra* note 165 (both favoring articulation of third-party interests), with Martha Minow, *Trends in Health Care Decision Making: Who's the Patient?*, 53 Md. L. Rev. 1173, 1180–81 (1994).

Chapter 5

1. Concerning the burdens and risks associated with kidney transplants, *see Hart v. Brown*, 289 A.2d 386 (Super. Ct. Conn. 1972); Janet B. Korins, *Toward a Clear Standard for Authorizing Kidney and Bone Marrow Transplants between Minor Siblings*, 16 Vt. L. Rev. 499, 502 (1992); Bryan Shartle, *Comment, Proposed Legislation for Safely Regulating the Increasing Number of Living Organ and Tissue Donations by Minors*, 61 La. L. Rev. 433, 437 (2001).

2. *See Lawse v. University of Iowa Hospital*, 434 N.W.2d 895 (Iowa App. 1988) (damage suit by kidney donor who claimed a lack of informed consent by the donor whose remaining kidney failed 13 years after the kidney donation).

3. Michael Morley, *Note, Proxy Consent to Organ Donation by Incompetents*, 111 Yale L.J. 1215, 1222 (2002) (describing the use of anesthesia and long needles in the course of bone-marrow extraction).

4. Concerning bone-marrow transplants, *see* Cara Cheyette, *Note, Organ Harvests from the Legally Incompetent: An Argument Against Compelled Altruism*, 41 B.C. L. Rev. 465, 475–78 (2000); Victoria Weisz, *Psycholegal Issues in Sibling Bone-Marrow Donation*, 2 Ethics & Behavior 185 (1992).

5. Rebecca Dresser, *Dementia Research: Ethics and Policy for the Twenty-first Century,* 35 Ga. L. Rev. 661, 664 (2001). *See also* Nancy M. P. King, *Defining and Describing Benefit Appropriate in Clinical Trials,* 28 J.L. Med. & Ethics, 332, 339 (2000) (commenting on how medical research diverts attention from the best interests of individual research subjects).

6. Robert J. Levine, *International Codes of Research Ethics: Current Controversies,* 35 Ind. L. Rev. 557, 559–62 (2002).

7. For commentary on the therapeutic and nontherapeutic dichotomy, *see* Charles Weijer, *The Ethical Analysis of Risk,* 28 J.L. Med. & Ethics 344, 346–48 (2000). Professional bodies and study commissions have customarily recognized the therapeutic/nontherapeutic distinction. American College of Physicians, *Cognitively Impaired Subjects,* 11 Annals Internal Med. 843 (1989); Belmont Report of the National Commission on the Protection of Human Subjects of Biomedical and Behavioral Research, 44 Fed. Reg. 23192 (April 18, 1979); Report of the National Bioethics Advisory Commission, *Research Involving Persons with Mental Disorders That May Affect Decisionmaking Capacity* (1998). *See also Grimes v. Kennedy Krieger Institute,* 782 A.2d 807, 837–38 (Md. 2001).

8. *E.g.,* Kendall Ann Desaulniers, *Legislation to Protect the Decisionally Incapacitated Individual's Participation in Medical Research: Safety Net or Trap Door?,* 13 Regent U.L. Rev. 179 (2000); Michelle Oberman & Joel Frader, *Dying Children and Medical Research: Access to Clinical Trials as Benefit and Burden,* 29 Am. J.L. & Med. 290, 316–17 (2003); David P. T. Price, *Contemporary Transplantation Initiatives: Where's the Harm in Them?,* 24 J.L. Med. & Ethics 139, 141 (1996); Weisz, *supra* note 4, at 198.

9. Jennifer S. Bard, *The Diagnosis Is Anencephaly and the Parents Ask about Organ Donation: Now What?,* 21 W. New Eng. L. Rev. 49, 91 (1999), *quoting from* Hans Jonas, *Philosophical Essays* (1974).

10. *See* Calif. Health and Safety Code § 24178 (1992); American Academy of Pediatricians, *Guidelines for the Ethical Conduct of Studies to Evaluate Drugs in Pediatric Populations,* 95 Pediatrics 286 (1995).

11. Charles Fried, Children as Subjects for Medical Experimentation, in *Research on Children: Medical Imperatives, Ethical Quandaries, and Legal Constraints* 113 (Jan van Eys ed., 1978).

12. Peter V. Rabins, *Issues Raised by Research Using Persons Suffering from Dementia Who Have Impaired Decisional Capacity,* 1 J. Health Care L. & Pol'y 22, 26–27 (1998).

13. Dresser, *supra* note 5, at 678–79; King, *supra* note 5, at 333.

14. *Id.* at 679; Ezekiel J. Emanuel, David Wendler & Christine Grady, *What Makes Clinical Research Ethical?,* 283 JAMA 2701, 2705 (2000).

15. Richard W. Garnett, *Why Informed Consent? Human Experimentation and the Ethics of Autonomy,* 36 Catholic Law. 455, 485–87 (1996); *see also* Rabins, *supra* note 12.

16. Angela Holder comments that a parent "should be able to consent to research so long as the risk of harm to the child is less than that to which a child of that age

is reasonably likely to be exposed in daily life." Angela R. Holder, *Legal Issues in Pediatrics and Adolescent Medicine* 149 (2d ed. 1985). *See also* Benjamin Freedman, Abraham Fuks & Charles Weijer, In Loco Parentis, *Minimal Risk as an Ethical Threshold for Research upon Children*, 23 Hastings Center Rep. 13, 16–17 (April 1993).

17. Report of the National Bioethics Advisory Commission, *supra* note 7, at 41. *See also* Angela Holder, *supra* note 16, at 141 n.11, 149.

18. *See* Jessica Wilen Berg, *Legal and Ethical Complexities of Consent with Cognitively Impaired Research Subjects: Proposed Guidelines*, 24 J.L. Med. & Ethics 18, 28, 34 n.117 (1996). *See also infra* pp 154, 194, commenting on the need for moral justification of even minimal-risk research.

19. *See McFall v. Shimp,* 10 Pa. D. & C.3d 90 (Pa. Common Pleas 1978) (court will not compel a cousin to provide bone marrow for a terminally ill cousin); *In re A.C.,* 573 A.2d 1235, 1243–44 (D.C. Ct. App. 1990) (dying woman will not be compelled to undergo Caesarian section to salvage a fetus).

20. *See, e.g.,* Cheyette, *supra* note 4, B.C. L. Rev. at 469–70; Mark Sheldon, Children as Organ Donors, in *Organ and Tissue Donation: Ethical, Legal, and Policy Issues* (Bethany Spielman ed., 1996), 111, 116–17. If a donation is impelled by pressure from others, altruism hardly exists. Forced altruism is an oxymoron.

21. Robert W. Griner, *Note, Live Organ Donations between Siblings and the Best-Interests Standard: Time for Stricter Judicial Intervention,* 10 Ga. St. L. Rev. 589, 600 (1994).

22. Robert Burt and Monroe Price have made a similar observation: "Does it truly serve important social purposes to bar conclusively the incompetent donor from exercising the right that the 'normal' population prizes as an ethical imperative— to give of one's self in order to help others?" Robert Burt & Monroe Price, Nonconsensual Medical Procedures and the Right to Privacy, in *The Mentally Retarded Citizen and the Law* 102–03 (Michael Kindred et al. eds., 1976).

23. Immanuel Kant, *Groundwork of the Metaphysic of Morals* (1785), *as quoted in* Deryck Beyleveld & Roger Brownsword, *Human Dignity in Bioethics and Biolaw* 52 (2001).

24. John Kavanaugh, *Who Counts as Persons? Human Identity and the Ethics of Killing* (2001), 119. *See* R. S. Downie & K. C. Calman, *Healthy Respect: Ethics in Health Care* 15 2d ed. (1994). "Exploiting a person for one's own ends by inflicting on him harm or suffering with disregard for his own needs, interests and desires is the paradigm violation of [the imperative not to treat a person solely as a means]" and therefore is the essence of disregard for human dignity. Meir Dan-Cohen, Defining Dignity, in *Harmful Thoughts: Essays on Law, Self, and Morality* 150, 161 (Meir Dan-Cohen ed., 2002).

25. Immanuel Kant himself may not have intended to apply his imperative to treatment of profoundly disabled persons who are mentally incapable of moral agency. It is not clear whether Kant confined his protective imperative to persons who possess a certain level of mental function—such as capability of moral reasoning—that would exclude the profoundly disabled. *See* Lois Shepherd, *Dignity*

and Autonomy after Washington v. Glucksberg: *An Essay about Abortion, Death, and Crime,* 7 Cornell J.L. & Pub Pol'y 431, 457 (1998). Itzhak England and many philosophers interpret Kant as attaching human dignity only to persons capable of rational agency. Itzhak England, *Human Dignity: From Antiquity to Modern Israel's Constitutional Framework,* 21 Cardozo L. Rev. 1903, 1921 (2000). Whatever Kant's original intention, many commentators apply the Kantian injunction to all human beings, deeming them all to be bearers of intrinsic human dignity.

26. Ronald Dworkin, *Life's Dominion* (1993), as quoted in Beyleveld & Brownsworth, *supra* note 23, at 49 n.1. *See also* Martha Minow, *All in the Family and in All Families: Membership, Loving, and Owing,* 95 W. Va. L. Rev. 275, 326 (1993). *But see* Evelyn B. Pluhar, *Beyond Prejudice: The Moral Significance of Human and Non-Human Animals* 125 (1995) (suggesting that humane treatment does not by itself satisfy the Kantian imperative).

27. Martha C. Nussbaum, *Objectification,* 24 Philosophy & Pub. Affairs 249, 265 (1995).

28. *Id.* at 257, 261–62, 290.

29. *See generally* William J. Curran, *A Problem of Consent: Kidney Transplantation in Minors,* 34 N.Y.U.L. Rev. 891 (1959); Lainie Friedman Ross, *Children, Families, and Health Care Decision-Making* 111–12 (1998).

30. 445 S.W.2d 145 (Ky. 1969).

31. *Id.* at 146–47. *See also* Charles J. Cronan, *Comment, Spare Parts from Incompetents: A Problem of Consent,* 9 J. Fam. L. 309, 310 (1969).

32. Lisa K. Gregory, *Annotation, Propriety of Surgically Invading Incompetent or Minor for Benefit of Third Party,* 4 A.L.R. 5th 1000, 1011–16 (1999); Thomas H. Murphy, Jr., *Minor Consent to Transplant Surgery: A Review of the Law,* 62 Marq. L. Rev. 149, 159 (1978).

33. 576 S.W.2d 493 (Tex. Civ. App. 1979).

34. *See also* Melvin D. Levine et al., *The Medical Ethics of Bone Marrow Transplantation in Children,* 86 J. Pediatrics 145, 148 (1975) (describing an unreported 1973 Massachusetts case involving a thirteen-year-old Down's syndrome donor).

35. 481 N.Y.S.2d 932 (N.Y. App. Div. 1984).

36. 289 A.2d 386 (Conn. Super. Ct. 1972).

37. *In re Richardson,* 284 So. 2d 185 (La. App. 1973).

38. *In re Pescinski,* 226 N.W.2d 180 (Wis. 1975).

39. *Curran v. Bosze,* 566 N.E.2d 1319 (Ill. 1990).

40. Curran was complicated by the fact that the minors' custodial mother opposed the idea of a bone-marrow transplant to her former husband's stricken child. The noncustodial parent therefore had a particularly heavy burden in seeking a medical procedure opposed by the primary guardian.

41. *See* Norman Fost, *Children as Renal Donors,* 296 N. Eng. J. Med. 363, 365 (1977); Jennifer K. Robbenolt, Victoria Weisz & Craig M. Lawson, *Advancing the*

Rights of Children and Adolescents to Be Altruistic: Bone Marrow Donation by Minors, 9 J.L. & Health 213, 243 (1994–95).

42. *E.g.,* Cheyette, *supra* note 4, at 504–05; Charles J. Cronan, *Comment, Spare Parts from Incompetents: A Problem of Consent,* 9 J. Fam. L. 309, 313 (1969); John D. Lantos, Children as Organ Donors: An Argument for Involuntary Altruism, in Primum Non Nocere *Today* (G. R. Burgio & J. D. Lantos eds., 1994), 67, 71; Lynn E. Lebit, *Note, Compelled Medical Procedures Involving Minors and Incompetents,* 7 J.L. & Health 107, 118–19 (1992–93); Deborah Mathieu, *Respecting Liberty and Preventing Harm: Limits of State Intervention in Prenatal Choice,* 8 Harv. J.L. & Pub. Pol'y 19, 42–44 (1985).

43. David Price, *Legal and Ethical Aspects of Organ Transplantation* 351 (2000).

44. 481 N.Y.S.2d 932 (N.Y. App. Div. 1984).

45. *See* Dorothy M. Bernstein & Roberta G. Simmons, *The Adolescent Kidney Donor: The Right to Give,* 131 Am. J. Psychiatry 1338, 1341 (1974); Cheyette, *supra* note 4, at 500–01; Weisz, *supra* note 4, at 185, 199.

46. The court in *Little v. Little* mentions the possibility that a transplant ordeal may be more burdensome for a disabled donor because of incomprehension, but the court then attributes no weight or significance to that element. 576 S.W.2d 493, 499 (Tex. Civ. App. 1979).

47. *See Hart v. Brown,* 289 A.2d 386, 388–89 (Conn. Super. Ct. 1972); *Little v. Little,* 576 S.W.2d at 496, 499 (use of an alternative donor would "significantly lessen" the chances of a successful transplant).

48. Keep in mind that using a less well matched donor necessitates an immunosuppressive regime that creates additional risks for the transplant recipient.

49. *Richardson,* 284 So. 2d 185. David Price contends that recent rates of success using cadaveric organs in transplant make it rare for an incapacitated relative to be the only possible source of an organ. Price, *supra* note 43, at 361.

50. James F. Childress, *The National Bioethics Advisory Commission: Bridging the Gaps in Human Subjects Research Protection,* 1 J. Health Care L. & Pol'y 105, 106–13 (1998); Jonathan D. Moreno, *Regulation of Research on the Decisionally Impaired: History and Gaps in the Current Regulatory System,* 1 J. Health Care L. & Pol'y 1, 14 (1998).

51. The Belmont Report of the National Commission on the Protection of Human Subjects of Biomedical and Behavioral Research, 44 Fed. Reg. 23192 (April 18, 1979). The Department of Health, Education, and Welfare issued regulations on medical research in 1981, the Department of Health and Human Resources revised them in 1983, and in 1991 those regulations were adopted by a number of federal agencies. The regulations became known as the Common Rule and were published at 56 Fed. Reg. 28012 (1991). *See* Desaulniers, *supra* note 8, at 185–88.

52. *See* Jessica Wilen Berg, *Legal and Ethical Complexities of Consent with Cognitively Impaired Research Subjects: Proposed Guidelines,* 24 J.L. Med. & Ethics 18 (1996); Dresser, *supra* note 5, at 687–88; Franklin G. Miller, *Research Ethics and Misguided Moral Intuition,* 32 J.L. Med. & Ethics 111 (2004).

53. Baruch A. Brody, *The Ethics of Biomedical Research: An International Perspective* 134 (1998); Diane E. Hoffmann, Jack Schwartz & Evan G. DeRenzo, *Regulating Research with Decisionally Impaired Individuals: Are We Making Progress?*, 3 DePaul J. Health Care L. 547, 603 (2000); Moreno, *supra* note 50, at 9, 62–63; Oberman & Frader, *supra* note 8, at 317.

54. Paul Ramsey, *The Patient as Person: Explorations in Medical Ethics,* 12 (1970) ("where there is no possible relation to the child's recovery, a child is not to be made a mere object in medical experimentation for the sake of good to come"). *See also id.* at 35–36. Thomas Murray quotes Ramsey as insisting that "fidelity to a human child includes never treating him as a means only, but also as an end." Thomas H. Murray, Research on Children and the Scope of Responsible Parenthood, in *Ethical Issues in Modern Medicine* 791, 796 (6th ed., Bonnie Steinbock, John D. Arras & Alex John London eds., 2003).

55. *See* Richard J. Bonnie, *Research with Cognitively Impaired Subjects,* 54 Archives of Gen. Psychiatry 105, 108 (1997); 43 Fed. Reg. 53956 (1978).

56. Council of Europe, *Recommendations Concerning Medical Research on Human Beings, printed in* Brody, *supra* note 53, at 241, 246.

57. *See* National Bioethics Advisory Commission Report, *supra* note 7, at 61–62; Dresser, *supra* note 5, at 677; Diane E. Hoffmann & Jack Schwartz, *Proxy Consent to Participation of the Decisionally Impaired in Medical Research: Maryland's Policy Initiative,* 1 J. Health Care L. & Pol'y 123, 149 (1998).

58. Berg, *supra* note 18, at 23, 34 n.117; Dresser, *supra* note 5, at 687–88.

59. 782 A.2d 807 (Md. 2001).

60. As to the degree of risk that is found to be unacceptable, the court would not tolerate "any articulated risk beyond the minimum kind of risk that is inherent in any endeavor." *Id.* at 862.

61. *Id.* at 852–53, 857.

62. Burt & Price, supra note 21, at 93, 104.

63. *See* John Fletcher, *Human Experimentation: Ethics in the Consent Situation,* 32 J.L. & Contemp. Probs. 620, 639 (1967).

64. 43 Fed. Reg. 53955 (November 17, 1978), discussing proposed 45 C.F.R. § 46.505.

65. *Id.* at 53956, discussing proposed 45 C.F.R. § 46.507. *See also* National Institutes of Health regulations, in Brody, *supra* note 53, at 300–01.

66. 43 Fed. Reg. at 53956.

67. Belmont Report, 44 Fed. Reg. 23192 (April 18, 1979), in Brody, *supra* note 53, at 286.

68. *Id.* at 23192, in Brody, *supra* note 53, at 283–84.

69. 45 C.F.R. § 46.111(a)(2) (emphasis added). The Common Rule, *Federal Policy for the Protection of Human Subjects,* 56 Fed. Reg. 28002 (June 18, 1991).

70. 45 C.F.R. § 46.406(a) (2003).

71. *See* Griner, *supra* note 21, at 606–07; Korins, *supra* note 1, at 506–07; Sheldon, *supra* note 20, at 119.

72. Fletcher, *supra* note 58, at 638; Richard W. Garnett, *Why Informed Consent? Human Experimentation and the Ethics of Autonomy*, 36 Cath. Law. 455, 485–87 (1996); Peter V. Rabins, *Issues Raised by Research Using Persons Suffering from Dementia Who Have Impaired Decisional Capacity*, 1 J. Health Care L. & Pol'y 22 (1998); Ross, *supra* note 29, at 94–95.

73. John Harris, Professional Responsibility and Consent to Treatment, in *Consent and the Incompetent Patient: Ethics, Law and Medicine* 37, 45–47 (S. Hirsch & J. Harris eds., 1998).

74. *See McFall v. Shimp*, 10 Pa. D. & C.3d 90 (Pa. Common Pleas 1978); David S. Lockemeyer, *Note, At What Cost Will the Court Impose a Duty to Preserve the Life of a Child?*, 39 Cleveland-State L. Rev. 577, 581–83 (1991); Price, *supra* note 43, at 145.

75. Prevention of a mother's "abandonment" of her dependent child was part of the justification for a court-ordered blood transfusion for a Jehovah's Witness in the Georgetown College case, Application of President and Directors of Georgetown College, Inc. 331 F.2d 1000 (D.C. Cir. 1964). More recent jurisprudence eschews this duty to dependents rationale so long as there is another parent or close relative who will be able to care for the child to be left behind if the parent declines medical intervention and dies. In theory, though, a court might still be willing to override a parent's rejection of life-sustaining medical intervention if the parent would be leaving behind a thoroughly dependent orphan.

76. Mary Anne Warren, *Moral Status: Obligations to Persons and Other Living Things* 8–9, 77 (1997).

77. *Id.* at 94–95; John Harris, The Philosophical Case Against the Philosophical Case Against Euthanasia, in *Euthanasia Examined: Ethical, Clinical, and Legal Perspectives*, ch. 3 (J. Keown ed., 1995).

78. American Medical Association Council on Ethical and Judicial Affairs, *The Use of Anencephalic Neonates as Organ Donors*, 273 JAMA 1614, 1616 (1995).

79. The Council on Ethical and Judicial Affairs later withdrew its recommendation, but it did so on the basis of a question about whether all anencephalic infants lack consciousness and feeling. They did not rescind the notion that an unconscious, anencephalic infant might be used as an organ donor. *See* Bard, *supra* note 9, at 62–63; Dorothy E. Vawter, Ethical Frameworks for Live and Cadaver Organ Donation, in *Organ and Tissue Donation: Ethical, Legal, and Policy Issues* 63–66 (B. Spielman ed., 1996).

80. *In re T.A.C.P.*, 609 So. 2d 588 (Fla. 1992).

81. *See In re Christopher I.*, 131 Cal. Rep. 122, 133–34 (Cal. App. 2003); *Care and Protection of Beth*, 587 N.E.2d 1377, 1382 (Mass. 1992); *Matter of Torres*, 357 N.W.2d 332, 340 (Minn. 1984); *Matter of A.B.*, 2003 N.Y. Misc. LEXIS 878 (N.Y. Probate 2003). *Cf. Brophy v. New England Sinai Hospital*, 497 N.E.2d 626 (Mass. 1986) (a case involving a formerly competent, permanently unconscious

patient in which the court stresses the patient's dignity interest in avoiding permanent unconsciousness). *See also* Ben Rich, *Reflections on the Social Constructions of Death,* 24 J. Legal Med. 233 (2003).

82. The reasons that profoundly disabled persons—even those lacking rudimentary reasoning capacity—have full moral status may be varied. Mary Anne Warren accords profoundly disabled persons "the same moral weight" as any competent human. Warren, *supra* note 76, at 164. She cites several factors as supporting this stance, including emotional abhorrence at doing otherwise and self-interest flowing from a realization that even a competent being can later deteriorate to a point of grave mental debilitation. *Id.* at 166. She also relies on what she calls "transitivity of respect"—a principle that society ought to respect the fact that some human beings love and attribute full stature to profoundly disabled beings. In other words, society ought to accept the moral significance that some persons choose to attribute to profoundly disabled beings regardless of their intrinsic moral status. *Id.* at 88, 170–71. I argue in chapter 1 that law cannot afford to differentiate about legal status among people with varying levels of intellectual function. The dividing lines are too imprecise and too unprincipled to follow that course. For another defense of the proposition that every human being has full moral status, *see* Kavanaugh, *supra* note 24, at 119–22, 125–31.

83. A number of commentators have observed this common slide from substituted judgment to best interests in the context of never competent persons. *See* Rachel M. Dufault, *Bone Marrow Donations by Children: Rethinking the Legal Framework in Light of* Curran v. Bosze, 24 Conn. L. Rev. 211, 226–27 (1991); Thomas H. Murphy, Jr., *Minor Consent to Transplant Surgery: A Review of the Law,* 62 Marq. L. Rev. 149, 156 (1978). Courts have also commented on the phenomenon. *See In re Grady,* 426 A.2d 467 (N.J. 1981); *Little v. Little,* 576 S.W.2d 493, 498 (Tex. Civ. App. 1979).

84. Norman Fost, an important commentator on medical issues involving children, contends that a child's best interests, as best approximated by assessing what a competent adult would want done if facing the circumstances of the minor potential organ donor, ought to determine a donation decision involving a young child. Benefits and risks would thus govern any donation decision on behalf of a child. *See* Norman Fost, *Children as Renal Donors,* 296 N. Eng. J. Med. 296, 365 (1977). *See also* Dan W. Brock, Ethical Issues in Exposing Children to Risks, in *Children as Research Subjects* 85 (M. Grodin & L. Glantz eds., 1994). However, it is not clear that a strong majority of competent adults would agree to tissue donation in the absence of capacity to experience personal satisfaction.

85. Robbenolt, *supra* note 41, at 238–39.

86. A mix of motivations, including some self-interested motivation, can underlie altruism. Price, *supra* note 43, at 331, 477–79.

87. Joseph Boyle, A Case for Sometimes Tube-Feeding Patients in PVS, in *Euthanasia Examined: Ethical, Clinical, and Legal Perspectives* 189, 198 (J. Keown ed., 1995). This is not to say that children can never experience the positive benefits of altruistic behavior. As children mature they no doubt acquire more and more

capacity to enjoy the rewards of contributing to others' well-being. *See* Dufault, *supra* note 83, at 238, 245; Robbennolt, *supra* note 41, at 226–28.

88. *See* Howard Klepper, *Incompetent Organ Donors*, 25 J. Soc. Philosophy 241, 294 (1994).

89. Boyle, *supra* note 87, at 198.

90. *See* Dufault, *supra* note 83, at 237–38; Michael T. Morley, *Note, Proxy Consent to Organ Donation by Incompetents*, 111 Yale L.J. 1215, 1233–34 (2002); Robbennolt, *supra* note 41, at 226–28.

91. *Id.* at 1234.

92. *In re Pescinski*, 226 N.W.2d 180, 184 (Wis. 1975).

93. *Id.*

94. Richard McCormick expresses a variation on this theme of charity as a part of intrinsic human nature. He argues that a surrogate may consent to nontherapeutic research on behalf of a never competent person because everyone, including profoundly disabled beings, ought to be willing to make modest sacrifices to promote the life and health of others. Richard A. McCormick, *Proxy Consent in the Experimentation Situation*, 18 Persp. Biology & Med. 2, 12–13 (1974). For me, some further explanation is necessary (beyond a deontological "ought") before ascribing altruism to never competent persons.

95. The perspective of these commentators is akin to the parallel claim (examined in chapter 2) that a profoundly disabled person has the same rights as a competent person. If a competent person can incur risks and perform an altruistic act, then a surrogate is entitled to choose similarly for an incapacitated ward. Yet here, as in chapter 2, the profoundly disabled person cannot have "the same right" to choice as a competent person who actually experiences and assesses the many factors in play.

96. *Matter of Jane A.*, 629 N.E.2d 1337, 1340 (Mass. App. 1994).

97. Shannon Jordan, *Decision Making for Incompetent Persons: The Law and Morality of Who Shall Decide* 79 (1985).

98. *See* Leonard H. Glantz, The Law of Human Experimentation with Children, in *Children as Research Subjects* 108–10 (M. Grodin & L. Glantz eds., 1994); Ross, *supra* note 29, at 43–44, 50–51, 252–54.

99. Murray, *supra* note 54, at 791, 800.

100. *See* James Dwyer & Elizabeth Vig, *Rethinking Transplantation between Siblings*, 25 Hastings Center Rep. 7, 10 (September–October 1995), for a description of various ways in which parents commonly impel siblings to sacrifice for the benefit of other siblings. *See also* Frederick Schoeman, *Parental Discretion and Children's Rights*, 10 J. Phil. & Med. 48 (1985); Robert M. Veatch, *The Patient as Partner: A Theory of Human Experimentation Ethics* 56–57 (1987).

101. *Hart v. Brown*, 289 A.2d 386, 390 (Conn. Super. 1972); *Nathan v. Farinelli* (Mass. 1974) (described in Glantz, *supra* note 84, at 110, and in Murray, *supra* note 54, at 160–62).

102. Glantz, *supra* note 98, at 110.

103. *See* Rebecca Dresser, *Standards for Family Decisions: Replacing Best Interests with Harm Prevention*, 3 Am. J. Bioethics 54, 55 (Spring 2003). *But see* George Hill, *Can Anyone Authorize the Nontherapeutic Permanent Alteration of a Child's Body?*, 3 Am. J. Bioethics 47 (Spring 2003) (questioning the ethics of neonatal circumcision).

104. The degree of deference that the law typically gives to family autonomy has aroused considerable objections from some feminists and children's advocates. Those sources lament the harmful and unjust conduct (short of abuse or neglect) that is permitted under a deferential approach to family decision making. *E.g., Martha Albertson Fineman, What Place for Family Privacy?*, 67 Geo. Wash. L. Rev. 1207, 1216–1219 (1999); Barbara Bennett Woodhouse, *The Dark Side of Family Privacy*, 67 Geo. Wash. L. Rev. 1247, 1255–56 (2000). *See also* Carl E. Schneider, *Rights Discourse and Neonatal Euthanasia*, 76 Calif. L. Rev. 151, 162–64 (1988).

105. This framework has been acknowledged by the U.S. Supreme Court in *Bowen v. American Hospital Association*, 476 U.S. 610, 627–28, 630 (1986).

106. *Troxel v. Granville*, 530 U.S. 57, 65–67 (2000).

107. *Wisconsin v. Yoder*, 406 U.S. 205 (1972). *See* David DeGroot, *Note, The Liberal Tradition and the Constitution: Developing a Coherent Jurisprudence of Parental Rights*, 78 Tex. L. Rev. 1287, 1312 (2000).

108. *Yoder*, 406 U.S. at 234.

109. *But see* Morley, *supra* note 90, at 1236–38, 1243–45 (arguing that parents have both a constitutional right and duty to consider the best interests of the family as a whole in deciding whether to derogate an incapacitated sibling's interests in favor of an ailing sibling).

110. *See* David D. Meyer, Lochner *Redeemed: Family Privacy after* Troxel *and* Carhart, 48 UCLA L. Rev. 1125, 1137–42 (2001).

111. Courts also make independent assessments of a child's best interests when parents are in conflict about what medical course to follow for their child or about which spouse should have custody of a child.

112. *E.g., Newmark v. Williams*, 588 A.2d 1108 (Del. 1991); *Weber v. Stony Brook Hospital*, 467 N.Y.S.2d 685 (App. Div. 1984). *See also Bowen v. American Hospital Association*, 476 U.S. 610, 627–28 (1986).

113. *Reno v. Flores*, 507 U.S. 292, 304 (1993).

114. Paul Ramsey, *The Patient as Person* (1970), 25, 36–38. *See also* William J. Curran & Henry K. Beecher, *Experimentation in Children*, 210 JAMA 77, 80 (1969).

115. *Id.* at 13.

116. Weisz, *supra* note 4, at 186: "The proxy decisionmaking power that our society invests in parents relative to each child authorizes parents to act in the best interests of that child. It does not authorize them to use that child's body for the benefit of another."

117. *Grimes v. Kennedy Krieger Institute*, 782 A.2d 807, 814–15, 852–53 (Md. 2001). *See also T.D. v. New York State Office of Mental Health*, 626 N.Y.S.2d 1015 (Sup. Ct. 1995), *modified*, 650 N.Y.S.2d 173, 191 (App. Div. 1996).

118. Brock, *supra* note 84, at 89–90; John D. Lantos, Children as Organ Donors: An Argument for Involuntary Altruism, in Primum Non Nocere *Today* 67, 73–74 (G. R. Burgio & J. D. Lantos eds., 1994); Ross, *supra* note 29, at 33, 68, 251. Charles Fried asserts that it is "open to parents as part of their care to enlist their children to do a reasonable and good thing [such as tissue donation] which they themselves would have done, so long as this is not against the will of the child." Fried, *supra* note 11, at 114.

119. "Requiring children to behave in certain ways in order to help them understand the importance of certain virtues is a parental responsibility." Lantos, *supra* note 118, at 74.

120. Weisz, *supra* note 4, at 185, 196.

121. Fineman, *supra* note 104, at 1214.

122. Brock, *supra* note 84, at 87; Dwyer & Vig, *supra* note 100, at 12; Morley, *supra* note 90, at 1242–44; Ross, *supra* note 29, at 3–5; Lainie Friedman Ross, *Moral Grounding for the Participation of Children as Organ Donors*, 21 J.L. Med. & Ethics 251, 252 (1993).

123. Ross, *supra* note 29, at 43, 50–51, 124, 252; Ross, *supra* note 122, at 252–54.

124. Gregory A. Loken, *Gratitude and the Map of Moral Duties toward Children*, 31 Ariz. St. L. Rev. 1121, 1176–77, 1181–82 (1999).

125. Martha Minow suggests that family members impliedly consent to intrafamily duties by remaining within the family unit. Minow, *supra* note 26, at 307. However, a profoundly disabled or young child cannot choose to leave the unit.

126. Cf. *In re Doe*, 481 N.Y.S.2d 93 (App. Div. 1984) (allowing an institutionalized disabled person to serve as a donor where the donee had been the person tending to the donor's affairs in the institutional setting).

127. *See* Norman Daniels, *What Do We Owe Our Parents?* 29 (1993); Minow, *supra* note 26, at 309, 322–55.

128. *See* Daniels, *supra* note 127, at 112–13; Loken *supra* note 124, at 1201. In theory, parents might vow to supply benefits *after* imposing a sacrifice on a profoundly disabled child, but we would not trust a previously neglectful parent to fulfill that prospective duty.

129. The case of anencephalics is different from the case of most disabled persons for a couple of reasons. First, any organ harvest is not for the benefit of a close relative but rather for a stranger.*See In re T.A.C.P.*, 609 So. 2d 588 (Fla. 1992). Second, the anencephalic will never live at home as part of a family unit. Parents who want to consent to organ donation on behalf of an anencephalic are typically "seeking a way of providing some meaning into the birth of their child and assuaging the parental grief." Julie Koenig, *Note, The Anencephalic Baby Theresa: A Prognosticator of Future Bioethics*, 17 Nova L. Rev. 445, 472 (1992).

130. Ross, *supra* note 29, at 55 n.32, 124, 174; Klepper, *supra* note 88, at 252–53; Morley, *supra* note 90, at 1220.

131. Ross, *supra* note 29, at 50–51, 114–19, 252.

132. *Id.* at 114–15.

133. Lantos, *supra* note 118, at 73.

134. McCormick, *supra* note 94, at 17. Robert Veatch also seems to subscribe to the notion that "there are some benefits to others that all individuals ought to desire." Robert M. Veatch, *The Patient-Physician Relation*, pt. 2, 230 (1991).

135. Robert Veatch, *The Patient as Partner: A Theory of Human Experimentation Ethics* 57 (1987).

136. Mark R. Wicclair, Ethics and the Elderly 185–86 (1993).

137. Can a social-justice argument—relying on benefits provided in return for any bodily imposition on a profoundly disabled research subject—be reinforced by taking a cross-generational perspective? The contention would be that a contemporary never competent person has reaped benefits from prior generations of incapacitated persons' participation in nontherapeutic research. Fairness then supposedly dictates that a contemporary research subject assume similar burdens for the good of future generations. Brock, *supra* note 84, at 91–92, discusses the notion of cross-generational fairness. *See also* Fried, *supra* note 11, at 113. Carl Coleman has made a similar point in comments to me.

There is some appeal to this notion of cross-generational fairness. If a person has in fact benefitted from the sacrifices of prior research subjects (an empirical question), then some moral debt seems reasonable. Yet I have hesitations about the whole argument. Even if prior generations of similarly situated persons did participate in medical research, was that prior participation itself moral? What justified using the first generation of never competent persons as subjects of nontherapeutic research? Finally, the whole cross-generational argument seems to prove too much. Every generation benefits from the sacrifices of its predecessors—from the taxes used to construct public facilities, from the labor invested in those facilities, and from the lives lost in protecting the country. If those considerable prior sacrifices justify extractions from contemporary citizens, there's virtually no limit to the burdens that could be imposed under the rubric of moral debt. It seems more fitting and more manageable to look to contemporary benefits extended to incapacitated persons in any calculation of fair return for benefits received.

138. For recognition of the incommensurate nature of personal sacrifices and social gains, *see* Ezekiel J. Emanuel, David Wendler & Christine Grady, *What Makes Clinical Research Ethical?*, 283 JAMA 2701 (2000).

139. 274 U.S. 200 (1927).

140. Of course, the senselessness of the sterilizations in issue makes them particularly offensive. If severe, unavoidable, inheritable deficiencies were shown, perhaps the practice of nonvoluntary sterilization could be deemed moral. I venture no opinion on that issue.

141. James W. Trent, Jr., *Inventing the Feeble Mind: A History of Mental Retardation in the United States* 230 (1994).

142. *See, e.g.,* Philip M. Bein, *Surrogate Consent and the Incompetent Experimental Subject,* 46 Food, Drug & Cosmetic L.J. 739, 755–58 (1991); Clarence J. Sundram, *In Harm's Way: Research Subjects Who Are Decisionally Impaired,* 1 J. Health Care L. & Pol'y 36, 41–42, 45 (1998).

143. *E.g.,* Lois Shepherd, *Face to Face: A Call for Radical Responsibility in Place of Compassion,* Pub. L. & Legal Theory Working Paper #77, p. 56 (April 2003).

144. Georgetta Glavis-Innis, *Organ Donation and Incompetents: Can They Consent?,* 10 Touro Int'l L. Rev. 155, 186 (2000).

145. *See* Newark Star Ledger, September 20, 2002.

146. *San Remo Hotel v. City of San Francisco,* 41 P.3d 87, 108 (2002).

147. *Harmelin v. Michigan,* 501 U.S. 957 (1991); *Hutto v. Davis,* 454 U.S. 370 (1982).

148. Later in this chapter, I attribute this requirement to a concept of respect for intrinsic human dignity and to the fact that profoundly disabled persons have full moral and legal status.

149. *See* Klepper, *supra* note 88, at 248–49. In any event, the surrogate decision maker who is considering whether to impose a measure of sacrifice on an institutionalized person would be a parent or other bonded guardian and not the institution itself. Because of the special interests and historical record of institutions for the mentally disabled, we would not trust the institution itself to make a sacrificial decision for a ward.

150. Jonathan D. Moreno, *Regulation of Research on the Decisionally Impaired: History and Gaps in the Current Regulatory System,* 1 J. Health Care L. & Pol'y 1, 64 (1998).

151. Deference to an incapacitated research subject's resistance is confined to the context of nontherapeutic research. Where a research protocol carries a reasonable chance to cure or improve the condition of an ailing person, overriding the will of a resisting, mentally incapacitated patient is more justifiable because an object is to directly benefit the patient.

152. Belmont Report, *supra* note 7. Commentators commonly recognize that justice precludes disproportionate utilization of helpless populations in human subject research. James F. Childress, *The National Bioethics Advisory Commission: Bridging the Gaps in Human Subjects Research Protection,* 1 J. Health Care L. & Pol'y 105, 118 (1998); Dresser, *supra* note 5, at 71; Veatch, *supra* note 135, at 68.

153. Richard Garnett makes a strong pitch for incorporating principles of human dignity into the framework of medical research. Garnett, *supra* note 15, at 498–503.

154. Human dignity certainly dictates that helpless persons are not infinitely exploitable to satisfy the interests of other human beings. Warren, *supra* note 76, at 228.

155. While intrinsic human dignity may have a universal inviolable core, cultures sometimes diverge in their members' assessments of the moral bounds of some practices. Circumcision provides an example. *See* Dena Davis, *Male and Female Genital Alteration: A Collision Course with the Law?,* 11 Health Matrix 487 (2001). There will also be some cultural variation as to acceptable practice in the context of research on human subjects. *See* Emanuel et al., *supra* note 138, at 2708; Benjamin Freedman, Abraham Fuks & Charles Weijer, In Loco Parentis: *Minimal Risks as an Ethical Threshold for Research upon Children,* 23 Hastings Center Report 13, 17–18 (April 1993).

156. As quoted in Garnett, *supra* note 15, at 470.

157. 45 C.F.R. § 46.406 (2003). *See also* President's Commission for the Study of Ethical Problems in Medicine and Biomedical Research, *Making Health Care Decisions* 177–79 (1983) (asserting that surrogates must be constrained by a judgment of reasonableness of risk even where the now incompetent ward previously consented to participate in medical research).

158. Veatch, *supra* note 135, at 31.

159. Brock, *supra* note 84, at 86; Weijer, *supra* note 7, at 350–52.

160. *See infra* pp. 149–50. *See also* Rebecca Dresser, *Dementia Research: Ethics and Policy for the Twenty-first Century*, 35 Ga. L. Rev. 661, 679 (2001); Jonathan D. Moreno, *Regulation of Research on the Decisionally Impaired: History and Gaps in the Current Regulatory System*, 1 J. of Health Care L. Pol'y 1 (1998).

161. Emanuel, *supra* note 138, at 2706: "There is no settled framework for how potential social benefits should be balanced against individual risks."

162. McCormick, *supra* note 94, at 15.

163. Emanuel, *supra* note 138, at 2706. Rebecca Dresser explains maximum-risk limitations as a moral imperative that is aimed at preventing society from imposing excessive burdens on vulnerable people. Dresser, *supra* note 160, at 689.

164. John Harris comments: "Because the advantage to be gained is future and speculative, we are entitled to demand that the risks imposed for such gains be genuinely negligible and that the discomfort, anxiety, and indignity of any research procedures be truly minimal." Harris, *supra* note 73, at 45.

165. Freedman et al., *supra* note 155, at 17; Weijer, *supra* note 7, at 356.

166. These examples are drawn from a 1991 report of the British Medical Research Council reproduced as an appendix in Baruch Brody, *The Ethics of Biomedical Research* 320–21 (1998).

167. American Academy of Pediatrics, *Guidelines for the Ethical Conduct of Studies to Evaluate Drugs in Pediatric Populations*, 95 Pediatrics 286 (1995).

168. American College of Physicians, *Cognitively Impaired Subjects*, 111 Ann. Internal Med. 843, 844–45 (1989). The ACP seemed to hold out the possibility that some national review body might be constituted to authorize important nontherapeutic research that carries more than minimal risk—but only with the consent of any mentally impaired subject. *Id.* at 847.

169. *See* Diane E. Hoffmann, Jack Schwartz & Evan G. DeRenzo, *Regulating Research with Decisionally Impaired Individuals: Are We Making Progress?*, 3 DePaul J. Health Care L. 547, 558 (2000). *See also* Curran & Beecher, *supra* note 114, at 83.

170. 45 C.F.R. § 46.406 (2003). The same regulation requires parental consent to the research on behalf of their child and that the child (where of appropriate age) assent. Concerning interpretations of Section 46.406, *see* Hoffmann et al., *supra* note 53, at 564; Jennifer Rosato, *The Ethics of Clinical Trials: A Child's View*, 28 J. L. Med. & Ethics 362, 366 (2000); Weijer, *supra* note 7, at 349. The

regulations also permit research that carries more than a minor increase over minimal risk if the researcher secures special approval from the Secretary of Health and Human Services.

171. *See* NBAC Report, *supra* note 7, at 41.

172. 43 Fed. Reg. 53956 (1978), speaking to a proposed section 46.507.

173. *See* Va. Code Annot. § 32.1-162.18 (1996); Hoffmann et al., *supra* note 53, at 589–90; Miller, *supra* note 52, at 113.

174. Dresser, *supra* note 5, at 680–81. At the same time, Professor Dresser worries about the vagueness of terms like "minor increase over minimal risk." She fears disparate interpretations by researchers and institutional research boards. Rebecca Dresser, *Mentally Disabled Research Subjects,* 276 JAMA 67, 70 (1996).

175. Holder, *supra* note 16, at 146.

176. *See* Hoffmann et al., *supra* note 53, at 561–63. Although the Department of Health, Education, and Welfare published a proposed regulation that authorized research with a minor increase over minimal risk, the department also announced that it was considering a ban on such research, at least where the prospective subject was incapable of assenting to the research. 43 Fed. Reg. 53956 (1978), discussing proposed Section 46.507(a)(4)(iii).

177. European Parliament Directive 2001/20/EC, Art. 5(e)(i) (April 4, 2001).

178. National Bioethics Advisory Commission, *supra* note 7, at 61–62. The report states that a surrogate, in the absence of prior indications of the patient's willingness to participate in research, can act only in the patient's best interests. *Id.* at 61. It is hard to regard nontherapeutic research as being in a patient's best interests. Berg, *supra* note 18, at 34 n.117.

179. 45 C.F.R. § 46.407 (2003). The section also requires parental consent to the research and assent by the research subject. Perhaps this last requirement (assent) excludes profoundly disabled persons from research that goes beyond a minor increase over minimal risk. An alternative reading, though, is that this section requires assent only where the potential subject is capable of understanding the nature of the research and its consequences.

180. Rosato, *supra* note 170, at 371.

181. Brody, *supra* note 53, at 130; Desaulniers, *supra* note 8, at 192, 212; Rabins, *supra* note 12, at 26.

182. European Parliament Directive, *supra* note 177, at Preamble and Article 4(e); Rosato, *supra* note 170, at 362–63, 371.

183. Weijer, *supra* note 7, at 356–58.

184. Court-appointed guardians are deemed to be officers of the court and hence may be subject to the best-interests standard that is commonly articulated for judicial decisions on behalf of incapacitated medical patients. And while institutions commonly rely on parents for routine medical decision making on behalf of profoundly disabled residents, they might insist that a parent be appointed formal guardian for purposes of consenting to nontherapeutic research.

185. Even as judicially appointed guardians, however, conscientious parents almost certainly get some deference from health-care providers while making surrogate decisions and probably get some deference from courts as well.

186. Separate study groups in two states—Maryland and New York—both concluded that a moderate degree of risk could appropriately be imposed on incapacitated research subjects. Dresser, *supra* note 5, at 676. The notion of moderate risk seems consistent with the minor increase over a minimal-risk standard. Thus, at least two study groups composed of experts have found this level of risk to be consistent with human dignity. *See also* Ross, *supra* note 29, at 95 (concluding that nontherapeutic research on children is moral so long as risk does not exceed more than a minor increase over minimal risk).

187. Under those guidelines, a precondition of nontherapeutic research on children or mentally incapacitated adults was that competent adults not be suitable subjects. *See* John Fletcher, *Human Experimentation: Ethics in the Consent Situation*, 2 J.L. & Contemp. Probs. 620, 631 (1967).

188. Brody, *supra* note 53, at 287–88. The National Commission that authored the Belmont Report (*supra* note 7) considered necessity to be present if the research was aimed at ultimately alleviating the same disease or disorder as that afflicting the incapacitated research subject. The theory was that some research regarding mental conditions could be performed only on persons having the condition. Desaulniers, *supra* note 8, at 214.

189. *See* N.Y.C.C.R.R. tit. 14, § 527.10(d)(6) (2002); American College of Physicians, *supra* note 7, at 845. All three expert panels that recently examined the bounds of ethical research concluded that mentally impaired research subjects should not be used if competent persons can be utilized. Dresser, *supra* note 5, at 667.

190. While the relevant cases often stress the considerable potential benefit to the donee, that emphasis is not pursuant to a simple weighing of benefits to the donee against burdens on the donor. There must be medical necessity for even considering an incapacitated person as a potential donor. And according to the cases, organ or tissue donation will not be authorized unless found to be in the donor's interests. *See* notes 32–38, *supra*.

191. Brody, *supra* note 53, at 285. Refusal to assent would then be honored unless the research promised an important potential benefit to the disabled subject. That is, authority to overcome the resistance of a never competent patient is much more justifiable where the proposed medical intervention is therapeutic in nature.

192. 45 C.F.R. § 46.402(b) (2003). *See* Brody, *supra* note 53, at 279–80; Hoffmann et al., *supra* note 53, at 149–50; Rosato, *supra* note 170, at 369.

193. Jessica Wilen Berg, *Legal and Ethical Complexities of Consent with Cognitively Impaired Research Subjects: Proposed Guidelines*, 24 J.L. Med. & Ethics 18, 24 (1996); Brody, *supra* note 53, at 124–25, 133; Holder, *supra* note 16, at 151; Dresser, *supra* note 5, at 667, 683; Stephan Haimowitz, Susan J. Delano & John M. Oldham, *Uninformed Decisionmaking: The Case of Surrogate Research Consent*, 27 Hastings Center Rep. 9, 10, 14 (1997); Price, *supra* note 43, at 360; Ross, *supra* note 29, at 82–87. *See also* Va. Code Annot. § 32.1-162.18 (1996); Cal. Health &

Safety Code § 24178 (1992); HEW Proposed Regulation regarding research on institutionalized persons, 53 Fed. Reg. 53951, 53955 (November 17, 1978).

194. National Bioethics Advisory Commission, *supra* note 7, at 58.

195. Ross, *supra* note 29, at 95.

Chapter 6

1. Previously competent persons who have articulated prior wishes and preferences may be accorded prospective autonomy, meaning that their advance expressions will be respected. Never competent persons do not have that prerogative.

2. *K.C.M. v. State*, 627 P.2d 607, 612 (Alaska 1981); *Matter of Moe*, 432 N.E.2d 712, 722 (Mass. 1982); *In re Grady*, 426 A.2d 467, 483 (N.J. 1981); *In re Terwilliger*, 450 A.2d 1376 (Pa. 1982). *See* Martha A. Field & Valerie A. Sanchez, *Equal Treatment for People with Mental Retardation* 99, 363 n.3 (1999).

3. Me. Rev. Stat. Annot., tit. 34-B, § 7011.9 (1988); Utah Code Annot. § 62A-6-108(3) (2000); Va. Code Annot. § 54.1-2976(5) (2002). *See* Field & Sanchez, *supra* note 2.

4. *See, e.g., Matter of Susan S.*, 1996 W.L. 75343 (Del. Ch. 1996) (partial hysterectomy); *Matter of R.H.* 622 N.E.2d 1071, 1076 (Mass. 1993) (dialysis); *In re Rogers*, 458 N.E.2d 308 (Mass. 1983) (psychotropic drugs); *Matter of Ingram*, 689 P.2d 1363 (Wash. 1984) (cancer treatment).

5. *See, e.g., In re C.D.M.*, 627 P.2d 607, 613 (Alaska 1981); *Matter of Jane A.*, 629 N.E.2d 1337, 1340 (Mass. App. 1994).

6. *See* Douglas O. Linder, *The Other Right to Life Debate: When Does Fourteenth Amendment "Life" End?*, 37 Ariz. L. Rev. 1182, 1201 (1995); Bruce J. Winick, *Competency to Consent to Treatment: The Distinction between Assent and Objection*, 28 Houston L. Rev. 15, 43 (1991).

7. H. Tristam Engelhardt, *The Foundations of Bioethics* 346 (2d ed. 1996). Not everyone agrees that irrational expressions should not govern decisions on behalf of incompetent persons. Martha Field argues that the preferences of incompetent retarded persons should be determinative—even as to major medical decisions such as sterilization—on the theory that they are likely to be as sound as the decisions of supposedly impartial arbiters. Martha Field, *Killing "the Handicapped"— Before and after Birth*, 16 Harvard Women's L.J. 79, 89 n.29 (1993). Professor Field concedes, though, that at some level of mental dysfunction a person cannot communicate an intelligible preference—at which point the incapacitated person's expressions should not be binding. Field & Sanchez, *supra* note 2, at 158–64, 191–93, 198.

8. *In re Hier*, 464 N.E.2d 959 (Mass. App. 1984); Winick, *supra* note 6, at 46.

9. Susan R. Martyn, *Substituted Judgment, Best Interests, and the Need for Best Respect*, 3 Cambridge Q. Health Care Ethics 195, 201–02 (1994).

10. I argue in chapter 1 that purposive behavior is a key determinant of human personhood.

11. Similar considerations apply in dealing with children. Seeking and listening to a child's perspective is a sign that parents and health-care providers respect the child. Lainie Friedman Ross *Children, Families, and Health Care Decision Making* 67–68 (1998).

12. For example, a mentally disabled patient may vigorously resist the needle pricks and discomforts associated with kidney dialysis. And that same patient may not comprehend the medical necessity for the bodily interventions, a fact that might exacerbate the distress that is being experienced.

13. *E.g., In re Baby Boy Doe,* 632 N.E.2d 326, 335 (Ill. App. 1994); *Cruzan v. Director,* Missouri Department of Health, 497 U.S. 261 (1990) (Justice O'Connor). *See also* Field & Sanchez, *supra* note 2, at 177–78.

14. Meir Dan-Cohen, Defending Dignity, in *Harmful Thoughts: Essays on Law, Self, and Morality* 163–64 (M. Dan-Cohen, ed., 2002).

15. *See R.H.,* 622 N.E.2d at 1075 (dialysis); *Ingram,* 689 P.2d at 1371 (cancer treatment).

16. President's Commission for the Study of Ethical Problems in Medicine, Making Health Care Decisions 181 (1983).

17. This pattern of limited deference to persons with limited capacity for self-determination applies in the context of medical decision making for minors. Surrogate decision makers and medical personnel will always solicit the input of minors who are capable of understanding the essence of the decision in issue. Colleen Sheppard, *Children's Rights to Equality: Protection Versus Paternalism,* 1 Ann. Health L. 197, 206 (1992). Minors who understand the factors in play and who display mature reasoning—for example, where the medical issue is tissue or organ donation—are likely to have their assent or dissent followed by care givers.

18. Winick, *supra* note 6, at 43–45, 52–53.

19. *Id.* at 42–45.

20. Jennifer L. Rosato, *The Ethics of Clinical Trials: A Child's View,* 28 J.L. Med. & Ethics 362, 368, 376 n.141 & n.142 (2000).

21. *See Lefebvre v. North Broward Hospital District,* 566 So. 2d 568, 571 (Fla. Ct. App. 1990) (stressing best interests as the governing factor).

22. *Conservatorship of Angela D.,* 70 Cal. App. 4th 1410 (1999) (applying California Probate Code Section 1958(h)).

23. Conversation with Peggy Dervitz, head of the Bureau of Guardianship Services within New Jersey's Department of the Developmentally Disabled (November 2002).

24. 45 C.F.R. §§ 46.401 et seq. (2003).

25. Rebecca Dresser, *Dementia Research: Ethics and Policy for the Twenty-first Century,* 35 Ga. L. Rev. 661, 667 (2001); Jonathan D. Moreno, *Regulation of Research on the Decisionally Impaired: History and Gaps in the Current Regulatory System,* 1 J. Health Care L. & Pol'y 1, 19 (1998); John W. Warren et al., *Informed Consent by Proxy: An Issue in Research with Elderly Patients,* 315 N. Eng. J. Med. 1124, 1128 (1986).

26. *See Estate of C.W.,* 640 A.2d 427, 430 (Pa. Super. 1994) (sterilization).

27. *Matter of Jane A.,* 629 N.E.2d 1337, 1339–40 (Mass. App. 1994) (abortion); *In re Kowalski,* 382 N.W.2d 861, 866 (Minn. App. 1986) (custody).

28. Jane Gross, *Striving for a Gentle Farewell,* New York Times, August 3, 2003, § 4, p. 1.

29. John Arras, *The Severely Demented, Minimally Functional Patient: An Ethical Analysis,* 36 J. Am. Gerontological Soc'y 938, 939 (1988); Joseph M. Foley, The Experience of Being Demented, in *Dementia and Aging: Ethics, Values, and Policy Choices* 39–42 (Robert Binstock et al. eds., 1992); Hilde Lindemann Nelson, What Child Is This? 32 Hastings Center Rep. 34 (2002).

30. *In re Hier,* 464 N.E.2d 959, 965 (Mass. App. 1984).

31. "When patients push away food or pull out feeding tubes, do such actions really mean that they do not want to be fed, or could they be uncomfortable, angry, depressed, or seeking attention?" Bernard Lo, Laurie Dornbrand, Leslie E. Wolf, and Michelle Groman, *The* Wendland *Case—Withdrawing Life Support from Incompetent Patients Who are Not Terminally Ill,* 346 New Eng. J. Med. 1489 (2002).

32. *In re Conroy,* 486 A.2d 1209, 1243 (N.J. 1986). "When Claire Conroy moaned as nurses moved her, was that a sound of pain or irritation or greeting, or was it merely a reflexive noise?" Peter Filene, In the Arms of Others 144 (1999).

33. "The behavior of individuals with dementia represents understandable feelings and needs, even if the individuals are unable to express the feelings or needs." Stephen Post, *Dementia in Our Midst: The Moral Community,* 4 Cambridge Q. Healthcare Ethics 146 (1995).

34. *In re Storar,* 420 N.E.2d 64 (N.Y. 1981); *Matter of O'Brien,* 517 N.Y.S.2d 346, 348 (Sup. Ct. 1986).

35. 20 Pa. C.S.A. § 5406 (2004).

36. *See* Official Code of Georgia Annotated § 31-36-5(c) (2000) (making an incompetent patient's wishes binding on a surrogate so long as the patient understands the nature of the health-care procedure in issue).

References

Ahronheim, Judith C., Jonathan D. Moreno, and Connie Zuckerman. *Ethics in Clinical Practice*. 2nd ed. Gaithersburg, MD: Aspen Publishers, 2000.

Allen, Richard C. *Legal Rights of the Disabled and Disadvantaged*. Washington, DC: U.S. Government Printing Office, 1969.

American Academy of Pediatricians. "Ethics and the Care of Critically Ill Infants and Children." *Pediatrics* 98 (1996): 149–152.

———. "Guidelines for the Ethical Conduct of Studies to Evaluate Drugs in Pediatric Populations." *Pediatrics* 95, no. 2 (1995): 286.

American College of Physicians. "Cognitively Impaired Subjects." *Annals of Internal Medicine* 11 (1989): 843.

American Medical Association Council on Ethical and Judicial Affairs. *Current Opinions* Ethical Standards Sec. 2.20. (1994).

———. "Persistent Vegetative State and the Decision to Withdraw or Withhold Life Support." *Journal of the American Medical Association* 263 (1990): 426.

———. "Treatment Decisions of Seriously Ill Newborns." <http://www.ama-assn.org.amal/upload/mm/369/431pdf>.

———. "The Use of Anencephalic Neonates as Organ Donors." *Journal of the American Medical Association* 273 (1995): 1614.

Ambrosio, Michael P. "A Moral Appraisal of Legal Education: A Plea for a Return to Forgotten Truths." *Seton Hall Law Review* 22 (1992): 1177.

Arras, John D. "The Severely Demented, Minimally Functional Patient: An Ethical Analysis." *Journal of the American Geriatrics Society* 36 (1988): 938.

———. "Toward an Ethic of Ambiguity." *Hastings Center Report* 14, no. 2 (April 1984): 29

Bard, Jennifer S. "The Diagnosis Is Anencephaly and the Parents Ask about Organ Donation: Now What?" *Western New England Law Review* 21 (1999): 49.

Battin, Margaret. *The Least Worst Death*. New York: Oxford University Press, 1994.

Beauchamp, Tom. "The Failure of Theories of Personhood." *Kennedy Institute of Ethics Journal* 9 (December 1999): 293.

Beauchamp, Tom L., and James F. Childress. *Principles of Biomedical Ethics.* 4th ed. New York: Oxford University Press, 1994.

Bein, Philip M. "Surrogate Consent and the Incompetent Experimental Subject." *Food, Drug, and Cosmetic Law Journal* 46 (1991): 739

Beltran, Joseph E. "Shared Decision Making: The Ethics of Caring and Best Respect." *Bioethics Forum* 12, no. 3 (Fall 1996): 17.

Berg, Jessica Wilen. "Legal and Ethical Complexities of Consent with Cognitively Impaired Research Subjects: Proposed Guidelines." *Journal of Law, Medicine, and Ethics* 24 (1996): 18.

Bernstein, Dorothy M., and Roberta G. Simmons. "The Adolescent Kidney Donor: The Right to Give." *American Journal of Psychiatry* 131, no. 12 (1974): 1338.

Berry, Roberta M. "From Involuntary Sterilization to Genetic Enhancement: The Unsettled Legacy of *Buck v. Bell.*" *Notre Dame Journal of Law, Ethics, and Public Policy* 12 (1998): 401.

Beschle, Donald. "Autonomous Decision Making and Social Choice: Examining the Right to Die." *Kentucky Law Journal* 77 (1989): 319.

Beyleveld, Deryck, and Roger Brownsword. *Human Dignity in Bioethics and Biolaw.* New York: Oxford University Press, 2001.

———. "Human Dignity, Human Rights, and Human Genetics." *Modern Law Review* 61, no. 5 (1998): 661.

Blatt, Burton. *The Conquest of Mental Retardation.* Austin, TX: PRO-ED, 1987.

Blum, Erika T. "Note, When Terminating Parental Rights Is Not Enough: A New Look at Compulsory Sterilization." *Georgia Law Review* 28 (1994): 977.

Blumenson, Eric. "Who Counts Morally?" *Journal of Law and Religion* 14, no. 1 (1999–2000): 1.

Bonnie, Richard J. "Research with Cognitively Impaired Subjects." *Archives of General Psychiatry* 54 (1997): 105.

Bopp, James, and Thomas Marzden. "*Cruzan:* Facing the Inevitable." *Law, Medicine, and Healthcare* 19 (1991): 37.

Boyle, Joseph. "A Case for Sometimes Tube-Feeding Patients in PVS." In John Keown, ed., *Euthanasia Examined: Ethical, Clinical, and Legal Perspectives.* Cambridge: Cambridge University Press, 1995.

Brock, Dan W. "Ethical Issues in Exposing Children to Risks in Research." In Michael A. Grodin and Leonard H. Glantz, eds., *Children as Research Subjects: Science, Ethics, and Law.* New York: Oxford University Press, 1994.

———. "Justice and the Severely Demented Elderly." *Journal of Medicine and Philosophy* 13 (1988): 73.

———. "What Is the Moral Authority of Family Members to Act as Surrogates of Incompetent Patients?" *Millbank Quarterly* 74, no. 4 (1996): 599.

Brody, Baruch A. *The Ethics of Biomedical Research: An International Perspective.* New York: Oxford University Press, 1998.

———. *Life and Death Decision Making*. New York: Oxford University Press, 1988.

Buchanan, Allen. "The Limits of Proxy Decision Making for Incompetents." *UCLA Law Review* 29 (1981): 386.

Buchanan, Allen E., and Dan W. Brock. *Deciding for Others: The Ethics of Surrogate Decision Making*. Cambridge: Cambridge University Press, 1989.

Buckley, Mary Ann. "Comment, *In re Wendland*: Contradiction, Confusion, and Constitutionality." *Journal of Law and Policy* 11, no. 1 (2002): 255.

Burt, Robert A. "Developing Constitutional Rights of, in, and for Children." *Law and Contemporary Problems* 39 (1975): 118.

———. "The Supreme Court Speaks: Not Assisted Suicide But a Constitutional Right to Palliative Care." *New England Journal of Medicine* 337 (1997): 1234.

Burt, Robert A., and Monroe Price. "Nonconsensual Medical Procedures and the Right to Privacy." In Michael Kindred et al., eds., *The Mentally Retarded Citizen and the Law*. New York: Free Press, 1976.

Byrne, Peter. *Philosophical and Ethical Problems in Mental Handicap*. New York: St. Martin's Press, 2000.

Cannon, William P. "The Right to Die." *Houston Law Review* 7 (1970): 654.

Cantor, Norman L. *Advance Directives and the Pursuit of Death with Dignity*. Bloomington, ID: Indiana University Press, 1993.

———. "Discarding Substituted Judgment and Best Interests: Toward a Constructive Preference Standard for Dying, Previously Competent Patients without Advance Instructions." *Rutgers Law Review* 48 (1996): 1193.

———. "A Patient's Decision to Decline Life-Saving Medical Treatment: Bodily Integrity versus the Preservation of Life." *Rutgers Law Review* 26 (1973): 228.

———. "The Permanently Unconscious Patient, Nonfeeding, and Euthanasia." *American Journal of Law and Medicine* 15 (1989): 381.

———. "Prospective Autonomy: On the Limits of Shaping One's Post-Competence Medical Fate." *Journal of Contemporary Health, Law, and Policy* 8 (1992): 13.

———. "Twenty-five Years after *Quinlan*: A Review of the Jurisprudence of Death and Dying." *Journal of Law, Medicine, and Ethics* 29 (2001): 182.

Caplan, Arthur. "Dignity Is a Social Construct." *BMJ (British Medical Journal)* 327 (2003): 1419.

Capron, Alexander, M. "Where Is the Sure Interpreter?" *Hastings Center Report* 22, no. 4 (July 1992): 26.

Cepko, Roberta. "Involuntary Sterilization of Mentally Disabled Women." *Berkeley Women's Law Journal* 8 (1993): 122.

Channick, Susan Adler. "The Myth of Autonomy at the End of Life: Questioning the Paradigm of Rights." *Villanova Law Review* 44 (1999): 577.

Charlesworth, Max. *Bioethics in a Liberal Society*. New York: Cambridge University Press, 1993.

———. "Disabled Newborn Infants and the Quality of Life." *Journal of Contemporary Health Law and Policy* 9 (1993): 129.

Cheyette, Cara. "Note, Organ Harvests from the Legally Incompetent: An Argument against Compelled Altruism." *Boston College Law Review* 41 (2000): 465.

Childress, James. "Dying Patients: Who's in Control?" *Law, Medicine, and Health Care* 17 (1989): 227.

———. "The National Bioethics Advisory Commission: Bridging Gaps in Human Subjects Research Protection." *Journal of Health Care, Law, and Policy* 1 (1998): 105.

Clifford, Matthew O., and Thomas P. Huff. "Some Thoughts on the Meaning and Scope of the Montana Constitution's Dignity Clause." *Montana Law Review* 61 (2000): 301.

Cohen, Michael H. "Toward a Bioethics of Compassion." *Indiana Law Review* 28 (1995): 667.

Cohn, Felicia. "The Ethics of End-of-Life Care for Prison Inmates." *Journal of Law, Medicine, and Ethics* 27 (1999): 252.

Cox, Stanley E. "Government as Arbiter, not Custodian: Relational Privacy as Foundation for a Right to Refuse Medical Treatment Prolonging Incompetents' Lives." *New Mexico Law Review* 131 (1988): 131.

Cranford, Ronald E., and David Randolph Smith. "Consciousness: The Most Critical Moral (Constitutional) Standard for Human Personhood." *American Journal of Law and Medicine* 13 (1992): 233.

Cronan, Charles J. "Comment, Spare Parts from Incompetents: A Problem of Consent." *Journal of Family Law* 9 (1969): 309.

Curran, William J. "A Problem of Consent: Kidney Transplantation in Minors." *New York University Law Review* 34 (1959): 891.

Curran, William J., and Henry K. Beecher. "Experimentation in Children." *Journal of the American Medical Association* 210 (1969): 77.

Dan-Cohen, Meir. "Defending Dignity." In *Harmful Thoughts: Essays on Law, Self, and Morality* (Chap. 5). Princeton: Princeton University Press, 2002.

Daniels, Norman. *Am I My Brother's Keeper? An Essay on Justice between the Young and the Old.* New York: Oxford University Press, 1988.

Davis, Dena S. "Male and Female Genital Alteration: A Collision Course with the Law?" *Health Matrix* (2001): 487.

———. "Old and Thin." *Second Opinion* 15 (November 1990): 26.

DeGroot, David. "Note, The Liberal Tradition and the Constitution: Developing a Coherent Jurisprudence of Parental Rights." *Texas Law Review* 78 (2000): 1287.

Desaulniers, Kendall Ann. "Legislation to Protect the Decisionally Incapacitated Individual's Participation in Medical Research: Safety Net or Trap Door?" *Regent University Law Review* 13 (2000): 179.

"Developments in the Law: Medical Technology and the Law." *Harvard Law Review* 103 (1990): 1519.

Deveterre, Raymond. "Neocortical Death and Human Death." *Law, Medicine, and Health Care* 18 (1990): 96.

Dew, Betty. "Do Those Who Cannot Speak Really Have a Voice?" *Law, Medicine, and Health Care* 20 (1992): 316.

Donnelly, Rachel. "Twin 'Critical But Stable' as Sister Dies." *Irish Times,* November 8, 2000, p. 12.

Downie, R.S., and K.C. Calman. *Healthy Respect: Ethics in Health Care.* 2nd ed. Oxford: Oxford University Press, 1994.

Dresser, Rebecca. "Confronting the Near Irrelevancy of Advance Directives." *Journal of Clinical Ethics* 5 (1994): 55.

———. "Dementia Research: Ethics and Policy for the Twenty-first Century." *Georgia Law Review* 35 (2001): 661.

———. "Mentally Disabled Research Subjects." *Journal of American Medical Association* 276 (1996): 67.

———. "Missing Persons: Legal Perspectives of Incompetent Patients." *Rutgers Law Review* 46 (1994): 609.

———. "Relitigating Life and Death." *Ohio State Law Journal* 51 (1990): 425.

———. "Standards for Family Decisions: Replacing Best Interests with Harm Prevention." *American Journal of Bioethics* 3, no. 2 (2003): 54.

Dresser, Rebecca, and John A. Robertson. "Quality of Life and Non-Treatment Decisions for Incompetent Patients: A Critique of the Orthodox Approach." *Journal of Law, Medicine, and Ethics* 17 (1989): 234.

Dufault, Rachel M. "Bone Marrow Donations by Children: Rethinking the Legal Framework in Light of *Curran v. Bosze.*" *Connecticut Law Review* 24 (1991): 211.

Duff, Raymond S., and A.G.M. Campbell. "Moral and Ethical Dilemmas in the Special Care Nursery." *New England Journal of Medicine* 289 (1973): 890.

Dworkin, Roger B. *Limits: The Role of the Law in Bioethical Decision Making.* Bloomington: Indiana University Press, 1996.

Dwyer, James, and Elizabeth Vig. "Rethinking Transplantation Between Siblings." *Hastings Center Report* 25, no. 5 (September–October 1995): 7.

Elliott, Carl. "Attitudes, Souls, and Persons: Children with Severe Neurological Impairment." In Carl Elliott, ed., *Slow Cures and Bad Philosophers: Essays on Wittgenstein, Medicine, and Bioethics.* Durham, NC: Duke University Press, 2001.

Ellis, James W. "Decisions by and for People with Mental Retardation: Balancing Considerations of Autonomy and Protection." *Villanova Law Review* 37 (1992): 1779.

Elshtain, Jean Bethke. "The Dignity of the Human Person and the Idea of Human Rights." *Journal of Law and Religion* 14 (2000): 53.

Emanuel, Ezekiel. "The Promise of a Good Death." *Lancet* 351 (1998): 4.

Emanuel, Ezekiel J., David Wendler, and Christine Grady. "What Makes Clinical Research Ethical?" *Journal of the American Medical Association* 283 (2000): 2701.

Engelhardt, H. Tristram, Jr. *The Foundations of Bioethics.* 2nd ed. New York: Oxford University Press, 1996.

Englard, Izhak. "Human Dignity: From Antiquity to Modern Israel's Constitutional Framework." *Cardozo Law Review* 21 (2002): 1903.

European Union. *European Parliament Directive 2001/20/EC.* April 4, 2001.

Evans, Daryl Paul. *The Lives of Mentally Retarded People.* Boulder, CO: Westview Press, 1983.

Fader, John. "Trends in Health Care Decision Making: The Precarious Role of the Courts." *Maryland Law Review* 53 (1994): 1193.

Feinberg, Joel. *Freedom and Fulfillment: Philosophical Essays.* Princeton, NJ: Princeton University Press, 1992.

Feldman, David. "Human Dignity as a Legal Value, Part 1." *Public Law* (1999): 682.

Field, Martha A. "Killing 'the Handicapped': Before and after Birth." *Harvard Women's Law Journal* 16 (1993): 79.

Field, Martha A., and Valerie A. Sanchez. *Equal Treatment for People with Mental Retardation: Having and Raising Children.* Cambridge, MA: Harvard University Press, 1999.

Filene, Peter G. *In the Arms of Others: A Cultural History of the Right to Die in America.* Chicago: Dee, 1999.

Fineman, Martha Albertson. "What Place for Family Privacy?" *George Washington Law Review* 67 (1999): 1247.

Finnis, John. "Euthanasia, Morality, and Law." *Loyola of Los Angeles Law Review* 31 (1998): 1123.

Fitzgerald, Wendy Anton. "Engineering Perfect Offspring: Devaluing Children and Childhood." *Hastings Constitutional Law Quarterly* 24 (1997): 833.

Fletcher, John. "Human Experimentation: Ethics in the Consent Situation." *Journal of Law and Contemporary Problems* 32 (1967): 620.

Fletcher, Joseph. "Four Indicators of Humanhood." *Hastings Center Report* 6, no. 4 (December 1974): 4.

Foley, Joseph M. "The Experience of Being Demented." In Robert Binstock, Stephen G. Post, and Peter J. Whitehouse, eds., *Dementia and Aging: Ethics, Values, and Policy Choices.* Baltimore: Johns Hopkins University Press, 1992.

Fost, Norman. "Children as Renal Donors." *New England Journal of Medicine* 296 (1977): 363.

Freeden, Michael. *Rights.* Minneapolis: University of Minnesota Press, 1991.

Freedman, Benjamin, Abraham Fuks, and Charles Weijer. "*In Loco Parentis:* Minimal Risk as an Ethical Threshold for Research upon Children." *Hastings Center Report* 23, no. 2 (April 1993): 13.

Frey, R.G. *Rights, Killing and Suffering: Moral Vegetarianism and Applied Ethics.* Oxford: Blackwell, 1983.

Fried, Charles. "Children as Subjects for Medical Experimentation." In Jan van Eys, ed., *Research on Children: Medical Imperatives, Ethical Quandaries, and Legal Constraints.* Baltimore: University Park Press, 1978.

Friedman, Paul R. *The Rights of Mentally Retarded Persons: The Basic ACLU Guide for the Mentally Retarded Persons' Rights.* New York: Avon Books, 1976.

Garnett, Richard W. "Why Informed Consent? Human Experimentation and the Ethics of Autonomy." *Catholic Lawyer* 36 (1996): 455.

Garrow, David J. "The Right to Die: Death with Dignity in America." *Mississippi Law Journal* 68 (1998): 407.

Garvey, John H. "Freedom and Choice in Constitutional Law." *Harvard Law Review* 94 (1981): 1756.

Gauthier, Candace Cummins. "Philosophical Foundations of Respect for Autonomy." *Kennedy Institute of Ethics Journal* 3 (1993): 21.

Gewirth, Alan. "Human Dignity as the Basis of Rights." In Michael J. Meyer and William A. Parent, eds., *The Constitution of Rights: Human Dignity and American Values.* Ithaca, NY: Cornell University Press, 1992.

Giannella, Donald. "Eugenic Sterilization and the Law." In Jonas Robitscher, ed., *Eugenic Sterilization.* Springfield, IL: Thomas, 1973.

Glantz, Leonard H. "The Law of Human Experimentation with Children." In Michael A. Grodin and Leonard H. Glantz, eds., *Children as Research Subjects: Science, Ethics, and Law.* New York: Oxford University Press, 1994.

Glavis-Innis, Georgetta. "Organ Donation and Incompetents: Can They Consent?" *Touro International Law Review* 10 (2000): 155.

Gostin, Larry. "Family, Privacy, and Persistent Vegetative State." *Law, Medicine, and Health Care* 17 (1989): 295.

Green, Ronald M. "Determining Moral Status." In Ronald M. Green, ed., *The Human Embryo Research Debate.* Oxford: Oxford University Press, 2001.

Gregory, Lisa K. "Annotation; Propriety of Surgically Invading Incompetent or Minor for Benefit of Third Party." *American Law Reports* (5th ed.) 4 (1999): 1000.

Griffith, Daniel B. "The Best Interests Standard: A Comparison of the State's *Parens Patriae* Authority and Judicial Oversight in Best-Interests Determinations for Children and Incompetent Patients." *Issues in Law and Medicine* 7 (1991): 283.

Griner, Robert W. "Note, Live Organ Donations Between Siblings and the Best-Interests Standard: Time for Stricter Judicial Intervention." *Georgia State Law Review* 10 (1994): 589.

Gross, Jane. "Striving for a Gentle Farewell." *New York Times,* August 3, 2003, sec. 4, p. 1.

Guevara, Angie L., student author. "Note, *In re K.I.*: An Urgent Need for a Uniform System in the Treatment of the Critically Ill Infant—Recognizing the Sanctity of the Life of the Child." *University of San Francisco Law Review* 36 (2001): 237.

Guggenheim, Martin. "Minor Rights: The Adolescent Abortion Cases." *Hofstra Law Review* 30 (2002): 589.

Hackett, John. "Note, Procreative Choice for the Incompetent Developmentally Disabled." *DePaul Law Review* 36 (1986): 95.

Haimowitz, Stephan, Susan J. Delano, and John M. Oldham. "Uninformed Decisionmaking: The Case of Surrogate Research Consent." *Hastings Center Report* 27, no. 6 (1997): 9.

Hamman, Ardath A. "Family Surrogate Laws: A Necessary Supplement to Living Wills and Durable Powers of Attorney." *Villanova Law Review* 38 (1993): 103.

Handler, Alan B. "Individual Worth." *Hofstra Law Review* 17 (1989): 493.

Hardwig, John. "The Problem of Proxies with Interests of Their Own." *Utah Law Review* 1992 (1992): 803.

———. Hardwig, John. "The Problem of Proxies with Interests of Their Own: Toward a Better Theory of Proxy Decisions." *Journal of Clinical Ethics* 4 (1993): 20.

Harmon, Louise. "Falling off the Vine: Legal Fictions and the Doctrine of Substituted Judgment." *Yale Law Journal* 100 (1990): 1.

Harris, John. "The Concept of the Person and the Value of Life." *Kennedy Institute of Ethics Journal* 9, no. 4 (1999): 293.

———. "The Philosophical Case against the Philosophical Case Against Euthanasia." In John Keown, ed., *Euthanasia Examined: Ethical, Clinical, and Legal Perspectives* (chap. 3). Cambridge: Cambridge University Press, 1995.

———. "Professional Responsibility and Consent to Treatment." In Steven R. Hirsch and John Harris, eds., *Consent and the Incompetent Patient: Ethics, Law and Medicine—Proceedings of a Meeting Held at the Royal Society of Medicine, 9 December 1986*. London: Gaskell, 1988.

Hartsell, Jennifer. "'Mother, May I . . . Live?' Parental Refusal of Life-Sustaining Medical Treatment for Children Based on Religious Objections." *Tennessee Law Review* 66 (1999): 499.

Heimer, Carol A. "Competing Institutions: Law, Medicine, and Family in Neonatal Intensive Care." *Law and Society Review* 33 (1999): 17.

Herald, Marybeth. "Until Life Support Do Us Part: A Spouse's Limited Ability to Terminate Life Support for an Incompetent Spouse with No Hope of Recovery." *Thomas Jefferson Law Review* 24 (2002).

Hill, George. "Can Anyone Authorize the Nontherapeutic Permanent Alteration of a Child's Body?" *American Journal of Bioethics* 3, no. 2 (Spring 2003): <http://www.bioethics.net/journal>.

Hoffman, Diane E., and Jack Schwartz. "Proxy Consent to Participation of the Decisionally Impaired in Medical Research: Maryland's Policy Initiative." *Journal of Health Care Law and Policy* 1 (1998): 123.

Hoffman, Diane E., Jack Schwartz, and Evan G. DeRenzo. "Regulating Research with Decisionally Impaired Individuals: Are We Making Progress?" *DePaul Journal of Health Care Law* 3 (2000): 547.

Holder, Angela Roddey. *Legal Issues in Pediatrics and Adolescent Medicine*. 2nd ed. New Haven, CT: Yale University Press, 1985.

Jaegers, Eric M., student author. "Note, Modern Judicial Treatment of Procreative Rights of Developmentally Disabled Persons: Equal Rights to Procreation and Sterilization." *University of Louisville Journal of Family Law* 31 (1992): 947.

Jecker, Nancy S. "Anencephalic Infants and Special Relationships." *Theoretical Medicine* 11 (1990): 333.

Jennings, Bruce. "The Liberal Neutrality of Living and Dying: Bioethics, Constitutional Law, and Political Theory in the American Right-to-Die Debate." *Journal of Contemporary Health, Law, and Policy* 16 (1999): 97.

Jordan, Shannon. *Decision Making for Incompetent Persons: The Law and Morality of Who Shall Decide.* Springfield, IL: Thomas, 1985.

Kadish, Sanford. "Letting Patients Die: Legal and Moral Reflections." *California Law Review* 80 (1992): 857.

Kamisar, Yale. "When Is There a Constitutional 'Right to Die'?" *Georgia Law Review* 25 (1991): 1203.

Kass, Leon R. "Death with Dignity and the Sanctity of Life." *Commentary* (1990): 33.

———. *Life, Liberty, and Defense of Dignity: The Challenge for Bioethics.* San Francisco: Encounter Books, 2002.

Kavanaugh, John F. *Who Counts as Persons? Human Identity and the Ethics of Killing.* Washington, DC: Georgetown University Press, 2001.

Kelley, Tina. "Ruling Supports Parents' Rights to Decide on Child's Life Support." *New York Times,* May 17, 2003, p. B-1.

Kelson, Gregory A. "In the Best Interests of the Child: What Have We Learned from Baby Jessica and Baby Richard?" *John Marshall Law Review* 33 (2000): 353.

Kennedy, Foster. "The Problem of Social Control of the Congenital Defective." *American Journal of Psychiatry* 99 (1942): 13.

Keown, John. *Euthanasia, Ethics, and Public Policy: An Argument Against Legalisation.* Cambridge: Cambridge University Press, 2002.

Keown, Rebecca M. "A Case-Based Approach to Sterilization of Mentally Incompetent Women." *Princeton Journal of Bioethics* 1 (1998): 94.

Kindred, Michael. "Guardianship and Limitations upon Capacity." In Michael Kindred et al., eds., *The Mentally Retarded Citizen and the Law.* New York: Free Press, 1976.

King, Nancy M. P. "Defining and Describing Benefit Appropriate in Clinical Trials." *Journal of Law, Medicine, and Ethics* 28 (2000): 332.

Klepper, Howard. "Incompetent Organ Donors." *Journal of Social Philosophy* 25 (1994): 241.

Kluge, E.W. *The Ethics of Deliberate Death.* Port Washington, NY: Kennikat Press, 1981.

Knepper, Kathleen. "Withholding Medical Treatment from Infants: When Is It Neglect?" *University of Louisville Journal of Family Law* 33 (1994): 1.

Koenig, Julie. "Note, The Anencephalic Baby Theresa: A Prognosticator of Future Bioethics." *Nova Law Review* 17 (1992): 445.

Kolber, Adam, student author. "Note, Standing Upright: The Moral and Legal Standing of Humans and Other Apes." *Stanford Law Review* 54 (2001): 163.

Koogler, Tracy K., Benjamin S. Wilfond, and Lainie Friedman Ross. "Lethal Language, Lethal Decisions." *Hastings Center Report* 33, no. 2 (2003): 37.

Korins, Janet B. "Toward a Clear Standard for Authorizing Kidney and Bone Marrow Transplants between Minor Siblings." *Vermont Law Review* 16 (1992): 499.

Krais, William A. "Note, The Incompetent Developmentally Disabled Person's Right of Self-Determination: Right to Die, Sterilization, and Institutionalization." *American Journal of Law and Medicine* 15 (1989): 333.

Krasik, Elaine. "Comment, The Role of the Family in Medical Decision Making for Incompetent Adult Patients: A Historical Perspective and Case Analysis." *University of Pittsburgh Law Review* 48 (1986): 539.

Kuczewski, Mark. "Narrative Views of Personal Identity and Substituted Judgment in Surrogate Decision Making." *Journal of Law, Medicine, and Ethics* 27 (1999): 32.

Kutz, Christopher C. "Just Disagreement: Indeterminacy and Rationality in the Rule of Law." *Yale Law Journal* 103 (1994): 997.

Lantos, John D. "Children as Organ Donors: An Argument for Involuntary Altruism." In G. Roberto Burgio and John D. Lantos, eds., *Primum Non Nocere Today*. New York: Elsevier, 1994.

Larson, Edward J., and Leonard J. Nelson. "Involuntary Sexual Sterilization of Incompetents in Alabama: Past, Present, and Future." *Alabama Law Review* 43 (1992): 349.

Lebit, Lynn E. "Note, Compelled Medical Procedures Involving Minors and Incompetents and Misapplication of the Substituted Judgment Doctrine." *Journal of Law and Health* 7 (1992–1993): 107.

Leschensky, William A. "Note, Constitutional Protection of the Refusal of Treatment." *Harvard Journal of Law and Public Policy* 14 (1990): 248.

Levine, Melvin D., Bruce M. Camitta, David Nathan, and William J. Curran. "The Medical Ethics of Bone Marrow Transplantation in Children." *Journal of Pediatrics* 86 (1975): 145.

Levine, Robert J. "International Codes of Research Ethics: Current Controversies." *Indiana Law Review* 35 (2002): 557.

Lewis, Melvin. "Kidney Donation by a Seven-Year-old Identical Twin Child: Psychological, Legal, and Ethical Considerations." *Journal of the American Academy of Psychiatry* 13 (1974): 221.

Linder, Douglas O. "The Other Right to Life Debate: When Does Fourteenth Amendment Life End?" *Arizona Law Review* 37 (1995): 1182.

Lizza, John P. "Persons and Death: What's Metaphysically Wrong with Our Current Statutory Definition of Death?" *Journal of Medicine and Philosophy* 18 (1993): 351.

Lo, Bernard. "Caring for Incompetent Patients: Is There a Physician on the Case?" *Law, Medicine, and Health Care* 17 (1989): 214.

Lo, Bernard, Laurie Dornbrand, Leslie E. Wolf, and Michelle Groman. "The *Wendland* Case: Withdrawing Life Support from Incompetent Patients Who Are Not Terminally Ill." *New England Journal of Medicine* 346 (2002): 1489.

Lockemeyer, David S. "Note, At What Cost Will the Court Impose a Duty to Preserve the Life of a Child?" *Cleveland State Law Review*39 (1991): 577.

Loken, Gregory A. "Gratitude and the Map of Moral Duties toward Children." *Arizona State Law Journal* 31 (1999): 1121.

Lomasky, Loren E. *Persons, Rights, and the Moral Community.* New York: Oxford University Press, 1987.

Lombardo, Paul A. "Medicine, Eugenics, and the Supreme Court: From Coercive Sterilization to Reproductive Freedom." *Journal of Contemporary Health, Law, and Policy* 13 (1996): 1.

Macklin, Ruth. "Dignity as a Useless Concept." *BMJ (British Medical Journal)* 327 (2003): 1419.

Martyn, Susan R. "Substituted Judgment, Best Interests, and the Need for Best Respect." *Cambridge Quarterly of Healthcare Ethics* 3 (1994): 195.

Mathieu, Deborah. "Respecting Liberty and Preventing Harm: Limits of State Intervention in Prenatal Choice." *Harvard Journal of Law and Public Policy* 8 (1985): 19.

Mayerfeld, Jamie. *Suffering and Moral Responsibility.* New York: Oxford University Press, 1995.

Mayo, Thomas. "Constitutionalizing the Right to Die." *Maryland Law Review* 49 (1990): 103.

Mays, David J., and Martin Gunderson. "Vitalism Revitalized." *Hastings Center Report* 32, no. 4 (July 2002): 14.

McCormick, Richard A. "Proxy Consent in the Experimentation Situation." *Perspectives in Biology and Medicine* 18 (1974): 2.

McKnight, Deborah K., and Maureen Bellis. "Foregoing Life-Sustaining Treatment for Adult, Developmentally Disabled Public Wards: A Proposed Statute." *American Journal of Law and Medicine* 18 (1992): 215.

Meehan, Johanna. "Plurality, Autonomy, and the Right to Take One's Life." *Drake Law Review* 47 (1998): 87.

Meilaender, Gilbert. "Bioethics and the Character of Human Life." *New Atlantis* 1, no. 1 (Spring 2003): 67.

Meisel, Alan. "Legal Issues in Decision Making for Incompetent Patients." In Hans-Martin Sass, Robert M. Veatch, and Rihito Kimura, eds., *Advance Directives and Surrogate Decision Making in Health Care.* Baltimore: Johns Hopkins University Press, 1998.

Meyer, David D. "Lochner Redeemed: Family Privacy after *Troxel* and *Carhart.*" *UCLA Law Review* 48 (2001): 1125.

———. "The Paradox of Family Privacy." *Vanderbilt Law Review* 53 (2000): 527.

Miles, Steven and Allison August. "Courts, Gender, and the Right to Die." *Law, Medicine, and Health Care* 18 (1990): 85.

Miller, Franklin G. "Research Ethics and Misguided Moral Intuition." *Journal of Law, Medicine, and Ethics* 32 (2004): 111.

Minow, Martha. "All in the Family and in All Families: Membership, Loving, and Owing." *West Virginia Law Review* 95 (1993): 275.

—. "Interpreting Rights: An Essay for Robert Cover." *Yale Law Journal* 96 (1987): 1860.

—. *Making All the Difference: Inclusion, Exclusion, and American Law.* Ithaca: Cornell University Press, 1990.

—. "Trends in Health Care Decision Making: Who's the Patient?" *Maryland Law Review* 53 (1994): 1173.

Moreno, Jonathan D. "Regulation of Research on the Decisionally Impaired: History and Gaps in the Current Regulatory System." *Journal of Health Care, Law, and Policy* 1 (1998): 1.

—. "Who's to Choose? Surrogate Decisionmaking in New York State." *Hastings Center Report* 23, no. 1 (1993): 5.

Morley, Michael T. "Note, Proxy Consent to Organ Donation by Incompetents." *Yale Law Journal* 111 (2002): 1215.

Morton, Bruce. "Right-to-Die." *Touro Law Review* 7 (1991): 409.

Murdock, Charles. "Civil Rights of the Mentally Retarded: Some Critical Issues." *Notre Dame Lawyer* 48 (1972): 133.

Murphy, Thomas H., Jr. "Minor Consent to Transplant Surgery: A Review of the Law." *Marquette Law Review* 62 (1978): 149.

Murray, Thomas H. "Research on Children and the Scope of Responsible Parenthood." In Bonnie Steinbock, John D. Arras, and Alex John London, eds., *Ethical Issues in Modern Medicine* (6th ed.). Boston: McGraw-Hill, 2003.

National Bioethics Advisory Commission. *Research Involving Persons with Mental Disorders That May Affect Decision-Making Capacity.* Washington, DC: Government Printing Office, 1998.

National Commission on the Protection of Human Subjects of Biomedical and Behavioral Research. "The Belmont Report." *Federal Register* 44 (April 18, 1979): 23292.

National Conference of Catholic Bishops. "Nutrition and Hydration: Moral and Pastoral Reflections." *Journal of Contemporary Health, Law, and Policy* 15 (1999): 455.

Nelson, Hilde Lindemann. "What Child Is This?" *Hastings Center Report* 32, no. 6 (2002): 34.

Nelson, Lawrence J., et al. "Forgoing Medically Provided Nutrition and Hydration in Pediatric Patients." *Journal of Law, Medicine, and Ethics* 23 (1995): 33.

New York State Task Force on Life and the Law. *When Others Must Choose: Deciding for Patients without Capacity.* Albany, NY: New York Department of Health, March 1992.

Neuman, Gerald L. "Human Dignity in U.S. Constitutional Law." In Dieter Simon and Manfred Weiss, eds., *Zur Autonomie des Individuums.* Baden-Baden: Nomos Verlagsgesellschaft, 2000.

Nussbaum, Martha C. "Objectification." *Philosophy and Public Affairs* 24, no. 4 (1995): 249.

Oberman, Michelle, and Joel Frader. "Dying Children and Medical Research: Access to Clinical Trials as Benefit and Burden." *American Journal of Law and Medicine* 29 (2003): 290.

Olick, Robert S. *Taking Advance Directives Seriously: Prospective Autonomy and Decisions Near the End of Life.* Washington, DC: Georgetown University Press, 2001.

Pappworth, M.H. *Human Guinea Pigs; Experimentation on Man.* Boston: Beacon Press, 1968.

Paredes, Teresa Harvey. "The Killing Words? How the New Quality of Life Ethic Affects People with Severe Disabilities." *Southern Methodist University Law Review* 46 (1992): 805.

Parent, William A. "Constitutional Values and Human Dignity." In Michael J. Meyer and William A. Parent, eds., *The Constitution of Rights: Human Dignity and American Values.* Ithaca: Cornell University Press, 1992.

Paust, Jordan. "Dignity as a Constitutional Right." *Howard Law Journal* 27 (1984): 145.

Pearlman, Robert A., et al. "Insights Pertaining to Patient Assessments of States Worse Than Death." *Journal of Clinical Ethics* 4 (1993): 35.

Pellegrino, Edmund D. "Patient and Physician Autonomy: Conflicting Rights and Obligations in the Physician-Patient Relationship." *Journal of Contemporary Health, Law, and Policy* 10 (1994): 47.

Peters, Philip. "The State's Interest in the Preservation of Life: From *Quinlan* to *Cruzan.*" *Ohio State Law Journal* 50 (1989): 891.

Plastine, Laura M. "'In God We Trust': When Parents Refuse Medical Treatment for Their Children Based upon Their Sincere Religious Beliefs." *Constitutional Law Journal* 3 (1993): 123.

Pluhar, Evelyn B. *Beyond Prejudice: The Moral Significance of Human and Nonhuman Animals.* Durham, NC: Duke University Press, 1995.

Pollock, Stewart. "Life and Death Decisions: Who Makes Them and by What Standard?" *Rutgers Law Review* 41 (1988): 505.

Post, Stephen G. "Dementia in Our Midst: The Moral Community." *Cambridge Quarterly of Healthcare Ethics* 4 (1995): 142.

Pratt, David A. "Too Many Physicians: Physician-Assisted Suicide after *Glucksberg/ Quill.*" *Albany Law Journal of Science and Technology* 9 (1999): 161.

President's Commission for the Study of Ethical Problems in Medicine. *Deciding to Forgo Life-Sustaining Treatment.* Washington, DC: Government Printing Office, 1983.

———. *Making Health Care Decisions.* Washington, DC: Government Printing Office, 1983.

Price, David P. T. "Contemporary Transplantation Initiatives: Where's the Harm in Them?" *Journal of Law, Medicine, and Ethics* 24 (1996): 139.

————. *Legal and Ethical Aspects of Organ Transplantation*. New York: Cambridge University Press, 2000.

Proctor, Robert. *Racial Hygiene: Medicine Under the Nazis*. Cambridge, MA: Harvard University Press, 1988.

Quinn, Adrienne E. "Who Should Make Decisions for Incompetent Adults." *Seattle Law Review* 20 (1997): 573.

Rabins, Peter V. "Issues Raised by Research Using Persons Suffering from Dementia Who Have Impaired Decisional Capacity." *Journal of Health Care, Law, and Policy* 1 (1998): 22.

Ramsey, Paul. *The Patient as Person: Explorations in Medical Ethics*. New Haven: Yale University Press, 1970.

Rendleman, Douglas R. "*Parens Patriae* from Chancery to the Juvenile Court." *South Carolina Law Review* 23 (1971): 204.

Rhoden, Nancy. "How Should We View the Incompetent?" *Law, Medicine, and Health Care* 17 (1989): 264.

————. "Litigating Life and Death." *Harvard Law Review* 102 (1988): 375.

Rhodes, Rosamond. "Futility and the Goals of Medicine." *Journal of Clinical Ethics* 9 (1998): 194.

————. "Treatment Dilemmas for Imperiled Newborns: Why Quality of Life Counts." *Southern California Law Review* 58 (1985): 1283.

Rich, Ben. "Reflections on the Social Constructions of Death." *Journal of Legal Medicine* 24 (2003): 233.

Riga, Peter. *Right to Die or Right to Live? Legal Aspects of Dying and Death*. Port Washington, NY: Kinnikat Press, 1981.

Roach, Cathleen A. "Paradox and Pandora's Box: The Tragedy of Current Right to Die Jurisprudence." *University of Michigan Journal of Law Reform* 25 (1991): 133.

Robbenolt, Jennifer K., Victoria Weisz, and Craig M. Lawson. "Advancing the Rights of Children and Adolescents to Be Altruistic: Bone Marrow Donation by Minors." *Journal of Law and Health* 9 (1994–1995): 213.

Robertson, John. "Assessing Quality of Life: A Response to Professor Kamisar." *Georgia Law Review* 25 (1991): 1243.

————. "*Cruzan* and the Constitutional Status of Nontreatment Decisions for Incompetent Patients." *Georgia Law Review* 25 (1991): 1139.

————. "Dilemma in Danville." *Hastings Center Report* 11 (October 1981): 5.

Robitscher, Jonas, ed. *Eugenic Sterilization*. Springfield, IL: Thomas, 1973.

Rosato, Jennifer. "The Ethics of Clinical Trials: A Child's View." *Journal of Law, Medicine, and Ethics* 28 (2000): 362.

————. "Using Bioethics Discourse to Determine When Parents Should Make Health Care Decisions for Their Children: Is Deference Justified?" *Temple Law Review* 73 (2000): 1.

Ross, Lainie Friedman. *Children, Families, and Health Care Decision Making*. New York: Clarendon Press, 1998.

———. "Moral Grounding for the Participation of Children as Organ Donors." *Journal of Law, Medicine, and Ethics* 21 (1993): 251.

Rothenberg, Karen. "Foregoing Life-Sustaining Treatment: What Are the Legal Limits in an Aging Society?" *Saint Louis University Law Journal* 33, no. 3 (1989): 575–602.

Sadurski, Wojciech. "Conventional Morality and Judicial Standards." *Virginia Law Review* 73 (1987): 339.

Scarry, Elaine. *The Body in Pain.* Oxford: Oxford University Press, 1985.

Schneider, Carl E. "Hard Cases." *Hastings Center Report* 28, no. 2 (March 1998): 24.

———. "Rights Discourse and Neonatal Euthanasia." *California Law Review* 76 (1988): 151.

Schoeman, Frederick. "Parental Discretion and Children's Rights." *Journal of Medicine and Philosophy* 10 (1985): 48.

Schriner, Kay, Lisa Ochs, and Todd Shields. "Democratic Dilemmas: Notes on the ADA and Voting Rights of People with Cognitive and Emotional Impairments." *Berkeley Journal of Employment and Labor Law* 21 (2000): 37.

Schrode, Kristi E. "Comment, Life in Limbo: Revising Policies for Permanently Unconscious Patients." *Houston Law Review* 32 (1995): 1609.

Scofield, Giles R. "Letters, *Dred Scott* Revisited." *Hastings Center Report* 21, no. 5 (September 1991): 44.

Scott, Elizabeth S. "Sterilization of Mentally Retarded Persons: Reproductive Rights and Family Privacy." *Duke Law Journal* 1986 (1986): 806.

Sharpe, Dana J., and Robert F. Hargest. "Lifesaving Treatment for Unwilling Patients." *Fordham Law Review* 36 (1968): 695.

Shartle, Bryan. "Comment, Proposed Legislation for Safely Regulating the Increasing Number of Living Organ and Tissue Donations by Minors." *Louisiana Law Review* 61 (2001): 433.

Sheldon, Mark. "Children as Organ Donors." In Bethany Spielman, ed., *Organ and Tissue Donation: Ethical, Legal, and Policy Issues.* Carbondale, IL: Southern Illinois University Press, 1996.

Shepherd, Lois. "Dignity and Autonomy after *Washington v. Glucksberg:* An Essay About Abortion, Death, and Crime." *Cornell Journal of Law and Public Policy* 7 (1998): 431.

———. "Face to Face: A Call for Radical Responsibility in Place of Compassion." Public Law and Legal Theory Working Paper # 77. April 2003.

Sheppard, Colleen. "Children's Rights to Equality: Protection Versus Paternalism." *Annals of Health Law* 1 (1992): 197.

Sherlock, Richard K., and Robert D. Sherlock. "Sterilizing the Retarded: Constitutional Statutory, and Policy Alternatives." *North Carolina Law Review* 60 (1982): 943.

Shultziner, Doron. "Human Dignity: Functions and Meanings." *Global Jurist* 3, no. 3 (2003): 5.

Singer, Peter. *Rethinking Life and Death: The Collapse of Our Traditional Ethics.* New York: St. Martin's Press, 1995.

———. *Writings on an Ethical Life.* New York: Ecco Press, 2000.

Singer, Peter A., Douglas K. Martin, and Merrijoy Kelner. "Quality End of Life Care: Patients' Perspectives." *Journal of the American Medical Association* 281 (1999): 163.

Smith, George P. "'Death Be Not Proud': Medical, Ethical, and Legal Dilemmas in Resource Allocation." *Journal of Contemporary Health, Law, and Policy* 3 (1987): 47.

Sofair, Andre N., and Lewis C. Kaldjean. "Eugenic Sterilization and a Qualified Nazi Analogy: The U.S. and Germany." *Annals of Internal Medicine* 132 (2000): 312.

Solnick, Paul B. "Proxy Consent for Incompetent Non-Terminally Ill Adult Patients." *Journal of Legal Medicine* 6 (1985): 1.

Somerville, Margaret. "Birth and Life: Establishing a Framework of Concepts." *Connecticut Law Review* 21 (1989): 667.

Splaine, Neal F. "Note, The Incompetent Individual's Right to Refuse Life-Sustaining Medical Treatment." *Suffolk University Law Review* 27 (1993): 905.

Stanley, John M., et al. "The *Appleton* Consensus: Suggested International Guidelines for Decisions to Forego Medical Treatment." *Journal of Medical Ethics* 15 (1989): 129.

Strasser, Mark. "Incompetents and the Right to Die: In Search of Consistent Meaningful Standards." *Kentucky Law Journal* 83 (1994–1995): 733.

Sulmasy, Daniel. "Heart and Soul: The Case of the Conjoined Twins." *America* (December 2, 2000). <http://www.americapress.org/articles/sulmasy.htm>.

Sundram, Clarence J. "'In Harm's Way': Research Subjects Who Are Decisionally Impaired." *Journal of Health Care, Law, and Policy* 1 (1998): 36.

Tansey, Bernadette. "UCSF Violated Patients' Rights." *San Francisco Chronicle,* July 28, 2002, p. A-1.

Tobin, Bernadette. "Did You Think about Buying Her a Cat? Some Reflections on the Concept of Autonomy." *Journal of Contemporary Health, Law, and Policy* 11 (1995): 417.

Tremper, Charles. "Respect for the Human Dignity of Minors: What the Constitution Requires." *Syracuse Law Review* 39 (1988): 1293.

Trenkner, Thomas R. "Jurisdiction of Court to Permit Sterilization of Mentally Defective Person in Absence of Specific Statutory Authority." *American Law Reports* (Vol. 74, 3rd ed., p. 1210) (1976).

Trent, James W. *Inventing the Feeble Mind: A History of Mental Retardation in the United States.* Berkeley: University of California Press, 1994.

Tribe, Laurence. *American Constitutional Law* (2nd ed.). Mineola, NY: Foundation Press, 1988.

Tucker, Bonnie P., and Bruce A. Goldstein. *The Legal Rights of Persons with Disabilities: An Analysis of Federal Law.* Horsham, PA: LRP Publications, 1991.

Ullrich, Dierk. "Concurring Visions: Human Dignity in the Canadian Charter of Rights and Freedoms and the Basic Law of the Federal Republic of Germany." *Global Jurist* 3, no. 1 (2003). <http://www.bepress.com/gj/frontiers/vol3/art/>.

Vawter, Dorothy E. "Ethical Frameworks for Live and Cadaver Organ Donation." In Bethany Spielman, ed., *Organ and Tissue Donation: Ethical, Legal, and Policy Issues*. Carbondale, IL: Southern Illinois University Press, 1996.

Veatch, Robert. "The Dead Donor Rule: True by Definition." *American Journal of Bioethics* 3, no. 1 (Winter 2003): 10.

———. "Ethical Dimensions of Advance Directives and Surrogate Decision Making." In Hans-Martin Sass et al., eds., *Advance Directives and Surrogate Decision Making in Health Care: United States, Germany, and Japan*. Baltimore: Johns Hopkins University Press, 1998.

———. *The Foundations of Justice: Why the Retarded and the Rest of Us Have Claims to Equality*. New York: Oxford University Press, 1986.

———. *The Patient as Partner: A Theory of Human Experimentation Ethics*. Bloomington, ID: Indiana University Press, 1987.

———. *The Patient-Physician Relation: The Patient as Partner, Part 2*. Bloomington, ID: Indiana University Press, 1991.

Wald, Patricia. "Basic Personal and Civil Rights." In Michael Kindred et al., eds., *The Mentally Retarded Citizen and the Law*. New York: Free Press, 1976.

Walters, James W. *What Is a Person? An Ethical Exploration*. Urbana, IL: University of Illinois Press, 1997.

Warren, John W., et al. "Informed Consent by Proxy: An Issue in Research with Elderly Patients." *New England Journal of Medicine* 315 (1986): 1124.

Warren, Mary Anne. *Moral Status: Obligations to Persons and Other Living Things*. Oxford: Clarendon Press, 1997.

Weber, Walter M. "Substituted Judgment Doctrine: A Critical Analysis." *Issues in Law and Medicine* 1 (1985): 131.

Webster, Walter L. "'Right to Die' Cases: A Model for Judicial Decision-Making?" *New York Law School Journal of Human Rights* 7 (1990): 140.

Weijer, Charles. "The Ethical Analysis of Risk." *Journal of Law, Medicine, and Ethics* 28 (2000): 344.

Weir, Robert F. *Selective Nontreatment of Handicapped Newborns: Moral Dilemmas in Neonatal Medicine*. New York: Oxford University Press, 1984.

Weiser, Benjamin "A Question of Letting Go; Child's Trauma Drives Doctors to Reexamine Ethical Role." *Washington Post*, July 14, 1991, p. A-1.

Weisz, Victoria. "Psycholegal Issues in Sibling Bone Marrow Donation." *Ethics and Behavior* 2, no. 3 (1992): 185.

Wennberg, Robert N. *Terminal Choices: Euthanasia, Suicide, and the Right to Die*. Grand Rapids, MI: Eerdmans, 1989.

Whitman, Thomas L., Cynthia L. Miller, and Deirdre Mylod. "Mental Retardation." In *Encyclopedia of Disability and Rehabilitation*. New York: Macmillan, 1995.

Wicclair, Mark R. *Ethics and the Elderly.* New York: Oxford University Press, 1993.

Winick, Bruce. "Advance Directive Instruments for Those with Mental Illness." *University of Miami Law Review* 51 (1996): 57.

———. "Competency to Consent to Treatment: The Distinction Between Assent and Objection." *Houston Law Review* 28 (1991): 15.

Wolf, Susan. "Toward a Theory of Process." *Law, Medicine, and Health Care* 20 (1992): 278.

Woodhouse, Barbara Bennett. "The Dark Side of Family Privacy." *George Washington Law Review* 67 (2000): 1247.

Wright, R. George. "Treating Persons as Ends in Themselves: The Legal Implications of a Kantian Principle." *University of Richmond Law Review* 36 (2002): 271.

Yuen, Michele. "Comment, Letting Daddy Die: Adopting New Standards for Surrogate Decision Making." *UCLA Law Review* 39 (1992): 581.

Index of Cases and Statutes

Index